DARKENED ENLIGHTENMENT

The premise of *Darkened Enlightenment* is to highlight the fact that there currently exist a number of socio-political forces that have the design, or ultimate consequence, of trying to extinguish the light of reason and rationality.

This book presents a critique of modernity and provides a socio-political and cultural analysis of world society in the early twenty-first century. Specifically, this analysis examines the deterioration of democracy, human rights, and rational thought. Key features include a combination of academic analysis that draws on numerous and specific examples of the growing darkness that surrounds us along with a balanced practical, everyday-life approach to the study of the socio-political world we live in through the use of popular culture references and featured boxes.

The general audience will also be intrigued by these same topics that concern academics, including: a discussion on the meaning of "fake news"; attacks on the media and a declaration of the news media as the "enemy of the people"; the rise of populism and nationalism around the world; the deterioration of freedom and human rights globally; the growing economic disparity between the rich and the poor; attempts to devalue education; a growing disbelief in science; attacks on the environment; pseudoscience as a by-product of unreasoned and irrational thinking; the political swamp; the power elites and the deep state; and the variations of Big Business that impact our daily lives. This book will make a great contribution to such fields as sociology, philosophy, political science, environmental science, public administration, economics, psychology, and cultural studies.

Tim Delaney is Professor and Department Chair of Sociology at the State University of New York (SUNY) at Oswego. Among his most recent book publications are *Common Sense as a Paradigm of Thought* (2019) and *Social Deviance* (2017).

DARKENED ENLIGHTENMENT

The Deterioration of Democracy, Human Rights, and Rational Thought in the Twenty-First Century

Tim Delaney

First published 2020
by Routledge
2 Park Square, Milton Park, Abingdon, Oxon OX14 4RN

and by Routledge
52 Vanderbilt Avenue, New York, NY 10017

Routledge is an imprint of the Taylor & Francis Group, an informa business

© 2020 Tim Delaney

The right of Tim Delaney to be identified as author of this work has been asserted by him in accordance with sections 77 and 78 of the Copyright, Designs and Patents Act 1988.

All rights reserved. No part of this book may be reprinted or reproduced or utilized in any form or by any electronic, mechanical, or other means, now known or hereafter invented, including photocopying and recording, or in any information storage or retrieval system, without permission in writing from the publishers.

Trademark notice: Product or corporate names may be trademarks or registered trademarks, and are used only for identification and explanation without intent to infringe.

British Library Cataloguing-in-Publication Data
A catalogue record for this book is available from the British Library

Library of Congress Cataloging-in-Publication Data
A catalog record has been requested for this book

ISBN: 978-0-367-46129-4 (hbk)
ISBN: 978-0-367-46130-0 (pbk)
ISBN: 978-1-003-02709-6 (ebk)

Typeset in Bembo
by Wearset Ltd, Boldon, Tyne and Wear

Dedicated to those who support enlightened, rational, reasoned, and scientific thought.

CONTENTS

List of boxes	*ix*
About the author	*x*
Preface	*xi*
Acknowledgments	*xiv*

1 Enlightened rational thought   1

Introduction 1
Antecedents to the Enlightenment 2
The Enlightenment (c.1700–1840s) 11
Critical thinking and higher education 26
Twentieth-century scientific achievements 28
Connecting enlightened rational thought with popular culture 31
Summary 33

2 The darkness that surrounds us: the deterioration of democracy and human rights   35

Introduction 35
Lies, falsehoods, and misleading claims 37
Declaring the news media as the "enemy of the people" 46
Populism and nationalism 54
The deterioration of freedom and human rights 75
Social stratification and economic disparity 82
Connecting enlightened rational thought with popular culture 89
Summary 90

3 **The darkness that surrounds us: unenlightened and irrational thinking**   91

Introduction 91
Attempts to devalue education 91
A disbelief in science 106
Attacks on the environment 116
Pseudoscience: a by-product of unreasoned and irrational thinking 131
Connecting enlightened rational thought with popular culture 137
Summary 139

4 **A flooded swamp**   141

Introduction 141
The political swamp 141
The swamp has not been drained; it is deeper and murkier 149
The Deep State 164
Too big to fail ... from flooding the swamp 177
Connecting enlightened rational thought with popular culture 192
Summary 194

5 **Will the light of rational thought chase away the darkness?**   196

Introduction 196
Signs of light 196
Signs of further darkness 199
The future 200

Bibliography   202
Index   231

BOXES

1.1	The Moon landing: "an epic moment in civilization"	31
2.1	"The press was to serve the governed not the governors"—from the film, *The Post*	89
3.1	Chernobyl: from nuclear accident to popular TV show and tourist attraction	137
4.1	"I Liked beer. I still like beer"—Brett Kavanaugh, US Supreme Court Justice	192

ABOUT THE AUTHOR

Tim Delaney is Professor and Department Chair of Sociology at the State University of New York (SUNY) at Oswego. He earned his BS in Sociology from SUNY Brockport, an MA degree in Sociology from California State University, Dominguez Hills, and a PhD in Sociology from the University of Nevada, Las Vegas. He has published 21 books (to date), numerous book chapters, journal and encyclopedia articles, and has been published on five continents. Among his book publications are *Common Sense as a Paradigm of Thought* (Routledge, 2019), *Social Deviance* (2017), *Sportsmanship: Multidisciplinary Perspectives* (editor, 2016), *Beyond Sustainability: A Thriving Environment* (co-author, 2014), *American Street Gangs, Second Edition* (2014), *Classical and Contemporary Social Theory: Investigation and Application* (2014), *Shameful Behaviors* (2008), and *Social Diseases: Mafia, Terrorism and Totalitarianism* (co-editor, 2004).

Delaney regularly presents papers at regional, national, and international conferences. His commitment to scholarly activity allows him to travel the world and learn first-hand the great diversity, and similarity, found among people from different cultures. He maintains membership in more than a dozen academic associations and has served as president of the New York State Sociological Association for three separate terms.

Tim Delaney has traveled much of the world seeking signs of light to triumph over the darkness. While there is great beauty in the world, alarmingly, he has seen first-hand the growing number of evil forces that have darkened enlightened thinking.

PREFACE

In my 2019 book *Common Sense as a Paradigm of Thought*, I discussed the four major paradigms of thought (my own categorization): tradition, faith, enlightened rationality, and common sense. Because the primary topic of that book was "common sense," it is likely that most readers expected me to conclude that common sense should be emphasized as the prevailing paradigm of thought to help guide society and individual decision making. However, in the concluding chapter of *Common Sense*, I put forth the notion that it was enlightened rational thought that should reign supreme.

The dedication statement in *Common Sense*—"to those who shine the light on the darkness and attempt to drain the swamp of ignorance"—was purposively used as a means of foreshadowing this current book. And that is because, in this book, I make the fuller case for rational enlightened thought as the paradigm of thought we should abide by in governing our behavioral choices. Common sense certainly has its value but it cannot compete with the logic of reason and science, and enlightened thought is certainly superior to tradition- and faith-based forms of thinking. It is further argued that while enlightened, rational thought is important at any point in history, it is especially important in the twenty-first century.

The premise of this book is to highlight the fact that there currently exist a number of socio-political forces that have the design, or ultimate consequence, of trying to extinguish the light of reason and rationality. The reference to a "flooded swamp" in this monograph centers primarily on the socio-political systems that are increasingly being filled with corrupt individuals and entities. These combined social forces have led to what I call "darkened enlightenment." *Darkened Enlightenment* offers a critique of modernity and provides a socio-political and cultural analysis of world society in the early twenty-first century. Specifically, *Darkened Enlightenment* examines the deterioration of democracy, human rights, and rational thought. A brief review of each chapter is described below.

In Chapter 1, the growth of enlightened, rational thought is highlighted from the time of the Renaissance era and the Scientific Revolution, continuing with the Enlightenment period and a review of some key European and American Enlightenment thinkers, the Age of Reason, the Century of Criticism and the conservative reaction, a discussion of the value of critical thinking and higher education, through to a sampling of scientific achievements of the twentieth century. These eras certainly had their own dim moments and many examples of "darkness" (e.g., challenges to enlightened thought, inequality among all people, and constant warring between nations), but it was during this timeframe that progressive and scientific thought came to the forefront more so than in previous centuries. More importantly, the path had been cleared for the twenty-first century to become the most progressive in the history of humanity.

Chapter 2 describes the darkness that surrounds us from the context of the deterioration of democracy and human rights. Utilizing primarily a socio-political perspective, the topics covered include the thousands of lies, falsehoods, and misleading claims of US President Donald Trump and their dangerous implications of darkness. Declaring the news media as the "enemy of the people" is a sure sign of an attack on democracy as the role of the press is to keep the power elites in check. The spread of populism and nationalism in the United States, Europe, and around the world highlights the deterioration of democracy that is occurring right before our eyes. Attacks on human rights globally and in the United States are an alarming display of autocracy or would-be autocracy. The extreme social stratification and economic disparity that exist in the world continue to assure poverty and global inequity.

The "darkness that surrounds us" theme continues in Chapter 3 with a focus on unenlightened and irrational thought. There are numerous examples of unenlightened and irrational thought but the focus of discussion in this chapter revolves around four general categories: attempts to devalue education; a disbelief in science; attacks on the environment; and utilizing pseudoscience. The many subtopics found within each of these four categories help to further illustrate the harm that can be caused by illogical and groundless thinking. Discussion begins with the social institution of education, its value, and the attacks on it.

A popular adage in American socio-political discussion is the idea that politics is like a "swamp," a dirty and murky environment that it is filled with vile corruption that contaminates all who enter. More specifically, the "swamp" refers to the unelected personnel that run the government. To "drain the swamp" would mean that one plans on rooting out corruption in politics, especially in Washington, DC. A flooded swamp, on the other hand, would imply that the world of politics is so dark that light cannot possible shine through. Chapter 4 describes the meaning of a flooded swamp, the history of this notion (which dates back to the 1870s) of politics as a swamp and the flooded White House that is filled with unqualified cabinet and judicial appointments. The concept of the "Deep State," "Big Business" (e.g., the fossil fuel industry and "Big Pharma"), and Big Banks and Wall Street are also discussed within the contexts of darkness trying to extinguish the light of reason and rationality.

In Chapter 5, the question of what lurks around the corner is pondered. That is to say, will enlightened rational thought prevail, or will the darkness that surrounds us in the early twenty-first century eventually lead to the deterioration of democracy, human rights, and reason?

Darkened Enlightenment is filled with academic analysis but is balanced with a practical, everyday-life approach to the study of the socio-political world we live in. The use of popular culture boxes helps to illustrate a specific topic area in an approachable manner. As a result of this style of approach, scholars, social thinkers, and laypersons alike will find this book quite fascinating and it will leave readers with plenty of food for thought about a subject area that encompasses much of our lives. Those with a background in sociology, political science, environmental science, public administration, economics, philosophy, and psychology will especially find *Darkened Enlightenment* valued reading.

Humanity is capable of such greatness. Why is it that we are failing in so many ways? As presented here, it is because an increasing number of people have turned their backs on enlightened, rational thought—the paradigm of thought everyone should embrace—and instead have turned to the dark side of thinking and behaving.

ACKNOWLEDGMENTS

I acknowledge the reviewers of this text for their valuable comments, suggestions, and support.

Special thanks to all the fine folks at Routledge, including Emily Briggs, Emma Harder, and Lakshita Joshi, the copy-editor Dan Shutt, and everyone else who helped to produce this book.

I would also like to acknowledge Professor Tim Madigan (Department Chair of Philosophy at St. John Fisher College) for his review of the first draft of the manuscript—your edits and comments are always welcomed and appreciated.

1
ENLIGHTENED RATIONAL THOUGHT

Introduction

Enlightened rational thinking evolved into a paradigm of thought following the emergence of the Enlightenment era. "The Enlightenment," also known as the "Age of Reason," is a collective term used to describe the politics, philosophy, and growth in science, social trends, and writings in Europe and the American colonies during the eighteenth and early nineteenth century. Spearheaded by the liberal sentiments of liberty, equality, and brotherhood, and the thoughts of many enlightened European and American social thinkers (i.e., Charles de Montesquieu, Francois-Marie Arouet (Voltaire), Jean-Jacques Rousseau, Immanuel Kant, Benjamin Franklin, John Adams, and Thomas Jefferson), the Enlightenment spirited a movement of social reasoning. The "enlightenment" metaphor was frequently employed by writers of this period as they were convinced that they were emerging from centuries of darkness and ignorance (as a result of the paradigms of thought of tradition and faith) into a new age of enlightenment by means of reason, science, and respect for humanity (Delaney 2019). The Enlightenment was a period of dramatic intellectual development and change in philosophical thought as a number of long-standing ideas and beliefs were being abandoned and replaced by new ideas that were influenced by science, reason, and the utilization of empirical research.

Enlightened thinkers argued that since the natural world could now be explained by science and reason, so too should the principles of rationality and reason be applied to the social world (Ritzer and Stepnisky 2018). Geoffrey Clive (1973) argued that the "Enlightenment consolidated the scientific breakthroughs of the great seventeenth-century thinkers by applying their method to the problems of society" (p. 23). He further presented the idea that the application of science and reason paved the way for the French Revolution of 1789. Indeed, the traditional system of feudalism had been metaphorically dismantled piece by piece during the rise of enlightened rational thought.

Antecedents to the Enlightenment

Most of human history played witness to the dominance of the paradigms of thought of tradition and faith. These forces shaped how social order should be structured. In a number of instances, these two forces worked symbiotically via such a doctrine as the "divine rights of kings." Elements of enlightened rational thought (e.g., discovery and explanation, innovation and invention, and theoretical speculation) had emerged from time to time over millennia and in a variety of geographic locations but in many cases, such discoveries represented practical improvements in technique and were less often a result of intellectual curiosity. Among the key antecedents of the Enlightenment are the Renaissance (*c*.1300–1600) and the Scientific Revolution (*c*.1600–1700).

The Renaissance (c.1300–1600)

The Renaissance is a period of time in European history that falls in between the Middle Ages and the Enlightenment. There is debate among scholars who have studied the Renaissance as to its exact time frame. As explained by Ernst Cassirer (1951), Jean le Rond d'Alembert's essay on the *Elements of Philosophy* describes the beginning of the Renaissance as the middle of the fifteenth century, with the Reformation reaching its climax in the middle of the sixteenth century. William Caferro (2011) describes how J.R. Hale wrote in *Renaissance Europe* (1971) that the Renaissance took place during the limited period of 1480–1520 but, at the end of his career (in *The Civilization of Europe in the Renaissance*), argued that the Renaissance actually spanned from 1450 to 1620—in essence, the "long" sixteenth century. As another example, Caferro (2011) explains that Wallace Ferguson first advocated that the Renaissance took place from 1300 to 1600 but later changed his mind to state that it took place from 1300 to 1520—with the terminal date corresponding to the deaths of Leonardo da Vinci (1519) and Raphael (1520) and the condemnation of Martin Luther (1521). Caferro further explains that

> Some scholars divide the Renaissance into stages or generations. They use rubrics "early, high, and late," the same employed by medievalists for their period. The stages represent degrees of penetration and diffusion of the movement. Petrarch, an early figure, is emblematic of a "limited," early Renaissance that involved few participants. Leonardo da Vinci (d. 1520) is representative of the "high" Renaissance, now a pervasive phenomenon most evident in terms of artistic developments.
>
> (p. 24)

Paul Oskar Kristeller (1951) puts forth the notion that the Renaissance was a period of Western European history that extends approximately from 1300 to 1600, although also makes the point that it was not the case that there was a specific event in 1300 or 1600 that represents a clear beginning and ending point, respectively. Kristeller offers a good explanation as to why there is such debate among scholars as to the exact time frame of the Renaissance—it was because of regional and social differences in the various European locales. For example, Kristeller states that there were cultural differences between Italy and Northern Europe that led to Italy's Renaissance being earlier than that of France. Adding to this explanation offered by Kristeller, Caferro (2011) states that a number of variables go into determining the labeling of Renaissance periods. For example, "The early Renaissance represented a period of 'hope': the late Renaissance an era of 'anxiety'" (p. 24). Peter Burke (1964) adds, "In the sixteenth century, the idea of the Renaissance was developed in several ways. It was divided into periods by Vasari; applied to music by Galilei, and to medicine by Vesalius; and extended to include printing, gunpowder, and voyages of discovery by Rabelais and Fernel" (p. 4).

One thing scholars seem to agree on is the fact that the Renaissance followed the Middle Ages (the period in European history from the collapse of the Roman Empire in the fifth century CE to the time of the Renaissance). Burke (1964) proclaims that the people living in the Middle Ages never knew they were the Middle Ages, but that the people in the Renaissance era did in fact know they were experiencing the Renaissance. As with Caferro, Burke describes Francis (Francesco) Petrarch (1304–1374) as a (*the*) early beginning point of describing the Renaissance.

> Christian writers had often divided history into two periods; an age of darkness and paganism, followed by an age of light and Christianity. Petrarch took over these terms but applied them differently; for him, it was the period before conversion of Constantine, the *aetas antiqua*, which was the age of light; and the *aetas nova*, the modern age which succeeded it, which was the age of darkness.
>
> *(Burke 1964:2)*

Johnson (2000) disagrees with Burke that those in the Renaissance were aware of this term.

> Needless to say, it is not those who actually live through the period who coin the term, but later, often much later, writers.... The term "Renaissance" was first prominently used by the French historian Jules Michelet in 1858.... The usage stuck because it turned out to be a convenient way of describing the period of transition between the medieval epoch, when Europe was "Christendom," and the beginning of the modern age.
>
> *(p. 3)*

Johnson also chronicles the beginning of Renaissance sculpture to the Italian Nicola Pisano, who lived approximately between 1220 and 1284 CE.

As Petrarch's name has been referenced twice already, it should be pointed out that Francis Petrarch is actually the Anglicized version of Francesco Petrarca (1304–1374). Petrarch was a Latin and Greek scholar and Italian poet whose poems influenced "much of Elizabethan lyric poetry, and Shakespeare's sonnets could not exist without Petrarch's previous sonnets and canzone" (Harvard University 2019). Petrarch's sonnets were admired throughout Europe during the Renaissance era. He was also among the earliest proponents of Renaissance humanism (to be discussed later in this chapter). Petrarch's interest in recovering and studying Latin writings and historical accounts helped to spark the Renaissance in Italy.

At the height of the Italian Renaissance, Florence-born Niccolo Machiavelli (1469–1527), a political philosopher, statesman, and secretary of the Florentine Republic, published his most famous works, *The Prince* and the *Discourse on Livy*, in which he laid out his political ideas. There was much turmoil in Italy during Machiavelli's lifetime. He was born in Florence during the Medici regime but this government was defeated during France and Spain's 1494 invasion of Italy. It was at this time that Machiavelli became a member of the Florentine government. His role with the government placed him in charge of the Republic's foreign affairs in subject territories. Machiavelli attempted to create the perfect system of government in Florence and restore the city to the position it had held in Tuscany prior to the French invasion (Schwoebel 1971). In 1512 the Florentine Republic was overthrown and the gonfalonier deposed by a Spanish army that Julius II had enlisted into his Holy League. (In the medieval Italian city-states, gonfalonier—"standard bearer"—was the title given to high civic magistrates, who generally were the commanders of the people's militia.) The Medici family returned to rule Florence, and Machiavelli, suspected of conspiracy, was imprisoned, tortured, and sent into exile in 1513 to his father's small property south of Florence. There, he wrote his two major works, both of which were published after his death (Mansfield 2019).

In *The Prince* (1513), Machiavelli

> believed that he was providing a scientific analysis of the practice of government based on experience and on the study of the past. He went beyond events and analyzed the characteristic behavior of men and institutions. His conclusions were stark and shocking. He said in effect that the way things had gone in Italy constitute political reality. And he went on to prescribe what the rulers of Florence must do in order to survive and prosper within that reality.
>
> *(Schwoebel 1971:xvii)*

To truly understand the nature of politics, Machiavelli believed, it would be necessary to examine and grasp the underlying motives of behavior. He concluded that men and states were equally aggressive, ambitious, and grasping. Change, disorder, and struggle were facts of life. The ruler of a republic would have to be able to control such social forces that directly affected the success of his plans. Until the Renaissance, most books upheld general notions of normative behavior, were non-empirical, and did not observe, describe, or analyze actual human behavior. *The Prince* shocked its readers and was widely censored and banned.

At nearly the same time as Machiavelli was shocking the establishment with his political discourse in *The Prince*, Martin Luther (1497–1546) was challenging the Catholic Church and its assertion that the only true interpretation of the Bible should come from the religious leaders. As a proponent of mass education, Luther believed that it was the right, even duty, of all Christians to interpret the Bible for themselves. In 1517, Luther publicly challenged the Catholic Church by nailing his 95 Theses to the door of the cathedral in Wittenberg, Germany, lighting the fires of the Reformation and Protestantism.

In addition to the open proclamation and challenge of the existing social order among a select number of Renaissance thinkers, there were also a few significant contributors to the scientific community during the Renaissance era, including Polish astronomer Nicolaus Copernicus (1473–1543). Copernicus proposed that the planets, including the Earth, revolved around the Sun, instead of the universally held belief that the Earth was the center of the universe (Redd 2018). It would take other astronomers to build upon Copernicus' work and prove that our planet was indeed just one of many planets to orbit the Sun and just one star in a vast cosmos of infinite others. However, as Edward Rosen (1971) explains,

> Before Copernicus, it [the Earth] was almost universally considered not to be a heavenly body. The earth was placed in a category apart from the heavenly bodies. This disjunction divided the universe into two separate layers. The planets and countless stars dotted the heavenly region. Far below it lay the sub-celestial zone of the earth, on which we spend our lives, miserable or happy.
>
> *(pp. 96–97)*

Copernicus would suffer the same fate as most other brilliant thinkers in the Renaissance, the Scientific Revolution, the Enlightenment, and the Modern eras who dared to speak the truth against long-held ignorant beliefs—being mocked and questioned and having to find others smart enough to verify his factual knowledge.

Scientific discovery would not be the central achievement of the Renaissance era. Instead, the key intellectual aspect of the Renaissance is *humanism*. Once again, however, scholars and historians seem to disagree as to its true meaning. (Still today there is much debate as to the actual meaning of the term "humanism" as almost any kind of discourse regarding human values is called "humanistic.")

> Humanism has long stood at the core of the Renaissance debate. Scholars have viewed it not only as an individual prime mover, but as a unifying feature by which the Renaissance was transmitted, received and transformed into a pan-European phenomenon.... But if humanism was a critical component of the Renaissance, its precise nature has been the source of much disagreement.
>
> *(Caferro 2011:98)*

Schwoebel (1971), for example, describes the importance of humanism during the English Renaissance period and credits the "spread of the new culture" of humanism to Thomas More (1478–1535), describing him as "one of its leading lights" (p. xv). Saint Thomas More's most famous publication, *Utopia* (1516), was a work of fiction primarily depicting an island on which social and political customs were entirely governed by reason. More used *Utopia* to point out that European society of his era was driven by self-interest and greed, and not reason (Delaney 2016).

As Kristeller explains, to understand the role of classical studies in the Renaissance, we must acknowledge the character of humanism.

> The most characteristic and most pervasive aspect of the Italian Renaissance in the field of learning is the humanistic movement. I need hardly to say that the term "humanism," when applied to the Italian Renaissance, does not imply all the vague and confused notions that are now commonly associated with it. Only a few traces of these may be found in the Renaissance. By humanism we mean merely the general tendency of the age to attach the greatest importance to classical studies, and to consider classical antiquity as the common standard and model by which to guide all cultural activities.
>
> *(Kristeller 1951:95)*

The true meaning of humanism during the Renaissance period is directly connected to Petrarch, who is generally considered the founder of humanism. The humanistic movement of early Italian humanism is centered on intellectual, philosophical, and cultural aspects of study designed to restore classical intellectual values (known today as the "humanities"). Renaissance humanism did not abandon religious thought but, rather, attempted to find a balance between religious and secular thought. As the "Father of Humanism," Petrarch's writings include well-known odes to Laura, his idealized love. His writings were also used to shape the modern Italian language (Biography.com 2019a).

Beginning with Petrarch and other early Renaissance social thinkers, the concept of "humanism" was really articulated by the term *humanista*.

> The term *humanista*, coined at the height of the Renaissance period, was in turn derived from an older term, that is, from the "humanities" or *studia humanitatis*. This term was apparently used in the general sense of liberal or literary education by such ancient Roman authors as Cicero and Gellius, and this was resumed by the Italian scholars of the late fourteenth century.
>
> *(Kristeller 1951:9)*

Humanism in this context, then, refers to the study of classical literature (i.e., Latin and Greek) and values liberal education; it emphasizes the importance and central role of the classics in the curriculum. "Thus, Renaissance humanism was … a cultural and educational program which emphasized and developed an important but limited area of studies" (Kristeller 1951:10).

Charles G. Nauert (1995) describes *studia humanitatis* as an implied broad general education, but one with a strong emphasis on the oratorical skills and the social attitudes most needed by a ruling elite: grammar, rhetoric, poetry, history (largely dealing with politics), and moral philosophy (which included the issue of political obligation). Nauert credits Petrarch for making humanistic education a popular ideal. However, Nauert also points out that the humanistic program of education proposed by Petrarch would be replaced by the Italian elite with an educational system based on practical ends. From Nauert's perspective, in the tradition of the humanistic Renaissance, to be among the educated elite was to have been trained in the humanities.

Petrarch's passion for the classics and for his own writing was brought about by his disdain for the darkness of the "Middle Ages" (a term that is often credited to Petrarch) and his hope for the future based on the heights of humanity's past accomplishments. Humanism, then, was the bridge from the classical past to the Renaissance era. "As one of the world's first classical scholars, Petrarch unearthed vast stores of knowledge in the lost texts he discovered, while his philosophy of humanism helped foment the intellectual growth and accomplishments of the Renaissance" (Biography.com 2019a).

It should be clear to see that the very foundation of modern higher education (colleges and universities) is directly connected to the concept of "humanism," the humanities and the liberal arts (the arts and sciences). The truly enlightened person is one who has achieved an advanced education in the humanities and arts and sciences. In this regard, the purpose of higher education is to provide knowledge from the humanistic perspective and to create classically trained graduates. This realization is a gift from the Renaissance to the contemporary era and the source of the credo that knowledge serves as the path to enlightenment.

As we summarize the Renaissance period, there is debate among historians and scholars as to the exact starting and ending points of the Renaissance era, but settling with 1300–1600 seems a safe determination. Scholars seem to agree that this was a legendary time for poetry, art, sculpture, architecture, and attempts of social change that provided hope for new lifestyles (e.g., urban, lay culture, commercial economy, and challenges to tradition and faith). The Renaissance brought about the first wave of humanism and as such a hope for a more enlightened society filled with hope, tolerance, and dignity for all. As Schwoebel (1971) explains,

> Old values and virtues no longer reflected the realities of social life. Renaissance man was hard put to reconcile the professed ideals of the received tradition and the way people actually lived. The creative and vital forces of the new culture were located in towns and cities that were centers of commerce, industry, [and] banking. Renaissance culture was essentially a civic and commercial culture. Yet the proponents of a traditional Christian ethic proclaimed the value of the ascetic life. The ideal Christian was one who lived apart from the world and who pursued neither wealth nor worldly renown.
>
> *(pp. ix–x)*

And yet,

> the Renaissance was also a restless and chaotic era, a period of accelerating change, and of discontinuity. It explained sharp demographic fluctuations and severe, recurrent economic and social dislocations. War, disease, hunger were constant scourges, with poverty, repression, and bigotry far more prevalent than wealth or individual freedom or toleration. For the great majority life was brief, harsh, and materially unrewarding.
>
> (Schwoebel 1971:viii–ix)

State leaders who rose to power promising a better life for the masses themselves turned into tyrants.

> Champions of human rights and liberty of conscience condemned and killed their opponents. Joan of Arc, John Hus, Savonarola were burned for what they believed. Henry VIII murdered royal wives and his lord chancellor, Thomas More. Protestants and Catholics massacred each other while they nursed a common enmity for Jews and Turks.
>
> (Schwoebel 1971:ix)

Thus, while the Renaissance gives us a glimpse as to how enlightened reason could play a positive role in transforming society, the nation states and religious leaders would not give up their hold on thought processes dominated by tradition and faith. In the search for a new moral authority, a new enlightened human species would have to be put on hold.

The Scientific Revolution (c.1600–1700)

The pursuit of a new enlightened humanity is exemplified by a number of early enlightened social thinkers, some of whom overlap with the end of the Renaissance era and others of whom were a part of the early stages of the development of the Enlightenment. This period between the Renaissance and the Enlightenment is often referred to as the "Scientific Revolution" era. As the name implies, scientists were promoting and utilizing the *scientific method* (the pursuit of knowledge involving the stating of a problem, the collection of facts through observation and experiment, and the testing of ideas/hypotheses to determine whether they appear to be "valid" or "invalid") to various fields of study, but especially in the natural sciences of mathematics, physics, astronomy, gravitation (i.e., Isaac Newton's theory of gravity as articulated in *Principia*), optics, biology and medicine, and chemistry. Systematic experimentation and empiricism (the reliance on observation and measurement as a way of acquiring knowledge—an approach in direct contrast to a reliance on tradition, faith, and common sense) are hallmarks of the scientific approach. Galileo is a good example of an early contributor to the Scientific Revolution era.

Galileo Galilei (1564–1642) was born in Pisa, Italy, and is known as an Italian natural philosopher, astronomer, and mathematician who made contributions to the sciences of motion, astronomy, and strength of materials, and to the development of the scientific method (Van Helden 2019).

> His formulation of (circular) inertia, the law of falling bodies, and parabolic trajectories marked the beginning of a fundamental change in the study of motion. His insistence that the book of nature was written in the language of mathematics changed natural philosophy from a verbal, qualitative account to a mathematical one in which experimentation became a recognized method for discovering the facts of nature
>
> *(Val Helden 2019)*

Galileo improved the telescope, made astronomical observations, and put forth the basic principle of relativity in physics (Boundless World History 2019).

A contemporary of Galileo was Francis Bacon (1561–1626; his full title was Francis Bacon, 1st Viscount St Alban, but he is also known as Sir Francis Bacon). Born in London, Bacon was a lawyer, statesman, and philosopher, and a master English literary speaker. Of greatest relevance to our discussion on the utilization of the scientific method, Bacon put forth (in his 1620 book *Novum Organum*, or *New Method*) an investigative method that was supposed to replace the methods put forward in Aristotle's *Organon*. "This method was influential upon the development of the scientific method in modern science, but also more generally in the early modern rejection of medieval Aristotelianism" (Boundless World History 2019).

One of the first to abandon scholastic Aristotelianism was René Descartes (1596–1650). Born in Touraine, France, Descartes was a French mathematician, scientist, and philosopher. He abandoned Aristotelianism because he

> formulated the first modern version of mind-body dualism, from which stems the mind-body problem, and because he promoted the development of a new science grounded in observation and experiment, he has been called the father of modern philosophy … Decartes' metaphysics is rationalist, based on the postulation of innate ideas of mind, matter, and God, but his physics and physiology, based on sensory experience, and mechanistic and empiricist.
>
> *(Watson 2019)*

Descartes was also a deep thinker. He believed that humans are capable of gaining certain knowledge on a wide variety of things (Crumley 2016). In *The Discourse on Method*, Descartes expressed one of the most famous concepts in the history of philosophy: "I think; therefore, I am." This profound statement has been interpreted by many scholars and laypersons alike, but essentially Descartes is making the point that he cannot doubt his own existence because he is the one doing the doubting in the first place. That he can ponder his own existence implies that he must exist in order to question his own existence.

Building upon the individualism put forth by Descartes ("I think; therefore, I am"), Wiltshire, England-born Thomas Hobbes (1588–1679) used the individual as the building block from which all of his theories sprang. Hobbes formulated his theories by way of empirical observation; he believed that everything in the universe was simply made of atoms in motion, and that geometry and mathematics could be used to explained human behavior (Delaney 2004). According to his theories, there are two types of motion in the universe: "Vital" (involuntary motions such as a heartbeat) and "Voluntary" (things we choose to do). Voluntary motion was further broken down into two subcategories that Hobbes believed were reducible to mathematical equations involving "desires" and "aversions." Desires are things one is moved toward or that are valued by the individual, while aversions are fears or things to be avoided by the individual. Further, individuals' appetites constantly keep them in motion, and in order to remain in motion, everyone needs a certain degree of power. Thus, the pursuit of power is the natural state of humans, as humans are in constant struggle for power and, above all else, they want to avoid a violent death (Delaney 2004).

Hobbes's observations about the role of humans within a given society, especially in light of his premise that each of us seeks some independence and freedom to keep in motion, led him to conclude that because social order is made by humans, they can also change it (Adams and Sydie 2001). Even under authoritarian rule, Hobbes believed that authority is given by the subjects themselves; that is, by their consent, the rulers maintain sovereign power. As a political and social theorist, Hobbes wondered what life and human relations would be like in the absence of government. In 1651, Hobbes published his greatest work, *Leviathan*. In this book, he provides a disturbing account of society without government. From his viewpoint, society would be filled with fear and danger of violent death, and the life of man would be solitary, poor, nasty, brutish, and short. In his brief introduction to *Leviathan*, Hobbes describes the state as an organism analogous to a large person. He demonstrates how each part of the state parallels the functions of the parts of the human body. Hobbes further asserted that "thinking in general is 'calculation' and that all calculation is either addition or subtraction also holds for all political thinking" (Cassirer 1951:19).

Hobbes's emphasis on the importance of the individual, his idea that government should derive from humans and not as some divine sense of purpose or birthright, certainly qualifies him as engaging in liberal thought—an important element of the Enlightenment. Since Hobbes is often referred to as the first liberal thinker, it is only fitting that our attention is now turned to John Locke, considered by some to be the father of liberal democratic thought.

Liberalism is centered on the belief that humans have basic innate rights, and deserve freedom from tyranny, moral self-determinism, happiness on Earth (instead of some promise of an afterlife), private property ownership, government policies that promote *laissez faire*, and the right to believe, or not believe, in God(s). Social thinkers such as John Locke and Montesquieu epitomize early liberal thought. Montesquieu, an Enlightenment social thinker, will be discussed later in this chapter.

John Locke (1632–1704) was born in a village in Somerset, England. In 1652, he attended Christ Church, Oxford, where he studied Aristotelianism; he remained a student there for many years. He would come to revolt against the medieval scholasticism of the Oxford curriculum and become more interested in the "new science" or "natural philosophy" introduced by Sir Robert Boyle, who ultimately founded the Royal Society (Thomson 1993). Locke became friends with Boyle (known as the father of chemistry) and many of the leading scientists of his era, including Thomas Sydenham and Isaac Newton (Ayers 1999). For many years, Locke pursued his medical studies but eventually shifted his attention to philosophy and the scientific questions of his time.

Locke embraced many, but not all, of the ideas presented by Hobbes in his theories on the state of nature and the rise of governments and societies. They shared a common view of the importance and autonomy of the individual in society: that people exist as individuals before societies and governments; that people have certain rights, including basic freedoms; and that individual freedom is important because it serves as the foundation for modern liberal democracy. Locke strongly believed that individuals have the right to own property. Locke's *Two Treatises of Government* (1690) has been viewed as the classic expression of liberal political ideas and is read as a defense of individualism and of the natural right of individuals to appropriate private property (Ashcraft 1987). It also served as a primary source for the American Declaration of Independence. The US Constitution, which is filled with liberal principles, was directly influenced by the many ideas of Locke, and this is especially true of his *A Letter Concerning Toleration* (1689). In this publication, Locke argues for the rights of humans and the necessity of separating Church and State. The principle of the separation of Church and State is another key element of enlightened rational thought.

This concludes our brief look at the antecedents of the Enlightenment. The coverage of the Renaissance and the Scientific Revolution and the many social thinkers who influenced the Enlightenment was never intended to be exhaustive, as that is beyond the scope and concern of this book. Instead, this review was meant to introduce the reader to the idea that many thoughts and ideas preceded the social thinkers of the Enlightenment era.

The Enlightenment (c.1700–1840s)

The "Age of Enlightenment" is a term used to describe the essence of the long eighteenth century in Europe and the American colonies (and the early United States). The collectivity of progressive and liberal ideas and alternatives to traditional ways of thinking was being advanced by "the leading intellectuals and propagandists of the day, unambiguously amounted to a decisive stage in human improvement" (Porter 1991:1). Cassirer (1951) states, "Perhaps no other century is so completely permeated by the idea of intellectual progress as that of the Enlightenment" (p. 5). The Enlightenment was a period of dramatic intellectual development and change in philosophical thought. A number of long-standing ideas and beliefs were being abandoned and replaced during this era. The Enlightenment thinkers kept a watchful eye on the social arrangements of society; "Their central interest was the attainment of human and social perfectibility in the here and now rather than in some heavenly future. They considered rational education and scientific understanding of self and society the routes to all human social progress" (Adams and Sydie 2001:11). Progress could be attained because humans hold the capacity for reason. Further, reason should not be constrained by tradition, religion, or sovereign power.

Through education, humanity itself could be altered, its nature changed for the better. A great premium was placed on the discovery of truth through the observation of nature, rather than through study of authoritative sources, such as Aristotle and the Bible. Although viewing the Church, especially the Catholic Church, as the principal force that had enslaved the human mind in the past, most Enlightenment thinkers did not renounce religion completely. They saw God as a "Prime Mover," a motivator of sorts (Garner 2000). Yet they still believed that human aspirations should be centered on improving life on Earth, and not on the promises of an afterlife. Worldly happiness was placed before religious promises of "salvation." No social institution was attacked with more intensity and ferocity than the Church; with all its wealth, political power, and suppressions of the free exercise of reason, it was deemed a logical target of secular scorn.

The Enlightenment was more than a set of ideas; it implied an attitude, a method of thought. There was a clear desire to explore new ideas and allow for changing values. And while most texts, including this one, devote their coverage to some of the biggest names of the Enlightenment, there were "a few thousand academicians familiar with 'the light'" that were involved in this intellectual movement (Jacob 1991:143). Furthermore, it is important to note that not all social writers and commentators of the Enlightenment that comprised the collectivity of enlightened reason were intellectuals. There were many popularizers engaged in a self-conscious effort to win converts to enlightened thinking. These nonacademic proponents of enlightenment were journalists, propagandists, and historians who were often described as *philosophes*. As Munck (2000) explains,

> [The] *philosophes* have often been regarded as 'outsiders,' both socially and politically—that is, their main impact was through criticism and through their influence on public opinion, rather than directly on government. This may be true of some of them, but the generalization does not always stand up to closer scrutiny. The physiocrats, in particular, came to exercise considerable direct influence, not just whilst one of their foremost contributors, Turgot, held the highest financial office of the state.
>
> *(p. 18)*

Porter (1991) describes the *philosophes* as deploring the way the French kingdom was constituted, as they considered it backward, repressive, and a failure on the international stage. Not surprisingly, they did not feel loyalty toward it. Porter adds, "The *philosophes* mocked narrow-minded nationalism along with all other kinds of parochial prejudice" (1991:51). The philosophes valued both education and practical knowledge and as a result they placed a great deal of emphasis on practical skills, such as how to farm, how to construct bridges and dams, and how to relate to fellow citizens (Adams and Sydie 2001).

In the following pages, we will take a look at representative European and American Enlightenment thinkers.

European Enlightenment thinkers

We begin our review of European Enlightenment thinkers with Charles-Louis de Montesquieu, Francois-Marie Arouet (Voltaire) and Jean-Jacques Rousseau, a trio described by Thomas Munck as the "Trinity of the Enlightenment."

Munck puts forth the notion that Montesquieu (1689–1755) was the key figure of European Enlightenment thinkers because of his *Persian Letters* of 1721, which set much of the tone of the Enlightenment way of thinking, and his substantial treatise on the *Spirit of the Laws* (1748), which remained one of the most frequently cited texts through the period of the American and French Revolutions. Munck, as with his contemporaries, enjoyed the literary style, wit, and satire, though less weighty in terms of systematic ideas, of Voltaire (1694–1778), who enjoyed a wide following and established a number of famous correspondents around Europe (Munck 2000).

> The trinity of the enlightenment was completed by Rousseau (1712–78), the most eccentric of the three—a perpetual rebel, a self-proclaimed spokesperson for truth and sincerity in an age prone to empty flattery, an educational reformer (in *Emile* of 1762), an early Romantic (in *La Nouvelle Heloise* of 1761), a communitarian (in theory if not by personal preference), and a political innovator (in *The Social Contract* of 1762).
>
> *(pp. 1–2)*

Let's take a closer look at this "Trinity of the Enlightenment." The first of these three, Montesquieu, was born near Bordeaux to a noble and prosperous family. His publication of the *Persian Letters* (while published anonymously, his authorship was an open secret) had a significant impact on the Enlightenment. An instant success, the volume made Montesquieu a literary celebrity.

> The *Persian Letters* is both one of the funniest books written by a major philosopher, and one of the bleakest. It presents both virtue and self-knowledge as almost unattainable. Almost all the Europeans in the *Persian Letters* are ridiculous; most of those who are not appear only to serve as a mouthpiece for Montesquieu's own views.
>
> *(Stanford Encyclopedia of Philosophy 2014)*

Spending a great deal of time in Paris, Montesquieu frequented the intellectual salons, listening and learning from other enlightened thinkers, during this time writing several minor works.

He spent years working on his masterpiece, *The Spirit of Laws*, a publication designed to explain human laws and social institutions. Montesquieu argued that laws should be adapted to fit the needs of the people for whom they are framed: the climate of each country (e.g., the quality of its soil); the primary occupations of the natives; the provision of their liberty; the religion of the inhabitants; the inclinations, wealth, and number of the people the laws governed; and the manners and customs of those people (*Stanford Encyclopedia of Philosophy* 2014). As Cassirer (1951) explains,

> The aim of Montesquieu's work is not simply to describe the forms and types of state constitutions—despotism, constitutional monarchy, and the republican constitution—and to present them empirically, it is also to construct them from the forces of which they are composed. Knowledge of these forces is necessary if they are to be put to their proper use, if we are to show how they can be employed in the making of a state constitution which realizes the demand of the greater possible freedom. Such freedom, as Montesquieu tries to show, is possible only when every individual force is limited and restrained by a counterforce.
>
> (p. 20)

The idea that every force should be presented with a counterforce led to Montesquieu's famous doctrine of the "division of powers" (Cassirer 1951).

Montesquieu should not be considered a utopian, by either temperament or conviction. Montesquieu said, "In the first place, I'm going to plant my feet firmly on the ground. I'm not going to aim at the blissful state of angels, so I shan't cry because I don't get it" (Hazard 1954:20). He believes that a stable, non-despotic government that leaves its law-abiding citizens more or less free to live their lives is a good one. Still, he proposed that for laws that are genuinely in need of reform, such reforms must be accomplished (*Stanford Encyclopedia of Philosophy* 2014). Furthermore, in an attempt to recognize all of the existing forms of government, he proposed a "mixed government" system as a means of safeguarding against despotism and assuring a balance of powers.

Born in Paris, Francois-Marie Arouet, known as Voltaire, was a writer, philosopher, poet, dramatist, historian, and polemicist of the French Enlightenment whose diversity of literary output is rivaled only by its abundance (Voltaire Foundation 2017). As proclaimed by the Voltaire Foundation, "The Age of Voltaire" is synonymous with "the Enlightenment." One of the greatest of all French writers, Voltaire's works was indeed very popular during the Enlightenment and a few of his publications are still read today. He was a crusader against tyranny, bigotry, and cruelty and often angered religious and political figures. "Through its critical capacity, wit, and satire, Voltaire's work vigorously propagates an ideal of progress to which people of all nations have remained responsive" (Pomeau 2019).

He was a polemicist who fought for liberal civil rights (e.g., the right to a fair trial, freedom of speech, and freedom of religion) and denounced the hypocrisies and injustices of the Ancien Régime. Voltaire embraced Enlightenment philosophers such as Newton, Locke, and Bacon who promoted the ideals of a free and liberal society, along with freedom of religion and free commerce (Biography.com 2019b). He believed the French bourgeoisie of his era to be too small and ineffective, the aristocracy to be parasitic and corrupt, the commoners to be ignorant and superstitious, and the Church to be a static force useful only to provide backing for revolutionaries. On the other hand, Voltaire also distrusted democracy because he saw it as propagating the idiocy of the masses; instead, he promoted a benevolent despotism, similar to that advocated by Plato (The Basics of Philosophy 2019).

Voltaire's *Essay on Manners* "assessed the cultural achievements of sixteenth-century Italy and tried to explain them, noticing that they took place at the same time as European prosperity, refinement of manners, and political achievement" (Burke 1964:7). The publication of Voltaire's *Letters on the English* (1733) angered the French Church and government, forcing the writer to flee to safer pastures. He spent the next 15 years with his mistress, Émilie du Châtelet, at her husband's home in Cirey-sur-Blaise (Biography.com 2019b).

Voltaire is often perceived as an atheist but there is some contradictory information about the extent of his views on religion. as Roy Porter (1991) writes, "Voltaire went onto the offensive against the evils of religion with what became a notorious catchphrase, *Ecrasez l'infame* (destroy the infamous one)" (p. 4). Geoffrey Clive (1973) states that Voltaire "was clearly opposed to religious fanaticism, superstition, metaphysical cant, and tyranny" (p. 31). However, in line with other Enlightenment thinkers of the era, Voltaire was a deist—not by faith, according to him, but rather by reason. "He looked favorably on religious tolerance, even though he could be severely critical towards Christianity, Judaism, and Islam" (Biography.com 2019b). His distrust in the people closest to him led Porter (1991) to state,

> Voltaire was notoriously convinced that it was essential that one's servants—one's wife, too—should be pious, otherwise, lacking the fear of God, such people would steal the spoons or be unfaithful. Recognizing thus the utility of devotion, many philosophes not surprisingly advocated a two-tier religious system, with a simple, pure, rational religion for the elite, and a melodramatic faith to regulate the minds and hearts of the plebs. Such beliefs eventually found expression in the cult of the Supreme Being, a modern, rational dechristianised object of worship, concocted during the French Revolution.
>
> *(pp. 35–36)*

Rousseau completes Munck's (2000) "Trinity of the Enlightenment." Jean-Jacques Rousseau was born in the city-state of Geneva (in Switzerland) and baptized into the Calvinist faith. A philosophical writer and political theorist, he passionately promoted his republican sentiments for liberty, equality, and brotherhood and his treatises and novels inspired the French Revolution and Enlightenment ideals.

Rousseau had a number of significant publications; a brief sample of his works is described below.

Rousseau's first published work was in 1750, entitled *Discourse on the Arts and Sciences*. This publication was a prize-winning essay written for the Academy of Dijon. He argued that the more science, industry, technology, and culture became developed and sophisticated, the more they carried human societies from decent simplicity toward moral corruption (Cranston 1986).

In his second publication, *Discourse on the Origin of Inequality* (1755), also known as *Second Discourse*, Rousseau described the process of how social institutions had developed the extreme inequalities of aristocratic France, where the nobility and the Church lived in luxury, while the poor peasants had to pay most of the taxes (Rousseau 1992). The theme of *Second Discourse* is that society alienates man from his natural self, thus creating a situation of inner dissension and of conflict with other men (Crocker 1968). This publication is viewed as one of the most influential works of the Enlightenment as Rousseau develops a theory of evolution that predates Darwinism and provides a theoretical view of the effects of civilization on human nature. Rousseau explains in the preface of his *Second Discourse* that it in order to judge rightfully the natural state of man, we must consider his development from his origin and follow through to the current times when laws have infringed upon the natural order of the human species. He also reveals a theme of his works that the first order of business for humans, since the dawn of the species, has been self-preservation.

In subsequent publications, Rousseau attempted to resolve the issues he raised in *Discourse on the Origin of Inequality*. In his *Discourse on Political Economy* (1755), also known as the *Third Discourse*, a forerunner of *The Social Contract*, Rousseau first makes his suggestions of remedies for the injustices described in *Second Discourse*. He recommends that the individual should choose to regard himself as a part of the whole society. In his *Third Discourse*, Rousseau argues that civil freedom must be accompanied by moral freedom. Rousseau states,

> Men are trained early enough never to consider their persons except as related to the body of the State, and not to perceive their existence, so to speak, except as part of the State's, they will eventually come to identify themselves to be members of the homeland; to love it with that delicate sentiment that any isolated man feels only for himself.
>
> *(Quoted in Cullen 1993:87)*

In 1762, Rousseau published his famous *The Social Contract*, which represents another attempt to resolve issues he brought up in his *Second Discourse*. According to Rousseau, society could only be accounted for, and justified, as a means of enabling men to advance to a higher level of achievement than could be arrived at in its absence. Rousseau's beliefs, including such phrases as "Man is born free and everywhere he is in chains," did not go over well with the Parisian authorities, resulting in the book being banned. Rousseau believed that nature ordained all men equal and that the State's conformity to natural law involved the maintenance of public order and the provision of opportunities for the happiness of individuals. Rousseau, therefore, believed that the State is to have a limited role in societal matters, with its primary function to protect the members from outside threats as well as internal self-concerning individuals. The proper role of the State is to secure the freedom and equality of its citizens and not to act in a manner that limits them.

It is clear that Rousseau wanted a democratic society, but he was also aware of the potential of individuals acting in their own self-interest. He believed that the only primitive instinct of individuals is the desire for self-preservation. Individuals will love what tends to conserve them and abhor what tends to harm them.

The ideals of Scottish Enlightenment are exemplified by David Hume (1711–1776) and Thomas Reid and Adam Smith (both to be discussed later in this chapter). Hume was a philosopher, historian, economist, and essayist, and perhaps the most radical and important of the so-called British Empiricists (New World Encyclopedia 2017). Possessing an interest in our beliefs about the world and a desire to attain truth and knowledge, Hume was willing to grant that we often get things right, that is to say, many of our beliefs about the world are undoubtedly true, or, at the very least, are likely to be true. However, he cautioned that if we use just one method of analyzing the world, while there may be a good reason to rely on such an approach, such a strategy may also be shown to be irrational. He recognized that often people think that their beliefs are rational simply because they find a way to rationalize them.

But how does this rationalization process work, Hume pondered? In his publication *An Enquiry Concerning Human Understanding* (1751), Hume puts forth the notion that all human knowledge comes to us through our senses, which leads to perceptions about things. Hume believed that there are two categories of perceptions: ideas and impressions. He defines these terms in *An Enquiry*:

> By the term impression, then, I mean all of our more lively perceptions, when we hear, or see, or feel, or love, or hate, or desire, or will. And impressions are distinguished from ideas, which are the less lively perceptions, of which we are conscious, when we reflect on any of those sensations or movements above mentioned.
>
> *(Quoted in* New World Encyclopedia *2017)*

Hume is associated with his advocacy of skepticism, although he promoted a relatively moderate version that entails "exercising caution and modesty in our judgments" and "restricting our speculation to abstract reasoning and matters of fact" (*Internet Encyclopedia of Philosophy* 2019).

Thomas Reid (1710–1796) was a Scottish philosopher who was interested in the fabric of the human mind and body; he promoted the research methodologies of observation and experimentation and is best known as the "father of common sense philosophy" (Delaney 2019). It was his renowned publication of *An Inquiry Into the*

Human Mind: On the Principles of Common Sense (1764) that helped Reid to garner such a reputation. Christopher Hookway (2002) says of Reid that he understood "common sense as a body of ill-defined but self-evident and certain principles which guide our actions and our beliefs, including philosophical ones" (p. 198).

Despite his promotion of common sense, Reid proclaimed that the best way to attain knowledge is through observation and experiment. Reid (2000) states:

> By our constitution, we have a strong propensity to trace particular facts and observations to general rules, and to apply such general rules to account for other effects, or to direct us in the production of them. This procedure of the understanding is familiar to every human creature in the common affairs of life, and it is the only one by which any real discovery in philosophy can be made.
>
> *(pp. 11–12)*

Reid did acknowledge that theories and conjectures help to spark the curiosity of man but warned of their limitations compared to actual scientific procedures.

Adam Smith (1723–1790) was a Scottish social philosopher and political economist who positioned himself as the leading economist of his day (and with an impact still today) with his publication of *An Inquiry into the Nature and Causes of the Wealth of Nations* (usually shortened to *The Wealth of Nations*) in 1776. Smith utilized the sentiments of the Enlightenment to berate

> governments for their traditional, "mercantilist" and "protectionist" policies, which (he argued) hamstring trade for the "fiscalist" purposes of raising revenue. Smith further attacked the traditional belief that war was the route to wealth; accused vested interests of supporting monopolies contrary to the public interest; and argued that, properly-understood, market mechanisms, would, in the long term, prove beneficial to all.
>
> *(Porter 1991:22)*

At the time of Smith's *The Wealth of Nations*, the strength of a nation's economy was generally measured by its reserves of gold and silver. Smith turned this around by suggesting that the nation's wealth should be measured by its total production and commerce, known today as the gross domestic product (GDP). Smith argued that the wealthiest nations were the ones with free trade and not necessarily better resources or a harder-working workforce. One of the most important aspects of Smith's economic treatise is the idea of "the invisible hand," a concept that suggests that the determination of pricing and value is determined by the market. If someone sells an inferior product or charges too much for a product they will not survive in the long run; conversely, when someone sells a better-quality product at a more reasonable price, the market will reward the seller with more customers.

Another important aspect of Smith's economic theory is the concept of *laissez faire*, which is a belief that economies and businesses function best when they are free from governmental interference. *Laissez faire* comes from the French meaning "to leave alone" or "to allow something to do as it wills." This theory is akin to an economics version of the "natural law" of market forces. The *laissez faire* notion took off as a guiding principle during the Industrial Revolution. Interestingly, as Smith's ideas of "the invisible hand" and *laissez faire* would take hold in the developing nation of the United States, they became the stimulus of capitalism, a very mercantile system of economics that would lead to a great divide between the haves and the have-nots (mercantilism).

A contemporary of the Scottish Enlightenment thinkers was the German philosopher Immanuel Kant (1724–1804). In 1784, Kant wrote his often-referenced essay "What is Enlightenment?"

> For Kant, enlightenment was man's final coming of age, the emancipation of the human consciousness from an immature state of ignorance and error. He believed this process of mental liberation was actively at work in his own lifetime. The advancement of knowledge—understanding of nature, but human self-knowledge no less—would propel this great leap forward.
> *(Porter 1991:1)*

The Enlightenment, from Kant's perspective, was a "process of discovery, the active and critical engagement of the individual, that mattered, not necessarily the end result" (Munck 2000:7). Borrowing from the Latin poet Horace, Kant would promote "*Sapere aude*" or "dare to know."

Kant was born in Konigsberg (today it is the Russian city of Kaliningrad), Prussia, near the southeastern shore of the Baltic Sea. He set the tone for much of nineteenth- and twentieth-century philosophy. Kant answered the fundamental question of his philosophy—how is nature possible?—by saying that nature was nothing but the representation of nature. Thus, the notion of the realm of nature, the sensible world, is organized by human understanding in accordance with certain *a priori* principles of knowledge. Kant argued that man could never attain "true" knowledge of things in themselves, but only a knowledge that was mediated through certain fundamental mental categories, or "givens."

Kant's philosophy was often a critical one. He outlined his fundamental idea of "critical philosophy" in his three *Critiques*: the *Critique of Pure Reason* (1781, 1787), the *Critique of Practical Reason* (1788), and the *Critique of the Power of Judgment* (1790) (*Stanford Encyclopedia of Philosophy* 2016). These three publications occurred toward the end of the European Enlightenment, and Kant was taking on an increasingly pessimistic view of human progress, believing that the antagonism between men was the ultimate driving force in history. As Coser (1977) explains, Kant believed that men were given to an "unsociable sociability." This conclusion was in contrast to his hope that sociability would promote democratic ideals as Kant posited the axiom that each individual should possess freedom to the extent that is compatible with the freedom of every other individual.

In his *Critique of Pure Reason*, Kant wrote about the possibility of metaphysics to be understood in terms of "the cognitions after which reason might strive independently of all experience" (*Stanford Encyclopedia of Philosophy* 2016). For Kant, metaphysics concerns *a priori knowledge*, or knowledge whose justification does not depend on experience, and he associates *a priori knowledge* with reason. The goal of his *Critique of Pure Reason* is an attempt to determine whether, how, and to what extent human reason is capable of *a priori knowledge* (*Stanford Encyclopedia of Philosophy* 2016). *A priori knowledge* is knowledge based on the power of deductive reasoning based on self-evident truths and/or logic. For example, a farmer upstream uses pesticides that kill fish near his farm, and a farmer downstream finds dead fish near his farm and concludes that the pesticides used upstream caused the death of these fish too. Kant argued, however, that we treat the world "as if" something is true because of past experiences ("givens"). This type of knowledge is known as *a posteriori knowledge*. An example of this is suspecting your significant other of cheating on you because they have cheated in their previous relationships. Using this form of thinking, Kant is saying that we come to "know" things (knowledge) as "true" based on past personal experiences and preconceived notions about things.

In his *Critique of the Power of Judgment*, Kant attempts to bridge what he believes is a chasm in philosophy that separates the domain of his theoretical philosophy (discussed in the *Critique of Pure Reason*) and the domain of his practical philosophy (discussed mainly in the *Critique of Practical Reason*). In essence, Kant was trying to come to grips with the growing power of science and its ability to explain things that had historically been unexplainable. He felt that science was threatening to undermine traditional moral and religious beliefs. "Kant's response is to argue that in fact these essential interests of humanity are consistent with one another when reason is granted sovereignty and practical reason is given primacy over speculative reason" (*Stanford Encyclopedia of Philosophy* 2016).

Kant put forth in the *Critique of the Power of Judgment* a number of ways in which reflecting judgment leads us to regard nature as purposive. Reflecting judgment allows us to discover empirical laws of nature. For example, Kant believed that Newton's science had provided adequate evidence that permanent "laws" existed in nature. Still, he questioned how such insights of nature were possible since nature does not provide any privileged access to its operation. Kant believed that man was capable of sorting data into categories of knowledge. The foremost of these categories were "space," "time," and "causality" (Hadden 1997).

The final European Enlightenment thinker to be discussed is the Italian criminologist and economist Cesare Beccaria (1738–1794). Beccaria's publication of *On Crimes and Punishment* (1764) became a definitive and enlightened (for its time) examination of the principles governing criminal punishment. He believed that humans are free to choose courses of action and that they are capable of making rational decisions. People can choose whether to follow the rules or be deviant. And while he spoke about the people and their free will to behave as they choose, with an implication that they are also aware of the possible repercussions for breaking the law, he felt that the government must be fair in handing out punishment.

Beccaria put forward the notions that

> the utilitarian principle that government policy should seek the greatest good for the greatest number. He lashed out at the barbaric practices of his day: the use of torture and secret proceedings, the caprice and corruption of magistrates, brutal and degrading punishments. The objective of the penal system, he argued, should be to devise penalties only severe enough to achieve the proper purposes of security and order; anything in excess is tyranny.
>
> *(Encyclopedia Britannica 2019a)*

Beccaria believed that the criminal justice system operates the best based on the certainty of punishment rather than on its severity. He was completely against capital punishment, believing it to be uncivilized.

His reformist attitude was based on the harsh realities of criminal punishment in his era.

> Throughout eighteenth-century Europe, savage torture and barbarous punishments, including branding and mutilations, were the order of the day. Nearly 200 different offenses were punishable by death. Punishments were determined by the status and relative power of the offender or the whim of the judge rather than by the nature of the crime. The prison population was a mixture of children and adults, men and women, sane and insane, guilty and innocent, thieves and murderers—all thrown in together.
>
> *(Thornton and Voigt 1992:154)*

The savagery of punishment in his day led him to characterize the system of justice and penology as irrational and ineffective.

American Enlightenment thinkers

It is the European Enlightenment that garners the most attention when one discusses "the Enlightenment," and this is for good reason, as the movement in Europe had a much greater overall impact on prevailing social thought and socio-political observations of the nature of society. In addition, political matters were far less complicated in North America than they were in Western Europe. As Munck (2000) describes, "The American intellectual politicians Benjamin Franklin (1706–1790) and Thomas Jefferson (1743–1826) may have had the easiest task, in that they were assisting in the construction of a new political system; in Europe, long historical memories and traditions complicated matters" (p. 19).

A relatively less complicated socio-political past allowed the United States to be assembled based on many enlightened ideals. "At least six ideas came to punctuate American Enlightenment thinking: deism, liberalism, republicanism, conservatism, toleration and scientific progress. Many of these were shared with European Enlightenment thinkers, but in some instances took a uniquely American form"

(Ralston 2019). *Deism* reflects the perspective of God among Enlightenment thinkers of this era as a creator on the basis of reason but not as a supernatural deity that interacts directly with humans and other creations. James Madison, Benjamin Franklin, John Adams, and George Washington were deists. *Liberalism* is a fundamental way of life for enlightened thinkers and the United States was founded on such liberal principles as rights for all humans, a focus on the middle class over the concerns of the upper class, government authority not as absolute but as based on the will and consent of the governed, and democracy. The Declaration of Independence and the US Bill of Rights both reflect liberal idealism. *Republicanism* refers to the idea that a nation should be set up as a republic wherein the State's highest officials should be determined by a general election, rather than determined through tradition (hereditary right) or faith (some sort of religious dispensation). *Conservatism* took hold in the United States toward the end of the Enlightenment (the conservative reaction to the Enlightenment will be discussed later in this chapter) and was rooted in such concerns as possible political instability (due to the citizens having too many freedoms) and, as James Madison promoted, the need for future generations to revisit the Constitution and make changes. *Toleration*, or tolerant pluralism, is an aspect of liberalism that led to the formation of tolerant institutions such as secular education and democratically organized religion (Ralston 2019). *Scientific progress* is an aspect of liberal, progressive thinking that encourages empirical testing, reason, and rationality. Franklin became one of the most famous American scientists during the Enlightenment period because of his many practical inventions, theoretical work on the properties of electricity, and his insistence on empiricism.

The following review of leading American Enlightenment thinkers will be much briefer than that of their European counterparts; chronological coverage begins with Benjamin Franklin, born in colonial Boston in 1706. Franklin ranks high as one of the greatest thinkers in American history. His self-taught education on the principles of European Enlightenment and life-long immersion in the works of the famous philosophers of the time, including Locke's "Essay Concerning Human Understanding," taught him many things including: the importance of the separation of morality from religion; opposition to organized religion; a belief in a supreme being; a reliance on science; the defense of the middle class against wealthy landowners; support of immigrants who came to America for their religious freedom (such as Franklin's friend Thomas Paine); and the desire to expand Enlightenment principles to colonial America and the eventual United States. His contributions to the early United States were immense and his idealism was inspired by enlightened thinking.

John Adams (1735–1826) was born in Braintree, Massachusetts and received a legal education from Harvard, obtaining his license in 1756. He immersed himself in the works of the Scottish Enlightenment thinkers and embraced many of their ideas, especially acknowledging the value of science and moral psychology. He blamed the English for introducing canon and feudal law to the colonies, referring to them as "the two greatest systems of tyranny" (Ralston 2019). In his "A Defense of the Constitutions of Government of the United States of America, Against the Attack of M. Turgot" (1787–1788), Adams offers an uncompromising defense of republicanism. He promoted the idea of a separation of powers between the branches of government and installed careful checks and balances on them. Still, he worried about "aristocrats" who might try to deprive liberty from the masses and thus concluded that a strong executive branch was necessary. He promoted the use of reason and justice for all (Ralston 2019).

Thomas Paine (1737–1809) was born in Thetford, Norfolk in England. In 1774 he met Benjamin Franklin in London, who advised him to emigrate to America. Heeding Franklin's advice, Paine arrived in Philadelphia in November 1774. He would work as a publicist and later as a co-editor of the *Pennsylvania Magazine*, in which his article "African Slavery in America" (1775) criticized slavery in the colonies as being unjust and inhumane. Paine quickly recognized the rising tension and spirit of rebellion in the colonies and supported the revolutionary cause in America (and Europe). In 1776, he published the internationally acclaimed *Common Sense*, which, among other things, advocated for the colonists' right to declare their independence as a matter of "common sense" based on the means of moral and political human dignity, the right for self-determination, and the belief that people should not be taxed without representation. Paine was also a proponent of pragmatism and republican sentiments (Delaney 2019). Having traveled to Paris in 1792 to oversee the French translation of *Common Sense*, Paine was threatened with execution by hanging when he was mistaken for an aristocrat. In 1793, Paine was arrested for treason because of his opposition to the death penalty, and most specifically the mass use of the guillotine. Due in part to the efforts of US President James Monroe, Paine was released (History.com 2019a).

Thomas Jefferson (1743–1836) is another member of the founding generation of Americans who was deeply influenced by the European social and intellectual European Enlightenment era. Jefferson particularly embraced the Enlightenment philosophy that stressed that liberty and equality were natural human rights (Thomas Jefferson Foundation 2019). As Adams and Sydie (2001) explain, Jefferson's preamble to the Declaration of Independence, a clear example of Enlightenment thinking, assumed that all "rational" individuals would agree with the "self-evident truths" that "all men are created equal" and endowed with "inalienable rights" of "life, liberty, and the pursuit of happiness."

> These rights justified the rejection of an unjust, tyrannical authority. Indeed, it was the duty of reasonable people to resist and reject such a government. This appeal to reason and "natural" rights as justification for resistance to traditional, religiously sanctioned authority was a profound challenge to the political status quo, especially in combination with the idea that government was a form of contract between the ruler and ruled. If the ruler did not fulfill the terms of the contract, then the subject had the right to reject the ruler and institute a new form of government.
>
> *(Adams and Sydie 2001:12)*

James Madison (1751–1836) was born near Port Conway, Virginia and is heralded as the "Father of the Constitution." He was also "a man of letters, a politician, a scientist and a diplomat who left an enduring legacy on American philosophical thought. Madison advanced his most groundbreaking ideas in his jointly authoring The Federalist Papers with John Jay and Alexander Hamilton" (Ralston 2019). Madison promoted the separation of powers among the branches of government and the implied checks and balances; he also warned of what he believed to be the inevitable dangers of political interest groups that would represent the needs of the few even at the cost of the many.

The last American to be discussed here is Benjamin Henry Day (1810–1889). Day is not a household name and perhaps not a person that comes to mind when discussing Enlightenment thinkers, but his contribution is very significant. Day was born in Springfield, Massachusetts and was an American printer and journalist who founded the *New York Sun*, the first "penny" newspaper in the United States. Having moved to New York City to run his own printing business in 1831, Day launched the *Sun*, a tabloid-type newspaper that showed the human side of the news, stressing crime and sensation while also including elements of pathos (demonstrating compassion and evoking pity) and humor (*Encyclopedia Britannica* 2019b). The significance of Day and the *Sun* to Enlightenment ideals comes from the fact that he sold his newspaper for a penny; most other newspapers cost six cents, making them too expensive for the average citizen. By selling his paper for a penny it was now possible for the middle class to become informed citizens. Many other newspapers would follow the *Sun*'s lead and also offer newspapers for a penny, leading to the expression the "penny press." While the *Sun* was sensational, it did provide news and information to the public. The enlightened founders of the United States made the value of having an informed public abundantly clear, assuring that political leaders did not act as tyrants by guaranteeing the freedom of speech and freedom of the press (along with freedom of religion and rights of assembly and petition) in the First Amendment to the US Constitution.

It has always been the role of the press to keep politically and economically powerful people in check and to keep the rights of the people at the forefront. A sure "red flag" of possible tyrannical behavior is displayed when a powerful person attempts to silence or discredit the press. From an Enlightenment perspective, a liberal press is one that promotes democracy and rights for all citizens while keeping a watchful eye of those who attempt to abuse their power. This also helps to explain why the most reputable sources of news today (based on research conducted by a number of diverse sources)—National Public Radio (NPR), *The Economist*, the Associated Press, Reuters, the Public Broadcasting Service (PBS), the British Broadcasting Corporation (BBC), the *Wall Street Journal*, *The Washington Post*, and Snopes.com (considered a watchdog for fake news more than a news source)—are generally labeled as liberal (the *Wall Street Journal* is considered a conservative publication) by their detractors. However, such a label is taken as a badge of honor by their supporters (Quora 2017; Myers 2017; Ralph and Relman 2018). (The press will be discussed in further detail in Chapter 2.)

The Age of Reason

As demonstrated in the discussion of Enlightenment thinkers, one of the most basic assumptions and beliefs of philosophers and intellectuals of the Enlightenment period, and perhaps the most important, was an abiding conviction in the power of human reason. The insistence on the ability of people to act rationally was anathema to Church and State (Hadden 1997). Social thinkers were impressed by Newton's discovery of universal gravitation. If humanity could so unlock the laws of the universe, God's own laws, why could it not also discover the laws underlying all of nature and society? Scientists came to assume that through a rigorous use of reason, an unending progress would be possible—progress in knowledge, in technical achievement, and even in moral values. Following the philosophy of Locke, the eighteenth-century social thinkers believed that knowledge is not innate, but comes only from experience and observation guided by reason (Delaney 2004). The use of reason would raise humankind beyond "savagery" and elevate it to a "civilization" or from "rudeness" to "refinement" (Porter 1991:18).

Cassirer (1951) puts forth the notion that the Enlightenment thinkers equated reason with progress. The use of reason itself was important even if the end results of a certain course of action did not pan out as hoped.

> The whole eighteenth century understands reason in this sense; not as a sound body of knowledge, principles, and truths, but as a kind of energy, a force which is fully comprehensible only in its agency and effects. What reason is, and what it can do, can never be known by its results but only by its function.
> *(Cassirer 1951:13)*

Progress can be attained because humans hold the capacity for reason and reason should never be constrained by tradition, faith, or a sovereign power.

The Century of Criticism

Just as the Enlightenment is referred to as "the Age of Reason," it is also known as the "Century of Criticism" (Cassirer 1951). The work of Enlightenment thinkers was not dispassionate inquiry, for they were deeply disturbed by the power of the Church and its secular allies in the monarchy. Freedom of inquiry and diversity of thought were not tolerated, and free-thinkers were often tortured and executed (Garner 2000). The Enlightenment is most readily characterized as "liberal individualism." It was a movement that emphasized the individual's possession of critical reason, and it was opposed to traditional authority in society and the primacy of religion in questions of knowledge (Hadden 1997). According to Seidman (1983), liberalism arose as a reaction against a static hierarchical and absolutist order that suppressed individual freedom. In addition, as Porter (1991) explains, "The philosophes claimed that critical reason would prove emancipatory. Reason and science, they proclaimed, would make people more humane and happy" (p. 8).

In the contemporary era, criticism sill plays a significant role in a democracy, for it is the responsibility of the citizens, along with the press, to call out all those who would violate the rights of others and those who would attempt to exceed their legal power.

The conservative reaction

History reveals that whenever a new and radical movement begins to challenge and ultimately changes the very core beliefs and values of an existing social structure, a corresponding, usually irrational and conservative (or reactionary), backlash will result. The Enlightenment created such a backlash. Intellectuals that represented the interests of the absolute monarchy and aristocracy wrote against the new ideas of freedom of thought, reason, civil liberties, religious tolerance, and human rights (Garner 2000). They argued for a return to rigid hierarchies, with fixed-status groups, established religion, and misery for the masses. Many of the conservatives questioned the legitimacy of individual freedom and rights, including the right to happiness. They argued that society is not a collection of individuals, but is instead a social unit in its own right, and must be protected from freedom of thought.

Extreme forms of irrationality among the conservatives included suggestions that society should go back to the medieval-era style of rule. Louis de Bonald (1754–1840), for example, was so upset by the revolutionary changes in France that he yearned for a return to the peace and harmony of the Middle Ages. De Bonald opposed challenges to traditional institutions such as patriarchy, the monogamous family, and the monarchy (Ritzer and Stepnisky 2018). He promoted a return to traditional religious beliefs, including one that promoted anti-Semitism. It was de Bonald who published one of the most violent anti-Semitic texts of the post-French Revolutionary period, *Sur les juifs* (*On the Jews*). He repeated the usual anti-Semitic accusations, that Jews were immoral and that the majority of them were parasites. De Bonald went so far as to argue that Jews must embrace Catholicism (Deutsch 2011). Identifying a category of people to use as a scapegoat for societal problems, or perceived social problems, is a typical response for extremist conservatives regardless of the era.

To counter the ignorance of the conservatism of this era came the promotion of critical thinking and higher education.

Critical thinking and higher education

Critical thinking and higher education go hand-in-hand as the purpose of attending college (at least traditionally) is twofold: to gain knowledge (both general knowledge and knowledge in one's chosen area of study that, ideally, can be used for employment purposes) and to learn how to think critically. Generally speaking, critical thinking is not a skill that comes naturally for people, as most folks think in a matter that is biased, distorted, based on limited information, uniformed, or factually incorrect. Critical thinking is different as it involves analyzing and evaluating thinking with the goal of becoming more informed. *Critical thinking* can be defined as intellectually disciplined thinking that is clear, rational, open-minded, centered on reason, and supported by evidence. It involves a mental process of skillful conceptualization, analyzing, synthesizing, and/or evaluating information gathered from, or generated by, observation, experience, reflection, questioning what biased others say is the truth, and an overall empirical grounding.

As articulated by Paul and Elder (2007), a well-cultivated critical thinker:

- raises vital questions and problems, formulating them clearly and precisely;
- gathers and assesses relevant information, using abstract ideas to interpret it effectively;
- comes to well-reasoned conclusions and solutions, testing them against relevant criteria and standards;
- thinks open-mindedly within alternative systems of thought, recognizing and assessing, as need be, their assumptions, implications, and practical consequences; and
- communicates effectively with others in figuring out solutions to complex problems.

(p. 4)

The Foundation for Critical Thinking (2019) states that

> Critical thinking can be seen as having two components: 1) a set of information and belief generating and processing skills, and 2) the habit, based on intellectual commitment, of using those skills to guide behavior. It is thus to be contrasted with: 1) the mere acquisition and retention of information alone, because it involves a particular way in which information is sought and treated; 2) the mere possession of a set of skills, because it involves the continual use of them; and 3) the mere use of those skills ("as an exercise") without acceptance of their results.

Formal education, especially higher education found in colleges and universities, is best equipped to help develop critical thinking skills of those seeking to attain a higher form of thinking based on reason and rationality. Formal education can be viewed as a process of teaching and learning in which some people (e.g., teachers and professors) cultivate knowledge, skills, intellect, and character, while others (students) take on the role of learner. The value of higher education is not simply the knowledge gained or the credentials (e.g., diplomas, certificates, security clearances, and powers of attorney) earned; it is the exposure to critical thinking techniques that enables people to better evaluate current events and matters of socio-political significance.

Formal education is a relatively new phenomenon. Martin Luther, as we learned earlier in this chapter, believed that everyone should have the right to learn to read and write. Specifically, Luther wanted all to be able to read the Bible for themselves and critically assess the meanings behind the readings. Mass education, however, did not begin until industrialization, as society needed literate people to operate machinery and develop further technology. In the United States, mandatory education laws were not instituted until the early 1900s. With the formation of community colleges and state universities during the twentieth century, far more opportunities became available for all Americans to attain a college education. Before the twentieth century, a college education was primarily restricted to those of the higher and privileged social classes.

Liberals and progressives want higher education to be more readily available to the masses so that subsequent generations have the knowledge and critical thinking skills necessary to challenge the power elites who try to dictate social policy to an uninformed populace. Conservatives would be less likely to endorse higher education and critical thinking as it does not work to the best interest of those in power to have challenges to the status quo (see Chapter 3 for a further discussion on this idea).

In brief, critical thinking is necessary in order to protect enlightened thought against those who prefer reactionary darkness.

Twentieth-century scientific achievements

The eras of the Renaissance and especially the Enlightenment helped to pave the way for a large number of significant scientific achievements in the twentieth century that would otherwise not have been possible without the guidance of reason, rationality, and science. Among the more momentous achievements of the twentieth century are the following: the airplane, the automobile, electricity and electrification, water distribution systems, electronics, radio and television, agricultural mechanization, the computer, the telephone, air conditioning and refrigeration, highways, spacecraft, the internet, imaging, household appliances, health technology, laser and fiber optics, nuclear technologies, high-performance materials, and petroleum and petrochemical technologies (National Academy of Sciences 2019a).

Let us briefly take a closer look at some of these achievements. At the start of the twentieth century not a single human being had ever flown in a powered aircraft, and yet by the end of the century it was so commonplace that billions of people had flown commercially and to all parts of the world. Consider that the International Air Transport Association (IATA) expects 7.2 billion passengers (many passengers are repeat flyers in any given year) to travel in 2035, a near-doubling of the 3.8 billion air travelers in 2016 (IATA 2019). The IATA (2019) states that the greatest passenger growth will occur in the Asia-Pacific region and that China will displace the US as the world's largest aviation market (defined by traffic to, from, and within the country) around 2024. This is a dramatic increase in air travel compared to the humble beginnings of this industry, which started with the Wright brothers' invention of the airplane in 1903. It is likely that humans have always contemplated flight and earlier attempts involved imitating birds (with built wings strapped onto the arms of individuals) and balloons filled with either hot air or hydrogen gas (Wright Brothers Aeroplane Company 2010). Prior to the Wright brothers' attempt at motorized air travel there had been a number of significant contributions from others, including Sir George Cayley, who made the first manned flight in a glider (1849), Félix du Temple, who made a steam-driven monoplane (1874), and Sir Hiram Maxim, who made a successful takeoff but not true flight in 1894 (Wright Brothers Aeroplane Company 2010). At the foundation of all successful (and unsuccessful) attempts of humankind flight was enlightened rational thought.

While airplanes criss-cross the skies across the globe, automobiles traverse across nearly all the land. Thomas Edison had predicted in 1895 (during a newspaper interview) that "The horseless carriage is the coming wonder. It is only a question of a short time when carriages and trucks in every large city will be run with motors" (National Academy of Sciences 2019b). Automobiles of all sorts help to ease the transportation needs of the more than seven billion people who crowd the Earth and the number of vehicles being produced continues to increase. Global sales of passenger cars alone in 2017 were forecast to reach nearly 79 million, and that is in addition to the hundreds of millions of cars already in existence (Statista 2019a).

Electricity and electrification have made life much better for humans in a variety of ways including heating, cooling, lighting, and power, and in the assistance of many products that rely on the use of electric power. In fact, we take the existence and availability of electric power so much for granted that we have come to view it similarly to the air we breathe; that is to say, we assume that electricity is always available to us for our many product usage needs. Electrical power is organized into a number of grids—a system of producers and consumers of electricity that runs through a system of substations, power lines, and transformers to deliver electricity.

With the availability of electricity and the creation of a large number of consumer products such as radio, television, and household products, the vast majority of humans are afforded an opportunity to take advantage of a world filled with comfort devices, and all because of rational enlightened thought. Furthermore, progressive, creative, and liberal thinking has led to the invention of all sorts of new technologies in many spheres of social life, including forms of communication. In the beginning, humans could only communicate with one another if they were face-to-face or in relatively close proximity to one another. Over time, humans found other ways to communicate, including via the telegraph, telephone, radio, television, and computer. The creation of computers allowed for the invention of the internet, which now allows for immediate long-distance social interactions through a series of networking sites. The internet has led to the creation of a virtual world (cyberspace) that has helped both personal and business interactions (Delaney and Madigan 2016).

One of the most significant contributions from scientific discovery and invention is found in the world of medicine. Mehta and Khan (2002) identify the ten greatest discoveries in cardiology during the twentieth century: electrocardiography, preventive cardiology, lipid hypotheses and atherosclerosis, coronary care units (CCU), echocardiography, thrombolytic therapy, cardiac catheterization and coronary angiography, open-heart surgery, automatic implantable cardiac defibrillators, and coronary angioplasty. Other medical and general health breakthroughs during the twentieth century include vaccination, motor-vehicle safety, safer workplaces, the control of infectious diseases, the decline in deaths from coronary heart disease and stroke, safer and healthier foods, family planning, fluoridation of drinking water, and the recognition of tobacco use as a health hazard (Centers for Disease Control and Prevention 1999). The use of vaccines is important to highlight as the practice has led to the eradication of many diseases, including this list of the top ten diseases eradicated in the twentieth century: typhoid fever, tetanus, polio, pneumococcal disease, pertussis, measles, malaria, invasive H. flu, diphtheria, and chicken pox (Said 2013).

This sampling of scientific achievements only begins to scratch the surface of the benefits that enlightened rational thought has bestowed upon humanity. And still, arguably, the greatest scientific achievement of the twentieth century, or any century to date for that matter, has yet to be discussed—space travel and humans walking on the Moon. The goal of sending humans to the Moon was sparked in earnest when President John F. Kennedy gave a speech before Congress on May 25, 1961 announcing his administration's aim to send an American safely to the Moon before the end of the decade. Kennedy stated, "We choose to go to the Moon in this decade and do other things, not because they are easy, but because they are hard..." It is true, however, that the motivation behind this lofty goal was not guided simply by progressive thought and instead by the fact that Kennedy felt pressure to have the United States "catch up to and overtake" the Soviet Union in the "space race" (NASA 2013a). The only means possible of achieving success in this mission were via scientific ingenuity. Four years earlier, Americans had been shocked when the Soviet Sputnik's cosmonaut Yuri Gagarin had become the first human in space. Sending humans successfully to the Moon and back was daunting in its own right but the fact that most rocket tests prior to this speech had failed made Kennedy's quest all the more improbable. Then again, scientific achievement often involves a steep learning curve, but that's what progressive liberal thought entails—attempts to improve humanity for further evolutionary growth despite harsh challenges. For more information on the Moon landing and the cultural backdrop of the era, see "Connecting enlightened rational thought with popular culture" Box 1.1.

With all of the achievements of rational and reasoned humans since the Middle Ages, the twenty-first century was primed to become the most enlightened one ever. However, instead of a universal embrace of enlightened rational thought, as logic and common sense would dictate, there are a number of threats confronting the human species. These threats come in the form of a darkness that surrounds us (e.g., anti-science/enlightened thinking; anti-higher education; anti-environment; anti-support of the press; a growing populist movement; pseudoscience; a general lack of humanity), a flooded swamp (e.g., the institutions of politics, Big Business, and banking), and an ever-increasing number of shameful behaviors that have led to a growing culture of shamelessness. These threats will be discussed in detail in the following chapters.

As presented here, it is argued that the many dark forces on full display in the early twenty-first century threaten the very survival of the human species and an increasing number of animal species and many forms of plant and vegetation life. We have the necessary forces (e.g., reason, rationality, and science) to overcome these threats, but the ultimate question is: will we?

Connecting enlightened rational thought with popular culture

BOX 1.1 THE MOON LANDING: "AN EPIC MOMENT IN CIVILIZATION"

Driven in great part by the achievements of the USSR and their ability to successfully send cosmonaut Yuri Gagarin into space, have him orbit the Earth, and return him successfully back to Earth, the United States felt the need to reach the Moon first. On July 20, 1969, the United States achieved the goal set by President Kennedy just eight years earlier as American astronauts reached the Moon, landed, and walked on the surface, and made it back to their orbiting spacecraft. This initial Moon walk represents one of the truly most epic moments in civilization. The science that went into this monumental accomplishment is a true testament to enlightened rational thought as such a quest involved technological advancement as well as the liberal spirit of the human mind to attempt something few dared to think could become a reality. "There is no denying the technical achievement of launching a rocket nearly 400,000 km towards the Moon, landing on the surface and returning the crew safely back to Earth, especially when you consider the computers used famously had less processing power than a modern smartphone" (Wiseman 2019).

It was the Apollo 11 mission that accomplished this epic moment in human history. "Launched from Earth on July 16, 1969, the three astronauts of Apollo 11 arrived in orbit of the Moon on July 19. The following day, Commander Neil Armstrong and Lunar Module Pilot Edwin 'Buzz' Aldrin climbed into their lunar module 'Eagle' and achieved humanity's first landing on another celestial body" (Tate 2012). The three astronauts were tightly fitted into the Apollo command module atop a three-stage Saturn V rocket to propel the spacecraft to a velocity of more than 25,000 miles per hour. The Eagle stood just 17.9 feet (5.5 meters) in height and weighed over 32,000 pounds and appeared ever so fragile, especially for its mission of landing on the Moon and returning back into orbit to dock with the command module. On final descent, Armstrong noticed that the automatic landing system was guiding the Eagle toward the "West Crater," an undesirable landing spot because of the crater's boulder-strewn floor; as a result, Armstrong took manual control and managed to land it on a flat plain. The Eagle had just 30 seconds' worth of landing fuel allocation remaining at touchdown (Tate 2012).

For many, this initial Moon landing is a matter of history; for others, we remember this event from our early childhood and recall the amazement and exhilaration we experienced while observing such a feat of mankind via live broadcast on television. In fact, televised broadcasts of the Apollo 11 mission began prior to lift-off with a series of interviews with the astronauts, the launch itself, and live reports from the astronauts inside the space capsule as they hurtled toward the Moon. Realizing the entertainment value of television, the astronauts not only provided factual accounts of their mission as it proceeded; they even performed "tricks" of science. The televised reports continued to be beamed back to Earth via live transmissions. The most classic moment, perhaps, for the viewing public and for humankind came when Armstrong took his first step on the Moon, saying "That's one small step for man, one giant leap for mankind." Interestingly, Armstrong maintained years afterwards that he had actually said, "That's one small step for *a* man ..." but people listening to the broadcast could not make out the "a" in his famous line (Wolchover 2012). Such a minor discrepancy in the actual sentence declared by Armstrong is of no (or minor) consequence and when one considers the limited television technology of 1969, it is amazing that those of us back on Earth were able to see and hear the event live before our very eyes.

The televised broadcast of the Moon landing and Moon walks itself became immortalized in the world of popular culture as this transcendental moment in time has been referenced in countless popular culture films, television shows, fiction and nonfiction books, magazines, comics, and songs. Among the movies that have referenced the Moon landing are "Apollo 13," "Transformers: Dark of the Moon," "Independence Day," "Men in Black 3," and "The Dish." A large number of TV shows including "The Simpsons," "Futurama," and "The Big Bang Theory" have all included storylines of the Moon landing. Viacom Media Network launched its flagship MTV (Music Television) in 1981, a network that originally aired music videos 24 hours a day and featured the image of an astronaut with a modified American flag planted on the surface of the Moon. The MTV Video Music Awards featured a trophy called the "Moonman" (a "man on the Moon" concept) that was bestowed upon the winners of various music video categories. From the time of its original on-air "launch," a voiceover proclaimed, "Ladies and gentlemen, rock and roll." As Pat Gorman, a lead designer for the MTV logo, explained, "We thought, we're like the guys landing on the Moon and claiming it. We claim this land for music" (Roth 2016). The Moon landing also inspired a number of popular food products, including Tang—the drink of astronauts.

There have been documentaries about the Moon landing as well, including the 1998 HBO series "From the Earth to the Moon." The 12-part series explained the science, politics, and difficulties of the Apollo program and astronaut selection. More recently, *ABC News* debuted a news program called "1969."

> In its first episode, "Moon Shot" (original air date, April 23, 2019), the docu-series highlighted the Apollo 11 mission in the context of popular culture (in addition to the science, politics, astronaut interviews, and challenges confronting NASA). The social backdrop of 1969 makes the Moon landing perhaps all the more inspiring as this pivotal year in American history included anti-Vietnam war protests, the hippie movement, the Manson murders, civil unrest in many urban areas, the women's movement, the Civil Rights movement, and general political unrest. The space race was, arguably, perfectly timed for 1969 as Americans needed something to unite them in a common cause. Attempting to land a man on the Moon caught the attention of a general public that seemed willing to accept the importance of enlightened rational thought. A number of television shows such as "The Jetsons" (1962–1963), "Lost in Space" (1965–1968), and "Star Trek" (1966–1969) had paved the path for the masses to embrace the science that could send humans to the Moon. Historian Douglas Brinkley (author of *American Moonshot*) appears on the "Moon Shot" episode of the television show "1969" to proclaim that humans had broken the shackles of Earth in order to be able to land on the Moon, stating that such an achievement was an "epic moment in civilization."

Summary

Enlightened rational thought developed over the centuries since the time of the Middle Ages. The Enlightenment period, also known as the Age of Reason, was especially important in the development of enlightened, scientific, rational thought. The Enlightenment had been preceded by the ages of the Renaissance and the Scientific Revolution, which had also had a strong impact on enlightened thinking.

The Renaissance (c.1300–1600) was a period of time in European history that fell between the Middle Ages and the Enlightenment. The Renaissance was characterized by poetry, humanism, scientific curiosity, and a number of social thinkers who made significant contributions to reasoned, liberal thought that challenged the domination of tradition and faith. Among the significant thinkers of this period were Francis Petrarch, Niccolo Machiavelli, Martin Luther, Nicolaus Copernicus, and Thomas More. The Renaissance gave us a glimpse as to how enlightened reason could play a positive role in transforming society; however, the nation states and autocratic and religious leaders would not give up their stranglehold on thought processes dominated by tradition and faith.

The Scientific Revolution (c.1600–1700) took place in between the Renaissance and the Enlightenment; however, as the exact dates of these three periods is debated among social thinkers, historians, and other scholars, they may have also overlapped. As the name of this time period would imply, scientists were promoting and utilizing the scientific method (the pursuit of knowledge involving the stating of a problem, the collection of facts through observation and experiment, and the testing of ideas/hypotheses to determine whether they appear to be "valid" or "invalid") to various fields of study, but especially in the natural sciences of mathematics, physics, astronomy, gravitation (i.e., Isaac Newton's theory of gravity as articulated in *Principia*), optics, biology and medicine, and chemistry. Systematic experimentation and empiricism (the reliance on observation and measurement as a way of acquiring knowledge, an approach in direct contrast to a reliance on tradition, faith, and common sense) are hallmarks of the scientific approach. Among the scientific social thinkers discussed are Galileo Galilei, Francis Bacon, Rene Descartes, Thomas Hobbes, and John Locke.

The "Age of Enlightenment" (*c.*1700–1840s) is a term used to describe the essence of the long eighteenth century in Europe and the American colonies (and early United States). The collectivity of progressive and liberal ideas and alternatives to traditional and faith-based ways of thinking were being advanced by leading intellectuals and scientists of the era in an attempt to improve the lives of all humans and not just the ruling class. The unifying idea of this time period was the general belief that progress could be attained because humans hold the capacity for reason. Educating the poor and the masses is a key aspect in assisting people to think rationally and scientifically. In this chapter, the ideas of a number of European and American Enlightenment thinkers were provided. Among the European thinkers discussed are Montesquieu, Francois-Marie Arouet (Voltaire), Jean-Jacques Rousseau, David Hume, Thomas Reid, Adam Smith, Immanuel Kant, and Cesare Beccaria. American Enlightenment thinkers discussed are Benjamin Franklin, John Adams, Thomas Paine (who was born in England but made significant contributions to early American history while living in the United States), Thomas Jefferson, James Madison, and Benjamin Henry Day. The Enlightenment era was characterized by reason and criticism (of existing social structures and ways of thinking) and these two topics were also discussed. The Enlightenment era was also known as "the Age of Reason," a period known for its reliance on rationality. A number of people did not like the intellectual challenges to the existing social structures and they spearheaded a negative conservative reaction toward a reliance on science, reason, and rationality. These conservatives argued for a return to rigid hierarchies, with fixed-status groups, established religion, and misery for the masses. Many conservatives questioned the legitimacy of individual freedom and rights, including the right to happiness.

The role of critical thinking and higher education was also discussed in the context of enlightened thinking. Critical thinking and higher education go hand-in-hand as the purpose of attending college is twofold: to gain knowledge (both general knowledge and knowledge in one's chosen area of study) and to learn how to think critically. A brief review of twentieth-century scientific achievements was also presented to highlight the positive impact of the Renaissance and Enlightenment eras on humanity.

The achievements of rational and reasoned thought embraced by enlightened thinkers since the Middle Ages had paved the path for the twenty-first century to become the most enlightened century ever. However, as the following chapters will highlight, instead of a universal embrace of enlightened rational thought, as logic and common sense would dictate, there are a number of threats confronting humanity.

2
THE DARKNESS THAT SURROUNDS US

The deterioration of democracy and human rights

Introduction

Fake news!
Alternative facts!
Truth isn't truth!

These are among the phrases uttered by shameful people over the course of the past few years and, not coincidentally, during the US presidency of Donald Trump. Trump himself loves to use the expression "fake news!" whenever he is confronted by undeniable truths reported by the news media that challenge his beliefs. Indeed, Trump is so enamored by the term that he claimed in an interview with former Republican governor of Arkansas Mike Huckabee, on his Trinity Broadcast Network show, to have created the expression "fake news" (Cillizza 2017). Trump said to Huckabee, "The media is really, the word, one of the greatest of all terms I've come up with, is 'fake.' I guess other people have used it perhaps over the years but I've never noticed it. And it's a shame" (Cillizza 2017). From this quote, it almost seems like Trump is claiming to have created the word "fake" and not just "fake news." The word "fake" has, of course, been in existence for hundreds of years but he is more accurate in claiming that he popularized the term "fake news." But again, he is far from the first person to have used this expression; there is evidence of the usage of "fake news" dating back to the end of the nineteenth century (Cillizza 2017).

Nonetheless, Trump's regular use of the term "fake news" is responsible for its current popularity and the fact that the phrase "fake news" was declared the official *Collins English Dictionary* "Word of the Year" for 2017 (Meza 2017). It is a dubious distinction to be known as the person who popularized the expression "fake news," as this is a clear indication that such a person has used the term repeatedly—reflecting the reality that others (e.g., the news media and scholars) have often pointed out the falsity of their statements.

US Counselor to the President Kellyanne Conway first used the phrase "alternative facts" during a *Meet the Press* interview on January 22, 2017, when she attempted to defend Trump's exaggerated claims about the size of the attendance at his 2017 inauguration. During his interview with Conway, *Meet the Press* moderator Chuck Todd asked, "Why put him out there for the very first time, in front of that podium, to utter a provable falsehood? It's a small thing, but the first time he confronts the public, it's a falsehood?" (Blake 2017). After a tense back-and-forth, Conway offered this shameful reply: "Don't be so overly dramatic about it, Chuck. You're saying it's a falsehood, and they're giving—our press secretary, Sean Spicer, gave alternative facts to that. But the point really is …" Astounded by this nonsensical response by Conway, a visibly frustrated Todd interrupts and states, "Wait a minute. Alternative facts? Alternative facts? Four of the five facts he uttered … were just not true. Alternative facts are not facts; they are falsehoods" (Blake 2017).

Todd is correct, of course, that there are facts and there are falsehoods but there aren't "alternative facts." From this point on, Chuck Todd was among the journalists on the top of Trump's media hate list; Trump has verbally (and his supporters have sometimes physically) attacked journalists who call out their falsehoods and claim that creating alternative facts is no big deal. Consider, for example, shortly after Conway uttered her infamous "alternative facts" phrase, pro-Trump CNN pundit Scottie Nell Hughes stated on *The Diane Rehm Show*, "One thing that's been interesting this campaign season to watch is that people that say facts are facts —they're not really facts.… There's no such thing, unfortunately anymore, as facts" (Blake 2017). Such a comment flies in the face of reason, rationality, science, and enlightened thinking. There exist an infinite number of facts. Unfortunately, there also exist an increasing number of shameful people who attempt to discredit facts as falsehoods.

The shameful phrase of "truth isn't truth" was uttered by former Republican New York City Mayor Rudolph "Rudy" Giuliani in 2018 while he served as one of Trump's attorneys. Once again NBC's *Meet the Press*, hosted by Chuck Todd, served as the platform for the launch of a phrase that makes rational people shake their heads. The backdrop was Giuliani "expressing his concerns about having Trump sit down for an interview with special counsel Robert Mueller as part of the probe into Russian meddling in the 2016 election" (Moore 2018). Giuliani stated, "I'm not going to be rushed into having him testify so that he gets trapped into perjury. And when you tell me he should testify because he's going to tell the truth —that he shouldn't worry—that's so silly because it's somebody's version of the truth, not the truth" (Moore 2018). Todd immediately countered by saying, "Truth is truth." Giuliani countered, "Truth isn't truth." "Mr. Mayor, the truth is the truth" Todd repeated (Moore 2018).

Todd then accurately predicted that Giuliani would become the brunt of mocking memes on social media for making such a ludicrous statement. In addition, the assertion that "truth isn't truth" topped the Yale Law School librarian's list of the most notable quotes of 2018 (Associated Press 2018c). The list is assembled by Fred Shapiro, an associate director at the library, who said that the quotes "are intended to reflect the culture of our time and often it's quotes that are not admirable but quotes that are silly or negative in some way. In our current world political scene, the United States maybe dominates that kind of quotation" (Associated Press 2018c). Such a statement is a sad commentary about the current American political culture. The shameful state of the current political climate is certainly not restricted to the United States, however.

All three of these ignominious quotes tie in neatly to the primary topics covered in this book, as they represent a challenge to reason, rationality, science, and facts (all are contributing factors in darkened enlightenment); they were uttered by power-hungry persons or staff members who possess blind allegiance to the powerful (an example of the flooded swamp, to be discussed in Chapter 4); such outrageous utterances represent a type of shameful behavior that is contributing to a "growing culture of shamelessness" (Delaney 2008).

The focus of this chapter is on the increasing darkness that exists in the world today and its threat to the light of reason and rational thought. Discussion begins with the spread of darkness via the telling of lies, falsehoods, and misleading claims.

Lies, falsehoods, and misleading claims

It is of little surprise that members of the Trump administration use such terms as "fake news," "alternative facts," and "truth isn't truth," as Trump himself has communicated (verbally or by tweet) many lies, falsehoods, and misleading claims throughout his presidency. Trump is not the only politician to spread lies, falsehoods, and make misleading claims but his are the most numerous and significant as he is the current US president.

As of December 10, 2019, Donald Trump averaged more than 14 untrue statements (lies, falsehoods, misleading claims) per day for a total of 15,413 mistruths during his presidency (Knowles 2019). As an attention-grabbing way of putting this in perspective, Cillizza (2019) informs us that Trump lies more often than a majority of Americans wash their hands. According to the American Cleaning Institute (2009), just 50 percent of Americans wash their hands in excess of ten times a day. Interestingly, women (62 percent) are more likely than men (37 percent) to wash their hands more than ten times per day and 41 percent of men compared to just 17 percent of women wash their hands six times a day or fewer.

While many of Trump's falsehoods are potentially damaging to Americans and American interests (as well as those who reside outside of the United States) he has also managed to entertain us with countless absurd statements (you can actually Google "stupid/dumb things Trump has said" and the search will provide many links to lists of gaffes). One of his classic blunders occurred during his 2019 Fourth of July "Salute to America" speech, when he praised the American military's effort in the Revolutionary War versus the United Kingdom: "Our army manned the air, it rammed the ramparts, it took over the airports, it did everything it had to do, and at Fort McHenry, under the rockets' red glare, it had nothing but victory" (Haynes 2019). Airports and airplanes are a twentieth-century invention and had nothing to do with the Revolutionary War. His reference to Fort McHenry and "rockets' red glare" actually occurred during the Battle of Baltimore, at which time the words to the "Star-Spangled Banner" were written, and took place during the War of 1812, not the Revolutionary War. Dumb things that Trump has said at other speeches include: "My fingers are long and beautiful, as it has been well documented, as are various other parts of my body"; "I have so many fabulous friends who happen to be gay, but I am a traditionalist"; "I've said that if Ivanka weren't my daughter, perhaps I'd be dating her"; "Sorry losers and haters, but my IQ is one of the highest and you all know it! Please don't feel so stupid or insecure. It's not your fault"; and "it's freezing and snowing in New York. We need global warming!" (Woolfson 2016).

As for more serious matters, when independent fact-checkers reveal his falsehoods on important matters Trump simply responds by blaming the "liberal" media as out to "get him" and follows up such outrageous claims with his greatest hit, "fake news." Trump's willingness to blame the media and cry "fake news" whenever he is caught lying is part of a well-established pattern and is summarized by Cillizza (2019) as follows,

1 Trump says something that is either misleading or totally refuted by known facts.
2 The media fact-checks him, presents the known facts as evidence that he isn't telling the truth.
3 He seizes on these media fact-checks as evidence that journalists are out to get him.
4 His followers believe him and question news agencies instead (i.e., asking such questions as, "How many times has CNN lied since Trump became President?").

This sequence continues over and over every single day. Any person who possesses the capacity for rational thought would see right through this cycle of lies. A slight majority of people do acknowledge this series of manipulative lying; unfortunately, there are enough people who believe whatever Trump says, resulting in a steady erosion of truth.

Citing data from *Washington Post*, Eric Alterman (2019) states that there is no discernible pattern to Trump's lies. As of mid-May 2019, Trump had lied 2,217 times at his rallies, 1,803 times on this Twitter feed, and 999 times in his speeches. His other false statements occurred while interacting with reporters. Trump has repeated 21 false claims 20 or more times, and more than 300 false claims at least three times (Alterman 2019; *Washington Post* 2019). The most repeated lie (and an unfulfilled campaign promise) is that "the wall" on the southern border of the

United States shared with northern Mexico is being built; he has repeated this lie 172 times (as of May 2019). (The biggest lie associated with "the wall" was Trump's promise that Mexico would pay for its construction, a campaign promise that anyone with common sense knew was a falsehood.) In fact, the only money allocated and the only construction occurring is bollard fencing and levee fencing, or the replacement of existing fencing. Trump refers to such fencing as his wall. Congress has funded about 175 miles of barriers, but this is not a part of Trump's promised border wall (*Washington Post* 2019). In July 2019, the conservative Supreme Court justices voted to give the Trump administration "approximately $2.5 billion in Defense Department money to replace existing sections of barrier in Arizona, California, and New Mexico with more robust fencing" (Gresko 2019:A5).

Another common lie repeated by Trump is his claim that he has accomplished more than "almost any administration in the history of our country." Trump repeated this claim to the United Nations General Assembly in September 2018 and the assembled audience of world leaders burst into laughter. Trump was briefly speechless and later admitted that he "didn't expect that reaction," but then changed his mind and fibbed yet again by claiming that he "meant to get some laughter" (Alterman 2019).

Trump has repeatedly bragged about his accomplishments in his role in lifting the economy so much that he claims full credit for US growth, all the while ignoring the reality of a huge and growing deficit. He touts his tax cuts (which helped the rich tremendously) as the reason for the American economic growth, but the truth is that the economy has been growing steadily for nearly ten years. The glee one can take from economic growth is offset by government borrowing as the federal deficit rose because of his tax cuts (Associated Press 2018a:A2).

> While the $1.5 trillion worth of tax reductions over the next decade are substantial, they're far from the largest in U.S. history as a share of the overall economy. The Trump tax cuts rank behind President Reagan's in the early 1980s, post-World War II tax cuts and at least several more, according to the Committee for a Responsible Federal Budget, which advocates for deficit Reduction.
>
> *(Associated Press 2018a:A2)*

Trump refuses to acknowledge that the current economic achievements and low unemployment rate (that started with Barack Obama's two terms as president) are both the result of steady and gradual recovery from the worst economic meltdown since 1929. The economic outlook of the US is not flawless. For example, the 2019 US deficit (the amount by which outlays exceed receipts in a given fiscal period has exceeded the $1 billion mark and the federal debt) is over $22 trillion (US Government Spending 2019). There are three primary reasons generally cited for the current budget deficit: military spending (nearly $1 trillion), which is greater than the spending of the next ten-largest government expenditures combined, four times greater than China's military budget and ten times bigger than Russia's military budget; tax cuts (which proponents of supply-side economics argue will recoup over the long term by boosting economic growth), which lowers the amount of money coming into the government's coffers; and mandatory spending (which does not include Social Security as that is funded through payroll taxes and the Social Security Trust Fund until 2034) such as Medicare, Medicaid, housing assistance programs, unemployment benefits, and retirement and disability programs for those who were former federal employees (e.g., civil servants, the Coast Guard, and the military) (Amadeo 2019).

Trump repeatedly claims that Russia did not interfere with the 2016 presidential election (in which Hillary Clinton won the popular vote by approximately 3 million votes) despite the fact that the US intelligence community has determined that Russia did indeed intervene to help Trump. The Senate Intelligence Committee supports the conclusions of the intelligence assessment released in 2017 (Associated Press 2018a:A2). During the Congressional Hearings of July 24, 2019 (with regard to the Mueller Report), Robert Mueller once again reiterated that Russia had interfered with the 2016 US presidential election; the hearings stated that Trump was not exonerated from any wrongdoing and that he could potentially face charges for obstruction of justice or other crimes after leaving office (Megerian and Haberkorn 2019).

In December 2018, Trump bragged to troops stationed in Iraq that he had secured for them a massive pay raise, repeating a false claim he's made repeatedly on the campaign trail. He went so far as to claim that he had authorized the first military pay increase in a decade, of 10 percent. The fact is, military pay has risen every year for three decades. It is true that the 2.6 percent increase scheduled for 2019 was the largest in nine years but it was a huge exaggeration to claim that this was a 10 percent pay raise (Stokols 2018a; Federal Pay 2019).

On July 22, 2019, Trump lied about having been invited by the Indian government to mediate in the long-running Kashmir conflict between India and Pakistan. Indian officials immediately denied the claims; "No such request has been made" said Raveesh Kumar, spokesperson for India's Ministry of External Affairs (Yeung and Liptak 2019). Trump's comments unleashed fury and indignation across Indian social media as well as in the United States. Democratic Representative Brad Sherman, who called Trump's statement "amateurish and delusional," added that anyone "who knows anything about foreign policy in South Asia knows that India consistently opposes third-party mediations regarding Kashmir (Yeung and Liptak 2019).

The above examples are a mere sampling of the lies, falsehoods, and misleading claims made by Trump during his first two-plus years as US president. But why should we care, you might ask? We should care because when a world leader can get away with so many lies, falsehoods, and misleading claims we have a clear example of darkness and a challenge to enlightened thinking. Andrew Coan, a professor of law at the University of Arizona, goes as far as to suggest that Trump is worse than former president Richard Nixon, a crooked politician who has the dubious distinction of being the only US president to resign the office (on August

9, 1974). Nixon interfered with an FBI investigation of the Watergate burglary and directed the CIA to shut down the investigation. Nixon also directed subordinates to pay hush money to subjects of that investigation, in which his campaign operatives broke into the Democratic National Committee headquarters. He then fired the first special prosecutor appointed to investigate these matters, hoping to protect himself and his senior advisors from possible criminal liability and untold political damage (Coan 2019; Farrell 2017; Brokaw 2019). Nixon's downfall served as a cautionary tale for subsequent presidents who might be tempted to interfere with a federal investigation for personal or political reasons. Firing a special prosecutor was especially understood to be political suicide as Watergate showed that the American public would not stand for a president who sought to place himself above the law.

Then came Trump. As the Mueller Report details, Trump asked FBI director James B. Comey to drop the investigation on national security advisor Michael Flynn. Before making this request, Trump cleared the room, strongly suggesting that he knew his actions were improper (Coan 2019). This action was similar to the "smoking gun" that sealed Nixon's fate. A few weeks later, in early March 2017, the Mueller Report showed how Trump had lobbied vigorously to prevent Attorney General Jeff Sessions from recusing himself in the Russia investigation. Trump wanted an attorney general who would protect him from any investigation. As Coan (2019:A9) explains,

> The report's most damning evidence of obstruction of justice concerns the special counsel's investigation itself ... [Trump] ordered White House Counsel Don McGahn to fire Mueller. The report describes "substantial evidence" that this was an attempt to obstruct the special counsel's investigation; Trump was acting to protect himself from potential criminal liability and political damage.

Coan goes on to detail other damaging evidence against Trump (e.g., Russian government inference in the 2016 presidential election and Trump's urging of Flynn, Paul Manafort, and Michael Cohen to stay strong as they would be "taken care of" if charges were pending against them for helping him) and provides a scary conclusion that if Trump escapes unscathed, future presidents will take notice. He states, "The cautionary tale of Watergate will be superseded by the Trump triumph and its very different lesson: In the hyperpolarized political environment of the early 21st century, the president is a law unto himself" (Coan 2019).

Michael D'Antonio (2018), a Trump biographer (*The Truth About Trump*, 2016), expressed a similar concern as Coan, claiming that Trump's crooked behavior is at a level on par with Nixon's darkest days. D'Antonio describes Trump's character as deviant and his conduct as delinquent. Such a negative portrayal of Trump's character and conduct is nothing new according to D'Antonio, as even as a child in the 1950s Trump had shown a stubborn tendency to deviate from the very principles that underpin civilization. "Trump explained to me in an interview that he felt most people are 'not worthy of respect,' and this was the attitude he would carry through life. He never felt that the rules applied to him or that he should take responsibility for any harm he caused" (D'Antonio 2018). In his biography of Trump, D'Antonio describes how the future president broke his deal of a seven-session interview process following the fifth interview simply because he had spoken to someone that Trump hated. Months later, one of Trump's lawyers, Michael Cohen, wanted to see a copy of the manuscript, as he was certain it was filled with errors. When D'Antonio refused the request, Cohen asked specific questions such as, "Does the book mention certain famous women?" "Does it say that he is a racist?" (D'Antonio 2018:ix). D'Antonio refused to cooperate with Cohen.

In the preface of his Trump biography, D'Antonio describes how the young Trump was disruptive and unruly while attending a genteel private school (Kew-Forest) (e.g., he once gave a teacher a black eye and continually refused to comply with basic rules). Donald and his family would sometimes attend the Marble Collegiate Church, led by the famous Reverend Norman Vincent Peale, who taught that salesmanship was next to godliness and ambition was practically a form of worship. Peale rarely spoke of sin or moral obligation and was very anti-Catholic, in opposition to John F. Kennedy's bid for the White House. Anti-Catholic sentiment has a long history in the United States and John F. Kennedy remains the only ever Roman Catholic president. "One leading Protestant minister from Dallas, Texas declared publicly that Roman Catholicism 'is not only a religion, it is a political tyranny'" (Shaw 2012). Kennedy had to repeatedly remind the public that he was not a Catholic candidate for president but instead was the Democratic Party's candidate for president, who happened also to be a Catholic. Among other irrational discriminatory fears that Kennedy had to address was concern put forth by a group of Protestant ministers led by Peale (and encouraged behind the scenes by Billy Graham) that he would instill Catholicism into public schools and break down the wall of separation between Church and State—it "is written in our country's constitution that church and state must be, in this nation, forever separate and free" (Shaw 2012). That Protestants were so adamant about the separate of Church and State decades ago is very ironic considering contemporary conservative Protestants want to instill religion (Christianity) in schools and other social institutions. In many of his speeches, Kennedy repeatedly reiterated that he "was no puppet of the Pope and danger to American democracy" (Shaw 2012). Listening to the hateful rhetoric spewed by Peale undoubtedly had an impact on Trump, and Peale's way of normalizing such bigotry has stuck with Trump throughout his life (examples to be provided later in this and other chapters of the book).

Trump reportedly bullied his schoolmates and teachers while in grade school. Following his college years, Donald settled in Manhattan,

> where he prowled the precincts of greed, deception, and depravity.... One of Trump's earliest close associates was mob lawyer and political hatchet man Roy Cohn, who was notorious for his racist and anti-Semitic (despite being Jewish himself) statements. Operating under Cohn's tutelage, Trump soon

demonstrated an ability for using the press to build a false image of success. With a little manipulation, he got the blessing of the *New York Times* … and he got attention from the city's most important TV talk shows.

(D'Antonio 2016:xviii–xix)

D'Antonio (2016) continues, "At every turn, whether he was looking for it or not, young Trump saw how those who were willing to violate old-fashioned notions of decency benefited.… And now, in 2016 … without a strong foundation of empathy and ethics, he exploits hatred, dabbles in misogyny, and tacitly encourages violence" (p. xix). These quotes from D'Antonio represent a sampling of Trump's temperament, which, Trump brags, hasn't changed since first grade (D'Antonio 2018).

A lifetime of bending the rules, bullying, and an eagerness to spread lies, falsehoods, and misleading claims are some of the things that have made Donald Trump the person he is today. Having learned the benefits of lying at an early age and honing his skills of manipulation, providing misleading information and a desire to crush his enemies are behaviors that Trump continues to employ because they have worked well for him his entire life. Most Americans, as well as informed people across the world, realize that Trump lies continuously and without shame but his supporters drink his Kool-Aid eagerly. As Max Boot (2018) wrote in the *Washington Post*, "Trump continues telling lies that not even a dimwitted child could possibly believe … his nonstop peddling of nonsensical conspiracy theories [is designed] to convince his acolytes that he is a victim of a Deep State plot" (p. E3). The notion of a "Deep State" will be discussed in further detail in Chapter 3, but for now it is helpful to think of this concept as a conspiracy theory that suggests the existence of a socio-political system within the legal political system that is designed to bring down certain elected officials, especially a sitting president. The belief in the existence of a "Deep State" has been around for centuries. Most recently, proponents of Barack Obama believed the Deep State was out to "get" him, and today proponents of Trump fear the same.

While it is shameful behavior enough in its own right that Trump lies more regularly on a daily average than most people wash their hands, it is equally troubling that millions of people simply accept or tolerate everything that he spews as the truth. And, as Lorraine Ali (2018) explains, Trump's willingness to lie and spread falsehoods is much worse than "fake news"; it is actually propaganda designed to brainwash the easily duped masses.

The state-sponsored spread of deliberate misinformation is not a "half-truth," "distortion of reality" or "the president's loose relationship with the facts," as many a mainstream news correspondent and pundit have it.… They [are] cases of purposefully manufactured narratives, disseminated from the highest levels of government, sometimes with the help of adversary nations, to sway public opinion, quash dissenting voices and consolidate power.

(Ali 2018)

Expanding on Ali's perspective on the harmfulness of spreading misinformation, Melissa Healy (2018:A5) states,

> In a modern democracy, peddling conspiracies for political advantage is perhaps not so different from seeding an epidemic. If a virus is to gain a foothold with the electorate, it will need a population of likely believers ("susceptibles" in public-health speak), a germ nimble enough to infect new hosts easily (an irresistible tall tale), and an eager "amen choir" (also known as "super-spreaders").

Healy (2018) uses a colorful description to incorporate the role of social media in spreading this epidemic of lies, falsehoods, and misleading claims: "Unleashed on the body politic, a falsehood may spread across the social networks that supply us with information. Facebook is a doorknob slathered in germs, Twitter a sneezing co-worker, and Instagram a child returning home after a day at school, ensuring the exposure of all." The solution to epidemics is to find a cure and in this case the medicine is fact-checking. The need for fact-checkers is critical as we confront the darkness that surrounds us. And there are great, reliable fact-checkers that can disprove the lies, falsehoods, and misleading statements unleashed upon us by Trump and countless other politicians and corporate leaders. The problem is, fact-checking has failed (for the most part) to change the minds of followers of ideologies peddled by those who lie to us because we chose to believe their falsehoods. In Donald Trump's case, his well-documented large number of daily false statements overwhelm those who would like to learn the truth. He has managed to use a large quantity of lies to suppress the poor quality of his presidency and repeated failures in business.

Combining the thoughts of Ali and Healy and the people that agree with their viewpoint of the current state of political affairs, we can draw a conclusion that the United States, as with much of the world, is currently confronted with a *propaganda epidemic*. And while Trump and some of his personnel are responsible for a great number of lies, falsehoods, and misleading claims, they do not own a monopoly on the bombardment of misinformation being forced upon the public. It would be easy to list below a number of specific lies from a variety of politicians (regardless of political affiliation) but I think we understand the primary point being made here. When politicians and others that serve the public, lie, create falsehoods, and make misleading claims, they erode the pretense of democracy, morality, and fair play and help to establish and maintain a darkness of unenlightened thought.

What, if anything, can be done to combat the spread of lies? Is it possible to outlaw lying, stating falsehoods, and making misleading claims? Should "honesty is the best policy" become a law applicable to politicians, businesses, advertisers, marketers, and so on? At first thought, this might seem like a good idea, even if an impossible law to enforce fully, fairly, and equally. A bigger problem than the challenge of trying to enforce such a law is the realization that those in power might attempt to establish the "truth" as they see it and not as based on empirical evidence. In Egypt, for example, scores of journalists, bloggers, social media users, and others have been detained for "disseminating false information" or spreading "fake news" (Islam 2018). The problem is that President Abdel Fattah Sisi is the one who decides what is real news and what is fake news, and this allows him to imprison his detractors. In 2018, Egypt jailed more journalists on legally defined fake news charges than any country in the world, according to the Committee to Protect Journalists, which tracks freedom of the press around the world (Islam 2018). When all potential criminal charges are considered (e.g., anti-state, censorship violation, defamation)—not just fake news charges—Turkey jails more journalists than any other country, followed by China and Egypt (Islam 2018). In 2018, 250 journalists were imprisoned, 63 were missing globally, and ten journalists were killed in the first half of 2019 (Committee to Protect Journalists 2019). During his reelection bid, Egyptian president Sisi blocked more than 500 websites that he claimed violated the cybercrime law and his administration identified 21,000 "rumors" that sought to undermine government stability. Autocrats like Sisi around the world have been inspired by Trump's use of the term "fake news" as a means of cracking down on dissension. Trump's constant attack of the media as the true enemy of the state becomes all the more alarming when we realize that he might be inspired by his friend Sisi; both share affection for one another that has been referred to by some in the media as a "bromance" (Lemon 2017).

One more example of a nation attempting to end the spread of misinformation is Singapore. In May 2019, the Singaporean government passed a law that imposes jail time and hundreds of thousands of dollars in potential fines for posting or failing to correct what it calls "online falsehoods" that harm the public interest (Pierson 2019a). Critics of the new law argue that the "Protection From Online Falsehoods and Manipulation" bill will have a ripple effect that goes beyond online platforms to potential censorship on freedom of expression and academic research, with the labeling of something as a falsehood being determined by the political party currently in power. It is worth noting that the Singaporean government has been dominated by one political party since the country gained independence from the United Kingdom more than 50 years ago (Pierson 2019a). The Ministry of Law said that the measure "targets falsehoods, not free speech. It will help ensure online falsehoods do not drown out authentic speech and ideas and undermine democratic processes and society" (Pierson 2019a). Critics counter by pointing out that the bill doesn't provide enough safeguards against government overreach, a valid concern as "Singapore ranks 151 out of 180 countries in a World Press Freedom Index published by Reporters Without Borders, rating worse than repressive nations such as Myanmar and Cambodia" (Pierson 2019a).

The Singapore law does not spare the big tech companies that have regional headquarters there either. Google, Facebook, and Twitter all use Singapore as their regional headquarters, and employ more than 2,000 people there. The tech executives are certainly aware of the low World Press Freedom Index rating of Singapore but they had hoped that they would be exempt from the law; they will not (Tripathi

2009). The larger number of "fake news" posts made on Facebook and Twitter could lead to some costly consequences for these tech companies.

Activists worry about autocratic governments that block the freedom of the press and the valuable word conducted by journalists. The Egyptian and Singaporean laws could inspire similar controls by other nations. Currently, governments in Russia, Malaysia, and France have introduced regulations seeking to stem the spread of fake news (Pierson 2019a).

Declaring the news media as the "enemy of the people"

The condemnation of the press via such expressions as "fake news," "alternative facts," and "truth isn't truth" are not only blatant attacks on the media and democracy itself; they are a sure sign of the growing darkness that surrounds us. The rich and powerful, including many politicians, and especially autocrats, attempt to control the media because they want to control the narrative of past, present, and future events. When someone claims the media is "out to get" them, it is generally a sign that such a person has been caught in their own web of lies, falsehoods, and misleading claims. The fact is, it is up to the news media to call out the lies of the powerful as it serves as a vanguard of democracy and as the voice of the people who want the truth. Any claim made against the news media as the "true enemy of the people" is a dangerous sign of autocracy.

While unacceptable in any civil society, we can understand why dictators, despots, and autocrats attempt to control the news media; however, when political leaders of democratic societies attempt to undermine the press such actions are deplorable and cannot be tolerated. Donald Trump has repeatedly attempted to control the flow of information so that he can continue to spread his false statements when he finds it necessary. Many times, Trump has referred to the press as the "enemy of the people"; below are a few examples.

Shortly after becoming President of the United States (inaugurated January 20, 2017), Trump let it be publicly known that he would not be acting in a presidential manner and would instead engage in such shameful behavior as to declare the media as "enemy of the American people." On February 16, 2017 Trump was engaged in a 77-minute news conference to criticize his press coverage. The following day he took to Twitter to write: "The FAKE NEWS media (failing @nytimes, @CNN, @NBCNews and many more) is my enemy, it is the enemy of the American people. SICK!" The message was quickly deleted, but 16 minutes later Trump posted a revised version wherein he had removed the word "sick," and added two more television networks—ABC and CBS—to his list of offending organizations (Grynbaum 2017). Trump had already referred to the media as the "opposition party" prior to this attack on a fundamental aspect of democracy— whose importance was clearly spelled-out in the US Constitution (to be discussed later in this chapter). To emphasize the importance of Trump's attack on the press, Grynbaum (2017) wrote, "The language that Mr. Trump deployed [in his tweet] is more typically used by leaders to refer to hostile foreign governments or subversive organizations. It also echoed the language of autocrats who seek to minimize dissent." Carl Bernstein, the journalist who helped to uncover the Watergate scandal, said of Trump's tweet: "Donald Trump is demonstrating an authoritarian attitude and inclination that shows no understanding of the role of the free press" (quoted in Grynbaum 2017). Historians have pointed out the similarities between Trump's descriptions of the press to those of Richard Nixon, who in 1972 told his national security adviser, Henry A. Kissinger, "The press is the enemy" (Grynbaum 2017). The general public and politicians regardless of their party affiliation should have demanded an end to this attack on the media and journalists and called out this shameful behavior, but that did not happen. Instead, Trump would continue to promote his mantra of the press as the enemy of the people.

Less than two weeks later, in fact, Trump repeated the attack on the press at a speech at the Conservative Political Action Conference—"They are the enemy of the people." As Bondarenko (2017) explains, "The phrase 'the enemy of the people' has a long history that Trump may or may not have known about. Over the course of the last century, it has been used repeatedly by dictators and autocrats to delegitimize foreign governments, opposition parties, and dissenters." The phrase can be traced back from the Roman era, when the Roman Senate declared Emperor Nero "an enemy of the people," to the German Third Reich's propaganda minister Joseph Goebbels, who referred to Jews as "a sworn enemy of the German people," and Vladimir Lenin and Joseph Stalin's use of the term "*vragnaroda*" (enemy of the nation/people) in Russia and the newly formed Soviet Union (Bondarenko 2017). Indeed, the use of the term "enemy of the people" has been used by many autocrats and casting the legitimate press under such a label is a very dangerous sign of darkness.

The attacks on the press would continue. In February 2019, Trump labeled the *New York Times* "a true enemy of the people" one day after an extensive report detailing the ways in which he has sought to influence the investigations into his presidency and allies. "The New York Times report is false," Trump tweeted. "They are a true ENEMY OF THE PEOPLE" (Samuels 2019). Trump did not provide any specific examples or counter-evidence of the *Times*' reporting. The *New York Times* publisher A.G. Sulzberger issued a statement later condemning Trump's use of the term "enemy of the people" as "dangerous" and inaccurate. "It is particularly reckless coming from someone whose office gives him broad powers to fight or imprison the nation's enemies," Sulzberger said (Samuels 2019). Sulzberger reports that he has spoken face-to-face with Trump numerous times about the mounting signs that this incendiary rhetoric is encouraging threats and violence against journalists at home and abroad (Samuels 2019).

Writing for the *Huffington Post*, Lee Moran (2019) states that Trump regularly attacks the "fake news media" in general with his vitriolic tweets and speeches, but he also claims that journalists "don't even call asking for verification" about stories they are planning to publish about his administration. The *New York Times* reporter Maggie Haberman, for whom Trump has particular disdain, responded that they always reach out to the White House about a planned story and countered that such requests generally go unanswered. "They [the White House] chose not to engage and then afterwards the president acts surprised" (Moran 2019).

In October 2018, following yet another mass shooting in the United States, this time at a Pittsburgh synagogue, and a series of mail bombings addressed to prominent Democrats (i.e., Barack Obama, Hillary Clinton, Joe Biden, Cory Booker, Kamala Harris, and Maxine Waters) and the CNN offices, Trump tweeted: "There is great anger in our Country caused in part by inaccurate, and even fraudulent, reporting of the news. The Fake News Media, the true Enemy of the People, must stop the open & obvious hostility & report the news accurately & fairly. That will do much to put out the flame …" (Breuninger 2018). President Trump often targets CNN by name. When asked if he would tone down his increasingly incendiary political rhetoric, Trump told reporters, "I could really tone it up" (Breuninger 2018).

It was previously written that the US Constitution makes apparent the importance of the role of the press. Evidence of this is found in the First Amendment (to the original seven articles), which states: "Congress shall make no law respecting an establishment of religion, or prohibiting the free exercise thereof; or abridging the freedom of speech, or of the press; or the right of the people peaceably to assemble, and to petition the Government for a redress of grievances." Of primary relevance to our discussion of the news media is the part of the First Amendment that guarantees that the freedom of speech and of the press cannot be reduced (abridged). Thus, the Constitution makes it very clear that press and freedom of speech are of vital importance to the country, an asset, and certainly not an enemy. It is the job of the president to protect and preserve all of the Constitution, and that includes the press. In fact, before entering the execution of the role of office, the newly elected president must take an oath: "I do solemnly swear (or affirm) that I will faithfully execute the Office of President of the United States, and will to the best of my Ability, preserve, protect and defend the Constitution of the United States." Attacking the press, as Trump routinely does, goes against this oath. That he is allowed to attack the press is a sign of the deterioration of democracy.

In a first of its kind, an example of an attack on the press that represents a sign of the deterioration of democracy in the United States was the US government's attack on the publisher of WikiLeaks; Julian Assange, co-founder of the whistleblower website, is facing 170 years in prison under the World War I-era Espionage Act. Ben Wizner, director of the American Civil Liberties Union's Speech, Privacy, and Technology Project, said of the indictment against WikiLeaks, "For the first time in the history of our country, the government has brought criminal charges against a publisher for the publication of truthful information. This is an extraordinary escalation of the Trump administration's attacks on journalism, and a direct assault on the First Amendment" (Goodman and Moynihan 2019c:A4).

Among other things, any attempt to silence the press and especially journalists is a sure sign of corruption. The importance of investigative journalism cannot be overstated as journalists are the ones who are paid to investigate corruption and other newsworthy stories. Often, investigative newspersons write such good stories that the unethical, immoral, and illegal activities of corrupt persons are revealed and consequences follow. Because their work involves revealing actions of people who wish to keep certain dealings private, journalists often come under attack and sometimes the lives of innocent people are disrupted. In most instances, however, journalists perform a valuable function in society. Not coincidentally, with the rise of social media and people's thirst for instant access to news, for free no less, professional journalists—especially those in the newspaper industry—began to lose their jobs in large numbers. Consider these statistics provided by the US Bureau of Labor Statistics (2017a): "From January 2001 to September 2016, the newspaper publishers industry lost over half of its employment, from 412,000 to 174,000. In contrast, employment in the Internet publishing and web search portals industry increased from 67,000 jobs in January 2007 to 206,000 jobs in September 2016." The inference from this is obvious and significant: more than half of those people trained in gathering news were replaced by billions of people (when we factor in that the only qualification needed to "report the news" online is a computer) with no journalistic job skills. The spread of misinformation, including lies, falsehoods, and misleading claims, became an epidemic in its own right. This reality compounds the previous problem of attacking journalists and real news outlets as "fake news" and "enemies of the people."

The press, especially newspapers, are one of our best hopes of curtailing political injustice and the corruption of the rich and powerful. Journalism must be protected by all means necessary and people have to stop looking at the internet as their primary source of news. The best place to find fact-based information is newspapers, according to extensive research conducted by the RAND Corporation. Based on a review of 27,000 front-page articles published between 1989 and 2017, RAND found that language and tone have been constant over that time. Television news, however, has experienced an increase in more subjective language and those differences become more pronounced when extracting television news that is posted on cable networks versus broadcast reports (Boyer 2019a; Kavanagh et al. 2019). In other words, broadcast (network) news is more objective than cable news. The sample size of digital-only news outlets was not as large as for television and newspapers since the content does not date back to 1989, but the conclusion for what was analyzed is similar to that of television (Boyer 2019a; Kavanagh et al. 2019). The key lesson to be learned from this is that newspapers provide the most objective news reporting, so make sure you keep a good amount of newspaper news in your life in addition to television and internet news sources. (See "connecting enlightened rational thought with popular culture" Box 2.1 for a closer look at the role of newspapers specifically, and the press in general, as servants of the governed, not the governors.)

The news in general, and newspapers specifically, are under threat in a number of ways, including a disturbing trend of newspaper conglomerate mergers, a decreasing number of people who read newspapers (preferring internet sources instead), an increasing amount of people who refuse to believe the truth even when presented with facts, and verbal and physical attacks on the industry and those who report the news. In August 2019, Gannett and GateHouse Media merged, signaling a very troubling attack on the freedom of the press. Gannett, already the nation's largest newspaper chain with more than 100 dailies and hundreds of weeklies, merged with GateHouse and its New Media Investment group, the second-largest chain in the US. GateHouse follows a disturbing business model that seeks to maximize financial returns by reducing the costs of production at the expense of newsroom employees and journalists who actually do investigative reporting and thus provide the public with factual information. "Nationally, the number of newsroom employees dropped from 71,000 in 2008 to 39,000 in 2017, a reduction of 45%" (Posner 2019). If the dramatic and devastating cut in news journalists itself was scary enough, Steven Waldman and Charles Sennott, the co-founders of Report for America (an initiative of the nonprofit media organization The Ground Truth Project), argue that the demise of local newspapers has a devastating effect on our democracy. Waldman and Sennott state, "The disintegration of community journalism leads to greater polarization, lower voter turnout, more pollution, less government accountability and less trust" (Posner 2019).

Interestingly, even when people are provided with true, albeit negative, stories, there is a certain segment of the population that will still shout "fake news" as if a wolf has entered their village of solitude from reality. According to a 2016 Gallup poll, 42 percent of Republicans consider accurate news stories that cast a politician or political group in a negative light to always be "fake news," while just 17 percent of Democrats feel this way (Wemple 2018). In a June 2017 Gallup poll, it was revealed that 72 percent of Democrats (up from 51 percent in 2016) report trust and confidence in the mass media to report news "fully, accurately and fairly." Independents' trust was a modest 37 percent, while Republicans' trust is unchanged at 14 percent (Swift 2017). It was speculated that the Democrats' trust and the Republicans' mistrust in the news media is driven by the perception that the news media serves as a watchdog over Republican president Trump.

A September 2017 Gallup poll revealed that 62 percent of Democrats compared to just 14 percent of Republicans report that the media "get the facts straight" (Swift 2017). It is the right wing that has intensified cries of "fake news," claiming that the mass media is biased or is making up news outright. This feeling has been promulgated by Trump, who has vowed to "continue to attack the press" (Swift 2017). A 2019 Pew Research study found that when respondents were asked who is to blame for the spread of made-up news, 57 percent cited political leaders, 53 percent said activist groups, and 36 percent blamed journalists (Boyer 2019b).

There are enough people that distrust, or in some cases hate, journalists that these professionals risk being attacked, arrested, or killed just because they attempt to report the truth. As established, President Trump regularly attacks certain segments of the news media. In fact, throughout the first year of his presidency, Trump and his administration had attacked various media outlets and journalists more than 400 times, specifically targeting CNN verbally and on Twitter dozens of times. The claims of the press as the enemy of the people have continued throughout Trump's presidency. Following Trump's lead, there is little surprise that conservative Republicans (87 percent) and moderate/liberal Republicans (80 percent) have a negative view of the national news media. In comparison, just 39 percent of liberal Democrats and 51 percent of conservative/moderate Democrats hold negative views of the news media (Pew Research Center 2017).

One of Trump's favorite punching bags is CNN's Jim Acosta, a reporter who had his White House credentials revoked on November 7, 2018. In doing his job as a journalist, Acosta would ask questions that Trump and his administrators would not care for and consequently it was deemed that he had failed to "treat the White House with respect" (Media Matters 2018). Recognizing that it is unconstitutional to revoke a reporter's press pass without providing a valid reason, Acosta's White House credentials were returned to him shortly thereafter (Epps 2018).

Having one's credentials taken away is on the mild side of harsh treatment journalists have endured in the past few years. Being arrested is the next step up. In Myanmar, for example, two Pulitzer Prize-winning journalists for Reuters were jailed while reporting on the country's violent suppression of Rohingya Muslims (Pierson 2019b). The journalists, Wa Lone and Kyaw Soe Oo, have been imprisoned since December 2017 and are serving seven-year terms for violating an obscure colonial-era state secrets law. The two were accused of obtaining secret documents (Pierson 2019b). "The case has brought widespread international condemnation of Myanmar's government and cast doubt on the country's commitment to democracy and the rule of law" (Pierson 2019b:A4). The journalists were freed in May 2019 (BBC News 2019b).

Public shaming (e.g., publicly revoking someone's press credentials) and imprisonment are still not the worst punishments facing journalists. Earlier in this chapter, data were given on journalists imprisoned in Turkey, China, and Egypt, total number of those missing globally, and those who were killed in the first half of 2019. Additional data are provided here. According to Reporters Without Borders, in 2017 there were 326 journalists imprisoned around the world for doing their work; 65 journalists were killed in the line of duty (the Society of Professional Journalists cites this number at 74); another 54 were held hostage by non-state actors (Chavern 2018). Roy Greenslade (2016), writing for the *Guardian*, reports that the new "global impunity index" reveals that Islamist groups have murdered a large number of reporters and photographers without fear of being punished. In 2018, agents working on behalf of the Saudi Arabian government assassinated Jamal Khashoggi, a Saudi dissident, journalist and contributing columnist for the *Washington Post*, and former general manager and editor-in-chief of the Al-Arab News Channel. The global impunity index was established by the Committee to Protect Journalists (CPJ). This index calculates the number of unsolved journalist murders as a percentage of each country's population; only nations with five or more unsolved cases are included in the listing (CPJ 2016). Cases are considered unsolved when no convictions have been obtained; cases in which some but not all perpetrators are held to justice are classified as partial impunity and are not included in the tally. When murder suspects are killed during apprehension they are classified as partial impunity (CPJ 2016). The Impunity Index is published annually on

November 2 to mark the International Day to End Impunity for Crimes against Journalists.

In 2016, the worse-offending country on the CPJ index, for the second year in a row, was Somalia (24), where the militant group al-Shabaab is suspected in the majority of media murders. Iraq (71) and Syria (17), where members of the militant Islamic State murdered at least six journalists in the past year, were ranked second and third on the list (CPJ 2016). (The number inside the parentheses represents the total number of unsolved murders that took place between September 1, 2006 and August 31, 2016.) The rest of the 2016 list includes the Philippines (41), South Sudan (5), Mexico (21), Afghanistan (5), Pakistan (21), Brazil (15), Russia (9), Bangladesh (97), Nigeria, and India (13). Despite their poor records in achieving justice for journalists, four of the countries listed on the Impunity Index—India, Mexico, Nigeria, and the Philippines—are on the governing council of the Community of Democracies, a coalition dedicated to upholding and strengthening democratic norms (Greenslade 2016). In 2018, there were 14 nations on the CPJ's Global Impunity Index. Now for the fourth year in the row, Somalia was ranked at number one, followed by Syria, Iraq, South Sudan, the Philippines, Afghanistan, Mexico, Columbia, Pakistan, Brazil, Russia, Bangladesh, Nigeria, and India (Witchel 2018).

It is noteworthy that there is another Global Impunity Index (GII) established by the University of the Americas Puebla (UDLAP) and the Center of Studies on Impunity and Justice (CESIJ) that is separate from the one created by the CPJ, which is specific to journalists. The GII attempts to measure, in quantitative terms, the impunity worldwide and its direct effect in other global issues such as inequality, corruption, and violence (Rappler.com 2017). There is an overlap among the worst-offending nations on both of the indexes. As for the GII, the Philippines was ranked as the leading offender of impunity violations due primarily to the increased violence related to organized crime and increased terrorist activities from local gangs linked to the Islamic State (Rappler.com 2017). Rounding out the top ten on the 2017 GII list were India, Cameroon, Mexico, Peru, Venezuela, Brazil, Columbia, Nicaragua, and the Russian Federation.

According to Reporters Without Borders (RWB), in 2017, there were 65 journalists (55 men and ten women) killed worldwide, a figure lower than the 79 journalists killed the year before. There were an additional 54 journalists being held hostage and two were missing. Twenty-six of the journalists (including 50 professional journalists, seven citizen-journalists, and eight media workers) were killed in the course of their work (the collateral victims of a deadly situation such as an air strike, an artillery bombardment, or a suicide bombing) and 39 were murdered and deliberately targeted because their reporting threatened political, economic, or criminal interests. The deliberate killing of journalists is the result of an attempt to silence them from reporting what they uncover (RWB 2017). The RWB (2017) provides two possible explanations as to why there was a decrease in the number of journalists killed in 2017: (1) activist campaigns to put pressure on news organizations to provide journalists with more protection and (2) journalists are abandoning countries that have become too dangerous. The RWB also reported that the two deadliest countries for reporters are Syria (civil war) and Mexico (drug cartels). Afghanistan, Iraq, and the Philippines are the next-deadliest countries for reporters, according to the RWB (2017).

The glimmer of hope that the deadly attacks on journalists might be decreasing was extinguished in the 2018 as UNESCO reported that in the first ten months of that year, 82 journalists had already been killed globally. (A total of 88 media workers were killed in 2018.) UNESCO also reports that, on average, 90 percent of crimes against journalists go unpunished. Furthermore, journalists are being silenced by such tactics as misuse of libel and counterterrorism laws, accusations of "fake news" and online harassment (IFEX 2018). International free speech organization ARTICLE 19 (a British human rights organization that defends and promotes freedom of expression) is calling on governments to take action over crimes against journalists. ARTICLE 19 executive director Thomas Hughes states, "Journalists around the world are assaulted and killed for exposing corruption, holding governments to account or simply expressing their opinions or beliefs. The perpetrators of these crimes largely go unpunished, whether they are state-sponsored actors, organized criminals or religious extremists" (IFEX 2018).

The preceding discussion helped to shine a light on the dangers confronting journalists and media personnel in some of the most dangerous nations in the world. However, as many activists including Freedom House (2019a; Freedom House describes itself as an independent watchdog organization to the expansion of freedom and democracy around the world) explain, the repression of the media is taking place in both authoritarian governments and democracies. The growing populist political currents and a lack of legal frameworks ensuring that journalists can conduct their work are helping to contribute to deteriorating media freedom around the world (Repucci 2019; Radu 2019). Among the key findings of the Freedom House investigation of the repression of the media are the following (Repucci 2019).

- Freedom of the media has been deteriorating around the world over the past decade.
- In some of the most influential democracies in the world, populist leaders have overseen concerted attempts to throttle the independence of the media sector.
- While the threats to global media freedom are real and concerning in their own right, their impact on the state of democracy is what makes them truly dangerous.
- The fundamental right to seek and disseminate information through an independent press is under attack, and part of the assault has come from an unexpected source—elected leaders in many democracies.

The world leader in promoting democracy is the United States and yet, as detailed in this chapter, many members of the US media are being attacked by President

Trump and other politicians. A key element of the Freedom House findings is clearly at play in the United States and many other parts of the world—and that is the role of populism.

Populism and nationalism

The concept of "populism" was just introduced and, undoubtedly, this is a term that nearly everyone has heard of, as its effects are being felt in multiple nations and in multiple ways.

Examining populism and nationalism

The concept of "popularism" often comes up when discussing populism so let's take a closer look at the meaning of these two notions. *Popularism* refers to any political ideology chosen to appeal to a majority of the electorate. *Populism* is a philosophy, political orientation, or standpoint that emphasizes the rights and powers of ordinary people with the general presumption that the people are exploited by the privileged elite, and champions their struggle to overcome this injustice. Muller (2016) expands on the anti-elites aspect of populism by stating that populists are always anti-pluralist as well. This anti-pluralist outlook often leads to the creation of an "us" (e.g., nativists) versus "them" (e.g., immigrants) scenario. Thus, populism represents "the people," but not all people. In his 2018 book *Them: Why We Hate Each Other—and How to Heal*, Senator Ben Sasse, Nebraska (R), puts forth the notion that nations are returning to tribal times wherein people are dividing themselves into categories of people (tribes) to take care of their own ("us") needs if it is at the expense of the other ("them"). Seeking common ground is what will unite the tribes into one nation and thus a more perfect union. This ideal used to be an American mantra (*e pluribus unum*—out of many, one) but populism threatens this concept.

Populism can take many forms and can be found in democratic or authoritarian movements. In democratic societies, populism seeks to defend the interests and maximize the power of ordinary citizens, through reform rather than revolution.

> In its contemporary understanding, however, populism is most often associated with authoritarian forms of politics. Populist politics … revolves around a charismatic leader who appeals to and claims to embody the will of the people in order to consolidate his own power. In this personalized form of politics, political parties lose their importance, and elections serve to confirm the leader's authority.
>
> *(Munro 2019)*

A common approach of populist leaders is to identify rallying points and provide scapegoats as a means of firing up and consolidating the fan base (the people who follow such leaders). Thus, "the people" can be, and generally are, defined along class, ethnic, and/or national lines (they become an "in-group"). The "elite," consisting of the political, economic, cultural, and media establishment is the enemy of the people (this "out-group" is viewed as a homogeneous entity). Donald Trump is a clear example of a populist leader who has, in addition to declaring the media as the enemy of people, identified specific categories of ethnic/racial group who then become a collection of out-group people (scapegoats). At its core, populism establishes a sharp distinction between friend and enemy in which populists' supporters (the in-group) are portrayed as the legitimate people while their opponents are the outsiders. Populists "claim to represent 'the true will of a unified people' against the domestic elites, foreign migrants or ethnic, religious or sexual minorities" (Banerji 2019).

The need to establish a true "us" versus "them" perspective, as described above, often reveals the nationalistic and nativist aspect of populism. Summarized from a variety of dictionaries, nationalism and nativism can be defined as follows. *Nationalism* refers to identification with one's own nation and support for its interests, especially to the exclusion or detriment of interests of other nations; it is an ideology and can be a social movement, and it may also be viewed as a doctrine that the interests of one national culture are superior to those of any other. An *ideology* is a system of ideas and ideals, especially one that forms the basis of a socio-economic theory and policy. *Nativism* is a policy favoring native inhabitants as opposed to immigrants. Nativism is a type of *xenophobic nationalism* (e.g., based on race/ethnicity/nation of origin or religion) that favors one category of people over another—a form of racism or some other type of prejudicial and discriminatory ideology. An important related term is ethnocentrism. *Ethnocentrism* is the belief that one's own ethnicity is superior to others (it is another aspect of nativism). In the United States, claiming to be a "native" is quite relative and is technically only accurate when referring to the indigenous people who lived here before the arrival of Europeans or other racial/ethnic people. It is particularly alarming that in a land of immigrants, nativism exists and is tolerated by so many people.

With the above discussions in mind, I would define *populism* as a socio-economic philosophy and political orientation or standpoint that emphasizes the rights of select categories of people who are generally anti-privileged, anti-pluralist, and anti-status quo and can be found in democratic or authoritarian nations that are headed by an authoritarian and/or charismatic leader who claims to embody the will of "the people" in order to consolidate his/her own power.

Are we in an "Age of Populism?"

In his book *What is Populism?*, Muller (2016) references Bulgarian political scientist Ivan Krastev, who nearly a decade ago wondered if we are in an "Age of Populism." Among other things, Krastev (2011) ponders how "a liberal democracy can function in an environment in which the elites will be permanently mistrusted, regardless of what they do or how transparent the mechanism of governing are."

Krastev took note of the growing tide of right-wing populist movements in the otherwise liberal and democratic Europe, proclaiming that "democracy is in a crisis in Europe" and that "at present European societies have vague hopes and clear fears as they observe the emergence of the threatened majority as the major political force in European politics" (p. 12). Muller's (2016) questioning of whether we are in an Age of Populism centers on the premise that "every politician—especially in poll-driven democracies—wants to appeal to 'the people,' all want to tell a story that can be understood by as many citizens as possible, all want to be sensitive to how 'ordinary folks' think and, in particular, feel" (p. 2). Muller is incorrect in this assumption, however. For one, every populist politician, even in a democratic society, is not concerned with the needs of *all* the people but rather with specific categories of people. For example, Donald Trump, an economic and cultural elitist himself, is leading a populist movement in the United States but he has purposively excluded the needs, desires, and rights of many Americans, especially recent immigrants, those seeking asylum and citizenship, liberals, pluralists, those pro-science, environmentalists, and so on. Populist leaders have an agenda designed to attract specific followers. In the United Kingdom, for example, Boris Johnson appeals to the pro-Brexit folks but he has mostly ignored the nearly equal number of people who are against Brexit. The controversial proposed exit from the EU took on an American flair as accusations of Russian interference in the 2016 Brexit referendum arose from detractors (King 2019e).

An argument in favor of the idea that we are in an "Age of Populism" comes from the fact that populist movements are springing up across the globe. As Carlos de la Torre (2018) explains, "Populism is no longer confined to Latin America, Asia, Africa or the Middle East. Nor is it at the margins of consolidated democracies. Nowadays, populists are in power in the U.S., and parts of Europe including Italy, Poland, Greece and Hungary" (p. 9). As the review of populism to this point has revealed, the idea of a popular movement could be quite democratic and could renew hopes of spreading democracy around the world. However, as also demonstrated, populism is quite different form popularism. De la Torre (2018) echoes this concern by stating that "most scholars are rightly concerned that populism could lead to the 'disfigurement of democracy' … or competitive authoritarianism" (p. 9).

Kenneth Roth, executive director of Human Rights Watch, warns against the rise of populism. He states that the new generation of populists is denying human rights to all the people from government abuse and neglect. Populists, Roth (2019) states, claim to speak for "the people," but in fact "they treat rights as an impediment to their conception of the majority will." Instead of protecting the rights of *all* the people of the country they represent, populist leaders encourage their followers to adopt the values and interests of a limited number of people who have a general discontent over the status quo, and those who feel left behind by technological change and the global economy (Roth 2019).

Arun Kumar Banerji's (2019) warning about populism is quite illuminating, as he compares this movement to the rise of communism.

More than 150 years after the publication of the Communist Manifesto, a new spectre is haunting vast swathes of Europe, Asia, Africa and America in the 21st century. It is the spectre of populist nationalism that thrives on exploitation of popular sentiments and undefined fears, with ominous portents for the very idea of liberal democracy.

Consider that the Group of 20 (G-20, a group of finance ministers and central bank governors from 19 of the world's largest economies and the European Union) have witnessed a striking counter-movement away from democracy and toward populism. "Populist parties—claiming to defend the common man against corrupt elites, valuing national unity above cosmopolitan inclusion, and offering simplistic solutions against complex policy debate—have been gaining strength since the global financial crisis a decade ago" (Orlik and Jimenez 2018). (Trump's inability to debate policy is yet another example that makes him the ideal example of a populist leader and a threat to liberal democracy.) Populists now comprise the largest bloc of the G-20 economies. The G-20 is divided into four categories of government: establishment democracy, populist democracy, weak democracy, and authoritarian. With Trump's election win in 2016, the United States was placed in the populist democracy category and China remains in the authoritarian category. The populist governments now control about 41 percent of the combined G-20 GDP of about $64 trillion; mainstream democracies only preside over about 32 percent. In 2007 they accounted for 83 percent (Orlik and Jimenez 2018). This shift in economic power gives prudence to the idea that we are in an "Age of Populism."

The populist movement is associated with nationalism. On November 11, 2018, French president Emmanuel Macron warned President Trump and more than 100 other world leaders at a gathering in Paris to celebrate the end of World War I (which was officially ended at the eleventh hour on the eleventh day of the eleventh month of 1918) of the "dangers of nationalism." Things such as Trump's "America First" populist movement ignores the painful lessons of history and the fragile global order. Without directly naming Trump or his "America First" mantra, Macron said, "By saying, 'Our interests first, who cares about the others?' we erase what a nation holds dearest, what gives it life, what gives it grace, and what is essential for its moral values." Macron continued, "Patriotism is the exact opposite of nationalism. Nationalism is a betrayal of patriotism" (Bierman 2018:A1). Referencing the resurgence of ethnic and religious hatreds that have led to devastating conflict, Macron stated, "Old demons are coming back to the surface" (Bierman 2018:A1). German chancellor Angela Merkel reminded everyone that peace could not be taken for granted and that it is something that must be worked at.

Populism in the United States

Populist movements are springing up in many parts of the world but the most dramatic example is the election of Donald Trump as President of the United States. Trump is a perfect example of a populist leader, as his "'America First' policy and the style of his governance are inconsistent with liberal democratic policies" (Banerji 2019). Norris and Inglehart (2018), authors of *Cultural Backlash: Trump, Brexit, and the Rise of Authoritarian Populism*, ask,

> How could such a polarizing and politically inexperienced figure win a major party's nomination—and then be elected President? He has been sharply attacked by conservatives such as George Will, establishment Republicans such as John McCain, Democrats such as Elizabeth Warren, and socialists such as Bernie Sanders. He has been described by some commentators as a strongman menacing democracy, by others as a xenophobic and racist demagogue skilled at whipping up crowds, and by yet others as an opportunistic salesman lacking any core principles. Each of these approaches contains some truth.

Norris and Inglehart answer their own question and view Trump "as a leader who uses populist rhetoric to legitimize his style of governance, while promoting authoritarian values that threaten the liberal norms underpinning American democracy." There have been other populists in US history (i.e., Joe McCarthy's witch-hunting of communists and George Wallace's white backlash against ending segregation policies) but none have succeeded in taking such a social movement all the way to the White House. Trump, with his angry nativist speeches, anti-establishment appeals, and racially heated language is similar to that of other populists of the contemporary era (examples to be provided later in this chapter).

Donald Trump did not win the popular vote in 2016; he became president because of the Electoral College system, which has worked against the will of the people and their majority vote four times since 1860. In all four of these elections, a Republican candidate was given the presidency over a Democrat who had secured a higher popular vote; in the 2016 election Democrat Hillary Clinton easily beat Donald Trump in the popular vote. While there is some debate over the origins of the Electoral College system, if we ignored modern interpretations of what really happened at the Constitutional Convention of 1787 we would see that the Electoral College was designed with two purposes: to separate the branches of government in an attempt to avoid "cabals," and to prevent foreign corruption. At least some of the framers of the Constitution assumed it would almost never actually elect a president (Spivak 2019). The modern interpretation of the establishment of the Electoral College considers it as due to the Constitutional Convention members not wanting a democratically elected president; since they feared the masses, they wanted the president to be chosen by their elite selves. The same interpretation argues that the Founding Fathers were afraid that a tyrant could gain power through the manipulation of public opinion.

The fact that Trump did not win the popular vote in the 2016 election reminds us that his populist movement is not popular among the majority of American voters. What Trump did accomplish (despite being part of the "cultural elite") was to tap into a large segment of the population that was not happy with the pluralistic, equality-for-all approach of the American democratic system. Interestingly, many of Trump's supporters represent some of the most oppressed Americans as a direct result of the actions of the socio-economic elite. Still, they support Trump. Karl Marx would refer to this as *false consciousness* (the inability to see where one's own best interests reside). The people who do support Trump do so because they feel as though he speaks for them and that he shares the same vision for America as they do. If that's the case, the United States really is surrounded by one element of darkness, as Trump not only spreads lies, falsehoods, and misleading claims and regularly attacks the press, but his detractors claim that he is also sexist, racist, and xenophobic. (Trump and his followers adamantly deny this claim.) His many critics, Amy Goodman and Denis Moynihan (2019a) among them, suggest that he gives new meaning to the name "White House" as he "hurls racist epithets via tweet while commanding armed agents to terrorize immigrants at the border and in communities from coast to coast" (p. A4). House Speaker Nancy Pelosi, a Democrat, has accused Trump of trying to "Make America White Again"—a reference to his political campaign of "Make America Great Again." As I described in *Common Sense: A Paradigm of Thought* (2019), this empty slogan (e.g., no substance, no policy implications) of "Make America Great Again" was embraced by millions of Americans because they were inspired by its conservative overtones. (Ronald Reagan used this same campaign slogan in 1980.) Never once did Trump explain which particular past era had been "great" or which particular era he wanted America to return to; we can only hope it was at least post-Civil War (which marked the end of slavery) and the Jim Crow era. However, his critics (e.g., Nancy Pelosi) would likely think this is not the case.

In July 2019, Trump verbally and via tweets attacked four Democratic Congresswomen of color: Alexandria Ocasio-Cortez (like Trump, a New York City native), Ilhan Omar (Minnesota), Ayanna Pressley (Massachusetts), and Rashida Tlaib (Michigan). He tweeted on July 14:

> So interesting to see 'Progressive' Democrat Congresswomen, who originally came from countries whose governments are a complete and total catastrophe … loudly and viciously telling the people of the United States … how our government should be run. Why don't they go back and help fix the totally broken and crime infested places from which they came.

And what crime-infested countries with "total catastrophe" governments did these women come from, you might ask? The United States would be the answer. Omar was actually born in Somalia but she came to the US as a political refugee when she was a child and has now been a US citizen longer than Trump's third wife, First Lady Melania Trump, a native of Slovenia. Collectively, these four women have become known as "The Squad." Individually, these four women easily won their districts' elections and are shaking up the Democratic Party, let alone bothering Trump. "The Squad" is often at odds with Democratic Party leader Nancy Pelosi and some have speculated that Trump is going after these women in an attempt to fracture the Democratic Party. He even tweeted, "I'm sure that Nancy Pelosi would be glad to quickly work out free travel arrangements" (King 2019a).

However, the attacks on these four women, which were viewed by a majority of Americans as racist (and perhaps sexist) harassment (a *USA Today* poll found that 68 percent of Americans found Trump's behavior offensive, but 57 percent of Republicans said they agreed with Trump) united the Democratic Party (Chapman 2019). On July 16, 2019, House Resolution 489 was passed. The resolution read, in part: "The resolution strongly condemns, as racist, the President's comments" (H.Res.489). As the week progressed, Trump doubled down on his verbal assaults of the four Congresswomen by accusing them of being socialists or communists, something that would certainly gain favor with his supporters. However, as Goodman and Moynihan (2019a) state, "Trump's use of McCarthy-era attacks should surprise no one, as his early mentor was Roy Cohn, who served as Sen. Joseph McCarthy's lead attorney when destroying thousands of lives through red-bating during the 1950s" (p. A4). (Roy Cohn was mentioned earlier in this chapter.) In a sure sign of things to come, Trump fired up his fan base while at a North Carolina campaign rally and mentioned the four women of color again and especially directed a tirade toward Omar. The crowd responded with the simplistic and racist chant of "Send her back! Send her back!" For 12 seconds Trump remained silent on stage to let the crowd enjoy their chanting; when the chants subsided he continued with his speech without condemning the chant. "The Squad" has not backed down, responding to Trump's attacks in a very strong manner and reminding everyone that they ran for office on a mandate to advocate for and to represent those ignored, left out, and left behind. In other words, they are representing the oppressed people of the United States and have their own populist movement.

The "send her back" chants shouted by many of Trump's supporters at the North Carolina rally echoed his own words when he had tweeted that these progressive Democratic Congresswomen should "go back" to where they came from. Shortly after the chanting ended, Trump said, "Hey, if they don't like it, let them leave, let them leave. Right? Let them leave" (Bierman 2019:A6). The "send her back" chant resembles the long-time acknowledged racist slogan of "go back to where you came from" used by racists for centuries in the United States (as well as some other nations). Jennifer Wingard, a University of Houston professor, traces this sentiment at least to 1798, when the US passed a series of laws—together known as the Alien and Sedition Acts (passed by the Federalist Congress and signed into law by President Adams) that were designed at making citizenship more difficult for immigrants and deportation easier for US authorities to carry out. The legislation was used in practice to remove immigrants who spoke against the US government (Dwyer and Limbong 2019). The most typically thought of application of the "go back to where you came from" sentiment used in the United States was directed toward freed black slaves following the Civil War. Unwilling to accept the idea of blacks being equal to whites, Southern states enacted Jim Crow laws to enforce racial segregation. Even though most blacks accepted the provisions of the

Jim Crow laws—in order to avoid being victims of violence—they were still confronted by whites who thought it best if they simply went back to Africa. Of course the freed slaves and their children and grandchildren had never been to Africa, so the idea of going back home to Africa was not only racist but ignorant. It is true, however, that a number of freed slaves did relocate to Africa prior to the Civil War (in particular to Sierra Leone and Liberia) (History.com 1820). The "go back home" sentiment was applied to Asians as part of the "Yellow Peril" in the late nineteenth century in Australia, New Zealand, South Africa, Canada and the United States. The "Immigration Act of 1924," or the Johnson–Reed Act (H.R. 7995), limited the number of Asians allowed to enter the US because they were considered an "undesirable" race.

A number of current Americans have ancestors that were greeted with the racist chant of "go back to your home country," including Irish immigrants who began to arrive in the US in the 1830s. The Irish, who were predominantly Catholic, faced a great deal of discrimination from the Protestant English and Scottish settlers, who had arrived in the US earlier and now considered themselves as the natives. Throughout many parts of the United States the iconic racist sign of "No Irish Need Apply" was found in places of business. When the Germans started to arrive after the Irish, they experienced racist discrimination as well. There was a clear divide between recent immigrants and the immigrants who were established and who now embraced the "nativist" label. There were secret societies of nativists (i.e., "The Order of the Star Spangled Banner"), with members told to deny any knowledge of societies' existence. When they claimed to "know nothing" of these societies, they eventually were pilloried as the "Know-Nothing" party (Elving 2019). For the Irish arriving in the United States during the late 1840s, it was especially tough to cope with English nativists who looked down upon these new immigrants just as the English had looked down upon the Irish for centuries back in their homelands. These Irish were escaping an English de facto genocide known as the "Irish Potato Famine" (1845–1850) wherein more than one million native Irish had died of starvation even as the island of Ireland exported food to England. In the US, the nativist Americans looked upon the starving immigrant Catholic Irish much in the same manner as Trump supporters are reacting to Spanish-speaking asylum-seekers on the US's southern borders—a campaign once led by the Know-Nothing party. In 1855, Abraham Lincoln wrote to a friend about the Know-Nothings warning of the racist consequences if they gained political power: "As a nation, we begin by declaring that 'all men are created equal.' We now practically read it 'all men are created equal, except Negroes.' When the Know-Nothings get control, it will read, 'all men are created equal, except Negroes, and foreigners, and Catholics'" (Lyons 2019:A4).

Trump and his supporters do not see anything racist in his controversial comments stating that the four progressive Congresswomen of color should "go back home." White House adviser Stephen Miller, in an interview with *Fox News* host Chris Wallace, defended Trump's comments, stating, "I think the term 'racist,' Chris, has become a label that is too often deployed by the left Democrats in this country simply to silence and punish and suppress people they disagree with, speech that they don't want to hear" (Tubman 2019). Then again, perhaps Miller should consider that "the left" is simply pointing out all the racist things Trump and many in his party are saying. Miller went on to say that when Trump criticizes Obama, the US trade deals, our foreign policy, our immigration policies, attacks the city of Baltimore as a "rat and rodent infested mess," and so on, it is out of love for America. However, when four Congresswomen criticized aspects of America, Trump labeled them as anti-American, as hating America, calling them socialists and communists (Tubman 2019). If it is okay for one American to criticize aspects of the United States (and the US Constitution guarantees that all Americans have the right to free speech), as Donald Trump has repeatedly, then it is okay for four Congresspersons to do so as well. For those who think that what Trump said to the four Congresswomen was not racist, imagine what would happen in most workplaces if one employee said to four women of color, "go back to your home country" or "go back to where you came from"; imagine how human resources would handle such a comment. The odds are high that some sort of reprimand would result.

Trump does not think he is a racist. He has often said that he does not have a racist bone in his body, and even that he is "the least racist person" reporters have ever interviewed (Associated Press 2018b). Perhaps there are some who do not know what racism is. So, let's define the term. First, we should realize there are two primary categories of racism; the most commonly referenced variation is interracism, or what most people simply call "racism." This type of racism involves any attitude, belief, behavior, or social arrangement that has the intent, or the ultimate effect, of favoring one racial category of people over another. Racism involves denying equal access to goods and services to all racial groups in society. A racist perspective denies the idea of equality among all people and promotes an ideology that one racial group is superior to another (Delaney 2012; Doob 1999). The presumed superiority of some groups and inferiority of others is subsequently used to legitimate the unequal distribution of society's resources, specifically, various forms of wealth, prestige, and power (Marger 2006). With this information in mind, you can ask yourself, "is Trump a racist?" His reference to certain countries as "shithole" nations (Associated Press 2018b) is another example of racism. A second category of racism is intraracism (sometimes referred to as colorism), which occurs between members of the same race who condemn those with darker or lighter skin tones than their own (Delaney 2012). For example, when light-skinned African Americans look down on dark-skinned Africans.

Accusations that Donald Trump is a racist have existed long before his political career began (e.g., with his real estate company in the 1960s and 1970s). According to Snopes.com (2016), Trump had been accused of racism many times before he announced he was running for president. On the campaign trail there were many documented examples of Trump as a racist including his infamous slanderous comment about Mexican immigrants as rapists and criminals, demanding a total and complete shutdown of Muslims entering the US, claiming that a federal judge of

Mexican ancestry could not be impartial when ruling on his proposed border wall, and so on (Finnegan and Barabak 2018). As president, Trump has said many racist things (prior to our discussion above) including the false claim that all Haitian immigrants have AIDS, that not all neo-Nazis are bad people, defending Confederate monuments, and disavowing NFL football players' right to take a knee during the anthem, as well as referring to Elizabeth Warren, who claimed Native American ancestry, as Pocahontas (Finnegan and Barabak 2018; Warren has since withdrawn the claim). These instances are but a few examples of his racist comments and come only from the 2015–2017 time period.

Michael Cohen, Trump's former personal attorney, testified before Congress' House Committee on Oversight and Reform in early 2019, saying, "I know what Mr. Trump is. He is a racist. He is a con man. He is a cheat" (Goodman and Moynihan 2019b:A4). Elaborating on his statement, Cohen continued, "The country has seen Mr. Trump court white supremacists and bigots. You have heard him call poorer countries s***holes.... In private he is even worse. He once asked me if I could name a country run by a black person that wasn't a s***hole" (Goodman and Moynihan 2019b:A4). In addition to Cohen's damaging claims against Trump, a Pulitzer Prize-winning historian, Jon Meacham, states that Donald Trump is now tied with Andrew Johnson as the "most racist president in American history" (Mazza 2019). This is a damning conclusion as Johnson said in a state message that African Americans were incapable of self-government and relapsed into barbarism if they weren't closely supervised (Mazza 2019). Johnson was the seventeenth president of the United States (1865 to 1869) who assumed the presidency as he was vice president at the time of the assassination of Abraham Lincoln. Meacham pointed to Trump's "birther" lies about former president Barack Obama as an early sign that his presidency would likely be one with a legacy of racism. Unfortunately, many past presidents have displayed racist attitudes and behaviors, regardless of political party affiliation. Nixon's racist views—on Jews, blacks, Irish, Italians—for example, are well documented, and recent revelations of Ronald Reagan's (see the National Archives) racism have come to light in the past two decades (Krakow and Elfrink 2019; Scott 2019).

Most likely, Trump does know what racism is, but he also knows what his primary fan base likes. "Trump is very aware that in 2016 white support for him was highest among those with negative views on America's increasing diversity, and that kind of white voter was a key factor in the swing districts that decided the election in 2016 and could well again in 2020" (Benjamin 2019). Consequently, it is a certainty that race-baiting and xenophobia will play a big role in Trump's 2020 re-election bid, especially because he cannot discuss policy achievements. "The Trump administration has aimed its rhetoric at a slice of aggrieved white Americans who are panicked about their demographic decline. When the courts or Congress or 'fake news' thwart his plans or call him out, that's just more evidence for the base that 'us' is under attack from 'them'" (Benjamin 2019). There are other detractors of Trump who claim he relies on childish, bullying tactics as a means of firing up his supporters. In a *Newsday* (2019) editorial there was a claim that "Trump's childish strategy to denounce opponents personally [is] because he can't debate policy" (p. A4). The *Newsday* editorial ended with an ominous conclusion, "Trump's message is a dangerous one, that the other, the person who is different from you, is not a real American. Soon enough, if Trump's hatred is not rejected, anyone who speaks against him will be the other" (p. A4). And there is evidence that Trump's message will continue to be fully accepted by his supporters as they simply disregard any accusations of racism directed toward Trump, or any other forms of criticism, as "fake news." When Trump was asked if he would back off his comments directed toward "The Squad" because critics viewed it as racism, he replied, "doesn't concern me because many people agree with me" (Colvin, Lemire, and Woodward 2019).

Populist movements in Europe

There are many populist movements in Europe and one of the primary reasons is the so-called "migrant flood" from Africa and the Middle East. In turn, a concern over immigration has led to right-wing nationalism and populist movements throughout Europe. In the following pages we will take a quick look at some examples of populist movements (as of mid-2019).

We begin with the United Kingdom and its vote to leave the European Union, known as "Brexit." On June 23, 2016, voters in the UK were asked to vote on a referendum that oversimplified many complicated issues: "Should the United Kingdom remain a member of the European Union or leave the European Union?" Led by conservative ideals held by many British people who felt leaving the EU would help secure the UK's cultural norms and values (cultural nostalgia), national identity (e.g., via limits on immigration), and independence from the rest of Europe (nationalism), the appeal of Brexit appealed to a certain segment of British society. According to Banerji (2019), the Brexit campaign was, in effect, for the idea of "Britain first," as it was after all a fear of "others," the jobseekers from other EU states, that was being exploited. The conservatives also warned about the ever-expanding jurisdiction of the EU over British citizens' sovereign rights.

The vote to leave the EU won by a margin of 52 to 48 percent. The UK was scheduled to officially depart from the EU on March 29, 2019 but this departure was delayed as a "divorce settlement" between the UK and EU failed to materialize. The failure of Theresa May to work out a departure deal (she repeatedly failed to get her ideas approved by the British Parliament) ended up costing the prime minister her position. (May's predecessor David Cameron also resigned because of Brexit.) May felt like she was acting responsibly by trying to work on such complicated matters as untangling decades of financial and legal connections between the UK and rest of Europe and whether or not exiting the EU would mean the return of a "hard border" between Northern Ireland (which is a part of the UK) and the Republic of Ireland (which will remain in the EU) (*Los Angeles Times* 2019a).

In July 2019, Theresa May was replaced by Boris Johnson, an "eccentric and unpredictable" politician with a populist touch who had helped lead the Brexit movement (Boyle and King 2019:A1). This populist leader did not gain his position via the popular vote. "Because of the quirks of the British political system, only dues-paying members of the governing Conservative Party—just 160,000 people—were eligible to vote in the leadership contest. That means that the new prime minister was in effect picked by less than 1% of the electorate, chosen by a group that is older, wealthier and more likely to be white than the average voter" (Boyle and King 2019:A1, A5). President Trump, a supporter of Brexit and Johnson, immediately offered his congratulations to the new prime minister. By the end of January 2020 the UK did leave the EU and entered the "transition period" as it attempts to finalize the exit details.

In Poland, it is the rise of the populist Law and Justice Party (PiS) that has the attention of the EU. In 2015, the PiS surprised many by returning to power with a populist platform, decrying a selfish elite and advancing policies that critics consider as illiberal and authoritarian. "What makes this election victory so shocking is that Poland is supposed to be the poster-boy of new post-communist Member States. Poland was the only EU member state to continue growing during the 2009 economic crisis and in 2017 had the highest economic growth in the EU" (Swallow 2018). The PiS have traditionally drawn support from religious, socially conservative areas in small towns and rural areas of eastern Poland as these regions have been hit hard by the collapse of state-owned enterprises in heavy industry and have fallen behind those making money in the new financial order.

Poland's right-wing populist movement comes with the seemingly requisite anti-immigration stance and finds a friend in Donald Trump (King 2017).

> Trump's Polish counterpart, President Andrzej Duda, shares some common policy ground with the U.S. president, including prospects for energy deal-making, a shared mistrust of Muslim immigrants and refugees and a degree of disdain for the European Union. But the country's most powerful political figure is Jaroslaw Kaczynski, the head of the nationalist-minded ruling Law and Justice party, which won the 2015 parliamentary elections.
>
> *(King 2017)*

Poland's populist movement also runs counter to the LGBTQ+ equal rights movement. During the 2017 Independence Day march, some participants carried racist and anti-Islamic banners calling for a "White Europe" and displayed white supremacist symbols like the Celtic Cross. There were also cases of violence against counter-protesters (Associated Press 2018d). Lawmakers in the European Parliament called the participants "fascists"—a label that has infuriated the conservative Polish government. Increasingly, the far-right nationalists have attempted to gain control of the celebration of independence (Associated Press 2018d). In 2019, analysts monitoring extremist groups have called the annual Independence Day march in Poland one of "Europe's biggest gatherings of ultra-fascists, extreme right-wingers and nationalists" (Hruby 2019:A3). Activists attribute the rise of far-right sentiments in Poland to the rise to power of PiS (Hruby 2019). We can see a couple of parallels to the United States with these last two Polish descriptions of right-wing populist supporters: (1) among Trump's supporters are neo-Nazis, pro-Confederate reactionists, and Alt-right white nationalists; (2) Trump has attempted to take control of US Independence Day celebrations in Washington, DC.

In 2018, an anti-migrant, Euro-skeptic populist coalition took power in Italy. Political novice Giuseppe Conte was sworn in as prime minister on June 1 along with his 18 cabinet ministers. The Italian government is now run by the anti-establishment Five Star Movement (M5S) and the far-right League party (Kirchgaessner 2018).

> [Matteo] Salvini, the bombastic and xenophobic leader of the League, who rose in recent years on the back of incendiary and racist statements about migrants and Roma, will take on the role of interior minister. Salvini has campaigned on the promise of mass deportations of migrants and said a new government would build detention centres around Italy.
>
> *(Kirchgaessner 2018)*

As a fierce critic of Brussels (the EU), he has called for closer ties to Russia. The M5S populist party is not like every far-right party as its position on such issues as environmental protection, public water, and sustainable transport are liberal concerns. One might wonder if the M5S and League parties can maintain their coalition given some of M5S's leftist stands but they share many typical far-right positions including their negative views on immigration, refugees, the euro, and the promotion of improved relations with Russia (Salhani 2017).

As an update to this story and a sign of light in Italy, far-right leader Matteo Salvini was replaced on September 4, 2019 by a career servant and specialist in migration policy, Luciana Lamorgese, a veteran of the interior ministry and a left-leaning pro-European politician who is working with a coalition aimed at curtailing the damage caused by Salvini's populist League party (Tondo 2019). "The coalition assembled by the prime minister, Giuseppe Conte, between centre-left Democratic party (PD) and anti-establishment Five Star Movement (M5S) also includes Roberto Gualtieri, an influential PD member of the European parliament, as economy minister" (Tondo 2019).

The Czech Republic is another European nation with a populist movement centered on calling out migration and Islam as major threats to Europe and expressing anti-EU sentiment. In April 2019, Europe's far-right leaders met in Prague. Marine Le Pen, leader of France's far-right National Rally party, and Geert Wilders, founder of the Dutch anti-Islam Party for Freedom, were the main draws of the right-wing Freedom and Direct Democracy party, the Czech member of the Movement for a Europe of Nations and Freedom. "All of the far-right politicians denounced migration and Islam, linking them to terrorist attacks and criticizing the current European Union. They vowed their alliance would seek a radical change in how Europe is run. The battle of Europe has begun," Le Pen announced, "Long live a Europe of sovereign nations" (Associated Press 2019a:A4). Le Pen also considers Islam "a medieval cult that denies freedom to others" and claims that "Islam and freedom are not compatible" (Associated Press 2019a:A4). The far-right rally was met with counter-protestors. The populist politicians are also targeting Czech journalists and media analysts. Members of the bodies supervising Czech news agencies are elected lawmakers and the concern among the media is political interference from populist nominees. SPD (Freedom and Direct Democracy) leader Tomio Okamura has repeatedly called Czech TV journalists "liars," while Czech prime minister Andrej Babis (who leads a minority center-left government of ANO and the left-wing Social Democrats) has dubbed them "a corrupt bunch" (Flemr 2019).

The next nation has a reputation for being an open, liberal country with a low crime rate and a strong social welfare system, and yet suddenly has played witness to the populist wave moving across Europe: Sweden. A far-right political group known as the Sweden Democrats is gaining electoral heights.

> Nearly 1 in 5 Swedish voters backed the party, which has fascist and white nationalist roots and advocates a hard-line stance on immigration. [The September 2018] election results in Sweden appear to reflect the broader political headwinds in Europe, which have seen right-wing populist parties such as the Sweden Democrats rise at the expense of traditional centrist parties such as the Social Democrats and the Moderates.
>
> *(Schultheis 2018:A3)*

The Sweden Democrats ran a campaign based on scare tactics and warnings of Sweden as a nation in decline as the result of the influx of refugees, advocating for a full halt on asylum-seekers. Sweden has taken in the highest per-capita number of refugees in Europe; a nation of just under 10 million, it took in 160,000 immigrants in 2015 alone. Critics of the Sweden Democrats believe that it is embarrassing for Sweden to have a party rooted in a Nazi racist culture (Schultheis 2018).

Perhaps the most extreme of the right-wing extremists in Europe is Viktor Orbán, the prime minister of Hungary (currently serving his third consecutive term) and head of the Fidesz party. "Although Hungary is a European Union member and a NATO ally, Orbán has become notorious for his attacks on the media, academia, the judiciary and other democratic institutions since he became prime minister in 2010" (King 2019b:A3). In May 2017, Orbán was invited to the White House to meet with President Trump, who praised "him as a respected leader, brushing aside expressions of alarm from human rights groups and Western governments" (King 2019c). Standing side-by-side at the White House,

> there was no mention of the Hungarian leader's sustained attacks on his country's democratic institutions, his conspiracist-style railing against Hungarian American philanthropist George Soros, or the Hungarian government's punitive campaign at nongovernmental groups with missions such as

help migrants. "Probably like me a little bit controversial, but that's OK," Trump said of Orbán.

(King 2019c)

While Trump has nurtured friendly relationships with an array of autocrats and global strongmen (i.e., Egyptian president Abdel Fattah Sisi; Philippine president Rodrigo Duterte; North Korean leader Kim Jong Un; Russian president Vladimir Putin), his friendship with Orbán is noteworthy because of his influence with populists in Europe. That Orbán embraces a nativist agenda especially endears him with Trump (King 2019b).

In 2015, when Europe struggled with an influx of refugees from Syria, Iraq and Afghanistan, he likened migrants to rapists and terrorists, echoing Trump's harsh rhetoric about migrants on the southern U.S. border. Orbán's harsh depictions of Muslims, whom he calls a threat to "Christian European culture," are part of a political agenda that he calls "illiberal democracy," one in which elections are held but traditional liberties erode.

(King 2019b:A3)

Orbán's particular interpretation of Christian values, coupled with his far-right anti-migrant rhetoric, has become a centerpiece of his increasingly authoritarian government's messaging, which he likes to call "Christian democracy" (Walker 2019).

Orbán visited Trump again in May of 2019, just prior to the Hungarian elections, as a strategic move to demonstrate to the Hungarian people that he had the backing of the United States, or at least of Donald Trump. It is interesting to note that although Hungary has received billions of euros in aid from the EU, Orbán is one of its leading critics. Orbán

> shares an antipathy with Trump, who has slammed the European Union as a "foe" on trade, boosted Brexit as a way to reset trade relations with Europe, and rattled NATO by suggesting it is obsolete.... Like Trump, Orbán is a fan of border barriers, erecting a formidable double fence topped with razor wire and bristling with sensors and watchtowers on Hungary's southern border. And like Trump, he has few qualms about demonizing his opponents.
>
> *(King 2019b:A3)*

Human Rights Watch has a very negative review of Hungary and states that the government fails to respect the rule of law and human rights. Its official statement on Hungary claims: "Government representatives are increasingly hostile to journalists and critics and engage in anti-migrant, anti-Muslim and xenophobic rhetoric including through publicly funded campaigns.... Asylum seekers are detained indefinitely in substandard border camps without a possibility to challenge their detention" (Human Rights Watch 2019a).

Greece is the next European country we will look at. In its 2019 elections, Greece replaced years of a populist-brand government for the New Democracy party, a center-right party. Kyriakos Mitsotakis became the new prime minster of Greece, with the populist leader Alexis Tsipras vowing a return to power. Tsipras had led his left-wing Syriza party to power in 2015 with promises that offered much hope to the Greek people—but that ultimately he could not keep. When he left office Greece had the highest unemployment rate in Europe and instead of ending austerity measures, as he had campaigned, he imposed more taxes (Al Jazeera 2019).

Mitsotakis promised that transparency and meritocracy would return to Greece, along with its voice in Europe.

> A liberal reformist, Mitsotakis promises to rebrand the country and change its image as Europe's problem child in wake of an eight-year depression that saw its economy slashed by 25%—the worst contraction in a developed economy since the end of World War II. Mitsotakis says his priority is to reignite the economy by slashing taxes and regulations, while attracting investment.
>
> *(Labropoulou 2019)*

Greece's brief relationship with populism resulted in bank runs and talk of Grexit (Greece's exit from the EU), banks closed for days, and capital controls were imposed. Greece has turned away from economic populism toward pragmatism, according to George Pagoulatos, a professor at the Athens University of Economics (Labropoulou 2019). Critics are hoping that what has happened in Greece will also take place throughout Europe and around the world. "Greece was the first country in the last decade to bring grand scale populism to the mainstream European arena. Now it is the first to firmly reject it, in an election result that may signal the beginning of the end for extreme populism in Europe" (Labropoulou 2019). At the very least, this new "age of pragmatism" will have to result in Greece's economic upswing or we are likely to see a return of populism. On the other hand, success in Greece could indeed shine a light bright enough to eliminate the darkness of discriminatory populism.

The final country to be discussed has a far-right autocratic leader and a large number of human rights violations (e.g., journalists jailed, censoring and blocking of websites, and incarceration of thousands of Turks for their social media posts) (Human Rights Watch 2019b): Turkey, whose president Recep Tayyip Erdogan Trump has befriended. When Trump had completed construction of his twin-skyscraper project in Turkey seven years ago, then-prime minister Erdogan attended the grand opening. Trump's daughter Ivanka praised him for doing so (Date 2019). Ivanka Trump is now a top White House aide. While it is no surprise that Trump supports right-wing fanatics and especially sides with countries where he maintains businesses, what did surprise political observers—even his fellow Republicans—was his abandonment of the Kurds—an American ally—in favor of Turkey.

The Kurds are a non-Arab minority ethnic category of people numbering around 20 million spread across four nations—10 million in Turkey, 6 million in Iran, 3.5 million in Iraq, and a little over 2 million in Syria (*The Post-Standard*

2019). The Kurds are overwhelmingly Sunni Muslim and speak an Indo-European language. They reside primarily in a 74,000-square-mile mountainous zone in the southeast of Turkey through northwest Iran. Trump's betrayal of the Kurds is not the first time they have been stabbed in the back, as following the Ottoman Empire's collapse after World War I they were promised an independent homeland in the 1920 Treaty of Sevres. The treaty was never ratified and "Kurdistan" was carved up. Since then, the Kurds have continuously rebelled in Iran, Iraq, and Turkey (*The Post-Standard* 2019). In 1991, the Kurds helped in the US-led Gulf War that liberated Kuwait from Iraqi forces and while then-President George H.W. Bush had never explicitly promised the Kurds their own land, a US-enforced no-fly zone over northern Iraq had helped to ensure a degree of Kurdish autonomy. Viewing the United States as an ally, the Kurds subsequently answered the American call for assistance in defeating ISIS in the Syrian region (*Post-Standard* 2019).

The Kurds provided most of the ground troops for the US war against the militant Islamic State. "More than 11,000 Kurds died in that campaign. The number of U.S. combat deaths reported in Syria: six" (McManus 2019b:A2). Other reports indicate that the Kurdish-Arab Syrian Democratic Forces (SDF) lost more than 12,000 lives fighting ISIS (*Post-Standard* 2019). With ISIS nearly defeated and confined to makeshift prisons guarded by Kurdish soldiers, Donald Trump shocked the world when he pulled out American troops from the region. This action would directly allow for, and lead to, a Turkish incursion into Syria (King 2019d). "That would leave Syrian Kurdish allies, who were instrumental in the fight against the Islamic State, vulnerable to being overrun or slaughtered by Turkish forces, who consider the Syrian Kurds to be allied with 'terrorist' counterparts in Turkey" (King 2019d:A3). In an absurd defense of his move, Trump referred to himself as possessing "great and unmatched wisdom" (King 2019d:A3). The US president tried to calm down the attacks he faced from fellow Republicans by warning Turkey that they better not try anything in Syria or he would punish them, including through economic means (King 2019d).

Trump announced his plans to withdraw US troops from Syria shortly after his October 6, 2019 phone call with Erdogan, and without consultation with the Pentagon, which had given assurances to the Kurds that they would be fully supported by the US (Cloud, Haberkorn, and Bulos 2019; Goodman and Moynihan 2019d).

> Trump argued that he doesn't owe anything to the Kurds despite Pentagon promises to them while they helped prevent Islamic State from becoming a direct threat to the United States. "The Kurds fought with us, but were paid massive amounts of money and equipment to do so" [Trump] tweeted. The Kurds weren't allies, it turns out; in Trump's view, they were subcontractors.
>
> *(McManus 2019b:A2)*

Trump's pullback on US promises to the Kurds continued his well-established record of abandoning America's allies. The Trump administration has criticized

Australia, South Korea, France, and other long-standing US partners while seemingly coddling foes and rivals like North Korea and Russia (Byman 2019). "Abandoning the Kurds, and doing so with no notice, is symptomatic of the Trump administration's disdain for allies, even those who are fighting and dying to keep America safe. Even the few supportive allies, such as Israel, are questioning the president" (Byman 2019). Trump's actions with regards to the Kurds is the latest example of his "approach to foreign policy that critics condemn as impulsive, that he sometimes reverses and that often is untethered to the advice of his national security aides" (Baldor, Lee, and Burns 2019:A6).

Just a few days after US troops had abandoned the Kurds, Turkey invaded the Kurdish-inhabited area. (Syrian forces would also attack the Kurds.) Erdogan said that he plans to relocate to the land claimed by the Kurds up to one million Syrian refugees, most of them Arab, in what the SDF commander warns will amount to "ethnic cleansing" (*The Post-Standard* 2019). Trump effectively green-lighted the Turkish invasion of the territory controlled by the SDF when he ordered the US troops out of Syria (Byman 2019). Trump would later defend his move to pull the troops out of Syria as part of a campaign promise that he made to the American people. As it turned out, however, the troops were moved to eastern Syria to protect the oil fields from potentially falling into the hands of Islamic State militants (Baldor and Burns 2019). These actions demonstrate, at least in part, Trump's loyalty to Big Oil over national allies.

Doubling down on his irrational behavior, Trump said that the US's allies the Kurds are "no angels" and that any fallout from a resurgence in ISIS would be Europe's problem and not the problem of the US (Kim and DeBonis 2019; Byman 2019). Senator Lindsey Graham, usually a strong Trump ally, warned, "The reemergence of ISIS is on the way. And if you think only Europe is threatened—you are sadly mistaken" (Byman 2019). Democratic presidential hopefuls all condemned Trump's troop withdrawal. The House was quick to adopt a resolution condemning Trump's move to pull US troops out of northern Syria. As an example of the overwhelming condemnation, the vote was 354 to 60 supporting the resolution.

Trump's erratic and illogical behavior and support of right-wing autocrats has dimmed the beacon of enlightened and rational thought that the United States once enjoyed. To many of its allies, the US is now viewed in a questionable and cautious manner; that is, at least until Trump is no longer president.

Populist movements in other parts of the world

As we continue with a quick look at populist movements, we turn our attention away from Europe and toward Africa. The diversity of Africa's governments clouds both democratic and populist attempts at running a nation as authoritarian regimes or civil war dominate many areas. On the other hand, there are some areas where popular unrest has altered governments, such the ouster of Sudanese president Omar Hassan Ahmed Bashir and Algerian president Abdelaziz Bouteflika. These developments could lead to increased migration north to Europe where, as already demonstrated, such migrants will face unwelcoming populations in many European nations; second, it could lead to an expansion of the Islamic State and Al Qaeda in northern Africa (Estelle 2019). The protest-backed coups in Algeria and Sudan are reminiscent of the original Arab Spring revolutions of 2011, which toppled governments in Tunisia, Egypt, Libya, and Yemen and led to civil war in Syria (Bulos 2019). On April 2, 2019, the 82-year-old Bouteflika resigned as the long-time president of Algeria in part because of poor health but also amid a growing dissent among Algerian opposition.

According to 2019 research conducted by the YouGov-Cambridge Globalism Project and the *Guardian*, South Africa is second behind only Brazil as the top nation fuelled by "populism" (Head 2019; Phillips, Burke, and Lewis 2019). In recent years, South Africa has experienced scandals and corruption. As a result, around 39 percent of South Africans have populist views and want to see an end to corruption, the domination of the elites, and power given to the people (See Table 2.1). In fact, all three major parties in South Africa are trying to come across as the best option for those in favor of the "for the people, and against the elite" sentiment. "With corruption essentially making up the fabric of South Africa's political landscape, populist sentiment is inescapable" (Head 2019).

In Namibia, it is a slow-developing economy that is triggering a rise in populism. Critics counter that meeting the demands of these nativists will do little to recharge a moribund economy (Hagenmeier 2017). Part of the economic problem in Namibia is the near-collapse of the construction industry, an economy that was government-funded, but because it could no longer afford to support such projects, the government cut the budget.

While Africa possesses some of the elements that fuel populist movements around the world, such as a nativism and demands for a stronger economy, much of Africa does not have an immigration problem and therefore is missing in one of the key elements of populism, anti-immigrant sentiment. There is the obvious exception of those who flee war-torn areas that may try to relocate to more stable

TABLE 2.1 Top ten nations with highest percentage of people holding populist views

Nation	Percent
1. Brazil	42.0
2. South Africa	39.0
3. Thailand	30.0
4. Mexico	29.9
5. Turkey	28.0
6. Poland	26.0
7. France	24.0
8. USA	23.5
9. Spain	22.0
10. India	21.0

Source: Head 2019; Phillips, Burke, and Lewis 2019.

and relatively prosperous African nations like Morocco, rather than venture to Europe. To date, Morocco has been accommodating to an influx of immigrants. Still, an anti-immigration platform has generally been a centerpiece of populist movements in the United States and Europe.

The last three examples of populist nations we will look at round out the top four nations ranked as the most populist (see Table 2.1): Brazil, Thailand, and Mexico. We begin with Brazil and its government led by far-right president Jair Bolsonaro, known as "Brazil's Trump."

> His populist agenda was much like the message that Trump rode to the White House, with plenty of anger-laced rhetoric and calls to clean up corruption and crack down on crime. He assiduously cultivated a tough-guy image, espousing torture, a restoration of the death penalty and looser gun laws. Critics called Bolsonaro racist, homophobic and misogynistic, but his extremist views did little to dent his popularity.
>
> *(King 2018a:A2)*

Bolsonaro even agrees with Trump's disbelief in the evidence provided by scientists regarding climate change. Environmentalists and others worry about Bolsonaro's views on the environment as Brazil has the planet's largest rainforests, which are often referred to as the "lungs of the planet."

Bolsonaro has expressed admiration for military dictatorships, has insulted women, people of color, and the gay community, has pledged to fight the teaching in schools of what he calls "the ideology of gender," believes he can end violence by shielding all police from prosecution for use of excessive force, and vows to "constantly ask God for guidance" (Wilkinson 2019a:A3). He has also targeted indigenous groups, descendants of slaves, and the LGBTQ+ community. At his inauguration, Bolsonaro promised, "This is the beginning of Brazil's liberation from socialism, political correctness and a bloated state" (Wilkinson 2019a:A3).

Ranked as the third-most populist nation is Thailand. In the early 2000s, Thailand was considered "one of the most democratic nations in the world" but this assessment was reappraised by Freedom House in 2006 as "not free" (Case 2017). In its annual "Freedom in the World" report, Thailand was rated as "Not Free" in 2018. The "Freedom in the World" rankings are composed of numerical ratings and supporting descriptive texts for 195 countries and 14 territories and have been published annually since 1973, allowing Freedom House to track global trends in freedom for nearly five decades (Freedom House 2018a). To compile its rankings, Freedom House combines on-the-ground research, consultations with local contacts, and information from news articles, non-governmental organizations, governments, and a variety of other sources.

Thailand's reputation as a democratically free state was altered following a military junta coup that was launched in 2014, since when its military government has exercised unchecked powers and has imposed extensive restrictions on civil and political rights, and suppressed dissent (Freedom House 2018b). Running

Thailand's government is the National Council for Peace and Order (NCPO) consisting of unelected junta members and King Maha Vajiralongkorn (since October 13, 2016), son of former King Bhumibol Adulyadej, as the royal family still exercises significant influence as an embodiment of power (CBS News 2019). On May 1, 2019, King Vajiralongkorn married his fourth wife, Queen Suthida. As an example of the military government's frequent use of the law to silence critics on any subject matter, the Thai public was reminded that "insulting the monarch, queen or heir apparent is punishable by three to 15 years in prison under Thai law" (CBS News 2019). Freedom House (2018b) states that "journalists, academics, and activists continue to face harassment or arrest for criticizing NCPO authorities or the monarchy."

Freedom House's "Freedom in the World 2018" profile ranks Thailand as "Not Free," with an aggregate score of 31/100 (0 = Least Free, 100 = Most Free). Thailand received a 6 for "Political Rights" (1 = Most Free, 7 = Least Free) and a 5 on "Civil Liberties" for an overall "Freedom Rating" of 5.57/7. This nation of over 63 million people ranks as "Not Free" on a wide variety of categories including political rights and civil liberties (Freedom House 2018b).

Coming in fourth place as the most populist nation according to the YouGov-Cambridge Globalism Project and the *Guardian* (see Table 2.1) is Mexico. Freedom House (2018c) has rated Mexico as "Not Free" since 2011 in its annual Freedom of the Press report primarily because of ongoing violence against journalists, which is carried out with impunity. Freedom House is working in Mexico in an attempt to help journalists better protect themselves from violence to protect free expression. Freedom House (2018c) ranks Mexico, a nation with 116 million people, as "Partly Free" overall with the internet as "Partly Free" and the press as "Not Free."

In its "Freedom in the World 2019" report, Freedom House (2019b) gave Mexico a "Partly Free" aggregate score of 63/100 (0 = Least Free, 100 = Most Free). Mexico received grades of 3 (1 = Most Free, 7 = Least Free) for "Freedom Rating," "Political Rights," and "Civil Liberties." While these scores are only partially discouraging, it is the "severe rule-of-law deficits that limit full citizen enjoyment of political rights and civil liberties" (Freedom House 2019b). The rampant criminal activities of drug cartels are another serious problem in Mexico. "Violence perpetrated by organized criminals, corruption among government officials, human rights abuses by both state and nonstate actors, and rampant impunity are among the most visible of Mexico's many governance challenges" (Freedom House 2019b).

In the 2018 general elections, left-wing populist candidate Andres Manuel Lopez Obrador was victorious. Lopez Obrador is overly nationalistic, pushes "Mexican people first" policies and peppers his speeches with anti-establishment slogans that thrill the working-class Mexicans who attend his rallies. "While his style might be distinctly Trumpian, his policy prescriptions could not be more different" (Rodriguez 2018). Lopez Obrador ran a campaign focused on themes of fighting corruption and providing social services to the people, and he attacked the establishment as a "mafia power" while pledging central government austerity and a crackdown on graft (Freedom House 2019b). Since his election, however, Mexico's criminal violence has continued to rise. Violence and threats of violence against political candidates, election officials, and campaign workers are among the problems in Mexico. The reality of criminal violence, which also extends to attacks on and the murder of journalists, combined with government corruption, which remains a serious problem in Mexico, harms its overall freedom rating and its hopes for a democratic society.

The deterioration of freedom and human rights

The "darkness that surrounds us" is meant to draw attention to, and identify, some of the key ways in which enlightened, rational, and reasoned thought are being challenged in the early twenty-first century. Examples of this darkness include: lies, falsehoods, and misleading claims made by political leaders, attacking journalists and the news media and in some cases referring to them as the "enemy of the people," and the rise of populism and nationalism. In their own way, each of these three subject areas contributes to the deterioration of democracy and human rights. There are many other examples of this deterioration and some of those topics will be described next.

Deterioration of freedom, globally

Previously in this chapter, the "Freedom in the World" calculations established by Freedom House were shared. The full for 2019 reveals that a total of 68 countries suffered net declines in "political rights" and "civil liberties" in 2018, while just 50 countries registered gains. Not only was there a net decline in freedom globally in 2018 but, according to Freedom House (2019c), 2018 marked the thirteenth consecutive year (2005–2018) that the global average of freedom has declined. The end of the Cold War facilitated a wave of democratization in the late twentieth century but a large number of newly independent countries could not maintain their democratic freedom (Freedom House 2019c).

> Social and economic changes related to globalization have contributed to a crisis of confidence in the political systems of long-standing democracies…. Hostile forces around the world continue to challenge the institutions meant to protect political rights and civil liberties and the damage has accrued over the past 13 years will not soon be undone.
>
> *(Freedom House 2019c)*

Among the examples of countries that went from "Free" to "Partly Free" in Freedom House's "Freedom in the World 2019" annual report are Hungary and Serbia. Hungary (as previously discussed in this chapter) was downgraded due to sustained attacks on the country's democratic institutions by Prime Minister Viktor

Orbán's Fidesz party, while Serbia's status declined due to deterioration in the conduct of elections, continued attempts by the government and allied media outlets to undermine independent journalists through legal harassment and smear campaigns, and President Aleksandar Vučić's de facto accumulation of executive powers that conflict with his constitutional role (Freedom House 2019c). Nicaragua and Uganda's status declined from "Partly Free" to "Not Free." In Nicaragua, the authorities' brutal repression of an anti-government protest movement, which has included the arrest and imprisonment of opposition figures, intimidation and attacks against religious leaders, and violence by state forces and allied armed groups that resulted in hundreds of deaths, led to its downward status. In Uganda, the downgrade is the result of long-ruling president Yoweri Museveni's government's restriction of free expression, including via surveillance of electronic communications and a regressive tax on social media use (Freedom House 2019c).

Other global examples of the deterioration of freedom and human rights include Romania's attempt to change its constitution to ban same-sex marriage in 2018. "It's a way of protecting our children in front of this whole concept of gender ideology," said Mihai Gheorghiu of the Coalition for Families, a consortium of religious nonprofit groups in Romania leading the charge on the referendum to deny rights to gay Romanian citizens (Ayers and King 2018). The referendum failed when only about 20 percent of registered voters cast ballots (a turnout of 30 percent was necessary for the vote to be valid). In Chechnya, members of the LGBTQ+ community have been killed or injured as a result of police torture and scores of others arrested as part of a crackdown on LGBTQ+ people living in the mostly Muslim North Caucasus republic (Ayers 2019). In Saudi Arabia, women now have the right to drive but they face verbal insults and acts of violence from Saudi men who do not approve of the idea that basic human rights should be fully extended to women (Bulos 2018). While there is warfare and conflict being waged across the globe it is sometimes hard to keep up with all the areas that need humanitarian emergency aid. Yemen is one of these often-forgotten regions. Here are some of the things facing the Yemeni people since 2015, the year in which the current civil war started: more than 10,000 people have been killed and many more wounded; two million have been driven from their homes because of the fighting between a Saudi-led coalition (composed of the Emirates, mercenaries, and a makeshift collection of militiamen including jihads) and Iranian-backed Houthi rebels (the US supports Saudi Arabia in the war against the Houthi movement); there are regular bombings from warplanes; 8.4 million Yemeni face famine; disease is spreading; there is a lack of clean drinking water (Bulos 2018). As Riedel (2017) states, "The war has created the worst humanitarian catastrophe in the world and threatens to turn into the largest famine in decades." In Venezuela, government security forces carry out "unjustified killings without any apparent consequences as the rule of the law in the country quickly vanishes" as the nation of over 28 million is confronted by "a deepening political and economic crisis marked by food and medicine shortages and soaring inflation that has driven thousands to flee the country" (Associated Press 2018e:A4).

The topic of the global deterioration of freedom is so extensive that it is impossible to give it full discussion here, but the point has been clearly made that there is indeed a shortage of human rights around the world.

Deterioration of freedom, the United States

Freedom House (2019c) states that there are certain challenges to American democracy that are testing the stability of the US's constitutional system and are threatening to undermine political rights and civil liberties worldwide. "While democracy in America remains robust by global standards, it has weakened significantly over the past eight years, and the current president's ongoing attacks on the rule of law, fact-based journalism, and other principles and norms of democracy threaten further decline" (Freedom House 2019c). Freedom House notes that similar patterns in the overall decline in freedom that it has observed in the past have led to authoritarianism and thus warns the United States not to take a cavalier attitude thinking that it couldn't happen there. "Prominent concerns have included Russian interference in US elections, domestic attempts to manipulate the electoral system, executive and legislative dysfunction, conflicts of interest and lack of transparency, and pressure on judicial independence and the rule of the law" (Freedom House 2019c). Other problems the organization cited include: an upsurge of civic action and demonstrations on a variety of issues; immigration policy; and mass shootings in schools.

The aforementioned problems with the American electoral system and Russian interference in US elections (especially the 2016 presidential election) are combined with another key threat to US democracy, namely, voter suppression. *Voter suppression* refers to a variety of tactics used to influence an election by lowering the number of, dissuading, or outright obstructing specific categories of people from voting in a particular election. These tactics can include: (1) removing voters from voting polls; (2) changing or reducing voting locations; (3) requiring IDs to vote; (4) running out of provisional ballots; and (5) "exact match" policies. In 2016, ten states put into place restrictive voting laws in time for the presidential elections. Collectively, these ten states are home to 80 million people who will determine 129 of the 270 electoral votes necessary to win the presidency (Ho 2016). Consider these examples designed to limit fair access to voting. In North Dakota, voter ID restrictions meant that in order to vote, a voter's driver's license had to have a residential address—something most Native Americans do not have because they live on reservations. Alabama, another state that requires specific forms of identification that can be obtained at a local Department of Motor Vehicles (DMV), closed nearly two-thirds of its DMV offices, obstructing many people's (especially minorities who were more likely to vote Democrat) access to voter registration. (Alabama Republican governor Robert Bentley claims that many DMVs were scheduled to close because of budget cuts.) In Indiana, many polling places in the poorer neighborhoods were moved out of local communities, meaning that those without cars could reach the polling stations (Abrams 2019). In Georgia, there were many allegations of voter suppression in the presidential election, including tens of thousands of voter registrations not being processed. Stacey Abrams (D), an African American woman who ran for Governor of Georgia in 2018, has claimed that over 50,000 black voters in the state were victims of voter registration fraud. Abrams cites this figure because Brian Kemp, the Republican candidate for governor and the then-secretary of state, put a temporary hold on the registrations of about 50,000 new voters; he also led a state drive to remove hundreds of thousands of infrequent voters from the rolls. Kemp, who won the hotly contested governor's race, was also the top official supervising elections (Savage 2018). Many people considered this unethical. This voter fraud, which affected many registered black voters, led Abrams to start an organization—"FairFight2020.org"—that wants to make sure all eligible voters are allowed to vote. The organization has three goals for all voters across the nation: access to voter registration, access to polling locations, and to have all votes counted. Voter suppression, regardless of who the victims are, is a sure sign of the deterioration of democracy and human rights.

Despite this less-than-rosy picture of the United States, Freedom House (2019d) does rate the United States as "Free" with an aggregate freedom score of 86 (Least Free = 0, Most Free = 100). The US scored 1.5 for "Freedom Rating," 2 for "Political Rights," and 1 for "Civil Liberties" (1 = Most Free, 7 = Least Free). The "86" rating places the US behind other major democracies such as France, Germany, and the United Kingdom, but it is still firmly in the "Free" category. However, its decline of eight points in as many years is significant. The United States' closest peers with respect to total Freedom in the World scores are Belize, Croatia, Greece, Latvia, and Mongolia (Freedom House 2019c).

The United States is, arguably, the world's oldest existing democracy with a strong rule-of-law tradition, robust freedoms of expression and religious belief, and a wide array of other civil liberties (Freedom Hose 2019d). "However, in recent years its democratic institutions have suffered erosion, as reflected in partisan manipulation of the electoral process, bias and dysfunction in the criminal justice system, flawed new policies on immigration and asylum seekers, and growing disparities in wealth, economic opportunity, and political influence" (Freedom House 2019d).

One thing in particular that the United States has messed up on is its immigration policy, and the mixed perception of the handling of immigrants on the southern border. Claims of "children in cages" do not help this perception. While the actual conditions that immigrant children are confined in vary based mostly on partisan lines, one thing that is clear is that the Trump administration does not want illegal border crossings. Most people would likely agree that there has to be some sort of accountability as to whom and how many people are entering the country (or any country, for that matter). People who lean left, such as California governor Gavin Newsom, are likely to point out that the United States was founded by immigrants and that this land has long been a safe haven for people fleeing tyranny, oppression, and violence. People who lean right are likely to say that they do not want any more immigrants entering the United States even if they seek legal immigration or asylum. Having promised stricter immigration laws and a more secure southern border while campaigning for president, Donald Trump leans far to the right. His position on immigration has only gotten stronger since he became president. Consider, for example, while visiting a section of the border wall with Mexico in Calexico, California on April 5, 2019, Trump renewed his push for border security and reaffirmed his anti-immigrant stance by declaring, "We can't take you anymore. Our country is full" (MSN 2019; Roberts and Roberts 2019a). "Trump's anti-immigrant rhetoric serves only one purpose: to energize his supporters by inflaming the nativist fears that have periodically engulfed the country throughout our history. He firmly believes those fears helped elect him once, and will again" (Roberts and Roberts 2019a:A4).

The war on immigration in the United States has ethical and moral implications. The largest number of refugees seeking to enter the US are fleeing conditions in their home countries and are so poor that they are willing to risk incarceration. A disturbing situation is the separation of children from their families. There are approximately 2,000 children living in detention centers, and in some cases US authorities have no idea who they are or the location of their families. In an editorial, the *Los Angeles Times* (2018) refers to the separation policy as "inhumane to children and their parents. It is a grotesque use of governmental power to abuse and traumatize families as a lesson to others. And it is crassly cynical to use the well-being of children as a political bargaining chip" (p. A8). The United Nations Human Rights Council compares the US policy of separating children from their families at the southern border to child abuse. "The thought that any state would seek to deter parents by inflicting such abuse on children is unconscionable," said Zeid Ra'ad al-Hussein, a Jordanian prince (Morello 2018:A12). Trump does not care about his critics on any topic, including his administration's "zero tolerance" immigration policy, saying, "The United States will not be a migrant camp, and it will not be a refugee-holding facility. Not on my watch" (Stokols and Bierman 2018:A1).

The immigrant children are being housed in the same facility as Apache leader Geronimo and some of the Japanese interned during World War II were held. Fort Sill in Oklahoma is one such detainee location, and a place where unaccompanied children were housed for four months during the Obama presidency (Brockell 2019). Some people have referred to the facilities housing separated children as "concentration camps," which in turn upset a number of Jewish people, who claimed that it is not nearly the same thing as what the Jews suffered during the Holocaust. The term "internment camp" seems more appropriate, as the Japanese during World War II and migrant children from south of the US have both experienced a historic mass incarceration. As the supposed global leader in democracy, it is important that the US government recognizes that even noncitizens entering the country, legally or illegally, have rights.

From an economic standpoint, it is safe to say that the United States "is not full." The continued economic growth of the US, especially where low-skilled workers are required, is dependent upon cheap migrant labor. Even Trump once admitted, "I got all these companies moving in [to the US]. They need workers. We have to bring people into our country to work these great plants that are opening up all over the place" (Roberts and Roberts 2019a:A4).

Worries for the human rights of immigrants entering the United States is just one of the problems confronting this democracy. Other freedom and human rights concerns include: a surge in anti-Semitism (e.g., Jewish worshippers massacred at the Tree of Life Synagogue in Pittsburgh, October 2018) (Kaleem 2018); Representative Steve Knight (R) of Palmdale, CA, posting dozens of racist, anti-Semitic, and anti-Muslim comments on Facebook, as well as his promotion of violence against journalists he sees as hostile to President Trump and his calls for citizen militias to turn their weapons on left-wing protesters (Finnegan and Sweedler 2019); Russia's invasion into US politics (Megerian 2018a); the sexist "Billy Graham Rule" that some Republicans, including Vice President Mike Pence, adhere to that is "supposed to help men avoid being tempted by women or being suspected of it, out of 'respect' for his spouse" (in other words, because they do not think they can control their sexual urges, they will discriminate against women rather than risk spending time alone with them during the course of their employment) (*Los Angeles Times* 2019b); and Mike Pence's wife Karen having taken a job at Immanuel Christian School, a private school in Virginia that doesn't admit or tolerate LGBTQ+ students or employees and discriminates based on gender identity (Porter 2019).

The United States' decision to leave the UN Human Rights Council in 2018 represents just one of the multinational institutions or accords that the Trump administration has abandoned, sometimes upending years of US policy. "Critics were quick to cite the withdrawal as further evidence that under President Trump, the United States is retreating from its position as the leading international advocate for human rights" (Wilkinson 2018a). The Trump administration justified its withdrawal by claiming that the 47-nation council has shown an "unconscionable" bias against Israel and a blind willingness to ignore abuse elsewhere. The US has continued to redefine its approach on human rights abroad under Trump and his top diplomat, Secretary of State Michael R. Pompeo, by "cozying up to some of the world's worst offenders and prioritizing religious freedom—particularly for Christians—often at the expense of poor women, gay people and other marginalized communities" (Wilkinson 2019b:A3). Critics also claim that Trump has a lack of transparency in light of his refusal to allow members of his administration to respond to subpoenas and other requests from Democrats and the Treasury Department's failure to comply with a House Ways and Means Committee request for six years of Trump's tax returns, even though the tax code makes it clear that the Internal Revenue Service "shall furnish" any return requested by the committee (McManus 2019a:A2). Trump has said on more than one occasion that he would take political dirt from a foreign government (i.e., Russia or China) on his opponents. He refers to such information as "opposition research." While it is common for political candidates to do research on their opponents, taking information from foreign governments has a number of potential drawbacks (although legally, it is not collusion): (1) it opens the president up to blackmail; (2) it openly invites foreign governments to do something that we spend billions of dollars trying to prevent; (3) it suggests that foreign governments can curry favor with the president by digging up dirt on his political opponents (Wolf 2019).

President Trump has often displayed his autocratic and anti-democratic views in favor of reaffirming his own socio-political agenda. In August 2019, he took the unprecedented move to pressure Israel's prime minister Benjamin Netanyahu to bar two US Democratic Congresswomen from entering Israel. These two women were half of "The Squad" (described earlier in the chapter), Representatives Ilhan Omar and Rashida Tlaib of Michigan. Both of these Congresswomen have been fiercely critical of Israel's treatment of Palestinians, which Trump interprets as a hatred for Israel and all Jewish people, which is not true. Trump tweeted that if Netanyahu allowed the women into Israel it would "show great weakness" (Wilkinson and Tarnopolsky 2019).

> Even the staunchly pro-Israel lobbying group AIPAC [The American Israel Public Affairs Committee] spoke out against the extraordinary diplomatic slap, saying all members of Congress should be welcome in the country.... The decision would harm U.S.-Israeli relations and set a bad precedent of disrespecting the U.S. Congress that other nations might follow.
>
> *(Wilkinson and Tarnopolsky 2019:A1)*

Responding to the Israeli snub, Congresswomen Omar said, "The irony of the 'only democracy in the Middle East' making such a decision is that it is both an insult to democratic values and a chilling response to a visit by government officials from an allied nation" (Wilkinson and Tarnopolsky 2019:A5). Bowing to international and domestic pressure, a few days after barring the Congresswomen, Netanyahu ignored Trump's anti-democratic stance and granted conditional permission (they would not be allowed to criticize Israeli policy while they were there) to the representatives to enter Israel. Oddly, or perhaps as her own political statement, the day after (August 16, 2019) gaining Israeli approval for her request for a "humanitarian" visit to the West Bank to see her Palestinian grandmother, Representative Tlaib said she wouldn't make the trip after all.

Meanwhile, at the same time this drama between Tlaib and Netanyahu was occurring in Israel, protestors in Hong Kong were in their tenth week of marching and staging sit-ins against the autocratic rule of the Chinese government. Many of the protestors waved American flags, as that is the sign of democracy. The protestors wanted democratic reforms and an investigation into alleged police brutally. But Trump, who has linked the pro-democracy, anti-Chinese government protests with his damaging trade war with China, showed sympathy with Chinese President Xi Jinping rather than the Hong Kongers. Trump praised the communist leader as "a good man in a 'tough business'" (Megerian 2019a). As the "leader of the free world," Trump should be aligning himself with any pro-democracy movement and not embrace the autocrats whose friendships he seems to so desire.

Social stratification and economic disparity

One of the reasons Donald Trump does not like the United Nations (UN) is because this global intergovernmental organization—tasked with the central mission of maintaining international peace and security and working with nations to prevent conflict—often criticizes the Trump administration. One such criticism from the UN came from Special Rapporteur Philip Alston as he presented his report on American poverty at the June 2018 Human Rights Council in Geneva. (A special rapporteur is an independent expert working on behalf of the UN.) Alston said, "In any country, but particularly a wealthy one, the persistence over a very long period of time of 40 million people living in poverty must be a cause for concern" (Jarvie 2018:A5). The US did not send a diplomat to the event to formally respond.

Alston's concern is a valid one, of course, as outside observers as well as many Americans often wonder how so much poverty can exist in the "greatest nation" on Earth. Sociologists have been studying the poverty issue globally since its beginnings as an academic discipline two centuries ago and in the United States specifically for well over a century. (The French social philosopher Auguste Comte coined the term "sociology" in 1838; he set the tone for this academic discipline, which literally means the "study of society.") Sociologists are not the only ones examining poverty and social stratification in the United States, as many politicians and activists are actively and regularly engaged in poverty issues. Solutions to poverty, however, are difficult and nearly impossible to come up with when there simply are not enough resources for the entire population. Even in the United States, where there are plenty of resources to go around, the socio-economic system of capitalism all but guarantees that there will always be some people who are very wealthy and some people that are very poor. Thus, to eliminate poverty in the United States the capitalistic system would have to be changed—and that is not likely to occur anytime soon, if ever.

Social stratification: wealth and income disparity

To better comprehend why poverty and economic disparity exists it is important to first understand the meaning of social stratification. *Social stratification* is a system for ranking members of a social structure into levels with different or unequal evaluations; it reveals patterns of social inequality found within a society. From a sociological perspective, social stratification may also be viewed as the hierarchal or horizontal division of society based on rank, strata, or social class. There are many examples of social stratification systems, including the military (rank and privilege is a built-in feature of this social institution), employment sectors (e.g., from entry-level positions to the president, CEO, or owner of a business), among college students (from freshmen to graduate students), sports teams (from bench players to star starting-position players), and so on.

Most societies have three major dimensions of stratification: social prestige, political power, and economics. The *social prestige* dimension of stratification, in the simplest terms, refers to what people think about others. The *political dimension* is usually expressed in terms of power, who has it and who does not, and to what degree certain people can make other people do things even against their will. The legal component of the political dimension of stratification is where legitimate power is exercised via such means as holding political office, voting, lobbying, contributing to campaigns, and participating in boycotts, strikes, and demonstrations. It is generally the *economic dimension* of stratification that holds most people's attention and focus. The economic dimension involves two key variables: income and wealth.

Income refers to the amount of money that a person or family receives over a period of time, generally a calendar year (e.g., reported income on a tax return). *Wealth*, on the other hand, refers to the total value of everything that a person or family owns, minus any debts owed. It is similar in meaning to the term "net worth." According to the United States Census Bureau (2018), the median household income in 2017 was $61,372; it was $68,145 for non-Hispanic whites, $50,486 for Hispanics, and $81,131 for Asians. Oddly, this press release did not mention the median household income for African Americans but data from the year earlier showed that the amount was just $40,232, a figure lower than in the year 2000 (Black Demographics 2019). Of great concern for sociologists is *income inequality*. There is a great deal of data that demonstrate just how much more money the richest of the rich earn compared to the masses. Consider, for example, that the richest 0.1 percent of Americans earn as much as the bottom 90 percent; that America's top 10 percent now average more than nine times as much income as the bottom 90 percent; Americans in the top 1 percent average 39 times more income than the bottom 90 percent; and that the nation's top 0.1 percent earn 188 times the income of the bottom 90 percent (Institute for Policy Studies 2019).

As of 2019, the United States was enjoying its eleventh straight year of economic expansion, the longest period on record. The economic boom has resulted in low unemployment, an overall increase in household wealth, a revived housing market, and an explosive rise in the stock market (Rugaber 2019). But, as the data above indicate, the richer you are, the more you are benefiting from this boom in the economy.

> After a decade of uninterrupted economic growth, the richest Americans now hold a greater share of the nation's wealth than they did before the Great Recession began in 2007. And income growth has been sluggish by historical standards, leaving many Americans feeling stuck in place. Those trends help to explain something unique about this expansion: It's easily the least-celebrated economic recovery in decades.
> *(Rugaber 2019:C3)*

Of the overall gains in household wealth (e.g., value of homes, stock portfolios, bank accounts, minus debt and loans) more than one-third ($16.2 trillion) of that gain went to the wealthiest 1 percent, while the bottom half of the population gained less than 2 percent in household wealth. The key economic lesson from this is the fact that as the economy grows, the wealth gap widens—or the rich get richer.

Sociologists are also very concerned with *wealth disparity*. In 2018, the total wealth of American households was over $98 trillion (with over $113 trillion in assets). (The dollar difference in these two variables illustrates how much total debt Americans carry.) If this $113 trillion amount was divided evenly across the US population of 329 million, it would result in over $343,000 for each person and, thus, for a family of three, that's over $1 million in assets (Sawhill and Pulliam 2019). However, given that wealth is not shared equally, any such notion to even contemplate equal distribution of wealth among all citizens would lead to screams of "communism" and "socialism" and certainly would be called "un-American." And this mindset helps to explain why there is such a high degree of wealth inequality in the United States as even those who are wealthy generally do not support a more equitable sharing of wealth. The wealthiest 20 percent of Americans held 77 percent of total household wealth in 2016, more than triple what the middle class held (Sawhill and Pulliam 2019). It is interesting to note that while socialism has never been too popular in the United States—and yes there is a small, perhaps growing, populist socialist movement currently—there are in fact a number of socialistic principles in play, including the reality that pooled resources are helping to pay for: police and fire departments; ambulances and first response; public schools; veterans' benefits; the National Weather Service; road and bridge construction; unemployment insurance; band deposit insurance; Medicare; Social Security; FEMA; the GI bill; the FDA; NASA; the CDC; hazardous waste disposal and clean-up; the maintenance of sewers; and the heavily funded military.

In case you were wondering, the five wealthiest Americans in 2019 were: Jeff Bezos and family ($131 billion, Amazon.com); Bill Gates ($96.5 billion, Microsoft); Warren Buffett ($82.5 billion, Berkshire Hathaway); Larry Ellison ($62.5 billion, Oracle); and Mark Zuckerberg ($62.3 billion, Facebook) (Statista 2019b). The Bezos family, Bill Gates, and Warren Buffett top the list of the wealthiest people in the world, followed by Bernard Arnault and family from France ($76 billion, LVMH Moët Hennessy, Louis Vuitton) and Carlos Slim and family from Mexico ($64 billion, América Móvil).

Poverty

Poverty can be defined as the lack of basic necessities, goods, or means of support. It prevents people from consuming, owning, or doing things that are an essential part of belonging to the society in which they live (Saunders 2005).

> At its core, poverty restricts people's ability to live a decent life because it imposes restrictions on what they can buy or do, and hence be. Those who are poor must devote all of their resources to meeting their basic needs, with nothing left over with which to exercise the freedom to consume and participate.
>
> *(Saunders 2005:59)*

As Saunders is suggesting, living in poverty compromises the overall freedom of the poor; it also compromises their basic human rights. In extreme cases, people may face destitution—a state of having absolutely none of the necessities of life. Widespread destitution is likely to occur in countries at war or facing famine or drought. Certainly destitute people are not enjoying the same human rights as others. As we know, poverty is not restricted to nations besieged by war on their soil or those who face famine or drought. The United States, one of the wealthiest nations in the world, has a relatively huge number of people living in poverty (something that UN Special Rapporteur Philip Alston pointed out).

Although the concept of "poverty" is straightforward, it is important, especially for governments, to establish clear parameters of its meaning in order to ascertain the degree and instance of poverty within their national borders so that they may be able to calculate the amount of money (if any) that will be allocated for financial assistance. In the United States, the number of "poor" is determined by using annually updated official "poverty thresholds" (a specified dollar amount considered to be the minimum level of resources necessary to meet the basic needs of a family unit). Poverty thresholds vary slightly depending by region (e.g., the 48 contiguous states and the District of Columbia—the data to be cited here—and Hawaii and Alaska). In 2019, the poverty thresholds were as follows: one-person household, $12,940; two-person household, $16,910; three-person household, $21,330; four-person household, $25,750; and so on (US Department of Health & Human Services 2019). If you're an American you know that these thresholds are not realistic as the thresholds are set very low. The US government does this on purpose, of course, because if they set the poverty thresholds to a more realistic dollar amount based on what people actually need to survive the poverty numbers would increase dramatically. As it is, the 2017 official poverty rate in the United States was 12.3 percent, which equates to 39.7 million acknowledged Americans living in poverty (US Census Bureau 2018). It is worth noting that the percentage of people without health insurance coverage for the entire 2017 calendar year was 8.8 percent, or 28.5 million (US Census Bureau 2018). Health care coverage is important because the very high medical costs in the United States means that one major hospital stay can lead to poverty.

The attack on collective bargaining and unions

All workers should support the rights of Americans to bargain collectively for higher income and to join a union. In fact, *all* Americans should support the rights of the people to bargain collectively and join a union as this is a clear example of democracy in motion. We the people have the right to assemble and we have civil rights as guaranteed in the Constitution of the United States of America. It has become fashionable for the far-right to take these rights away from the people and such acts represent a sure sign of the deterioration of democracy and human rights specifically and of the overall darkness that is surrounding us in general.

In the United States, more than three quarters of a century ago, labor laws were passed that gave every worker the right to organize a union in their workplace to negotiate wages and working conditions with their employers. In the 1950s, when the largest percentage of private-sector workers were in unions, the economy grew and the gap between high- and low-income Americans dramatically dropped. Collective bargaining and growth of the labor movement were the principle engines that led to the creation of the American middle class, the growth of wages for workers, the 40-hour work week, and the weekend (Creamer 2013). Workplace gains for union workers carried over to non-union settings if employers hoped to attract workers. In short, the right to collective bargaining and to join a union is something that benefits all workers. The only ones who should be against a strong unionized workforce are those who control the means of production as that means slightly less profits for them. And yet, in the past decade (in particular), the GOP has led many attacks on collective bargaining unions. Why would the GOP work against the rights of the workers unless they are fighting for the rich and powerful, the cultural elites?

In 2011, then-Senator Shannon Jones (Ohio, 2009–2016) introduced SB5, which limited collective bargaining for public workers. Jones tried to blame public employee salaries and pensions for budget shortfalls. Many other states have used the same lame excuse to attack the rights of workers. Poor management of state budgets before the economic collapse of 2008 and bad investments have been the more probable reasons for economic shortfalls (Long 2011). In 2013, Republicans in Nevada attacked working families with their proposals to upend collective bargaining; they would not be successful for long. In June 2019, the first-year Democratic governor of Nevada signed SB135, which returns to workers the collective bargaining rights lost years before. The bill includes arbitration rights to resolve disputes; however, the law also gives lawmakers and the governor the ability to control or opt out of any raises and other things backed by an arbitrator (Dornan 2019). In Wisconsin, Republican governor Scott Walker was able to pass Wisconsin Act 10, which prohibits public workers from bargaining over anything except wages. Local unions have fought this violation of workers' First Amendment rights (Zantow 2018). As with Nevada, Wisconsin now has a new governor, Tony Evers (D). In Alaska, the public university system faced a 41 percent reduction in state funding imposed by the governor in 2019 in an attempt to the balance the budget. If the proposed reduction goes in effect, Alaska's public university system would likely have to close campuses across the state and endanger the university's accreditation and a large number of rural and lower-income students would likely not be able to attend college (AAUP 2019).

GOP leaders are also directly attacking unions in an effort to undermine the collective action of workers. Republican leaders in New Hampshire, Missouri, and Kentucky were working on so-called "right-to-work" measures that allow workers to opt out of joining a union and out of paying union dues. Twenty-six states already have right-to-work laws on the books. A number of consequences occur at right-to-work workplaces: (1) some workers save a little bit of money by not paying union dues; (2) those in the union paying dues are likely to resent non-union workers who have the same salary and benefits (a GOP "divide and conqueror" tactic); (3) eventually, and the ultimate goal of the GOP, the union will fail. One variation of the "right-to-work" legislation is Pennsylvania's Senate Bill 166, cleverly called "Public Employee Paycheck Protection," which restricts unions from deducting any portion of union dues that underwrite political activity and union political action committee contributions from paychecks of unionized workers (Novak 2017).

Perhaps the two biggest attacks on workers' rights are the appointment of Republican conservative Brett Kavanaugh to the Supreme Court and President Trump's nomination of Eugene Scalia for Secretary of Labor. Scalia has made his reputation in Washington as a lawyer for big corporations resisting labor regulations; he helped Wal-Mart overturn a Maryland law mandating minimum contributions by big employers for workers' healthcare, and has written extensively against a federal regulation expanding ergonomic safety requirements (Hiltzik 2019). Organized labor was very much against the appointment of Kavanaugh to the Supreme Court as he routinely rules against working families, regularly rejects employees' rights to receive employer-provided health care, too often sides with employers in denying employees relief from discrimination in the workplace, and promotes overturning well-established US Supreme Court precedent (Gomez 2018).

There have been signs of a backbone among American workers and politicians that are willing to stand by the workers' rights to collective bargain and join unions. According to Gallup, which has been polling peoples' opinions about human rights since 1936, union approval was at 61 percent in 2017—the first time it had hit the 60 percent mark since 2003. Union support was at 65 percent among young people aged 18 to 34, and other than Democrats the group that likes unions the most is college graduates, with 70 percent support (Clawson 2018).

The right to bargain collectively and to join a union is something that helped to develop a strong middle class in the United States. It hardly seems like a coincidence that the middle class has been dwindling since the attack on collective bargaining and unions was begun, primarily by conservative politicians acting in the best interests of the owners of the means of production rather than looking out for the best interests of the workers. Attacks on collective bargaining and unions have also contributed to economic stratification and disparity. The right to bargain collectively extends beyond the United States, as the United Nations' Universal Declaration of Human Rights (adopted in 1948) states that every worker has the right to bargain collectively and the right to join trade unions for their own protection. To deny workers these rights is to downgrade them to second-class citizens, or worse.

Global economic inequality

It is beyond the scope of this book to provide extensive coverage of global economic inequality; as a result we will take a snapshot view. As with the United States, there is great economic inequality globally. The wealthiest 1 percent of the world's population owns more than half of the world's wealth; the total wealth in the world grew by 6 percent during 2017 to $280 trillion; globally it is the world's millionaires that are doing the best. There are 36 million millionaires in the world and that number is expected to increase to 44 million by 2022 (Frank 2017). Inequality.org (2019) claims mostly similar data as cited by Frank (2017), stating that the world's richest 1 percent (those with more than $1 million) own 45 percent of the world's wealth. Adults with less than $10,000 in wealth make up 64 percent of the world's population but hold less than 2 percent of global wealth. The "ultra-high-net-worth individuals"—people worth more than $30 million—hold a very significantly disproportionate share of global wealth. These ultra-high-wealth people hold 11.3 percent of the total global wealth and yet represent only a tiny fraction (0.003 percent) of the world's population. Further analysis shows that the world's ten richest billionaires, as according to Forbes, own $745 billion in combined wealth, a sum greater than the total goods and services most nations produce on an annual basis. There are 2,208 billionaires globally (Inequality.org 2019).

At quick glance there would appear to be a different outlook among the significant agencies tracking global inequality as to in which direction inequality is trending. The International Monetary Fund (IMF) (2017) states, "At the global level, inequality has declined substantially over the past three decades." Inequality.org (2019), however, states that "Inequality has been on the rise across the globe for several decades." A closer look reveals that the IMF tends to use "extreme poverty" as a barometer for measuring financial inequality whereas Inequality.org looks at the actual disparity between the richest and the poorest people. The World Poverty Clock (2019) provides a fascinating visual account as to in which direction "extreme poverty" is headed and, like the IMF, concludes that it is decreasing. As of July 31, 2019, the number of poor living in extreme poverty was under 600 million. The World Bank (WB) defines "extreme poverty" as living on $1.25 or less per day. The WB (2018) utilizes a different dollar value for determining poverty: living on $5.50 a day in upper-middle-income countries and $3.20 per day in lower-middle-income countries. The World Bank (WB) (2018) adds, "Economic advances around the world mean that while fewer people live in extreme poverty, [however] almost half of the world's population—3.4 billion people—still struggles to meet basic needs." A key point here is that, while the number of people living in extreme poverty is going down, the number of people living in poverty remains high and is trending upward. Thus, all of these entities are correct in the way in which they analyze global inequality and we should remember that no matter how global inequality is framed, it is a very real social problem.

Global inequality is a problem for the poor who seek to meet their daily needs, of course, but it is also a problem for the world in general. The IMF (2017), for example, states, "While some inequality is inevitable in a market-based economic system, excessive inequality can erode social cohesion, lead to political polarization, and ultimately lower economic growth." Our previous discussion on immigration has a starting point here when we realize that the very poor will often seek a better life in wealthier nations and will risk everything in pursuing this goal.

Connecting enlightened rational thought with popular culture

> **BOX 2.1 "THE PRESS WAS TO SERVE THE GOVERNED, NOT THE GOVERNORS" — FROM THE FILM, *THE POST***
>
> In director Steven Spielberg's film "The Post" (2017), the real-life drama of "The Pentagon Papers" is told within a context of coming to grips with the role of the press, especially when the story to be told is damning to the government. "The Post" refers to the *Washington Post* newspaper. It is described by IMDb (2019a) as follows: "A cover-up that spanned four U.S. Presidents pushed the country's first female newspaper publisher and a hard-driving editor to join an unprecedented battle between the press and the government." Meryl Streep stars as Kay Graham (owner of the *Washington Post*) and Tom Hanks as Ben Bradlee (the newspaper's editor).
>
> The IMDb (2019a) "Storyline" description of the film starts by introducing us to the importance of Daniel Ellsberg, an American military analyst for the RAND Corporation who has discovered the depths of the US government's deceptions about the futility of the Vietnam War and becomes so disgusted by this discovery that he copies top-secret documents that would later become known as the Pentagon Papers. (The photocopying occurred over a three-month period in 1969. He would copy documents and return the originals the next day.) In 1971, he sent 7,000 pages exposing the government's lies about the war to the *New York Times* (Gajanan 2017). Kay Graham, who has just recently taken over the *Washington Post* following her husband's death (suicide), is informed by Bradlee that the *New York Times* has scooped them with an explosive exposé on those papers. the *New York Times* had started to publish bits of the story when it was hit with a temporary publishing ban. Shortly after, the papers appear at the *Washington Post*. The *Post* now has to decide whether or not to publish its damning story—the editors only have a short period of time in which to decide. Meanwhile, President Nixon and his administration are working hard to keep the information from going public, even taking the case to the Supreme Court. The *Post* is served with a federal restraining order that could get the its staff indicted for contempt. Graham must decide whether to back down for the safety of the paper or publish the article that will expose three decades of government secrets spanning four US presidents, and fight for the "freedom of the press." Graham decides to proceed. "In doing so, Graham and her staff join a fight that would have America's democratic ideals in the balance" (IMDb 2019a).
>
> Ultimately, the Supreme Court sides with the right of the press to tell the truth. In a six-to-three vote, the court rules that the government did not adequately prove that it had the right to bar the newspapers from publishing the classified history of the Vietnam War (Gajanan 2017). Writing for the majority, Judge Hugo Black said, "In the First Amendment, the Founding Fathers gave

> the free press the protection it must have to fulfill its essential role in our democracy. The press was to serve the governed, not the governors." This quote is a powerful moment in the film. It is also a great reminder that the press works for the people and any challenge to the right of the press to report stories, or claim that the press is the enemy of the people, goes directly against the US Constitution.

Summary

The "darkness that surrounds us" is meant to draw attention to, and identify, some of the key ways in which enlightened, rational, and reasoned thought are being challenged in the early twenty-first century. The focus of this chapter is on the general theme of the deterioration of democracy and human rights.

The first example of darkness to cloud rationality and reason is the willingness of political leaders to constantly tell lies and make false statements and misleading claims. To make matters worse, when confronted with undisputable factual information that proves their falsehoods, often the response is to go on the offensive with claims of "fake news!," "alternative facts!," and "truth isn't truth!"

A very disconcerting sign of a deteriorating democracy is attacks on journalists and the press. In the United States, the Constitution guarantees the freedom of speech and of the press. It is up to the president to assure that the rights of the press are being upheld and protected. Instead, President Trump repeatedly attacks the press and refers to them as "the enemy of the people." In other parts of the world, journalists are being kidnapped, physically attacked, tortured, and murdered.

The concepts of populism, nationalism, and nativism were discussed as there is a clear trend that populist movements exist across the world, including in the United States. Inevitably, an "us" versus "them" scenario develops, leading to discriminatory, sexist, and racist behaviors. In many populist nations immigration is a key social issue with nativist populists very much against new immigrants entering their country.

Specific examples of the deterioration of freedom in the United States and globally were described. Data results from Freedom House's "Freedom in the World" calculations were provided. A number of measures were analyzed including political rights and civil rights (e.g., the rights of LGBTQ+ persons) and a categorization of the degree of freedom particular nations have (e.g., "Free," "Partly Free," and "Not Free").

Social stratification and economic disparity were also discussed in their relationship to the deterioration of democracy and human rights. In the United States and across the globe, there is great income and wealth disparity leading to a very small number of wealthy elites controlling a very large and disproportionate share of the total assets when compared to the masses. While a limited few enjoy the many luxuries that life can offer, approximately half the world's total population struggle to meet their daily basic needs and nearly 600 million people live in "extreme poverty."

3
THE DARKNESS THAT SURROUNDS US
Unenlightened and irrational thinking

Introduction

In the previous chapter, we explored the darkness that surrounds us from the context of the deterioration of democracy and human rights. In this chapter, we look at the darkness that comes in the form of unenlightened and irrational thinking. There is, of course, some cross-over between these two general contexts as there is a prevalent theme of the darkness that threatens enlightened, rational, and reasoned thought.

As presented in this chapter, unenlightened and irrational thought threaten the very foundation of the enlightened principles of rationality, reason, and science. In the early twenty-first century there are many social currents underfoot that lean the pendulum of thought and social action back to the "Dark Ages." Irrational thought, such as blind loyalty to a politician, celebrity, or religious leader, can lead individuals to traverse all sorts of paths of darkness rather than utilizing the light of reason. In some instances, unenlightened and irrational thought and behavior harm just the self, but in other cases the harm can extent to many others.

There are numerous examples of unenlightened and irrational thought but the focus of discussion in this chapter revolves around four general categories: attempts to devalue education; a disbelief in science; attacks on the environment; and utilizing pseudoscience. The many subtopics found within each of these four categories helps to further illustrate the harm that can be caused by illogical and groundless thinking. Discussion begins with the social institution of education, its value, and the attacks on it.

Attempts to devalue education

Despite the fact that the value of higher education is a matter of common sense, let alone rational and reasoned thought, there are those who do not share this perspective. Before we examine some of the attempts to devalue the positive role of education a review of some of the many positive aspects that education provides to individuals and society will be presented.

The multi-faceted value of higher education

As a long-time university professor I have taught thousands of students. In entry-level courses (e.g., introductory sociology) I would often ask my students, "Why are you attending college?" Over the years, the increasingly likely, number-one response from most students has been a rather pragmatic one: "To get a job." Idealistically, I wish that students would respond, "To increase my level of knowledge and develop critical thinking skills so that I can speak intelligently on a number of diverse topics." Realistically, however, I do realize that most students are attending college to find a job—although I remind them that if all they wanted was a job, they should be working instead of attending college! What students really mean, of course, is that they want a "good" job, and in most cases, that means a job as a professional (and not as a laborer) and one that pays well. Society certainly needs laborers and those skilled in the trades but most university students want a decent or high-paying career that allows them to utilize their brains rather than their brawns.

To be fair, some young people attend college for the social life; after all, there is a common adage, at least in the United States, that one's college years are "the best years of your life!" Is there anything wrong with someone going to college to have a fun social life? I would suggest that it is fine to do so, as most of us will work for 40 years of our lives—so why not have fun while we are young and more apt to be free from many of the major adult responsibilities (e.g., raising a family)? It seems reasonable enough. However, it becomes irrational to attend college (especially with the financial costs involved) with the sole mindset of "partying" all the time while failing to do the requisite schoolwork, only to drop out in debt and without a degree. Finding the balance between enjoying an active social life and doing well academically is the key to success in college. A social life is important because of the contacts one makes, as any one of your classmates (especially those in your major) might help you secure a career in the future. Joining academic and special-interest clubs is another way to make important contacts. Participating in college athletics builds social bonds between teammates and may also lead to future employment opportunities, either directly (a career in sports) or indirectly (contacts that might help you secure a career).

Let's take a step back for a moment and examine what exactly is meant by "education." *Education* involves learning; it is an act or process of acquiring knowledge and it can be accomplished informally or formally. *Informal education* occurs outside of a structured curriculum; it can take place anywhere and can be accomplished spontaneously via conversations with others, watching the news, exploring different environments and places (e.g., travel, museums, and libraries), paying close attention to details, and it can occur via self-taught methods (e.g., by reading and studying particular subjects). Ideally, informal education is something that is a regular occurrence with the vast majority of people as any one of us is capable of learning something new without the assistance of formal educators. Say, for example, you decide to start gardening but you have never had your own garden before. You can ask other people with gardens for tips on how to garden; you can watch gardening shows on television or YouTube; you can ask for advice from people at home and garden shops; and you can try your hand at gardening via trial and error. If you want to learn more about World War II you can read books and watch documentaries on the subject.

Generally, when one talks about "education" as a topic, as it is being discussed here, it is formal education that is being referenced. Formal education involves training and developing people in knowledge, skills, intellect, and character, in structured and certified programs. Thus, *formal education* can be viewed as a process of teaching and learning in which some people (e.g., teachers and professors) cultivate knowledge, skills, intellect, and character, while others (students) take on the role of learner. The value of formal education lies not simply in the knowledge one gains but the provision of *credentials* (e.g., academic diplomas, certificates, identification documents, security clearances, powers of attorney, and academic, peer-reviewed publications, especially books published by reputable publishers) that are needed in a technologically advanced society. A credential is issued by a third party with the relevant authority or assumed competence to do so. It indicates that the recipient is competent to perform or is qualified for a specific job or position.

There are different types of formal education, including apprenticeships, trade schools, and institutions of higher education. Apprenticeships and trade school education evolved over time into what we have today. Historically, different categories of people, such as the early hunters and gatherers, transmitted the skills necessary for survival from one generation to the next. In agrarian societies, agricultural skills were also passed down from generation to generation. This transmission of specific skills-training for specific occupations has, in most cases, become formalized—this is especially true in developed nations and less true in some developing areas of the world. An *apprenticeship* is a paid job with training in which the apprentice learns from a master the essential skills necessary in a given field. Electricians, carpenters, plumbers, ironworkers, and machinists are generally associated with apprenticeships. Some apprenticeships, known as "dual-training programs," combine on-the-job training with classroom instruction (Doyle 2019). Apprenticeships have become successful in Germany and are becoming increasingly popular in the United States with about a half-million people in apprenticeship programs (Smith 2019).

Trade school, vocational school, or *technical school* training refers to skills training for a specific type of trade at an educational institution, which in some cases is known as secondary or post-secondary education. Trade schools can be public or private, but many are for-profit businesses. Trade schools offer hands-on training and marketable skills to prepare students for a specific career. Examples of trade schools include maritime academics, culinary schools, automotive repair training programs, and training for medical technicians.

Our concern here resides primarily with higher education that is administered via formal training at colleges and universities. *Higher education* involves a process of teaching and learning and as students gain new knowledge they not only increase their level of knowledge but also come to better understand the world they live in. Higher education is a relatively new phenomenon as, historically speaking, people were far too busy securing their basic survival needs to worry about intellectual pursuits on general subject matters. Eventually, with the development of written language, a privileged few were taught to read and write. The masses, for the most part, were left to toil while select members of society began to learn about philosophy, the humanities, and the laws of mathematics and science.

Universities and colleges were few in number until the last couple of centuries. I had the pleasure to recently visit the world's first, and thus its oldest, degree-granting university—the University of al-Qarawiyyin—in Fez, Morocco. This university was founded in 859 CE and it continues to operate as an institution of higher education; it is designated as the world's oldest university by UNESCO and the Guinness Book of World Records (2019). The University of al-Qarawiyyin was founded by a wealthy Arab woman named Fatima al-Fihri, who also commissioned a mosque and madrasa (an institution of higher education). Its library was constructed in 1359 CE and contains manuscripts that are among the earliest in Islamic history (Maguder and Page 2017). The university is nestled within the city's medina (the ancient and historical part of North African cities) and is only 30 years younger than the city of Fez itself. Most of the oldest universities are located in Europe, with the University of Bologna, Italy, founded in 1088, being the oldest (Guinness Book of World Records 2019). It is worth noting that the University of Taxila or Takshashila in Ancient India (now Pakistan) was founded in 600 BCE and operated until 500 CE. Universities would slowly appear in most countries throughout the Middle Ages and became far more common by the 1800s and early 1900s.

With all the colleges and universities that exist around the world today there surely must be some benefit to the students who attend and graduate from them—isn't there? The answer is a resounding, "yes!" In fact, the value of higher education is multi-faceted.

One of the values of higher education is the increased likelihood of social mobility via the significant economic benefits associated with one's level of education. And this is a good thing especially for the many students who attend college with the hope of finding a good-paying job. The data in Table 3.1 illustrate the median weekly earning rates by educational attainment for 2017 (in the United States). As the table shows, the more you learn, the more you earn. Citing Bureau of Labor Statistics (2017b) data, Elka Torpey (2018) states,

> Median weekly earnings in 2017 for those with the highest levels of educational attainment—doctoral and professional degrees—were more than triple those with the lowest level, less than a high school diploma. And workers with at least a bachelor's degree earned more than the $907 median weekly earnings for all workers.

TABLE 3.1 Median weekly earnings by level of education, 2017

Level of education	Median weekly earnings (US$)
Doctoral degree	1,743
Professional degree	1,836
Master's degree	1,401
Bachelor's degree	1,173
Associate degree	836
Some college, no degree	774
High school diploma, no college	712
Less than a high school diploma	520

Source: Bureau of Labor Statistics 2017b.

As show in Table 3.2, a second value of higher education is the fact that the higher the level of education, the lower the unemployment rate. Compare unemployment by education level in 2017 with the overall unemployment rate of 3.6 percent.

The significance of comparing one's level of education with median weekly earnings (see Table 3.1) and the unemployment level (see Table 3.2) illustrates the economic value of higher education for the educated individual but also hints at the overall value to society. Certainly, individuals with higher education, on average, earn more than those with limited education. With this increased salary comes greater economic freedom to move beyond assuring that the basic needs of life are met to now enjoying luxury items such as a new car, taking a vacation, having a swimming pool installed, and so on. Taken as a whole, society in general benefits from greater numbers of highly educated people because they can purchase an even greater amount of consumer goods—a necessity in capitalistic economies. As logic would dictate, individuals who are unemployed will have less money coming into the household and are more likely to struggle to "make ends meet" (the ability to secure the basic needs of survival). Furthermore, when a large percentage of people in a society are unemployed there is less money being spent on consumer goods and the government pays out more in unemployment benefits, which causes the economy to suffer.

TABLE 3.2 Unemployment rate by educational attainment, 2017

Level of education	Unemployment rate, in percent
Doctoral degree	1.5
Professional degree	1.5
Master's degree	2.2
Bachelor's degree	2.5
Associate degree	3.4
Some college, no degree	4.0
High school diploma, no college	4.6
Less than a high school diploma	6.5

Source: Bureau of Labor Statistics 2017b.

While the data in Table 3.1 reveal that median weekly earnings, on average, increase as the level of education increases, it is important to note that graduates in some fields of study do much better than graduates from other academic disciplines. Citing data provided by PayScale.com, the *US News & World Report* (Somers and Moody 2019) provides a list of the top ten majors with the highest median starting salaries (for those with a bachelor's degree) and from this ranking we find that the highest median starting salary is awarded to those who majored in petroleum engineering ($97,689). See Table 3.3 for a complete listing of the top ten highest median starting salary majors and the starting salary associated with their respective degrees.

A quick look at Table 3.3 reveals that none of the top ten majors for starting salaries include the social sciences or humanities and instead consist solely of STEM majors. STEM stands for science, technology, engineering, and mathematics and the subjects that fall under these academic disciplines. There are variations to STEM (i.e., STEAM, which adds an "A" for applied arts) but it is generally agreed upon that specific subjects such as aerospace engineering, biochemistry, biology, chemical engineering, chemistry, civil engineering, computer science, electrical engineering, mathematics, physics, and statistics are examples of STEM. While there are a number of institutions of higher education that have been known to cater to specialized STEM majors (e.g., institutes of technology), in recent years it has become in vogue to promote STEM courses in liberal arts colleges. In many high schools it has become common to offer STEM educational programs designed to prepare primary and secondary students for college. Under Republican Betsy DeVos, the head of the US Department of Education, STEM is now an official federal strategy of higher education. Implemented at the end of 2018, the Department of Education's five-year strategic plan for STEM education is one that is based on a vision for a future where all Americans will have lifelong access to high-quality STEM education (US Department of Education 2019).

The first two aspects of higher education that provide value to individuals and society involved the practical economic considerations of earning a good salary and

TABLE 3.3 Highest median starting salary with a bachelor's degree, 2019

Academic major	*Starting salary, in US$*
Petroleum Engineering	97,689
Nuclear Engineering	73,267
Chemical Engineering	72,126
Computer Engineering	70,120
Electrical Engineering	69,039
Aerospace & Aeronautical Engineering	68,142
Systems Engineering	68,018
Materials Engineering	67,385
Mathematics & Computer Science	66,499
Mechanical Engineering	65,619

Source: PayScale.com, quoted in Somers and Moody 2019.

avoiding unemployment. The next two aspects of higher education involve the idealistic or "true" mission of colleges and universities, which are: to increase the intellectual knowledge of students and to impart students with critical thinking skills. With regard to intellectual knowledge, we must first come to understand the meaning of the concept of "intellect." *Intellect* refers to the mind's ability to know or understand objectively, by matter of reason, especially with regard to abstract or academic matters. Knowing and understanding something is distinguished from feeling or wishing something to be true. Intellect, then, is a matter of reasoned comprehension rather than an emotional reaction (to a given stimuli or matter). An intellect is likely to pursue intellectual knowledge as he or she places a high value on the knowledge of complex forms, which requires a great deal of disciplined thinking. In this regard, *intellectual knowledge* is associated with understanding abstract things, concepts, theories, and the interpretations of such complex ideas. It is higher education that allows for the development of intellectual knowledge.

A fourth value of higher education is the development of critical thinking skills. The connection between critical thinking and higher education was discussed in Chapter 1, but a few points are worth restating here. At all points of time in history the need for people to think critically has been important, but it is perhaps most significant today as there are so many sources of misinformation that are being shared (e.g., via social media sites and biased cable news networks) by agenda-minded purveyors of falsehoods, consumed by a gullible public that does not take the time to fact-check or think critically. Because critical thinking is not a skill that comes naturally for most people it is the responsibility of institutions of higher education to teach people how to analyze, evaluate, and fact-check information in an effort to cultivate a higher level of thinking. As stated in Chapter 1, critical thinking is intellectually disciplined thinking that is clear, rational, open-minded, centered on reason, and supported by evidence. Critical thinking is a mental process of skillful conceptualization, analyzing, synthesizing, and/or evaluating information gathered from, or generated by, observation, experience, reflection, questioning what biased others say is the truth, and an overall grounding in empiricism. In the social sciences, especially in the academic discipline of sociology, professors have students write term papers on subject-related topics wherein ideas and observations are supported by peer-reviewed academic sources. Academic, peer-reviewed publications increase the probability of factual information as such publications have been reviewed and verified as accurate by experts in the field. It is not a fool-proof system, but is certainly much better than relying on a source that does not consist of peer-reviews by subject authorities.

As centers of academic thinking, colleges and universities are the institutions of higher education best designed to help develop the critical thinking skills of those seeking to attain a form of accepted wisdom that is based on reason and rationality. This is especially true at liberal arts schools as the type of education stressed is designed to educate the whole person. That is to say, to provide general knowledge and cultivate overall intellectual abilities such as reason and rationality and judgment via critical thinking. It is the social sciences (e.g., cultural or social anthropology, economics, political science, social psychology, and sociology) and humanities (e.g., archaeology, comparative religion, ethics, history, languages and linguistics, literature, and philosophy) that are best suited to accept this task of development. A liberal arts education prepares students for many fields in the contemporary workplace. In contrast, a STEM-focus education, and especially a vocational/trade/apprenticeship a form of education, is designed to prepare students for specific occupations and is less likely to have emphasized critical thinking skills that are applicable to a wide range of social topics. As Fain (2019) explains, STEM degrees tend to have a "straight line" toward employment whereas the liberal arts have more of a "swirl"—in other words, the path to a career may take longer.

For the liberal arts, attaining knowledge through critical thinking is of utmost importance. Thus, the process of learning is as important as actually learning factual knowledge. Let us use Albert Einstein to illustrate this point. In his response to Thomas Edison's statement that a college education should be directed toward learning relevant facts, Albert Einstein said,

> It is not very important for a person to learn facts. For that he does not really need a college. He can learn them from books. The value of an education in a liberal arts college is not the learning of many facts, but the training of the mind to think something that cannot be learned from textbooks
>
> *(Frank 1947:185)*

In response to his inability to immediately answer the question, "What is the speed of sound?" Einstein replied, "I don't know, I don't burden my memory with such facts that I can easily find in any textbook" (*New York Times* 1921). As a university professor, I do want students to know facts but it is correct, of course, that many facts, such as the speed of sound, can easily be looked up in a book as Einstein suggested, and certainly can be found on reliable internet sites. It is more important to know the significance of the speed of sound than its measurable speed. (I suspect many readers, like myself, decided to look up the speed of sound—and if you did, you discovered that the speed of sound is variable depending upon whether we are talking about sound in dry air or in water, and even if in dry air, we still need to know the air temperature! So, why bother trying to memorize all these facts when we can use a "speed of sound calculator?")

As a means of highlighting the traditional mission of college, I share this 1898 quote from Syracuse University chancellor James Roscoe Day, who was addressing unruly behavior between members of the senior and junior classes the day before: "You are here, not for fraternities, not for social life and not for athletics, but for college. The world demands the scholar. The aim of the university is towards the highest level of scholarship" (Croyle 2018).

Attacks on higher education

Described above were a number of examples of the value of higher education both to individuals and to society as a whole. Historically, colleges and universities were interested in educating the whole student so that the graduate possessed new knowledge, critical thinking skills, and increased intellect in preparation for life as a productive member of society. It was indeed the aim of higher education to develop scholars who could intelligently discuss a number of topics with diverse members of the population.

Despite what should be treated as a given—the need for a highly educated populace—there are a variety of "attacks" on the institution of higher education including an over-emphasis on STEM disciplines at the expense of the social sciences and humanities; some politicians and people that question the value of a higher education; the increased costs of attending college and what to do about it; the growing culture of college administration interference; and power elites that view an educated populace as a danger to their agendas.

Let's be clear, the value of STEM subjects is to be treated as much as a "given" as the need to promote critical thinking skills. Skilled technicians in the STEM fields will make scientific discoveries that will lead to the development of new technologies that may help humanity in a number of ways for years to come. Thus, it is not the STEM disciplines themselves that are attacking higher education; it is the over-emphasis of STEM (by many college administrators and politicians, and a number of people from the general public) at the expense of the social sciences and humanities that represent a problem to the mission of colleges and universities to develop critical thinking skills that are applicable to a variety of social currents and events. The academic disciplines themselves (in the social sciences and humanities), the professors and students found in the social sciences and humanities, suffer in a variety of ways, including lower salaries for professors, fewer full-time faculty hires granted by administration for the departments resulting in fewer total courses that can be offered, which in turn frustrates interested students and ultimately leads to a decrease in the number of majors, which then gives ammunition to administrators to further cut financial support to the non-STEM disciplines.

Granted, there are a number of factors that justify the attention given to the STEM majors, including the realization that these fields have been established mainstays at colleges and universities for centuries and will surely remain so into the future. That many students today enter college not to become scholars or well-rounded persons (thus, explaining, in part, the recent decrease in the number of students choosing the social sciences and humanities as majors), preferring instead the higher-paying occupations associated with STEM degrees, is another factor that seems to justify the attention given to STEM disciplines.

The social sciences and humanities (the liberal arts), as varied as they are, examine culture, literature, politics, and all the social institutions found in society; they also prepare students for such professions as law, business, and creative fields such as art, film, and literature, as well as encouraging learning for the sake of learning. In other words, they serve a vital role in society and, thus, in higher education. And yet, there are an increasing number of people who think that certain degrees are a waste of money. As previously stated, a number of these people include college administrators and politicians. This attack on certain academic disciplines of higher education has caused great concern to such mainstays of colleges and universities as history, philosophy, comparative literature, and the classics. And it has led to such questions as, "Should an ambitious examination of English literature come at the cost of acquiring fluency in coding, digital marketing and the like?" (Bruni 2018a). A number of colleges and universities are either eliminating majors in the liberal arts or they are combining certain majors as a sort of compromise that allows such disciplines to exist in some form but not as true majors. The University of Illinois, for example, combines anthropology and linguistics with computer science; Assumption College is doing away with a host of traditional majors such as art history, geography, and the classics in order to make room for data analytics, actuarial science, and concentrations in physical and occupational therapy; the University of Wisconsin at Superior announced that it was suspending nine majors including sociology and political science and warned that others may also be cut; and the University of Wisconsin at Stevens Point has proposed dropping 13 majors, including philosophy and English, to make room for programs with "clear career pathways" (Bruni 2018a). Wisconsin Stevens Point might just as well become a vocational or trade school if it does not want to offer traditional academic majors. Colleges and universities need to embrace the nonvocational mission of higher education: to cultivate minds, prepare young adults for enlightened citizenship, give them a better sense of their perch in history, and connect them to traditions that transcend the moment (Bruni 2018a). It is the attack on higher-education majors in the social sciences and humanities that represents unenlightened and irrational thinking.

Many people question the direction higher education is moving toward and these perceptions can lead to attacks on the institution. The National Association of Student Financial Aid Administrators (NASFAA) reports that, "Despite a body of research showing many Americans recognize the value of higher education, most say that the nation's postsecondary education system is heading in the wrong direction" (Bidwell 2018). Citing Pew Research data, Bidwell (2018) reports that 61 percent of survey respondents said that they think higher education in America is off-track; however, when it comes to the reasons why they think this, a clear political affiliation divide is revealed. Republican respondents believe higher education is headed the wrong way because they think professors bring their political and social views into the classroom (79 percent of respondents said this) and 75 percent of respondents believe there is an over-concern and over-protection of students from views that they may find offensive (75 percent). For Democratic respondents, the percentages were 17 and 31, respectively, for the same two questions (Bidwell 2018). For Democrats, their number-one complaint about higher education heading in the wrong direction is high tuition costs (92 percent). Nearly all Republicans over 65 (96 percent) said that their number-one complaint was due to professors' social and political views, compared with 58 percent of those between 18 and 32 (Bidwell 2018).

Citing data from a New America (a centrist think tank) survey, *Forbes* reports that there is a big difference between how Republicans and Democrats view how and why higher education should be funded. Most Democrats (76 percent) indicated that "the government should fund higher education because it is good for society," while a slight majority of Republicans (52 percent) said that "students should fund their own education because it is a personal benefit" (Cooper 2018). This disparity indicates that Democrats believe that more people going to college generates benefits to society in general and not just those who attend college, while Republicans in contrast feel that the benefit of college is enjoyed by the individuals who attend, and not society as a whole. Other demographic breakdowns such as race and income produced just moderate divides on the issue of higher education (Cooper 2018).

When it comes to viewpoints about the openness of higher education to offer a wide range of opinions and viewpoints, there is quite a difference based on political affiliation/leanings. According to 2019 Pew Research higher-education survey results, Democrats (34 percent "very open," and 53 percent "somewhat open") are much more likely than Republicans (15 percent, 30 percent) to say that colleges and universities are open to differing views. Republicans (49 percent) are far more skeptical than Democrats (71 percent) to say that community colleges are open to a wide range of viewpoints (Laloggia 2019). Those who have a bachelor's degree or higher—and especially those with a postgraduate degree—are more likely than other adults to view colleges and universities as open to a wide range of opinions and viewpoints (Laloggia 2019).

A clear indicator that higher education is under attack is the response to a national survey conducted by the Pew Research Center (2017) revealing that a majority of Republicans and Republican-leaning independents (58 percent) said that colleges and universities have a negative effect on the country. Imagine that, higher education as a detriment to society. Thirty-six percent of Republicans said that it has a positive effect. Reflecting their ideological differences with Republicans, wide majorities of both liberal Democrats (79 percent) and conservative and moderate Democrats (67 percent) say colleges have a positive impact (Pew Research Center 2017).

Over the past few years, many Republican politicians have attacked the liberal arts, generally under the pretense of supporting STEM majors. Here is a sampling compiled by Patricia Cohen in 2016.

- Kentucky governor Matt Bevin (R) suggested that students majoring in French literature should not receive state funding for their college education.
- Governor Patrick McCrory (R) of North Carolina (he is now the former governor) proposed that higher-education funding should not be based on "butts in seats, but on how many of those butts can get jobs"
- Florida Senator Marco Rubio (R) has called for "more welders and fewer philosophers."
- Florida Governor Rick Scott (R) believes that students who major in certain disciplines such as history, philosophy, anthropology, and English should pay more than in tuition than engineers and other majors he referred to as "strategic." This, despite the fact that it costs more to run STEM courses than non-STEM courses.

As we have learned here, in some cases the liberal arts are being attacked, especially by Republicans, because of a support for STEM but in other cases because of a general belief that higher education does not serve a positive role in society. If this isn't a sign of darkness, unenlightened thought, and irrational thinking, then we are left to ponder: what is?

Another attack on higher education comes in the form of financial burdens to students, and often many of their parents who go into debt to cover the costs of tuition, room and board, and general expenses. But this attack includes some gray areas. So, let's begin with a problem that is very real for millions of Americans and many millions of students around the world. *Student loan debt* is a form of financial debt that is owed by an attending, withdrawn, or graduated student to lending institutions (e.g., banks or loan companies) that was borrowed for the purpose of higher education. Students (and/or their families) incur this cost because "Attending college is considered an investment in human capital with expectations of returns in the future for employment and financial well-being" (Henager, Wilmarth, and Mauldin 2016). It is this hope for employment and financial well-being that drives millions to attend college every year and as the data in Tables 3.1 and 3.2 reveal, this hope is, on average, met with reality. But, this reality is confronted by another reality—student loan debt. In 2019, student loan debt affected an estimated 40 million people who owed on average $29,000 (Investopedia 2019a). Forbes describes an even bleaker look at student loan debt, stating that there are more than 44 million borrowers who collectively owe $1.5 trillion in student loan debt in the US alone. The average student loan debt for the Class of 2016 is $37,172 (Friedman 2018). While some federally backed student loans—such as Direct Subsidized Loans and Federal Perkins Loans—can be discharged or forgiven (Investopedia 2019a), many students struggle to pay back their loans and may delay getting married and buying a home. In extreme cases, the student may become delinquent or default on their loan (the 2018 student loan delinquency or default rate was 10.7 percent).

One of the biggest contributing factors in the rise of student loan debt is the corresponding increase in tuition costs. A second significant factor in the rising levels of student loan debt is the result of state budget cuts that are often passed on to state university systems. Alaska provides us with an example of the latter scenario. In July 2019, Alaska governor Mike Dunleavy (R), a graduate of the University of Alaska, put his *alma mater* on the financial brink when he vetoed $130 million allotted for the University of Alaska system, a nearly 41 percent decline in state funding. "The unprecedented cut has left university leadership, faculty and students scrambling to persuade the Republican-led legislature to override the veto. If not, the university warns, it many dismiss as many as 2,000 people, slash programs, shutter campuses and lose students to other states" (Bohrer 2019:A8). Alaska is largely reliant on the oil industry for revenue but due to declining oil prices, there is a shortfall in the budget. Things are likely to get worse for Alaska as the United States slowly moves away from its archaic dependence on fossil fuels (petroleum, coal, and natural gas) to more efficient forms of renewable energies.

As it generally does with any significant social issue, politics plays a huge role in what to do about college affordability in the United States. We have already learned that some politicians, especially Republicans, question whether students in the liberal arts should be granted the same amount of assistance as STEM majors and a number of colleges and universities are eliminating or combining liberal arts majors. The current approach of assisting students with higher-education financial needs was established under the Nixon (R), Ford (R), and Carter (D) administrations and supported by most state governments and had as a fundamental goal that every student should be able to afford college (Astin 2019). In the years since the big federal aid programs were put in place, state and especially federal aid have failed to keep pace with ever-rising college costs, causing the burden to fall on colleges and students. Ironically, colleges, especially the private schools, have raised tuition, in part, to raise enough financial aid to help poorer students (Astin 2019).

A number of Democratic politicians have promoted the idea of "free college for all" as a way for all students to afford higher education. Proponents of universal free college often cite the high dropout rate as a good justification for free college. Data provided by the National Center for Education Statistics (NCES) (2019) report that the six-year graduation rate for first-time, full-time undergraduate students who began a bachelor's degree at four-year degree-granting institutions in fall 2011 overall was 60 percent. The six-year graduation rate was 60 percent at public institutions, 66 percent at private nonprofit institutions, and just 21 percent at private for-profit institutions. Females (63 percent) graduated at a higher rate than males (57 percent). Graduation rates were higher (87 percent) at institutions that were the most selective (e.g., those with acceptance rates of less than 25 percent) and lowest (31 percent) at institutions that were the least selective (e.g., those with an open admissions policy). Overall, the college completion rates have increased slightly since 1990 and some education researchers attribute this to improved student performance or to lower standards for graduation (Smith 2019; Nadworny 2019). Opponents of universal higher education point to this data arguing that the high dropout rate is not the result of tuition hikes and, therefore, that the four-year college track isn't for everyone (Smith 2019). Opponents also point out that with a "free college for all" system, the wealthiest families would receive a huge subsidy, and that the burden of paying for free education would fall on all taxpayers and especially the already-strapped middle class (Astin 2019). The banking and loan institutions would also fight any change to this lucrative system that benefits them so much.

This leads us to conclude that "universal free college" sounds like a good idea but certain versions of this approach may not be advisable. One additional variable worth looking at is the discrepancy in graduation/dropout rates based on race/ethnicity. Data show that Asian and white students are more likely to get a degree than their African American and Hispanic classmates. "For all black students who started college in 2012, just 41 percent earned a degree in six years. For Hispanic students, it's 49.5 percent. Much of that discrepancy is related to where black and Hispanic students tend to go: community colleges and for-profit schools"

(Nadworny 2019). Minority students also tend to have more loans and if they drop out, the burden to pay them off is a heavy one (Jackson and Reynolds 2013).

Throughout history various political and religious leaders have attempted to keep education and especially higher education inaccessible to the masses. Recall in Chapter 1, for example, where we learned that Martin Luther promoted mass education in the 1500s so that all Christians could read the Bible for themselves. Instead, the Catholic Church, supported by the various rulers, insisted that the masses did not need to be educated as the Church would tell the faithful the meaning of the stories in the Bible. The rich and powerful often prefer a naive, gullible, and uninformed populace as they are easier to keep in line when the message cannot be challenged by enlightened thought. When the masses can be duped it not only helps to maintain the status quo; it also allows for the cliché often repeated throughout the centuries that "the rich get richer and the poor get poorer." Interestingly, this adage can be found in the Bible itself:

"For whosoever hath, to him shall be given, and he shall have more abundance: but whosoever hath not, from him shall be taken away even that he hath" (Matthew 12:12, King James version).

It stands to reason that an enlightened populace is a greater threat to the status quo (the powers that be) and those who seek to benefit from it. Political leaders and Big Business in particular attempt to dupe the gullible and less educated (consequently, restricting equal access to higher education becomes a ploy of the social elite). At the political level especially, the uneducated person begins to believe simple answers to complex problems. Political leaders and their Big Business co-conspiracists retell basic talking points repeatedly until eventually certain segments of the population believe such clichés to be true. This strategy is a classic one used to promote propaganda. Autocrats and would-be autocrats such as Donald Trump employ this technique to keep their followers energized and believing in the messenger as much as the message itself. Trump repeatedly uses words such as "invasion," "aliens," "killers," "animals," and "criminals" when describing immigrants who hope to enter the US and become citizens. According to a *USA Today* analysis of Trump's transcripts from his 64 campaign rallies from 2017 through mid-Summer 2019, this populist president used the word "invasion" at least 19 times and "killer" nearly three-dozen times. In all, he has used the words "predator," "invasion," "alien," "killer," "criminal," and "animal" at his rallies while discussing immigration more than 500 times. In reference to immigrants, mostly, Trump has also used the phrase "[get] the hell out of our country" at least 43 times during his rallies in this same time period (Fritze 2019a). According to Ruth Ben-Ghiat, a history professor at New York University who has studied propaganda, Trump does not talk the way he does by accident; she states, "The use of repetition—a propaganda mainstay—points to an intention by Trump to impose a way of thinking about his designated targets" (2019a). Trump's detractors believe that his language is incendiary and as an example of the danger of his rants point to the 2019 El Paso mass shooting gunman who wrote in his manifesto (posted online) that his actions were sparked by "the Hispanic invasion of Texas" (Fritze 2019a).

The manner in which Trump speaks and the messages that he repeats are all a part of a well-orchestrated plan that was revealed throughout his 2016 presidential campaign bid and that have continued since his election via the Electoral College. Trump realized years ago that he had tapped into a frustrated segment of the US population that was ready to embrace far-right conservatism and, as a result, he espoused all the contemporary conservative talking points (many of which would have resonated with conservatives in the pre-Enlightenment era) by promoting such ideas as a return to the reactionary paradigms of thought of tradition (even though he lacked the traditional qualifications for the office of the president) and faith via such fundamental conservative ideas as Christianity as the true religion of the United States (the US does not have an "official" religion), de facto endorsing a system of patriarchy, advancing "family values" and the idea of a monogamous family (even though he himself has already had more divorces than all the past presidents combined), attacking all those who would challenge his rule, especially his political opponents and the news media, downplaying the importance of higher education (even though often referring to himself as a "genius" and "a very stable genius" without providing any evidence of such alleged intelligence—he has never produced copies of his college transcripts and has not allowed any of his educational records to be released), and the promotion of an anti-science agenda (e.g., that scientists are wrong when they say humans contribute to global warming).

The matter of education is most relevant here, and there is a reason why Trump said during his presidential campaign, "We won with the poorly educated. I love the poorly educated" (Hafner 2016): they love him. According to the Pew Research Center, a wide gap in presidential preferences emerged between those with and without a college degree in the 2016 presidential race. College graduates backed Hillary Clinton by a nine-point margin (52 to 43 percent), while those without a college degree backed Trump (52 to 44 percent). The biggest margin of victory for Trump over Clinton came from non-college whites, 67 percent to 28 percent, a 39-point advantage for Trump (Tyson and Maniam 2016). And therein lies the core conservative voting bloc, the uneducated, white male. The lower education level of many Trump supporters combined with his propaganda style of speech explains this revealing and disturbing fact that Trump communicates at the lowest grade level of the last 15 presidents, according to an analysis of speech patterns of presidents going back to Herbert Hoover. The analysis assessed the first 30,000 words each US president spoke in office, and ranked them on the Flesch-Kincaid grade level scale and more than two-dozen other common tests analyzing English-language difficulty levels. Trump's level of communication was at the mid-fourth-grade level. At the top of the list were Hoover and Jimmy Carter, who spoke at the eleventh-grade level; Barack Obama came in third with a high ninth-grade level of communication. Trump also uses the fewest average syllables. Obama, on the other hand, rated as the most fluent of the past 15 presidents (Burleigh 2018; Gordon 2018; Delaney 2019). The utilization of simplistic language helps the poorly educated and the ignorant to understand things easier, linguists report (Gordon

2018). Trump's style of speech, which includes fragmented sentences and simple vocabulary, is more relatable to the less educated because that is the manner in which many people speak in everyday life.

A disbelief in science

Science comes about as the result of the intellectual and systematic study of human behavior (social science) or of the natural world (natural science) that leads to new knowledge that is supported by data; as a result, it is a critical aspect of the enlightened, rational thought paradigm. The Age of Enlightenment (c.1700–1840s) was a period in history when social thinkers were convinced that society was emerging from centuries of darkness and ignorance into an age of scientific reason and the ability of people to act rationally (see Chapter 1 for a more in-depth discussion on this topic). This optimistic belief in humanity led to a great deal of progressive thinking that was reinforced by scientific discovery and technology. Enlightened thought nurtured by reason and rationality would in turn stimulate further scientific advancements that assisted in the evolutionary growth of humanity. In all, the belief in science is equated to a commitment to progress and cultural evolution. Conversely, a disbelief in science would be equated to the decline in humanity. Populists, for example, who feel left behind by pluralism, technological change, and the global economy, tend to be disbelievers. Disbelievers of science often yearn for a return to some past era (reactionary thinking) when things were simpler and less complicated. Looking at the past with rose-colored glasses leads some people to think that society would be better off it were dominated by the faith and tradition paradigms of thought. Well, we've already had such a period of time wherein conservative idealism of leaders was combined with Christian religious dominance and this period of time is known as the "Dark Ages." No one should want a return to the darkness of the Middle Ages but that is what we are headed toward due to unenlightened and irrational thinking. If someone truly wants to live in a society dominated by faith and tradition there are plenty of monarchies and autocracies from which they may choose (i.e., Afghanistan, Iran, Saudi Arabia, Sudan, United Arab Emirates, Yemen) but let's keep enlightened, rational thought as the primary paradigm of thought in the United States, the Western World, and any other area of the world that prefers to embrace rational and reasoned thinking and avoid autocratic rule.

A disbelief in science in the United States

True science does not bother itself with concerns of politicians or of people who fret over factual knowledge that undermines their beliefs. On January 8, 1790, less than a year into his first presidential term, George Washington stood in front of a joint session of Congress in New York City and delivered what would be the first message to the United States Congress on the state of the union. In this brief speech (1,089 words), devoid of partisan clapping and grandstanding, Washington stated,

"There is nothing which can better deserve your patronage than the promotion of science and literature. Knowledge is in every country the surest basis of public happiness" (Clark 2015). Washington went on to describe science as "essential" to our nation. Nine scores later (220 years), Barack Obama vowed to "restore science to its rightful place" (Fisher 2013). Obama's insinuation plays into the common perception in the media, electorate, and research community that Republicans are "anti-science." And there certainly are a number of Republicans with very unenlightened and irrational forms of thinking with regards to science, including Paul Broun of Georgia (an MD no less), who in 2012 declared that evolution, the Big Bang theory, and embryology are "lies straight from the pit of hell" (Williams 2012). That Broun believes in something as irrational as a "Hell" is one thing, as many people believe in an afterlife with a "good place" (i.e., Heaven) and a "bad place" (i.e., Hell), but what is worse is the fact that Broun served as a member of the House of Representatives' science committee (Williams 2012). (Broun was a member of the House of Representatives from July 17, 2007 to January 3, 2015.) Among his other bizarre beliefs, Broun claims "as a scientist" that he has found data that shows the Earth is no more than 9,000 years old and was created in six days. The Earth, of course, is approximately 4.5 billion years old. Broun is scared of scientific truths because they challenge his belief that he, and others like him, need a "savior" (Williams 2012). Wisconsin Representative Jesse Kremer (R) espoused unenlightened and irrational thought regarding the age of the Earth by claiming that the planet is only 6,000 years old. He was immediately bashed by enlightened people, including the media, against who, in typical fashion, he chose to lash out by referring to them as the "elitist media" because they lost their minds over someone with a different opinion (Opoien 2017). It is not an opinion, Representative Kremer; it is a fact that the Earth is approximately 4.5 billion years old. It is inconceivable that people such as Kremer and Broun can get elected to government offices in the United States but such is the extent of the darkness that surrounds us. At least Kremer had the good sense not to seek reelection. (Examples of other disbelievers' unenlightened and irrational views will be discussed later in the chapter, when the topic of pseudoscience is covered.)

Any further review of the pro- or anti-science stands of American politicians would pale in comparison to the importance of the president's views. There is a great deal of evidence that indicates Donald Trump is not a strong supporter of the importance of science in contemporary American society. Writing for the *Los Angeles Times*, Melinda Welsh (2019) describes how science takes a back seat in American policy under Trump, stating, "President Trump and members of his revolving-door cabinet have shown no letup since 2017 in their disdain for scientific truths, mischaracterizing them as opinions that are somehow partisan in nature and expendable" (p. A11). Welsh is correct that there is a revolving door in Trump's cabinet (it is fairly common in most presidential cabinets but not as troublesome as has been the case in Trump's administration) but of particular relevance here is the lack of appointees with a science background. (See Chapter 4 for a further analysis of Trump's troubled cabinet appointments.)

The Union of Concerned Scientists (UCS) (2019) explains some of the many ways this administration is weakening processes that guide the use of science in policymaking. "The Trump administration over its first two years has shown a pervasive pattern of sidelining science in critical decision making, compromising our nation's ability to meet current and future public health and environmental challenges" (UCS 2019). Specific examples of "sidelining expertise and independent science advice" and compromising public protections detailed by the UCS (2019) include the following.

- Circumventing guidance from scientific experts by shutting out scientists from the decision making process, leaving science positions vacant, disbanding or compromising advisory committees, or sidelining independent expertise.
- Suppressing scientific studies when their findings undercut the administration's political agenda.
- Politicizing scientific grants by allowing political appointees to review them, which undercuts the scientific process and deters progress of the wider scientific enterprise.
- Eliminating climate change policy development. The administration has repeatedly ignored, dismissed, or suppressed climate change science, limiting the ability of federal scientists to study it or speak about it and removing mentions of climate change from official agency documents and websites.
- Undermining protections from hazards at work and home (e.g., weakening chemical safety laws and air pollution rules, limiting public access to information on fracking, and rolling back collection of data on workplace injuries).
- Endangering the environment. The administration has pushed science out of the environmental protection for national parks and other protected areas, curtailed or canceled environmental impact reviews, and undermined the Endangered Species Act.
- Restricting scientists' communications and interactions with reporters and omitting important scientific information from news releases.
- Restricting federal scientists from presenting their data at scientific conferences.

This is a chilling review provided by the Union of Concerned Scientists and certainly illustrates the anti-science attitude of Donald Trump. Trump's dismissive approach to utilizing empirical data and scientific expertise on matters related to climate change is his most damning and dangerous tendency.

The UCS report was preceded by other documentations and warnings of Trump's anti-science moves. *Scientific American*, for example, provided a top-five listing in 2017 (Marks 2017), as follows.

- Trump's pick for the head of the US Environmental Protection Agency, Scott Pruitt, was an Oklahoma attorney general who has long been opposed to environmental regulations and who has questioned the science behind climate change. As an update to this original story and following a long record of "misdeeds and malfeasance" and "numerous scandals," Pruitt was replaced by Andrew Wheeler in 2018 (Turrentine 2018). What are Wheeler's qualifications to head the agency responsible for protecting the environment, you might ask? "Well, for starters, his most recent job was as an energy lobbyist. His biggest clients included Murray Energy Corporation, which proudly bills itself as the largest coal mining company in America, and whose CEO, Robert E. Murray, vigorously fought the Obama administration's attempt to reduce carbon emissions and strengthen environmental and public health laws" (Turrentine 2018). *Fox News* (2019) reports Wheeler's work as a backer of coal mining interests—he was a coal industry lobbyist—as a "Fun Fact" in its description of him in a review of Trump's cabinet. There's nothing "fun" about a coal lobbyist working as the head of the EPA.

- Trump chose former Texas governor Rick Perry to be the Department of Energy (DofE) Secretary. Perry, who is not a scientist, advocated for the dismantling of the DofE during his 2012 presidential bid. Perry oversees the department that maintains the US nuclear arsenal.
- He chose former ExxonMobil chief executive Rex Tillerson for secretary of state and while Tillerson acknowledges that climate change is a problem, he has been accused of hiding climate change research from Exxon shareholders—something he denies. Tillerson was replaced in April 2018 by Mike Pompeo, a former CIA director.
- Trump, who has tweeted that there are "many cases" of children who become autistic after receiving vaccinations, met with Robert F. Kennedy, Jr. (a vaccine skeptic himself, who has also repeatedly said that vaccinations have caused an increase in the number of cases of autism) to discuss a possible formation of an autism commission. Since this concern was raised by *Scientific American*, Trump has decided, for now, not to create this commission.
- When Trump first became president, his transition team sought the names of and information on the employees of the Energy Department who had worked on issues related to climate change.

Trump has done (e.g., cabinet appointments) and said many things that fly in the face of science. As complied by Eli Stokols (2019), Trump has demanded "god dammed steam" to power the Navy's aircraft and he prefers a wall to drones and other technology to secure the country's southern border. He has rejected the scientific consensus on climate change and has repeatedly, wrongly, pointed to occasional wintry weather as proof he is right. In March 2019, amidst the Boeing 737 Max 8 and Max 9 airplane safety scare, Trump complained that modern jets are "too complex to fly" and, "I see it all the time in many products. Always seeking to go one unnecessary step further, when the old and simpler is far better" (Stokols 2019:A2). Trump, a septuagenarian who tweets yet doesn't email, text, or use computers, displays a backward-looking approach that is at the core of his nostalgia-based appeal to voters longing for a supposedly simpler past era of American greatness. Looking to the past instead of the future is yet another way Trump has differed from his predecessors that have held the office of the president. Not only that, in countless ways he has acted less presidential than his predecessors as well. He just says whatever he thinks, like a child, before gathering data or evidence or facts and in this regard he is a dangerous threat to national security, according to John P. Holden, director of the White House Office of Science and Technology during the Obama administration (Stokols 2019). His threat to national security extends to his disbelief that humans are contributing to climate change, despite all the scientific evidence and common sense that indicates the opposite. And in instances where automation has replaced many traditional jobs, he prefers to blame immigrants or unfair foreign companies, or companies that move operations overseas.

As a proponent of the environmentally damaging fossil fuel energy industry, Trump has repeatedly bashed renewable energy sources as viable alternatives. His defense would be laughable were it not for the seriousness of the issue. For example, on April 2, 2019, Trump stepped up his attacks against wind power, claiming that the structures decrease property values and that the noise they emit causes cancer. Delivering remarks at the National Congressional Committee's annual spring dinner, Trump said, "If you have a windmill anywhere near your house, congratulations, your house just went down 75 percent in value. And they say the noise causes cancer" (Burke 2019). He offered no evidence to support these claims. Trump also said that wind turbines are a "graveyard for birds" even though the Department of Energy has noted that bird deaths from the structures are rare. Just a month earlier, Trump said at a Michigan rally that wind power doesn't work because the wind doesn't always blow. Sounding like a simpleton to make his point, Trump said, "If it doesn't blow, you can forget about television for that night. 'Darling, I want to watch television.' 'I'm sorry! The wind isn't blowing.' I know a lot about wind'" (Burke 2019).

A number of commentators have pointed out that Trump hated windmills long before his inaccurate claim that they cause cancer.

> His feud with wind power started in 2006, when Trump was developing plans to build a golf course in Balmedie, Scotland, just as a renewable energy group was developing a multimillion-dollar offshore wind farm close by. The idea of windmills spoiling the view on his gold course put Trump on the offensive, and he threatened to pull out of the deal—a move that prompted more wind farm proposals and social in-fighting.
>
> *(Melendez 2019)*

Trump argued that the installation of windmills on the Scottish coast was more damaging than any event in Scottish history. He has been on a Twitter rant ever since. Apparently, Trump has no idea about Scottish history, the country's desire to eliminate a dependence on fossil fuels in favor of "a cleaner, greener tomorrow" (Scotland.org 2019), and the science behind how windmills work—turning kinetic energy from wind into electricity. As for birds dying because of the structures, some do, but the rate is much far lower than the rate for other energy sources. Fossil-fuelled power plants kill birds (and bats) at nearly 15 times the rate of wind turbines (Chapman 2017). While Trump has claimed that wind turbines cause cancer, he ignored the science on things that do cause cancer, such as: asbestos, whose use he deregulated; beryllium, for which he delayed regulation; and coal, which he promotes.

It is important to point out that Trump's energy secretary Rick Perry promotes the benefits of wind, which supplies about 20 percent of the electricity in his home state of Texas (*Los Angeles Times* 2019c). While Trump has said that windmills are not working that well, the US has added more than 15 gigawatts of capacity since he took office in 2017, enough to power half of New York State (*Los Angeles Times* 2019c). The wind industry includes 114,000 full-time jobs in the US and it is also the cheapest source of electricity in many regions of the US. It is also true that wind energy does have some shortcomings. In early August 2019, for example, the wholesale power prices in Texas "surged 40,000%, in part because output from wind farms fell during a heat wave" and "in the U.K., more than a million homes lost power on Aug. 9 after turbines in the North Sea tripped offline" (*Los Angeles Times* 2019c).

It is clear that Trump needs lessons on science and how things work. A stronger background, or any background at all, in science would, hopefully, stop him from stating lies, falsehoods, and misleading claims and reduce the perception of how ignorant he comes across to those with even basic knowledge of science. But learning about science and prepping his statements on important issues would go against his typical way of going about things as he hates to prepare for meetings of any kind. For example, when asked in 2018 before his summit with Kim Jong Un of North Korea about his preparation, Trump replied that "attitude" is more important than preparation. "I don't think I have to prepare very much. It's about attitude. It's about willingness to get things done" (Miller, Colvin, and Lucey 2018). More than a year later and North Korea was still launching test missiles into the Sea of Japan.

Disbelievers in the validity of science tend to be either too ignorant to understand how it works, realize that the truth will interfere with their socio-political agendas, or fear that factual, scientific information disproves their unenlightened and irrational thinking. As far as not being able to understand how science works, it is possible that people get confused by its basic principles: select a specific topic to be studied; define the problem and establish the parameters; review the literature; formulate hypotheses; select research method(s) to be used (in data collection); actually collect data; analyze the data; and state conclusions and share the results (via publication or conference presentation). Ideally, a research project is designed clearly enough so that others can attempt to replicate the study. Replication allows other researchers to duplicate the original study so that they can either support or challenge the original conclusions. Replication also allows for the testing of reliability and validity of the original research. Scientific researchers are cautious to say that their data "prove" that their theory is correct until it can replicated to the point where it becomes known as a scientific fact.

As an example of a concern that the truth will interfere with a socio-political agenda, consider the case of President Trump and the Republican Party's argument against immigration reform and the corresponding argument for building a huge wall on the southern border as predicated by the entry of murderous and criminal immigrants into the US from Mexico (and other Central American countries). Trump kicked off his presidential campaign on June 16, 2015 with a speech in which he labeled immigrants from Mexico "rapists" and criminals. Trump said, "When Mexico sends its people, they're not sending their best. They're not sending you. They're sending people that have lots of problems, and they're bringing those problems with us. They're bringing drugs. They're bringing crime. They're rapists. And some, I assume, are good people" (Edelman 2016). A couple of weeks later he accused Mexican immigrants of being "killers" and "rapists" (Edelman 2016). (See Chapter 2 for a more in-depth look at the political views of Trump and other world leaders on immigrants and immigration.) While there have been some isolated examples of violence committed by illegal immigrants in the United States—which certain politicians use to "support" their worries about immigration—numerous studies have shown that illegal immigration has been at historic lows since 2000 and that an "overwhelming correlation exists between immigrants and low crime rates" (Carcamo, Fry, and Knoll 2018:B1). One study conducted by Michael T. Light, a sociology professor at the University of Wisconsin, indicates that "As the undocumented population increases, the violent crime rate tends to go down. And we see this across the four main measures we think of with violent crimes—robbery, rape, homicide and assault" (Carcamo, Fry, and Knoll 2018:B1). A 2015 study released by the Cato Institute (a libertarian public policy research organization) examined 2015 data from the Texas Department of Public Safety and found that homicide conviction rates for illegal and legal immigrants were 16 percent and 67 percent below those of native-born residents, respectively. The Department of Homeland Security revealed that the number of people who are apprehended each year trying to cross the southern US border climbed steadily from the 1970s through the 1990s, peaking at 1.64 million in 2000, but noted an opposite trend since this peak year, with 396,579 people apprehended in 2018 (Carcamo, Fry, and Knoll 2018). Among the points of this information worth highlighting is the fact that the scientific data paint a much different picture of the immigration issue in the United States than Trump and his supporters would care to acknowledge. An anti-science backlash ensues and cries of "fake news" are meant to keep the populist base fired up, as the last thing a politician like Trump wants to accept is the truth, which counters his belief and messaging.

A third proposed explanation as to why someone would disbelieve science is the idea that scientific information disproves their unenlightened and irrational thinking. A couple of examples come to mind right away. The first involves people who do not think humans are contributing to climate change and/or the deterioration of the environment. Scientists across the globe have concluded that the Earth's atmosphere is getting warmer because people are pumping carbon dioxide into the air (primarily from burning fossil fuels). They have followed the scientific research model approach so often that this assertion has now become fact. How anyone can deny this is beyond common sense and reason. And yet, an astounding and frightfully high number—60 percent—of Americans did not believe this to be true in 2015 (Rosoff 2015). A few years later, and as a sign of light, a surging number of Americans (more than 70 percent) understood that climate change is real and could harm their family and the country according to a 2018 poll from Yale and George Mason University (Meyer 2019). (The topic of humans harming the environment will be discussed further later in this chapter.)

The second example of unenlightened and irrational thinking has to do with childhood vaccinations and the misguided belief that they lead to autism. Scientists see no connection between the two and yet a number of people believe that there is. Why? Many people cite a single study (one that was not replicated or validated) by Andrew Wakefield that was submitted to the esteemed medical journal *The Lancet*. In this research paper (which has been retracted and the research conducted by the author deemed false and unethical—part of the costs of his research were paid for by lawyers of parents seeking to sue vaccine makers for damages), Wakefield claimed a connection between the measles-mumps-rubella (MMR) vaccine to the onset of autism, a neurodevelopment disorder characterized by impaired social interaction. While medical professionals quickly discredited Wakefield's conclusion, there are enough people who still believe in this discredited research that they have refused to have their children vaccinated. As a result, a disease, the measles, that was declared eradicated, has returned. Through November 2019, there were nearly 1,300 cases of measles in the United States, the largest number of such cases in 27 years (Stobbe 2019). Interestingly, it is the "liberal" Pacific Northwest that has played witness to the greatest number of people who are ignoring science and proclaiming "My child, my choice" (Baumgaertner 2019).

Meanwhile, in the northeast part of the US, a number of ultra-Orthodox Jewish families in New York's Rockland County are citing "individual autonomy" and "free exercise of religion" (Baumgaertner 2019) as a reason for not getting vaccines deemed completely safe by the scientific community. New York officials declared a public health emergency in parts of Brooklyn in April 2019, establishing mandatory vaccinations in an effort to stop the city's worst measles outbreak in almost 30 years. Health advocates pointed to what they believe is a major source of vaccine misinformation in the affected neighborhoods—*The Vaccine Safety Handbook*, a magazine published by an anonymously led group called Parents Educating and Advocating for Children's Health, or PEACH (Zadrozny 2019). The 40-page magazine filled with cartoons mocks the medical establishment and inaccurately suggests vaccines are made up of "toxins." Without providing evidence, it claims that vaccines are the nation's greatest threat to public health, linked to autism, ADHD, Sudden Infant Death Syndrome (SIDS), miscarriage, and other maladies (Zadrozny 2019). PEACH has also claimed that vaccines are in opposition with Jewish religious law, which is false (Koerner and Reinstein 2019).

114 Unenlightened and irrational thinking

In July 2019, a group of five New York State families had reached out to Robert F. Kennedy, Jr. (an anti-vaccination sympathizer) in hopes of reinstating a religious exemption to vaccine mandates. The exemption had been repealed a month earlier in the face of the nation's worst measles outbreak in decades. Critics of the old exemption say religious beliefs shouldn't outweigh overwhelming scientific evidence showing that vaccines work to protect individuals and communities from disease (Associated Press 2019b). In addition to the reemergence of measles, North Carolina is experiencing its worst chickenpox outbreak in decades as 36 children have been diagnosed at a private school where many families claim religious exemption from vaccines. It's the largest outbreak in the state since the varicella vaccine, which protects against chickenpox, was introduced in 1995 (CBS News 2018).

It is hard to fathom that in the early twenty-first century the enlightened form of thinking that is science is subject to protests from those who are unenlightened and irrational in their thinking.

A disbelief in science around the world

It would be a Herculean task to try and cover all the examples of anti-science in the many countries around the world; thus, we will limit our focus to two main topics —the anti-vaccine movement and countries that deny the fact that humans contribute to climate change and therefore cling to their dependency on fossil fuels. As described previously, the United States has its *anti-vaxxers* (a term for those who are against vaccine immunizations), but this is hardly the only country facing such darkness in thinking. So serious is the global anti-vaccination sentiment that the World Health Organization (WHO) has declared it as one of the world's top-ten gravest threats to global health. WHO refers to the reluctance or refusal to vaccinate despite the availability of vaccines as *vaccine hesitancy*. Vaccine hesitancy threatens to reverse progress made in tackling vaccine-preventable diseases. According to WHO (2019a), "Vaccination is one of the most cost-effective ways of avoiding disease—it currently prevents 2–3 million deaths a year, and a further 1.5 million could be avoided if global coverage of vaccinations improved." Just as the number of cases of measles has increased in the United States, so too has it risen globally—30 percent according to WHO (2019a). As an aside, the other health threats facing the world in 2019 are: air pollution and climate change; noncommunicable diseases (e.g., diabetes, cancer, and heart disease); the global influenza pandemic; fragile and vulnerable settings (e.g., areas with drought, famine, conflict, and population displacement—affecting 22 percent of the global population); antimicrobial resistance (as a result of the development of antibiotics, antivirals, and antimalarials); Ebola and other high-threat pathogens; weak primary health care; vaccine hesitancy; Dengue fever (a mosquito-borne disease) in Asia; HIV (the anti-science leadership in South Africa 15 years ago that led to the lack of antiretroviral drugs being distributed to the population is largely to blame for more than 300,000 deaths) (Birnbaum 2017; Stobbe 2019; WHO 2019).

Italy, the country with the second-highest (behind only Romania) figure of reported measles cases (5,004) in Europe (in 2017)—according to the European Centre for Disease Prevention and Control (ECDC)—did what logic would dictate and mandated ten routine vaccinations when enrolling children in nurseries or preschools (Mezzofiore 2018). One year later, Italy acted in an unenlightened and irrational manner by removing the mandatory vaccination requirement and sent shock waves through the country's scientific and medical community. The 5,000+ reported cases of measles in Italy account for 34 percent of measles cases reported by countries in the European Economic Area, according to the ECDC (Mezzofiore 2018). Italy's far-right political group League voiced opposition to compulsory vaccinations with its leader and interior minister Matteo Salvini stating that such vaccinations, which include measles, tetanus, and polio, "are useless and in many cases dangerous, if not harmful" (Mezzofiore 2018). Italy's measles vaccine coverage was on a par with Namibia and lower than that of Ghana before the 2017 mandatory vaccination law, the World Health Organization reported. WHO recommends that every country should have at least a 95 percent level of immunization to ensure "herd immunity" (Mezzofiore 2018). The reluctance of many Italians to have their children immunized is the result of a court ruling in Rimini that established a link between autism and the combined measles-mumps-rubella vaccination. While the ruling was overturned three years later, it helped to fuel the anti-vaccination craze across Italy and other parts of the world (Mezzofiore 2018).

From January 2018 through October 2019, there were more than 3,440 measles cases and nine measles-related deaths in Uganda, according to the World Health Organization (Mahr 2019). Uganda is not the only African nation facing a resurgence of measles cases. "A massive outbreak in the island nation of Madagascar off the coast of Mozambique, where more than 150,000 cases have been reported and more than 1,000 people have died due to low vaccination rates and a vaccine shortage once the outbreak took hold" (Mahr 2019:A2). Once again, the primary explanation for the measles outbreak in Africa is the fact that people are opting out of giving children immunization shots.

The ill-advised anti-vaccine movement, rooted in suspicions of modern medicine and a belief in unsubstantiated rumors fueled by social media, has led to children in Pakistan being infected with a disease that had been all but wiped out (Bengali and Ali 2019). Polio's disturbing comeback in Pakistan is being driven by some of the same troubling forces that have led to the return of measles in the United States. "Two years after health officials declared they were on the verge of eradicating the crippling childhood disease from Pakistan, one of the last countries where it remains endemic, at least 58 children [had] tested positive for the virus since January [2019]" (Bengali and Ali 2019:A1). This is an extraordinarily high figure in just a nine-month period and it represents nearly five times the total number of reported polio cases in all of 2018. A shocking two million Pakistani households have refused immunizations for children since April 2019. Most of the 2019 cases of polio in Pakistan came from the Khyber Pakhtunkhwa province and the adjacent tribal belt along the border with Afghanistan, "the world's last major corridor of polio transmission" (Bengali and Ali 2019:A4). Afghanistan had recorded 13 cases of polio in the same time period as reported here and represents the only other country where the disease continues to infect children (Bengali and Ali 2019).

With regard to fossil fuels dependency and the questioning of its link to climate change, the United States is not the only nation touting "alternative facts" as opposed to scientific ones (Birnbaum 2017). Sadly and irrationally, there is a climate change denial movement across the globe and generally it's connected to the elite's desire to hold onto the outdated form of energy provided by single-use fossil fuels. According to data compiled by the World Atlas (2019a), there are at least 29 countries that source more than 90 percent of their energy from fossil fuels. "The consumption rate seems to be rising most sharply in developing economies with or near rich oil reserves, such as India and Singapore, over the last ten years … India's dependence on the consumption of fossil fuel has risen to levels almost three times those seen in 1990" (World Atlas 2019a). The nations of Oman, Qatar, Kuwait, Saudi Arabia, and Brunei source fossil fuels for 100 percent of their energy use. Trinidad and Tobago (99.93 percent), Bahrain (99.92 percent), the United Arab Emirates (99.91 percent), Algeria (99.86 percent), and Iran (99.93 percent) round off the remaining top ten fossil fuel-dependent nations (World Atlas 2019). The United States does not crack the World Atlas top 50 ranking for fossil fuel dependency. At near 80 percent dependence on fossil fuels, the US has little to brag about, but it is positive to note that despite the Trump administration's disdain for protecting the environment, there is a green movement in the country that is spearheading a charge toward developing more renewable energy sources.

The countries least dependent on fossil fuels for energy are Iceland (89.0 percent of its energy comes from alternative and nuclear energy), Tajikistan (64.1 percent), Sweden (48.5 percent), France (47.0 percent), Switzerland (39.5 percent), Costa Rica (38.7 percent), Norway (34 percent), El Salvador (33.8 percent), New Zealand (31.5 percent), and Kyrgyzstan (29.5 percent) (World Atlas 2019b). While a dependency on fossil fuels as a primary source of energy represents unenlightened and irrational thinking, using renewable energy represents enlightened thinking. As the World Atlas (2019b) states, "Renewable energy is advantageous in that it is derived from sources that are never ending and can be replenished time after time. Renewable energy is considered clean energy as it does not cause adverse environmental pollution."

Attacks on the environment

One of the primary attacks on the environment comes from those who promote a dependency on fossil fuels, which, in turn, has a direct effect on climate change and contributes to the deterioration of the environment. The *environment* itself "refers to the totality of social and physical conditions that affect nature (land, water, air, plants, and animals) and humanity and their influence on the growth, development, and survival of organisms found in a given surrounding (e.g., a limited proximity of the Earth as a whole)" (Delaney and Madigan 2014:6). Undoubtedly, readers have heard the term *sustainability* (the ability to be maintained at a certain rate or level) applied to the environment. However, after conducting a great deal of research on the subject of the environment, my colleague Tim Madigan and I have published a textbook on the topic wherein we promote the idea of "thrivability." And for good reason; after all, if the environment is already compromised—which it surely is— why would anyone want to maintain it at its current given state of condition? Promoting "environmental sustainability" is not adequate for anyone who wants to see a flourishing environment. Thus, we promote the idea of "environmental thrivability." *Thrivability* refers to "a cycle of actions which reinvest energy for future use and stretch resources further; it transcends sustainability by creating an upward spiral of greater possibilities and increasing energy" (Delaney and Madigan 2014:6). Protecting the ecosystem is the primary goal of environmentalists and environmental social movements. The *ecosystem* refers to "the ecological network of interconnected and interdependent living organisms (plants, animals and microbes) in union with the nonliving aspects found in their immediate community, including air, water, minerals and soil" (Delaney and Madigan 2014:8). It could be argued that the entire planet is an ecosystem but the term is generally applied to specific and limited spaces. The word "ecosystem" was coined by the British botanist Arthur Tansley in his 1935 article "The Use and Abuse of Gestational Concepts and Terms." He stressed that one should not focus solely upon organisms, but rather upon the interactions between organisms and their environment.

The importance of protecting the environment from a multitude of human attacks cannot be understated as nothing, and I mean literally nothing, is more important than protecting the environment—not the economy, the stock market, employment, religion, politics, or anything else compares to our need to have access to clean drinking water, oxygen, and all the other critical elements related to the Earth's ecosystems. Things are so dire right now that we are in the era of the sixth mass extinction. A *mass extinction* occurs when the planet loses more than three-quarters of its species in a geologically short interval of time, usually during a few hundred thousand to a couple of million years (Barnosky et al. 2011). Then again, a critical event such as an all-out nuclear war or significant meteorite impact could trigger a mass extinction in a much shorter period of time. The Earth has already endured five mass extinctions, which are all named after the geological time period during which they occurred (see Table 3.4). The most commonly cited mass extinction is the one that killed the dinosaurs approximately 65 million years ago, long before humans roamed the planet.

A mass extinction occurs about every 65–70 million years and can last for millions of years. If you are thinking we must be close to the next mass extinction period you are correct; in fact, we are in the early stages of the sixth mass extinction right now. The evidence of this is all around us and includes such indisputable facts as the regular loss of animal species, something that has happened at a much quicker pace since human existence; the many forms of pollution compromising our environment on a daily basis; and the rise in the planet's CO_2 count. Humans were

TABLE 3.4 The Earth's five mass extinctions

Number	Name/time period	Cause(s)
1	End-Ordovian/440 million years ago	Glaciation
2	Late-Devonian/365 million years ago	Glaciation and global cooling
3	End-Permian/250 million years ago	Asteroids and volcanoes
4	End-Triassic/200 million years ago	Volcanoes
5	End-Cretaceous/65 million years ago	Meteorites/asteroids/volcanoes*

Source: Delaney and Madigan 2014; Andryszewski 2009.

Note

* New evidence indicates that volcanic eruptions triggered by the meteorites and asteroids may have contributed to killing the dinosaurs and nearly all land animals during this period.

not around, of course, during the first five mass extinctions, but our species represents the greatest threat and contributor to the current mass extinction. Depending on one's definition of what constitutes a "human," archaeologists estimate that our species has been on this planet for about 200,000 years. Humans are a member of the bipedal primate species in the Hominidae (great ape) family, having diverged from apes six million to eight million years ago, and are a dozen humanlike species removed (PBS 2001; Pickrell 2006).

Dependency of fossil fuels and climate change

The Earth has a limited "carrying capacity" to support life. *Carrying capacity* refers to the maximum feasible load, just short of the level that would end the environment's ability to support life (Catton 1980). The carrying capacity, then, is tied to the number of organisms that can be supported in a given area (ecosystem) based on the natural resources available without compromising present and future generations. Once the environment is sullied, the carrying capacity shrinks, thus negatively altering its ability to sustain life.

> Over the generations, but especially recently, the Earth's carrying capacity has been stretched to its limit due to a number of threats to the environment. These threats include, but are not limited to, urban sprawl, the spread of deserts, the destruction of forests by acid rain, deforestation, the stripping of large tracts of land for fuel, radiation fallout, and the many areas where the population is exceeding the carrying capacity of local agriculture.
>
> *(Delaney and Madigan 2014:26)*

Overpopulation in particular is a leading threat to the thrivability of the Earth's environment as the more people there are on the planet, the greater the demand for natural resources. At the start of industrialization (*c.*the late 1700s), there were just one billion humans on the planet and the Earth was not compromised as a result. At the end of 2019, there were well over 7.7 billion people on the planet. At this current rate of population growth, there will be over ten billion people by 2055. We are struggling to feed all the people we have today; how will we feed another two billion? Humans have also relied heavily on the burning of fossil fuels to meet their primary energy needs but this finite source will be exhausted sooner or later —and certainly sooner, as the number of people in the world continues to expand.

Our dependency on fossil fuels has been mentioned throughout this chapter but it is important to put it in its proper context here. To get an idea of the power of Big Oil and other proponents of fossil fuel dependency, consider the following unenlightened and irrational form of thinking. On May 28, 2019 the US Department of Energy posted a press release about liquid natural gas exports by referring to natural gas as "freedom gas" and as "molecules of U.S. freedom" (Wu 2019). The burning of fossil fuels causes many specific problems, beginning with compromising the Earth's ozone layer, which extends about ten to 30 miles above our planet and serves a shield protecting people and the environment from the Sun's harmful ultraviolet radiation. Without a healthy ozone the planet will suffer dramatic environmental change and life will not be the same as we know it. Many life forms, including humans, will suffer tremendously. A compromised ozone will cause an increase in the number of people who will suffer from asthma, lung problems, chest pain, coughing, shortness of breath, and so on. A further deterioration of the ozone can cause catastrophic levels of death. And yet, humans compromise the ozone on a regular basis by emitting toxic chemicals into the air, the chief among them from used fossil fuels. These "freedom gases" are really just potential molecules of death.

The effects of the compromised ozone layer are made evident in a number of ways, including ice cap and glacier thawing in Greenland, the Arctic, and Antarctica. The Arctic is especially important as it acts as the Earth's refrigerator, keeping the planet cool enough for life to exist. In its annual "Arctic Report Card," the National Oceanic and Atmospheric Administration (NOAA) indicated that the surface air temperatures in the Arctic continue to warm at twice the rate relative to the rest of the globe. The Arctic air temperatures for the years 2014–2018 have exceeded all records kept since 1900. In 2018, Arctic sea ice remained younger, thinner, and covered less area than in the past (NOAA 2019a). The NOAA (2019b) also warns about the Southern Hemisphere sea ice, which is at dangerously low levels. In addition to the concern over ice melt is the corresponding rise in sea levels, which could have a crippling effect on coastal cities around the world. Furthermore, as the ice melts, dangerous amounts of greenhouse gases trapped below thawing permafrost will likely seep into the air over the next several decades, accelerating and amplifying global warming (Borenstein 2011).

The ripple effect of relying on fossil fuels also has a direct bearing on climate change. Climate change refers to a long-term change in the Earth's climate, especially due to shifts in average atmospheric temperatures. There is overwhelming evidence to indicate that global warming is occurring now and it is likely to be a contributor to the sixth mass extinction. There should be no debate as to whether or not humans are contributing to climate change; the only question is, to what extent? The primary concern with climate change is global warming and the manner in which humans directly contribute to this problem is through the output of carbon dioxide (CO_2), which is measured in terms of parts per million (ppm). Scientists warn that the atmospheric CO_2 count needs to be at 350 ppm (maximum) in order to halt global warming and avoid catastrophic weather patterns that could spell the demise of human civilization. Scientists also calculate that the global level of CO_2 before the Industrial Revolution was about 280 ppm (Porter 2013). According to the NOAA (2019c), the atmospheric carbon dioxide level was 411.77 ppm in July 2019; it had been 408.71 just one year earlier. Record heat (July 2019 had the highest monthly global temperature reading in the Earth's recorded history), rising global water levels, flood deluges, and an increase in wildfires are just a few natural by-products of the rise in CO_2.

The increased output of CO_2 not only gives way to global warming; it also contributes to ocean acidification. Ocean acidification should not elicit less of a concern than climate change; it is a twin concern. The ocean absorbs about a quarter of the CO_2 emitted into the atmosphere every year. As the overall CO_2 level increases, so too does the amount of carbon emissions in our oceans increase, making the oceans more acidic, and as a result this poses a serious threat to biodiversity and marine life. With these notions in mind, *ocean acidification* (OA) is the term given to the chemical changes in the ocean as a result of carbon dioxide emissions (NOAA 2019d). If left unchecked, OA could destroy all our coral reefs by as early as 2050. It also has the potential to disturb other ocean ecosystems, fisheries, habitats, and entire food chains (Ocean Acidification 2012).

Climate change also leads to the greenhouse effect. The *greenhouse effect* refers to circumstances where the short wavelengths of visible light from the Sun pass through the atmosphere, but the longer wavelengths of the infrared re-radiation from the heated objects are unable to escape the Earth's atmosphere. The trapped long-wavelength radiation (infrared light) leads to more heating and a higher resultant temperature, thus contributing to global warming. The major greenhouse gases are carbon dioxide, chlorofluorocarbons (CFCs), methane (CH_4), and nitrous oxide (N_2O) (Drake 2000).

When we combine all of these threats—damage to the ozone layer, ice cap and glacier thawing, ocean acidification, and the greenhouse effect—which are causing climate change and accelerating the sixth mass extinction process, it should be a no-brainer that we must cut our dependency on fossil fuels and reduce our CO_2 output. Instead, we have many governments and people ignoring science. Leading the charge of this unenlightened thinking is Donald Trump, who has placed the United States (the second-highest producer of CO_2 behind only China) in the precarious situation of being an unrepentant mass producer of CO_2. Trump rejected the 2015 Paris Agreement signed by 195 nations to mitigate greenhouse gas emissions. This setback is especially chilling in light of a 2018 global warming prediction that the devastating effects of climate change will hit harder—and decades sooner—than previously expected (King 2018b). While Trump keeps his head buried in the sand with regard to fossil fuel dependency and the threat from climate change, "Networks and organizations representing more than 7,000 institutions of higher and further education around the world have a signed a letter declaring a 'climate emergency' and committing to tackle it," according to the UN (Associated Press 2019c). The agreement "commits the institutions to support a three-point plan that calls for mobilizing resources for climate change research, increasing education on preserving the environment, and going carbon-neutral by 2030, or 2050 at the latest" (Associated Press 2019c). While agreeing to try and do the right thing is commendable, setting a deadline of 2030 *or* 2050 is not a real commitment.

Human contributions to the sixth mass extinction

Earlier in this chapter, the topic of mass extinctions was introduced, and for good reason, as we are currently in the sixth such era. It was also pointed out that a mass extinction era can extend over a period of up to millions of years, or under dramatic conditions it can occur in a short period of time. That we are in the sixth mass extinction period does imply that the "sky is falling" tomorrow, the next day, or even in our lifetimes. However, the signs of impending doom are plentiful and some of the big worries have already been discussed. The seriousness of our dependency on fossil fuels and climate change means that humans are contributing to this current mass extinction and these contributions may lead to a sooner, rather than later, demise.

Before we look at the harm humans are causing the planet it would be remiss not to acknowledge the negative impact that nature can have on the environment. We have learned that there were five mass extinctions already and none of them involved humans. Threats from the environment include: volcanic eruptions (the cause, or partial cause, of three past mass extinctions), especially because of the ash and toxins—such as carbon dioxide, sulphur dioxide, hydrogen sulphide, hydrogen chloride, and so on—that they spew into the air; lighting strikes, which can destroy natural or manmade items and cause wildfires; wildfires, a natural phenomenon that occurred long before the dawn of humanity, which can destroy large chunks of the environment or entire local ecosystems; invasive species (non-native species that have found their way into habitants that have no defense against them), which can destroy entire ecosystems and species of animals, marine life, or plant life; and vapors from sulfur springs and the decay of dead species, which may lead to the release of deadly fumes, often undetectable until too late, and can destroy ecosystems. We are essentially powerless against the forces of nature, which makes it all the more imperative that we do not harm it any further and throw it off-balance all the more. What we can do, however, is curtail harmful human activities that negatively impact the environment.

Human contributions (beyond a reliance on fossil fuels) to the sixth mass extinction are plentiful. Our review will start with a look at how the advent of industrialization changed the course of human history forever, including negatively impacting the environment, through urbanization and the building of cities. Urbanites live in an environment with a limited ecosystem. Despite the existence of parks and trees and scattered lawns and gardens, cities are mostly concrete. To get to this point, humans destroyed diverse ecosystems, including by cutting down massive numbers of acres of trees, clearing large tracts of land, plowing prairies for crops, and the allocation of huge tracts of land for ranching, cultivating natural grass growth to conform to well-manicured lawns, and reducing the biological diversity of living things that exist in "wild" ecosystems (Delaney and Madigan 2014). Human overpopulation has already pushed the Earth's carrying capacity to point of unsustainability but it has also endangered countless ecosystems and the overall environment. Over nearly 250 years of industrialization, humans have come perilously close to altering the Earth's fragile ecosystems in a very harmful manner (Delaney 2005).

As a species, humans have harmed the environment via a wide variety of forms of pollution including air, water, land, chemical, nuclear, solid waste, noise, and celestial. We begin our look at the different types of pollution with air pollution. *Air pollution* refers to the presence in or introduction into the air of a substance, either particulates or microscopic biological molecules or gases, with harmful or poisonous effects. The air is an invisible gaseous substance surrounding the Earth that consists mainly of oxygen and nitrogen. As common sense dictates, all living species need oxygen to survive. Oxygen is a colorless, odorless, tasteless gaseous chemical element that appears in great abundance on the Earth because it is trapped by the atmosphere. The air we breathe, however, may be polluted and cause harm to those who breathe it in. According to WHO (2019), nine out of ten people breathe polluted air every day. In fact, WHO considers air pollution as the greatest environmental risk to health.

> Microscopic pollutants in the air can penetrate respiratory and circulatory systems, damaging the lungs, heart and brain, killing 7 million people prematurely every year from diseases such as cancer, stroke, heart and lung disease. Around 90% of these deaths are in low- and middle-income countries, with high volumes of emissions from industry, transport and agriculture, as well as dirty cookstoves and fuels in homes.
>
> *(WHO 2019)*

The primary cause of air pollution is, of course, the burning of fossil fuels. If our reliance on fossil fuels is not drastically reduced soon we risk our own extinction, along with countless other plant, marine, and animal species.

Addressing water pollution is nearly as important as addressing air pollution. *Water pollution* occurs when water supplies are contaminated. Sources of water pollution include industrial waste, harmful agricultural run-offs (e.g., chemical fertilizers and manure), sewage, fracking fluids, pharmaceutical products, pesticides, animal and human waste and decay, and plastics. Our dependency on oil has led to a number of off-shore drilling sites, which, on occasion, spring leaks of petroleum into the bodies of water that house these rigs. The shipping of petroleum has led to spills into the water as well (i.e., the 1989 Exxon *Valdez* spill). While we can only go without oxygen for seconds or minutes, most humans can live between three to eight or more days (depending on such variables as how much water-rich foods, such as fruits, juices, or vegetgables, the person consumes in their regular diet and the environmental conditions the person is exposed to) without water. That is of little consolation once we reach the breaking point of dehydration. Since water constitutes a basic essential of life, reason and rationality dictate that we do all that we can to keep it clean and assure that everyone has access to clean drinking water. In the United States, Trump has been on a mission to curtail all the good that former president Obama accomplished in his two terms. In effect, Trump has declared war on the environment. In September 2019, the Trump administration revoked an Obama-era regulation that shielded many US wetlands and streams from pollution. "The 2015 Waters of the United States rule defined the waterways subject to federal regulation," putting an end to a patchwork of clean water regulations (Flesher 2019:A6). Denying waterways with the necessary protections needed from developers and farmers potentially subjects millions of Americans to less safe drinking water, increases the chances that the wetlands will be damaged due to flooding, and inhibits natural filtering of pollutants that can harm multitudes of fish, waterfowl, and other wildlife, environmentalists contend (Flesher 2019).

A third type of pollution is land pollution. Assuming we have breathable air and drinkable water, the next thing humans need to secure is shelter and food. As land creatures, we tend to find our shelter and most of our food supplies on land. We build our homes, domesticate animals, establish businesses, and so on, all on land. We also grow our food and have our animals (which will be consumed by humans) graze on land. Vegetarians and vegans find most of their food on land too. So, what exactly is land and land pollution? *Land* is defined as the thin layer of topsoil on the Earth's surface that forms continents and islands. *Land pollution*, then, refers to the deposition of solid or liquid waste materials on land or underground in a manner that can contaminate the soil and groundwater, threaten public health, and cause unsightly conditions and nuisances. Land pollution often has a carry-over effect to water pollution as deposited contaminants tend to run off into bodies of waters (e.g., streams, rivers, lakes, seas, and oceans). Land pollution results in the deterioration or destruction of the Earth's land surfaces that is often directly or indirectly as a result of human activities, especially the use of pesticides. Examining all the data on pesticide use across the globe is maddening and far too extensive to review here. Suffice it to say, there are tens of thousands of different pesticides in use and many of these not only cause harm to air, water, and land, but are harmful and potentially deadly to humans and other animal species. Consider this one example from July 2019 when the EPA approved broad new applications for a controversial insecticide that contains compounds (e.g., sulfoxaflor, which acts as a neurotoxin to affected insects through contact or ingestion) responsible for eviscerating the US's bee population (Dennis 2019). Farmers will now be able to apply this new pesticide to a wide range of crops, including citrus, strawberries, pineapples, pumpkins, corn, and soybeans. And while this is a "highly effective" tool for farmers, it is also "very highly toxic" to bees and has been linked to developmental disorders and neurological damage in humans (Mohan 2019). The EPA decision, which environmentalists and beekeepers vow to fight, comes at a very bad time as commercial honeybee colonies are declining at a startling rate (Dennis 2019). Bees, in case you are unaware, are easily among the most important insects to human food production (they help provide us with our favorite fruits and vegetables); they pollinate wildflowers and thus benefit biodiversity and beautify landscapes and gardens. It should be noted that in August 2019, the state of California took formal legal steps to ban the use of this pesticide that had been rescued from elimination by the Trump administration. This move to protect the environment, bees, and humans is unlikely to be challenged by the EPA as California "often goes its own way on environmental matters, including auto emissions and climate regulation" (Mohan 2019:C1).

We have already seen how deadly chemicals can cause air, water, and land pollution so it stands to reason that chemical pollution is another thing that can harm the environment. We cannot escape the influence of chemicals on our life. If you smoke cigarettes you already know that you purposively consume over 4,000 chemicals, including 43 known cancer-causing carcinogenic compounds and 400 other toxins that include nicotine, tar, carbon monoxide, formaldehyde, ammonia, hydrogen cyanide, arsenic, and DDT. Smoking affects the smoker and second-hand smoke affects anyone in immediate proximity to the smoker. These 4,000 chemicals represent just a small percentage of 83,000 chemicals identified in the Toxic Substances Control Act (TSCA) Inventory. As new chemicals are commercially manufactured or imported, they are added to the list (EPA 2018). Mass-produced chemicals represent a potential large-scale problem, but so too do small-scale chemical operations (e.g., illegal drug labs).

Trying to lessen our dependency on fossil fuels means that we must find alternative energy sources. There are many challenges to reaching this goal: some governments are not looking for alternatives; we are good at developing energy from fossil fuels; for now, there seems to be a large supply of fossil fuels; the rich and powerful are getting richer and more powerful by keeping the world dependent on fossil fuels; the development of alternative energy sources is slowed by the lack of a huge financial commitment to accomplish a break from fossil fuels; and alternative sources have certain drawbacks themselves. One such alternative energy source is nuclear energy. Globally, nuclear energy provides about 11 percent of the world's electricity from about 450 power reactors (World Nuclear Association 2019). Nuclear energy has one big advantage over the burning of fossil fuels: it does not release carbon dioxide into the atmosphere. There are, however, many potential problems associated with nuclear energy, including: industrial accidents and nuclear meltdowns; radioactive waste; the high economic cost of running a nuclear power plant; and the concern over nuclear sources of energy being converted into weapons of mass destruction that might get into the "wrong hands." Nuclear waste becomes the key aspect when defining nuclear pollution. With these ideas in mind, the Organization for Economic Cooperation and Development (OECD) (2001) defines nuclear waste pollution as pollution "created by mishandling and inappropriate storage of spent nuclear fuel rods, and pieces of protective clothing and tools that have become contaminated, and by insecure transportation of highly radioactive material over long distances to a processing plant." Nuclear accidents such as the one that occurred in Pripyat, Ukraine at the Chernobyl Nuclear Power Plant in 1986 highlights fears that many people have about nuclear energy. (See Box 3.1 for a further discussion of the Chernobyl disaster.)

When combined, the nearly 8 billion people in the world consume vast amounts of food and consumer products that eventually become solid waste. Solid waste is often a polite way of describing garbage. The New York State Department of Environmental Conservation (2019) defines solid waste as

> any garbage, refuse, sludge from a wastewater treatment plant, water supply treatment plant, or air pollution control facility and other discarded materials including solid, liquid, semi-solid, or contained gaseous material, resulting from industrial, commercial, mining and agricultural operations, and from community activities, but does not include solid or dissolved materials in domestic sewage, or solid or dissolved materials in irrigation return flows or industrial discharges....

The lengthy definition goes on to include statute information but, suffice it to say, while many things constitute solid waste, according to the State of New York not everything we might consider garbage falls under the umbrella. We can view *solid waste pollution* as any garbage that is not properly disposed of or recycled and ends up on land or in water resulting in a negative impact on the environment.

Of all the forms of pollution found on our planet, noise pollution is the least likely to quicken our demise due to the sixth mass extinction and yet it is a very real irritant and a cause of poor health for many. *Noise pollution* is any unwanted or disturbing sound. Noise becomes unwanted when it interferes with normal activities such as sleeping, conversation, or in any way that compromises one's quality of life. While noise pollution is generally considered an urban problem because of the unrelenting clash of sounds in the environment it can affect people and other species wherever there is a loud source of noise (e.g., a manufacturing company, high-traffic areas, and large farms). Noise pollution has been attributed to stress-related illnesses, high blood pressure, speech interference, hearing loss, sleep disruption, and lost productivity. Noise pollution does not affect just humans; instead, many animal species are bothered by loud noises. If you own a dog, chances are you already know how much the sounds of fireworks adversely affect your pet.

The final form of pollution to be discussed does not occur on the planet's surface but instead exists in the celestial world. *Celestial pollution* refers to space debris or "space junk" that can be both natural (meteoroid) and artificial (man-made). NASA (2013b) makes a general distinction between space junk that is natural as "orbital debris," as it arrived in the Earth's atmosphere as a result of coming into contact with our gravitational pull, and man-made junk. Man-made space junk circling our planet comes in the form of rocket fragments, used-up boosters, Soviet nuclear reactors, and obsolete satellites. This space trash orbits our planet at speeds of up to 17,500 mph, fast enough for a relatively small piece of orbital debris to damage a satellite, the International Space Station, space shuttles, and other spacecraft with humans aboard. (If President Trump follows through on his "space force" idea, the potential sixth branch of the US military, the threat of celestial pollution cannot be ignored as those military personnel stationed in space would be at risk of space debris.) NASA takes the threat of space debris very seriously. NASA (2013b) has

> a long-standing set of guidelines on how to deal with each potential collision threat. These guidelines, part of a larger body of decision-making aids known as flight rules, specify when the expected proximity of a piece of debris increases the probability of a collision enough that evasive action or other precautions to ensure the safety of the crew are needed.

NASA (2013b) estimates that there are more than 20,000 pieces of debris larger than a softball orbiting the Earth. Any space debris currently in orbit, or future debris (e.g., additional satellites and rockets and potential space force military-related weaponry), could find its way crashing to the Earth's surface, causing harm to ecosystems.

The review of the primary types of pollution is critical for the overall understanding of the harm that humans are causing the environment. While there somehow exist people who question the legitimacy of the scientific evidence that proves climate change is real and that humans contribute to it, there is no denying the legitimacy of the existence of pollution and its harm on the environment. And yet, there may still be people who think the environment is fine even with climate change and pollution, so let's provide more evidence of the attacks on the environment as a result of human action. Discussion begins with hydraulic fracturing.

Hydraulic fracturing, commonly known as hydrofracking, combines the dangers associated with the dependency on fossil fuels and water, air, and land pollution. In other words, it represents a blatant attack on the environment and contributes to the sixth mass extinction. This is the type of "daily double" we are better off without. *Fracking* involves a controversial method of drilling for natural gas. On the plus side, of all the types of fossil fuels, natural gas is the cleanest burning, but it still is a fossil fuel and its drilling methods are what cause harm to the environment. The method used to drill for natural gas involves the hydraulic fracturing of layers of rock with an infusion of water and hundreds of potentially deadly toxins to allow for maximum extraction. The hydraulic fracture is formed when a fracking fluid is pumped down the well at pressures that exceed the rock strength, causing open fractures to form in the rock. Environmentalists, medical practitioners, and residents of communities near fracturing sites have expressed numerous concerns as a result of fracking. Among these concerns are undersurface disturbances (e.g., earthquakes); land surface disturbances; the high volume of water used during the course of the fracking process; exposure to deadly chemicals; the release of high levels of methane; the potentiality of underground and standing water contamination; the destruction of aesthetic beauty in the fracking areas; and the overall cost-benefits analysis of hydraulic fracking. Not surprisingly, proponents of fossil fuels and the power elites that support Big Oil discount all these harmful claims. There is encouraging news for those who want to protect the environment for present and future generations and that is the fact that many countries, including Ireland, France, Germany, Romania, and Bulgaria, have banned fracking.

Demonstrating the depths that he is willing to go in order to win his war against the environment, on August 29, 2019 Trump announced his far-reaching plan to cut back on the regulation of methane emissions, a major contributor to climate change (Friedman and Davenport 2019). The Environmental Protection Agency, a once well-respected government agency until the Trump Administration got its hands on it, aims to "eliminate federal requirements that oil and gas companies install technology to detect and fix methane leaks from wells, pipelines and storage facilities. It will also reopen the question of whether the E.P.A. even has the legal authority to regulate methane as a pollutant" (Friedman and Davenport 2019). This insane idea is a sure sign of the growing darkness that surrounds us. "Methane, the main component of natural gas, is an extremely powerful greenhouse gas, as much as 80 times more potent than carbon dioxide in its impact on the climate.… Leaks from equipment and pipelines release it into the atmosphere" (Diaz 2019:A7). The Obama administration adopted a rule in 2016 that ordered the oil and gas industry to step up its monitoring to look for leaks and to take new steps to prevent them (Diaz 2019). Trump, as stated previously, is eager to eliminate the environmental protections established by his predecessor and supports the fossil fuel industry, environment be damned. While carbon dioxide is the most significant greenhouse gas, methane is a close second and currently makes up nearly 10 percent of greenhouse gas emissions in the United States. A significant amount of this methane comes from the oil and gas industry and other leading sources include cattle and agriculture (Friedman and Davenport 2019).

The next area of concern involves the use of plastics. In the 1950s and 1960s, the production of plastics first boomed. Plastics had all sorts of consumer and industrial applications. They seemed to make life so much easier. While a glass container of milk would break if you accidentally dropped it, a plastic container would not. It seemed as though plastics were a major achievement in human ingenuity. *Plastics* are chains of like molecules linked together. Each molecule can have thousands of atoms bound together. Chains of linked molecules are referred to as polymers—which is why the names of many plastics begin with "poly," such as polyethylene, polystyrene, and polypropylene. These plastic materials contain various elements such as carbon, hydrogen, oxygen, nitrogen, chlorine, and sulfur (American Chemistry Council 2019). *Plastic pollution* refers to the harmful accumulation of plastic products on land and water. Plastic pollution harms the environment by adversely affecting wildlife, wildlife habitat, and humans.

Until recently nearly all plastics were non-biodegradable, meaning that every piece of plastic ever made still exists. In 2017, there was 348 metric tons of plastics produced (*Statista* 2019). The *National Geographic* (2018) reports that 91 percent of all plastics are not recycled. Of the 78 million metric tons of plastics produced in the United States annually, 32 percent flow into our ocean—the equivalent of pouring one garbage truck of plastic into the ocean every minute (EarthDay.org 2018). Scientists have recently discovered high levels of microplastics in the seemingly pristine Arctic that were likely carried north by the atmosphere (Khan 2019). Discarded plastics are found in our oceans and they have washed up on the shores of remote islands. There is so much plastic trash in the Pacific Ocean that an island larger than the size of Texas exists—it is known as the Great Pacific Garbage Patch. Much of our plastic consumption is unnecessary, including plastic bottles (e.g., humans buy one million plastic bottles per minute; Americans purchase 50 billion water bottles per year), plastic bags (there are an estimated four trillion plastic bags used worldwide annually and only 1 percent are returned for recycling), drinking straws (half a million straws are used in the world every day), cups (500 billion disposable cups are consumed every year), and so on.

Plastic pollution is so serious and so undeniable that there is a social movement to help eliminate our dependence on plastics that actually is beginning to gain results. Plastic straws and bags are banned at an increasing number of grocery stores and restaurants and a growing number of people are drinking water from reusable bottles.

Food waste is the next topic. *Food waste* includes uneaten portions of meals and trimmings from food preparation activities in kitchens, restaurants, fast-food chains, and cafeterias (Miller 2012). Anyone who has worked at a restaurant, especially a buffet restaurant, or a school cafeteria has an idea of how much food is wasted. Food waste also occurs during industrial processing and distribution. *Food waste pollution* refers to food waste that ends up in landfills resulting in the production of methane (a more powerful greenhouse gas than even CO_2) (MoveForHunger.org 2019). Food waste causes biodiversity loss at the global level because in order to maximize agricultural yields, farmers have increasingly invaded wild areas in search of more fertile lands to grow food. Unconsumed food accounts for approximately 1.4 billion hectares of land, constituting almost one-third of the planet's agricultural land. Because of wasted food, a corresponding amount of freshwater was also wasted (Conserve Energy Future 2019a). As this snapshot view of food waste reveals, when food is wasted it represents not only food that a hungry person could have consumed but harms the environment in many significant ways.

Another detrimental activity of humans that contributes to a deteriorating environment is harmful agricultural practices. Trying to find the balance of feeding the more than 7.7 billion in the world and doing it in an environmentally friendly manner has become increasingly difficult and eventually something will have to give. These consequences could include billions of people literally starving to death, the outbreak of wars to find food, mass immigration to escape famine, or the lack of land to grow food (especially as it is connected to food waste). *Agricultural pollution* is the result of trying to develop means of farming and agriculture to feed all the people of the world and comes in many forms including the following: the use of pesticides and fertilizers (the introduction of unnatural chemicals to ecosystems);

the use of contaminated water for irrigation (other forms of pollution find their way into underground reservoirs, canals, and rain); soil erosion and sedimentations (due to inefficient farming practices the top soil is open to erosion); livestock grazing on agricultural land that could grow a much higher food yield in the form of vegetables (this is a topic that has become quite political in the United States as some people are comparing the "threat" to take away their sources of meat akin to trying to take away their guns); and pests and weeds that choke off attempts to grow food and often result in the use of deadly pesticides (like those that kill honeybees described earlier) (Conserve Energy Future 2019b).

The next human attack on the environment is deforestation. Deforestation refers to the clearing, or permanent removal, of the Earth's forests on a massive scale, almost always resulting in damage to the quality of the land, causing soil erosion, poor water quality, reduced food security, impaired flood protection, and an even greater number of people moving to urban areas (Smith 2012). Trees are so important to life and yet, as the world seeks to slow the pace of climate change, preserve wildlife, and support billions of people, the mass destruction of trees (deforestation) continues, sacrificing the long-term benefits of standing trees for the short-term gain of using trees for building purposes (Nunez 2019). The good news is that forests still cover about 30 percent of the world's land area, but the bad news is that they are disappearing at an alarming rate—between 1990 and 2016, the world lost 502,000 square miles (1.3 million square kilometers) of forest. Trees are critical in that they absorb not only the carbon dioxide that we exhale, but also the heat-trapping greenhouse gases that human activities emit (Nunez 2019). The biggest culprit in deforestation is Brazil and its treatment of the Amazon rainforest. The Amazon rainforest extends across a huge part of South America with approximately 60 percent of it located in Brazil. The Amazon rainforest is considered so important to the Earth that it is referred to as the "lungs of our planet." As a true sign of the human threat to the environment, Brazil elected Jair Bolsonaro in 2018 as the new president. Bolsonaro—sometimes called the Trump of the Tropics—promised to open up the Amazonian rainforest to agriculture and industrial development (Wernick 2019). He has also said with regard to the many indigenous tribes that live in the Amazon that he wishes the Brazilian cavalry had been "as efficient as the U.S. in exterminating Indians" (Hance 2019). Like Trump, Bolsonaro likes to make cabinet appointments that are extreme. His foreign minister, Ernesto Araujo, for example, believes that climate change is part of plot by "cultural Marxists" to stifle Western economies and promote growth of China. Araujo also blogs about the "criminalization of red meat, oil and heterosexual sex" (Watts 2018). It looks like the rainforest in Brazil will be subject to the unenlightened and irrational whims of those who would prefer to hasten the sixth mass extinction.

Unfortunately, as early as August 2019 we found out just how dangerous unreasoned thought can be as Brazil's rainforest was confronted with a record number of fires. The National Institute for Space Research said there had been an 83 percent increase compared to the same period in 2018 and more than half of those fires occurred in the Amazon rainforest (BBC News 2019a). A combination of

Bolsonaro's disregard for the environment and cattle ranchers burning large tracts of the forest (an example of a harmful agricultural practice) so that their cattle could have grazing pasture were among the primary culprits of these fires. Cattle need a great deal of pasture to graze; it is generally recommended that two to five acres per cow be allocated. Bolsonaro has repeatedly "been accused of harming the Amazon rainforest and indigenous peoples in order to benefit loggers, miners and farmers who helped get him elected" (Garrand 2019).

Our next topic is marine debris. *Marine debris pollution* is defined as "any persistent solid material that is manufactured or processed and directly or indirectly, intentionally or unintentionally, disposed of or abandoned into the marine environment or the Great Lakes" (NOAA 2019e). NOAA (2019e) reports that no place on Earth is immune to marine debris and that a majority of the trash and debris that covers our beaches comes from storm drains and sewers, as well as from shoreline and recreational activities such as picnicking and beachgoing. Abandoned fishing gear is another significant problem as it can entangle, injure, maim, and drown marine wildlife and damage property. As described with the review of plastics, marine debris is illustrated by the "Great Pacific Garbage Patch," or "Garbage Island" for short. This "island" is a floating landfill of trash and marine debris in the Pacific Ocean north of Hawaii. Garbage Island is harmful to the environment in general but also to a great number of specific sea creatures such as sea turtles, seabirds, and seals, and marine vegetation life such as coral reefs (Howell et al. 2012).

Think of all the electronic devices (e-devices) you own. Now think about all the e-devices you have owned in your life. How did you dispose of your past e-devices and how will you dispose of your current e-devices when they need to be upgraded? While many people are conscientious and try to dispose of e-devices the "right way" by taking them to centers that collect such devices as televisions, computers, and smartphones, what happens to them after that? These are just a few of the questions that surround e-waste (electronic waste). *E-waste* refers to refuse created by discarded electronic devices and components as well as substances involved in their manufacture or use that can be hazardous, including heavy metals and glass (EPA South Australia 2019; Rouse 2019). The amount of e-waste is staggering. In 2013 the world produced nearly 54 million tons (49 million metric tons) of used electrical and electronic products. "That's an average of about 43 lbs. (20 kg), or the weight of eight bricks, for each of the 7 billion people on Earth" (Lewis 2013). E-waste contains toxins that pose risks to humans and other living species. Mercury, for example, a toxin found in fluorescent lamps, printed circuit boards, laptops, and LCD screen backlights, can adversely affect human health, marine life, and vegetation. When e-waste is collected for managed disposal it is often exported to foreign facilities that specialize in tearing apart electronic devices for recyclable parts such as the components of circuit boards. E-waste represents a serious problem in the future as its negative carry-over effect is felt on land, in water, and in air.

The final topic to be discussed with regard to unenlightened and irrational thought on matters of the environment is medical waste. Medical waste is a much bigger problem than most people realize. However, if you work in the medical profession or have had a prolonged hospital visit, you begin to get a sense of just how much medical waste is created and must be disposed of. *Medical waste* includes all waste generated by health institutions, research institutes, and laboratories; it also includes the waste originating from health care done at home (e.g., dialysis, insulin injections, and blood sugar tests) (Brasovean et al. 2010). A great deal of medical waste is hazardous and contains toxins or chemicals and poses environmental threat. Proper disposal is critical as the last thing anyone wants is to go to the beach and see that medical waste such hypodermic needles have washed ashore, as has happened on occasion. For example, in 2018, hypodermic needles and other medical waste washed ashore on several beaches on the South Shore of Long Island (ABC7 2018).

Pseudoscience: a by-product of unreasoned and irrational thinking

In this chapter we have examined the darkness that surrounds us from the perspective of unenlightened and irrational thought that has led people to attack the value of higher education, question the validity of science, ignore warnings of our dependency on fossil fuels, and continue to the destroy the planet we live on. This willingness to ignore factual information provided by science is often compounded in unreasoned thought via the acceptance of pseudoscience.

Believing in false science

Pseudoscience is a system of beliefs, theories, assertions, and practices mistakenly regarded as scientific when, in fact, they are not. Pseudoscience literally means false science as the Greek root *pseudo* means false and the English word *science* from the Latin word *scientia* means knowledge. Pseudoscience, then, can be viewed as fake science and false knowledge. The common example provided to explain the difference between science and pseudoscience is that astronomy is a science, but astrology is a pseudoscience. Other examples of pseudoscience are psychokinesis, clairvoyance, fortune telling, and palm reading.

People believe in pseudoscience much for the same reasons as many believe in religion: they are looking for answers to questions that are designed to give hope and faith. The failure to accept the death of a loved one may lead the grieving person to seek help from a religious leader or it may lead to the search of a fortune teller who serves as a sort of life consultant. People believe in fortune telling or any form of pseudoscience just as religious people believe in a religion—because they need to believe. Let's take a brief look at some of the variations of pseudoscience, beginning with astrology.

Astrology is a pseudoscience that involves the study of the movements and relative positions of celestial bodies that are interpreted as having an influence on human activities. A horoscope helps to predict a number of things relative to specific persons born under an astrological sign (i.e., the Zodiac). Alyson Mead (2015) states, "Astrology is the study of the planets and how they relate to us on Earth and to one another in the sky. Each planet exerts an influence and with astrology, these planetary influences are simpler to interpret when you understand how to read the birth chart" (p. 9). Juliana McCarthy (2018), an astrologist, believes that astrology is a language much like mythology that provides stories to help people keep on-track in life or help them to get back onto the right path. "By learning the language of the sky, we can commune with planets and stars, discovering important messages about who we are. The stars are speaking to us—astrology teaches us how to listen" (McCarthy 2018:1). The correct path in life is predicated by one's astrological birth chart, according to McCarthy.

The practice of astrology has been around for nearly four millennia. "Astrology is an ancient practice, originating more than two thousand years ago. In the second millennium BC, the Babylonians became the first to develop an organized system of astrology. Initially, they used it to predict the seasons and the weather. Later, it became a form of celestial divination" (McCarthy 2018:4). (The *practice of divination* involves uncovering hidden knowledge by supernatural means.) Nine centuries later, the Chinese began to use a system of astrology and other civilizations followed suit (Mead 2015). Despite the lack of credible scientific validity, astrology remains popular, perhaps as much because it serves as a form of entertainment as it does as the pretense of science. "Today, astrology seems to be more popular than ever. There are close to ten million astrologers working in the United States, over two million websites that mention astrology, and an increasing number of universities including astrology in their curricula" (McCarthy 2018:6). It is one thing when people check their astrological forecast for entertainment purposes, but another thing entirely when a US president relies on an astrologer to help determine his schedule, as was the case with Ronald Reagan and his astrologer Joan Quigley. Reagan's wife Nancy had first enlisted Quigley's astrological advice on a regular basis via frequent telephone conversations following the assassination attempt on the president on March 30, 1981, but before long she had the president's ear as well (Associated Press 2014).

A second variation of pseudoscience is clairvoyance. From the French, *clair* means "clear" and *voyance* means "vision." Thus, *clairvoyance* refers to the ability of gaining knowledge not present to the senses but instead via extrasensory perception, acute intuitive insight, or perceptiveness. Chauran (2014) adds, "Psychic perception simply means that you receive information through your senses other than your usual five" (p. 3). Weschcke and Slate (2013) make a distinction between religion and psychic empowerment by claiming that religion teaches a "greater power" that is external to us whereas a true understanding of self must come from an internal or "personal power." Psychic empowerment techniques help people to reach their inner selves. Clairvoyance is the key to finding our self-empowerment, Weschcke and Slate propose. "Clairvoyance is not a specific psychic ability but rather is—along with astral projection—a master system and faculty that functions in the background of all forms of divination" (Weschcke and Slate 2013:xiv). The popularity of this unreasoned form of thinking is demonstrated in a number of ways including that "Psychic empowerment programs are being developed for application in everyday activities—in business & professional training, in creativity and communications work, in sales and customer service, and in areas still thought of as 'paranormal' but rapidly become *normal*" (Weschcke and Slate 2013:xiv). It is proposed here that it is a belief in science that should be "normal," not a belief in pseudoscience.

Psychics claim to possess a type of clairvoyance that allows them to speak with the dead; they may also claim to have visions of the future and to communicate with the living telepathically. *Mediums* also claim to have clairvoyance but their abilities are limited to a communication between the dead and living human beings. *Mediumship* refers to this process of contact. Mediums claim to channel the spirits of the deceased that the living, usually grieving family members who have recently lost a loved one wish to contact. As grieving people tend to be quite emotional and distraught and desperate to find some sort of solace, there is a great deal of fraud associated with psychics and mediums who will gladly accept payment for a service that is very much a pseudoscience.

The next type of pseudoscience to be discussed is fortune telling. *Fortune telling* involves forecasting future events about a person's life. A *fortune teller* is a person who foretells a personal future. There are at least 50 different techniques that may be used in an effort to predict future events, including: aeromancy (fortune telling using the weather), astrology, capnomancy (assigning meaning to the shapes formed in smoke from candles, fire, burning herbs, or incense), casting or bone reading (throwing charms and interpreting how they land in relation to each other or how they fall on a divination board), crystal ball reading, domino divination (using regular domino tiles), fortune cookies, iching (throwing coins multiple times), numerology (the use of numbers), Ouija (using Ouija boards—once a popular form of entertainment with the upper classes), palmistry (commonly known as palm reading), Tarot (reading Tarot cards), and tasseomancy (tealeaf reading) (DivinatioandFortuneTelling.com 2017). Some sort of fortune telling has been going on for thousands of years as people in pre-Enlightenment eras had difficulty understanding a number of events and attempted to find solace in those who could provide reassurance that their futures would be fine. In some cases, however, predictions of a bright future were not offered. While some people believed in the validity of fortune telling in past centuries it was done mostly for entertainment purposes. Touchkoff (1992) describes how in pre-Revolution (1917) Russia it was common for families to attend church on Sundays and then return home for a reading. "One person would do a reading, while the rest of the family or friends would sit around the table, listen and make contributions. This was a time before table games or encounter sessions were developed" (p. 3). In this regard, it was clear that fortune telling was a form of entertainment and a community bonding practice.

Today, there are many US states that have made fortune telling illegal. In New York State, for example, NYS Section 165.35 makes fortune telling illegal unless it is specified by the fortune teller that the session is for entertainment purposes only. The laws that make various types of fortune telling illegal are generally centered on the idea that fortune tellers must claim that what they do is something that is not scientifically verifiable. Then again, the people who believe in fortune tellers are generally looking for non-scientific answers to their problems.

Another variation of pseudoscience is psychokinesis. *Psychokinesis*, or *telekinesis*, can be defined as the alleged psychic ability of a person to use their mind over matter to manipulate physical objects with the mind. Seemingly defying the laws of science, psychokinesis challenges what is perceived to be physical "reality" (Hawking 2018). Hawking (2018) believes in the power of psychokinesis and has claimed to witness many such examples that "demonstrated the power of consciousness in a manner not so much defying the classic laws of physics as making them seem irrelevant, and thereby revealing the presumed mechanical laws of nature to be no more than intellectual concepts or 'models,' as physicists call them." There is no conclusive evidence that psychokinesis is real and it therefore falls under the domain of pseudoscience. But, as Scott Lilienfeld writes in the foreword of *Pseudoscience: The Conspiracy Against Science* (2019), "We find ourselves living increasingly in a 'post-truth' world, one in which emotions and opinions count for more than well-established findings when it comes to evaluation assertions" (p. xi). And this statement helps to connect the darkness that surrounds us with pseudoscience.

A particularly interesting variation of pseudoscience is voodoo. The word "voodoo" means "spirit of God" (Alvarado 2011). *Voodoo* is "a fusion of religious practices from Africa that takes on different characteristics and emphases when practiced in various locations" (*Religious Facts* 2019). In Louisiana, voodoo is heavily influenced by French, Spanish, and Creole populations that reside in the state and it is also influenced by Christianity, especially Roman Catholicism. Haitian voodoo is heavily influenced by African slaves from France, and also by Christianity, especially Roman Catholicism. West African voodoo represents the origin these religious practices and has as a primary influence Christianity and particularly Roman Catholicism (Religious Facts 2019). Voodoo generally involves the use of religious amulets believed to ward off evil spirits and other variations utilize objects such as the popularized voodoo doll. Much of voodoo is the result of folklore and the oral tradition of indigenous knowledge. Those skilled in the voodoo magic are referred to as priestesses and priests, mambos, Santeros, and houngans, and perform ritualistic behaviors as a service, especially for healing (Alvarado 2011). While there isn't any scientific proof of the validity of voodoo, most people are uncomfortable if a voodoo priestess curses them or creates a voodoo doll that resembles them.

Undoubtedly, everyone has heard of witchcraft. *Witchcraft* involves the practice, or craft, of using magical and supernatural powers via the use of invocations in order to control people or events. Elaborating on the meaning of witchcraft, Anastasia Greywolf (2016) states, "Witchcraft means many different things to many different people. But on the whole, it is the study of how to harness energies as well as unleash the power within" (p. 3). To harness these energies, witches will utilize magic, spells, and potions. Some proponents of witchcraft view it as a religion. As Buckland (2002) states, "Witchcraft is not a step backward; a retreat into a more superstition-filled time. Far from it. It is a step forward. Witchcraft is a religion far more relevant to the times than the vast majority of established churches" (p. xvii). Buckland adds, "The Craft is a religion of love and joy. It is not full of the gloom of Christianity, with its ideas of original sin, with salvation and happiness possible only in the afterlife" (p. 11). Just as the term "witchcraft" has many meanings, so too does the concept of "witch." Generally, a *witch* is a woman who is thought to have magical or supernatural powers, especially evil ones, and practices the dark arts (magic used mainly to cause harm, exert control over, or even kill the intended targeted victim). In some instances, males might also be witches but they are more likely to be viewed as warlocks. Some people view witches in a more positive light such as that of healer, teacher, giver, seeker, and protector (Celtic Connection 2019).

Within the world of witchery, there is a disagreement about whether or not witchcraft is a religion. According to Celtic Connection (which states on its homepage that it has been "Serving the Wiccan and Pagan Community Since 1997"), there is a distinction between Wicca and witchcraft: Wicca is a religion while witchcraft is not. (This counters Buckland's above claim.) *Wicca* is a belief system and way of life based upon the reconstruction of pre-Christian traditions (paganism) originating in Ireland, Scotland, and Wales (Celtic Connection 2019). *Wiccans* profess a deep appreciation and awe of nature and show reverence to Mother Earth; they perform rituals and celebrate outdoors to further strengthen their connection to nature.

While proponents of Wicca and witchcraft claim both to be based on religious principles they are also both based on a system of magic.

And finally, we have superstition. *Superstition* is a belief, notion, or practice resulting from irrationality, ignorance, fear of the unknown, trust in magic, chance, or the supernatural, and a false conception of causation. It is this misguided belief in magic as a false belief in causation that makes superstition an example of pseudoscience. *Superstitious* persons find causal relations between certain behaviors and outcomes where they do not really exist (a type of *post hoc* reasoning). Many people, for example, worry about a "jinx" as if it is real. Pointing out someone's good fortune (e.g., you are the healthiest person I know) is interpreted by superstitious persons as a sure sign of a jinx or hex that will now bring about bad health (causation). Superstitious behavior can be found around the world and the sportsworld in particular is ripe with superstitious beliefs and behaviors. Akin to the health jinx just described, it is bad protocol in American baseball to tell a pitcher he only needs to get three more outs in the ninth inning to complete the rare and highly valued no-hitter. The pitcher and his (or her) teammates might assume a jinx has been uttered and that the pitcher will now allow a base hit in the ninth inning. Athletes may only eat a certain meal on game day, prepare in the locker room a certain way, play only specific music prior to the start of the game, and so on. Sports fans may wear a "lucky" cap or shirt on game day, sit in a specific spot while watching the game, eat specific foods before/during/after the game, engage in chanting rituals, and so on. While most people recognize that there is not a direct correlation between a fan wearing a certain article of clothing and a favorable outcome, they engage in superstitious behavior because they feel as though they are a part of the game. Athletes engage in superstitious behaviors because it may give them confidence to perform well on the playing field.

A belief in religion and prayer is similar to superstitious behavior in that people are looking for some sort of magical or divine intervention. While there are occasions when engaging in ritualistic behaviors does accompany a favorable outcome, there are far more times when it does not. But in either scenario, there is no scientific evidence of cause and effect.

German sociologist and philosopher Max Horkheimer, a proponent of reason and enlightened thought, believed that the enlightened person would not be bothered by superstitious beliefs and other irrationalities. Horkheimer (1947) states, "If by enlightenment and intellectual progress we mean the freeing of man from superstitious belief in evil forces, in demons and fairies, in blind fate—in short, the emancipation from fear—then denunciation of what is currently called reason is the greatest service reason can render" (p. 187).

Thinking that is devoid of reason

Often, people seem to engage in "ignorant" and "stupid" behaviors, as if they are not thinking at all. Ignorance refers to a lack of knowledge, awareness, or information on a topic, whereas stupidity refers to behavior that shows a lack of good sense or judgment. Ignorance and stupidity are two important reasons why formal education is so important. People who act in an ignorant or stupid manner seem to violate common sense, let alone rational and reasoned thought. In my book *Common Sense* (2019), I discuss many impediments to common sense, including a belief in pseudoscience (described above), poor socialization, lack of a formal higher education, overly emotional and irrational fear, believing in weird things (e.g., pseudoscience, superstitions, and other oddities), and ignorance and stupidity. Discussion here will be limited to two specific case examples of thinking that demonstrate a complete lack of scientific thinking—that the Earth is flat and that humans and dinosaurs roamed the Earth together just 6,000 to 9,000 years ago.

Trying to argue with people who lack common and scientific sense is both easy (when you are armed with scientific truths, you know your argument is correct) and frustrating (many people do not want their beliefs countered by facts and dig in with their irrational viewpoint every step of the way). Perhaps one of the oddest beliefs that one can hold, and certainly one that is devoid of reason, is the idea that the Earth is flat. We can skip a long, drawn-out conversation by simply stating our closing remarks—if the world were flat, wouldn't we have found the end edges by now?! To be flat and not to have found the edges would imply that the Earth has an infinite land mass that no one has yet been able to navigate. Satellite photos and photos taken from the Moon and other planets (via space probes) also clearly reveal that the Earth is round. And yet, there are still a few people who think the world is flat but provide no empirical evidence (they do have maps but fail to explain how we cannot find the literal edge). There is a home for such irrational people who believe in a flat Earth and that place is the Flat Earth Society. On their website is this mission statement: "The mission of the Flat Earth Society is to promote and initiate discussion of Flat Earth theory as well as archive Flat Earth literature. Our forums act as a venue to encourage free thinking and debate" (Flat Earth Society 2016). The site adds, "The Flat Earth Society mans the guns against oppression of thought and the Globularist lies of a new age." The term "globularist" to describe those who believe the Earth is spherical is clever but unreasoned nonetheless. (An interesting note: the Flat Earth Society website has not been updated in three years; infer from this what you will.)

One other example of thinking that is devoid of reason is the belief that the Earth is less than 10,000 years old. Earlier in this chapter we learned that former Representative Paul Broun (R, Georgia) believes that the Earth is no more than 9,000 years old and that it was literally created in six days. We also learned that Representative Jesse Kremer believes that the planet is only 6,000 years old. Where do people come up with such unreasoned notions when science has repeatedly proven that the planet is approximately 4.5 billions years old? The most common reply to this question is a belief in creationism. Former Alaska governor Sarah Palin, the 2008 Republican running mate of presidential hopeful Senator John McCain (Arizona), is a creationist and she too believes that the planet has only existed for less than 10,000 years. While mayor of Wasilla, Alaska, Palin revealed that she was a Young Earth creationist, accepting both that the world was about 6,000-plus years old and that humans and dinosaurs walked the Earth at the same time (*Canberra Times* 2008). There are so many things wrong with such a belief—where do we begin to point out the errors? For one, Palin is the daughter of a science teacher and she is a supposed energy expert (*Canberra Times* 2008), so how is it possible to have oil from fossil fuels if the planet and the existence of dinosaurs is only thousands of years old?

From their website, we can gather that the biblical Young Earth Creationist perspective is rooted in the readings of such books as the Bible and Qur'an, which both contain nearly parallel accounts of a six-day creation, a belief in Adam and Eve in the Garden of Eden, and Noah's flood (NW Creation Network 2019). The site uses a number of pseudoscience arguments to try and convince people of the validity of the Young Earth belief, but in every case legitimate science has an answer.

Connecting enlightened rational thought with popular culture

BOX 3.1 CHERNOBYL: FROM NUCLEAR ACCIDENT TO POPULAR TV SHOW AND TOURIST ATTRACTION

In this chapter we learned that while nuclear energy has certain advantages over fossil fuel, the concern over potential nuclear accidents scares many people away from pushing for a reliance on this option. Thankfully, serious nuclear accidents have been few and far between (UCS 2011). Among the more notable accidents are: the Three Mile Island (Middletown, PA) March 28, 1978 partial meltdown, considered the most serious nuclear accident in US history, although it resulted in only small radioactive releases; the Fukushima Daiichi (Fukushima, Japan) March 2011 serious nuclear accident on the northeastern coast of Japan caused by an earthquake and tsunami that struck the plant, cutting off power to the reactors and crippling the reactor cooling systems that caused fuel in three of the reactor cores to melt down, releasing radiation contaminating a wide area surrounding the plant, and forced the evacuation of nearly half a million residents; and the Chernobyl Nuclear Power Plant (Pripyat, about 65 miles north of Kiev in Ukraine) April 26, 1986 nuclear disaster, considered the world's worst nuclear disaster to date (UCS 2011).

The Chernobyl accident occurred as a result of an explosion and fire that destroyed Unit 4, allowing massive amounts of radiation to escape and spread across the western Soviet Union and Europe, resulting in approximately 220,000 people being relocated from their homes (UCS 2011). Unit 4 was in the process of being shut down for routine maintenance, but miscommunication and the lack of adequate precautions led to a divergence from safety procedures (UCS 2011). The explosion and subsequent meltdown claimed thousands of lives, caused countless birth defects, and unleashed a thyroid cancer epidemic on the region (Cohen 2018). It took years for the full story of the catastrophe to emerge to the worldwide community. The nearby town of Pripyat—which was not evacuated until 36 hours after the explosion—was blanketed by a lethal cloud of radioactive material. Soviet officials tried to keep the disaster under wraps, but on April 28, 1986 (two days after the nuclear accident) Swedish monitoring stations located more than 800 miles from Chernobyl reported radiation levels 40 percent higher than normal (Cohen 2018).

In 2004, I met a graduate student at Moscow State University who told me that as a child she grew up in the Pripyat area at the time of the accident and she expressed serious concerns about "going through the changes" in her future. This expression roughly translated to English referred to the fact that many nearby residents of the Chernobyl plant went through biological changes as their bodies reacted to the poisonous radiation contamination that affected people even years after the meltdown. She was especially worried about whether or not to have children as she feared that they might have birth defects, as was the case with people she knew. By 2019, she was still doing well and had two young children that thankfully appear to be very healthy.

The Chernobyl nuclear accident became a matter of popular culture as a result of the HBO show appropriately named "Chernobyl." "Chernobyl" was a five-episode miniseries that reached its finale on June 3, 2019. The series, which premiered on May 6, 2019, chronicled the power plant's 1986 disaster. The show was filmed on location in Lithuania and Ukraine. According to IMDb (2019), this highly regarded television series (9.4/10.0 IMDb rating) was created by Craig Mazin and starred Jessie Buckley, Jared Harris, and Stellan Skarsgard. "Chernobyl" received 19 Emmy nominations, including one for best

"Limited Series" (White 2019). "Chernobyl" is extremely detailed and high-quality and is seen as being impressively historically accurate (Chagaeva 2019).

As a result of the popularity of the "Chernobyl" television show and the world we live in, wherein Instagram "influencers" attempt to cash in on anything trendy, it became in vogue to visit Pripyat. Pripyat is now a mostly abandoned ghost city (Chagaeva 2019). There have been Pripyat tours for a number of recent years (be sure to wear your protection gear) but the HBO mini-series has made this city a destination site for those with a certain type of curiosity. A number of social influencers (people who have a large social media following and/or are regarded as an "expert" in a particular niche) who enjoy "extreme tourism" are going to Pripyat and the site of the nuclear power plant to take selfies, especially sexy shots (Chagaeva 2019). In some cases, people have been going to this nuclear disaster location for photo shoots. As reason, let alone common sense, should tell us, removing one's radiation protection suit for a sexy photo is not very enlightened and is another sign of the darkness that surrounds us.

Summary

In this chapter we have examined the darkness that surrounds us from the perspective of unenlightened and irrational thought that has led people to attack the value of higher education, question the validity of science, ignore the warning signs of our dependency on fossil fuels, demonstrate our willingness to the destroy the planet we live on, and express a willingness to ignore factual information provided by science via the acceptance of pseudoscience.

Higher education involves a process of teaching and learning and as students gain new knowledge they not only increase their level of knowledge, but they also come to better understand the world they live in. Higher education has a multi-faced value to both those who graduate from college and society as whole. These values include: the increased likelihood of social mobility via the significant economic benefits associated with one's level of education; a decreased likelihood of being unemployed as one's level of education increases; people in employment with a decent income spending more money, keeping the capitalistic system strong; a general increase in one's level of intellect; and the development of critical thinking skills. Among the attacks on higher education are: an over-emphasis on STEM disciplines at the expense of the social sciences and humanities; some politicians and people questioning the value of a higher education; the increased costs of attending college and what to do about them; and power elites that view an educated populace as a danger to their agendas.

A sure sign of unenlightened and irrational thought is a disbelief in science. Numerous examples of this disbelief in science in the United States and around the world were provided. The populist movement, a failure to accept climate change and the role that humans play in contributing to it, and the fear of scientific information disproving unreasoned thought were among the specific problems discussed. The disbelief in science and a failure to accept the science on climate change have a direct connection to the attacks on the environment, especially in our irrational continued reliance on fossil fuels as our primary source of energy. Why anyone would not want to save the environment goes beyond unenlightened and irrational thinking. Helping the environment thrive should be the number-one priority of every government, business, and populace around the world. It is especially important to curtail our negative impact (e.g., via many forms of pollution, hydraulic fracturing, the use of plastics, food waste, harmful agricultural practices, deforestation, marine debris, and e-waste) on the environment as we are currently in the sixth mass extinction period.

Some people who shun science turn to pseudoscience. Pseudoscience is a system of beliefs, theories, assertions, and practices mistakenly regarded as scientific when, in fact, they are not. Among the variations of pseudoscience discussed in this chapter were: astrology; clairvoyance, such as psychics and mediums; the many variations of fortune telling; psychokinesis, or telekinesis; voodoo; witchcraft; and superstition. The chapter concluded with a look at proponents of a belief in a flat Earth and Young Earth Creationists who believe the planet was formed less than 10,000 years ago as examples of thinking that is devoid of reason.

4
A FLOODED SWAMP

Introduction

What image comes to mind when you hear the word "swamp?" Do you think of a wetland surrounded by trees, or perhaps alongside a large river or lake? If you do, you are thinking about a low-lying area where water collects, like a bog or a marsh, or an area that is prone to flooding. To qualify as a swamp, a wetland area must often be partially or intermittently covered with water with poor drainage that is bordered by woody vegetation. Swamps are tracts of wet, spongy land that is unfit for cultivation. These wetlands contain their own ecosystems, characterized by animal and plant life. As this is a text on the socio-political realities of the twenty-first century, the concept of a "swamp" takes on an entirely different meaning. In this chapter, the idea of a "swamp" refers to the political realm, wherein unelected persons working for the government have power and influence over people.

The political swamp

Trying to find a clear explanation as to what exactly is meant by the "swamp" in political terms is as murky as its name implies. Some people seem to think that the White House itself was built atop a geological swamp and, thus, the metaphor of politics in Washington as akin to a swamp because of its foul stench and corruption has persisted. In truth, Washington, DC was not built on a swamp, despite being built in a low-lying area between the Anacostia and Potomac Rivers (Harrington 2016). George Washington, who led a three-member commission to pick the site for the nation's capital, knew that he wanted the new federal district and city to be near the head of navigation on the Potomac River, adjacent to the thriving port town of Georgetown and well away from the "squishy" margins of the Chesapeake Bay (Abbott 2017). Washington knew this region well because his of nearby home at Mount Vernon. Washington, DC, like other early American cities such as Philadelphia and Cincinnati, was built on a firm and dry riverbank. "The land sloped steadily upward away from the Potomac between Rock Creek and the Anacostia River, then called the Eastern Branch of the Potomac" (Abbott 2017). With the realization that Washington, DC and any reference to a "swamp" has nothing to do with marshlands, we turn to other explanations as to its meaning.

The meaning of the swamp

The political swamp is an aspect of politics and the government; at the federal level it does specifically mean Washington, DC. Politics itself is usually viewed as the guiding influence of governmental policy. The political system operates on behalf of the government. The *government* is the political unit that exercises authority via laws and customs. Collective actions, such as voting, marches, and rallies, are also considered to be political if the state is the target of such mass activity (Armstrong and Bernstein 2008).

Present-day political systems can be categorized in a number of ways, but the most critical distinction is based on power distribution. Political systems that limit power to a few, or one absolute leader, are referred to as authoritarian governments, whereas systems that give power to the people are known as democratic governments. Authoritarian governments expect unquestioned obedience to authority. With authoritarian governments, great power is given to political leaders; the people have little or no say in who their leaders will be. Monarchies are the oldest form of authoritarian government; other examples include totalitarian regimes, dictatorships, military juntas, and oligarchies. It is important to point out, however, that even in authoritarian governments where absolute power is in the hands of a sole person (or a limited few), there is still a reliance on a network of government officials to make sure that all of the system's needs are being met and are functioning properly. As governmental duties are diffused throughout the hierarchy and the different branches of the system, the development of a web of persons with a limited amount of authority emerges. As the system grows in complexity, so too does the need for lower-level officials to help run the government. Such a scenario represents the beginnings of a political swamp.

In a democracy, the political system is designed to empower the people, and leaders are chosen periodically, in contested elections, to represent the needs of the people. Democracy literally means, after all, "rule by the people." In a democracy the power rests with the position held (e.g., president, mayor, councillor) and not with the elected person. Although most people think of the United States as a democracy, it is not; it is a *representative democracy*—meaning that people elect others to make decisions for them. The people are allowed to vote for a number of propositions wherein total votes matter the most (a democracy), which is in contrast to a representative democracy, which has such components as an electoral college wherein total votes are rendered as a secondary concern. In a democracy, there are many levels of government and large numbers of people who help to run the very complicated bureaucracy associated with large social systems. Once again, complexity assures the need for many non-elected persons to help run the government. Such a scenario guarantees a large political swamp of people with some degree of power to make decisions over others even though they were not voted into office.

From this perspective, a political swamp exists in all societies because it is necessary for the non-elected (in democracies) and non-autocrats (in authoritarian governments) to help manage the seemingly countless daily operations of running a government.

Jeffrey Lord is more concerned with the political than the functional aspects of the swamp. Lord (2019) views the notion of the "swamp" in a similar manner as did Robert Bork (a Supreme Court nominee under President Ronald Reagan in 1987 and the author of *The Tempting of America: The Political Seduction of the Law*) who believes that a political war is being fought for the "control of culture" and a "class struggle about social and political values." Lord and Bork limit their view of the political swamp to the idea that such an entity is the result of political parties that fight for control of a society's culture. It certainly is true that political parties exist to promote a certain ideology. In fact, a *political party* is defined as an organization designed to gain power for itself via its candidates and to promote a prevailing ideology. However, the political swamp, as presented here, does not form and reform solely based on who is in power; the political swamp has a life of its own regardless of which party has the most power at a given time. Still, who is in power does have a great deal of importance with regard to the political swamp when it comes to cabinet and judicial appointments (a topic that will be discussed later in this chapter).

For some, the swamp refers to the Washington, DC political "establishment" and the old ways of doing things. A key feature of this interpretation of the swamp is "lobbying." *Lobbying* involves advocating on behalf of some cause or special interest via the means of influencing, or attempted influencing, of government officials who actually or potentially have decision making authority over that activity. A *lobbyist* is a person who tries to influence legislation on behalf of a special-interest agency. Individuals and interest groups alike can lobby governments, and governments can even lobby each other (The Free Dictionary 2019a). The lobbying process works at all levels of government and the attempted influence to gain favor of government officials can also be extended to the attempted influence over the public (e.g., the gun lobby, which attempts to associate gun control with attacks on the Second Amendment). The practice of lobbying, while often perceived negatively, is in fact an essential aspect of the proper functioning of the US government that is specifically protected by the First Amendment to the US Constitution (The Free Dictionary 2019a). All lobbyists are not equal, as some yield far more power than others and some, because of past associations within the government, have more connections to government officials than others. Thus, the lobbying playing field is not equal. The money at the disposal of lobbyists also varies a great deal. For example, the tobacco and oil industries have huge sums of money to fund lobbying efforts. "Contemporary lobbying methods include political action committees, high-tech communication techniques, coalitions among groups and industries sharing the same political goals, and campaigns to mobilize constituents at the grassroots level" (The Free Dictionary 2019a).

Eric Bolling (2017) examines the concept of the "swamp" in terms of presidential scandals. Among the examples he describes is one that involves President Hoover, who essentially blackmailed rivals and allies alike that he might release secrets about them if they did not cooperate with him. Political scandals contribute negatively to the reputation of the specific politician and to the political party to which he or she belongs, but this is a far too limited view of a political swamp to give any justice to a comprehensible explanation of its existence and function.

Thomas L. Krannawitter (2017) explains "the swamp" in terms that help us to clearly understand the depths of its meaning. He points out that the *swamp* is really the "Big Bureaucracy," administrative staffs that consist of unelected government employees who have the power to issue and enforce regulations as if they are law. These employees of the "swamp" number in the millions. "Today, at the federal level alone, the United States government includes 15 executive branch 'departments.' Virtually all federal regulatory and administrative agencies—which number in the hundreds, and employ directly around 3 million non-military, unelected, civil service bureaucrats—fall under the authority of one of these departments" (Krannawitter 2017:17). In the chronological order in which they were created, they are as follows: the Department of State; the Department of the Treasury; the Department of Justice; the Department of the Interior; the Department of Agriculture; the Department of Commerce; the Department of Labor; the Department of Defense; the Department of Health & Human Services; the Department of Housing & Urban Development; the Department of Transportation; the Department of Education; the Department of Energy; the Department of Education; the Department of Veterans Affairs; and the Department of Homeland Security.

While the above represent the "swamp" at the federal level, there are still many more employees, all unelected bureaucrats that work at the state, county, or local levels of government.

> In many states, for example, K-12 public education systems employ more non-teaching bureaucrats than teachers. The realm of public higher education, including colleges and universities at the undergraduate and graduate levels, has also seen a spike in the rate of hiring non-teaching bureaucrats that has dwarfed increases in the numbers of students and professors, combine.
> *(Krannawitter 2017:18)*

As a long-time professor, I can certainly attest to the alarming number of non-professors hired at my state university, which comes at the expense of hiring professors who can offer more classes to students, just so that they can graduate "on time." At my university there are many dozens (that I am aware of) of positions and administrative departments that are nonessential to the true mission of a university.

(The hiring of many nonessential administrators also results in a dramatic increase in student tuition in order to pay these bloated salaries.) Thus, the "swamp" exists on my college campus, like most others.

This is just the beginning of the swamp. Krannawitter goes on to identify that there are many regulators, inspectors, administrators, clerks, and bureaucrats of all kinds employed by state, county, and local governments. Add this up and the total reaches between 20 and 25 million Americans who work for the government at some level. "To put this in perspective: Approximately twice as many Americans are employed by [the] government today—as unelected bureaucrats—as are employed by all manufacturing companies added together" (Krannawitter 2017:18). Data provided by the Bureau of Labor Statistics (BLS) support Krannawitter's claims; "There were 21,995,000 employed by federal, state and local government in the United States in August, according to BLS. By contrast, there were only 12,329,000 employed in the manufacturing sector" (Jeffrey 2015). Among those employed by the government are contractors and grant recipients. Krannawitter (2017) explains,

> Much government work is performed by government contractors and government grant recipients—from weapons developers to "non-profit," tax-exempt charities, to big government political advocates, to organizations that launder government money and return it to politicians who vote reliably in support of more bureaucracy, more bureaucrats, and bigger government budgets. Often, taxpayers fund most or all of the work of these contractors and charitable grantees.
>
> *(pp. 19–20)*

If we add up all of these people, we see that according to BLS statistics a whopping 19 percent of employed Americans work for the government in one way or another, directly or indirectly. And there's your "swamp"—one out of five American employees work for the government. This explains why Krannawitter describes the "swamp" as a leviathan. The concept of the "leviathan" comes from Thomas Hobbes' (1588–1679) publication *Leviathan* (1651), wherein he describes what life and human relations would be like in the absence of government. He speculated that society would be filled with fear, danger of violent death, and that the life of humans would be filled with fear—nasty, brutish, and short. He therefore argues for a social contract between an absolute sovereign and its subjects in order to maintain a peaceful coexistence in society. Hobbes also recognized that such a sovereign government would become huge and oversee all aspects of social life. Such a government would be so intrusive, however, that it would become like a "monster." (From mythology and biblical references, a leviathan was viewed as a sea monster.) This monster is actually even larger when you consider that the BLS data cite only civilian employees. That means that many others—the millions of Americans serving in the United States military and employees of the Central Intelligence Agency, the National Security Agency, the National Imagery and Mapping

Agency, and the Defense Intelligence Agency—are actually employed by the US government and are excluded from this count (Federal Reserve Economic Data 2019).

It is common to refer to the "political swamp" simply as the "swamp" and thus, with the above discussion of the swamp in mind, it can be defined as an environment wherein a variety of non-elected persons, including cabinet and judicial appointees, lobbyists, diplomats, bureaucrats, and administrative staffs who help run the countless daily operations of a government and who have power to issue and enforce regulations as if they are law hold positions of quasi-authority. The vast majority of those working in the swamp are people who work for the government in an attempt to keep it running smoothly. Appointees to certain political offices reflect the values and ideology of the person (e.g., the US president) who appointed them, and lobbyists attempt to influence those who work for the government on the behalf of some other entity. Diplomats are sometimes career politicians and sometimes they are appointed by presidents who want to reward them as friends and political campaign donors. Gordon Sondland, the US ambassador to the European Union, for example, had no diplomatic experience but received his position after donating $1 million to Trump's inauguration (Fritze 2019b). One might wonder if diplomats are even necessary, as political leaders can communicate with one another very easily in the advent of technology. However, as Ivo Daalder (2019) explains, "foreign policy is about more than [making] decisions. It's also about building enduring relationships, deepening understanding of how other countries and governments operate, getting insight into the perspectives of other nations and their leaders and gauging where collaboration is possible and confrontation necessary" (p. E3). Such qualifications are found with career politicians and sociologists (a much better choice for such important work as diplomacy).

The concept of the swamp exists in every country around the world as all governments have non-elected personnel working on behalf of the government and instituting quasi-authority over others. A possible indicator of a swamp could be a bloated government. According to the Organization for Economic Cooperation and Development (OECD), government spending provides an indication of the size of government across countries. The OECD (2018) identifies six countries that spend more than half of their GDP on government: Finland (57 percent), France (56.8 percent), Denmark (54.5 percent), Belgium (53.7 percent), Greece (53.5 percent), and Austria (51.1 percent). Three more countries spend around half of their GDP on government: Italy (50.3 percent), Hungary (50.1 percent), and Sweden (49.6 percent). By comparison, the United States is at 37.9 percent. While this criterion is not the same thing as the US concept of the swamp, it does give us a measurement of the bloated size of governments. Dan Mitchell (2016) claims that when a government becomes too large, politicians and bureaucrats become "so focused on redistributing money to various interest groups that there's not enough attention given to fulfilling the few legitimate functions of government." As an example, Mitchell cites a Belgian counterterrorism official who claimed that due to the small size of the Belgian government and huge numbers of open investigations, virtually every police detective and military intelligence officer in the country was focused on international jihadi investigations. Mitchell (2016) finds this hard to believe because "Belgium has one of the biggest and most bloated governments in the world."

The concept of a bloated government as an indicator of swamp-like conditions is complicated by the realization that the term "bloated government" itself needs to be defined; this is not as simple as it should be, possibly because of the political overtones. Bloated means to be swollen or puffed up (like a bloated stomach), but when applied to a government the definition seems to be limited by including such parameters as "larger than is normal or desirable" (The Free Dictionary 2019a). Who decides what is larger than "normal" or "desirable?" People who wish to limit the role of government would have a much lower tolerance for the size of the government; they would also be among the proponents chanting "drain the swamp" (to be discussed later in this chapter). People who view the government *as* the people might be less likely to demand a decrease in its size. Regardless of where one stands politically, the idea of a political swamp is tied to the number and quality of government employees (this idea will be expanded upon when discussing the flooded White House).

The longevity of the swamp

It is hard to say exactly when the swamp concept was first applied to politics but it likely goes back to the beginning of government itself. Certainly the swamp was not nearly as deep in the early days of government as it is today. In addition, the concept of a "swamp" is a newer phenomenon. So, how do we trace the longevity of the political swamp concept when there is some ambiguity as to its exact meaning and origin of its initial application?

The concept of the "swamp," if we use the meaning of the concept to include unelected persons employed by the government, has been around since the 1870s, according to Krannawitter (2017). Initially, it was felt as though unelected "experts" were better suited for key positions than the potential "rubes" who were elected based on campaign promises that they could never accomplish. Because many elected officials come and go it was felt that "permanent government" workers could do a better a job than people with no experience in government. This idea is akin to the notion that if you need a doctor, plumber, electrician, mechanic, and so on, you hire a professional who has been trained in that field; you would not hire a novice to do such specialized work. Thus, a rational person would want a person experienced in political affairs serving in a government capacity; certainly, a position such as the President of United States should fall upon a person who is heavily experienced and qualified in political matters.

If we use the number of people working for the government as a criterion for determining the depth of the swamp, the BLS reports that as early as August 1941 there were nearly five million (4,821,000) people employed by the government in the US, equalling 1 for each 27.7 people in the overall population of 133,402, 471

(Jeffrey 2015). Clearly, there were millions of government workers prior to 1941 as well, thus indicating their prevalence. With this criterion in mind, one could conclude that the swamp has been around for a long time. Furthermore, one could argue that as the number of government employees increases, so too does the swamp get deeper. As BLS data reveal, that is certainly the case. "The BLS has been publishing seasonally-adjusted month-by-month employment numbers for both government and manufacturing going back to 1939. In the first 50 years of the 76-year span since then, manufacturing out-employed government. But, in August 1989, government overtook manufacturing as a U.S. employer" (Jeffrey 2015).

The history of the political swamp concept can be simplified to the realization that some version of its presence has been in existence since the earliest governments were formed and that it has only expanded in size over the years. It is also safe to assume that the swamp, in one variation or another, will continue to exist well into the future.

"Drain the swamp"

It has become increasingly popular for people to demand that the swamp be drained and for a number of politicians to promise that they will indeed "drain the swamp." The expression "drain the swamp" is a metaphor that means to root out corruption and eliminate non-essential governmental jobs.

As Harrington (2016) explains, the expression "drain the swamp" has roots in when malaria was a problem in the US (dating back to as early as 1882) and Europe and the idea of draining swamps as an effective means of killing mosquitoes that bred there and spread the disease. It wasn't long after that this expression was applied to Big Business. Harrington (2016) states that the first person to apply this term of "draining the swamp" to politics was a Democrat, Winfield E. Gaylord, in 1903.

> According to etymologist Barry Popik, "drain the swamp" was originally used metaphorically in 1903 by Social Democratic Party organizer Winfield R. Gaylord in a letter discussing how socialists wish to deal with big business: "Socialists are not satisfied with killing a few mosquitoes which come from the capittalist [sic] swamp, they want to drain the swamp."
>
> (Caldwell 2017)

President Ronald Reagan used the expression "drain the swamp" to refer to bureaucracy in Washington, DC, and created the Grace Commission, which identified $424 billion of wasteful government spending that could be cut (Harrington 2016). The Grace Commission was authorized in Executive Order 12369 on June 30, 1982. Immediately following the September 11, 2001 attacks, Republican Defense Secretary Donald Rumsfeld pledged to "drain the swamp" where terrorists reside. In 2006, Democratic Congresswoman Nancy Pelosi announced she would "drain the swamp" after being elected Speaker of the House of Representatives following ten years of Republican control of Congress. On October 23, 2015,

Republican presidential candidate Ben Carson released a campaign ad titled "Drain the Swamp" calling upon voters to elect him to clean up the United States government (Caldwell 2017). On October 17, 2016, Republican presidential candidate Donald Trump first used the expression "drain the swamp" in Green Bay, Wisconsin. Trump specifically targeted lobbyists. He also used the phrase to lash out at seemingly every aspect of the Washington, DC establishment, from the press corps to Senate Minority Leader Chuck Schumer (Meyer 2017).

While the corruption in Washington, DC may indeed be in need of a good scrubbing, it is highly unlikely that a complete cleanse will take place anytime soon, or ever. Those who think that the swamp is going to be drained to any great extent are either delusional or have no idea what is truly meant by the swamp. The swamp is too large to be drained any time soon and the functions of those working in the swamp are too intertwined with the daily activities of a given country. Writing for *Forbes*, Mike Patton applied a GE/P ratio, with "GE" as government employees and "P" as the percentage of the population. A higher ratio indicates a higher percentage of government employees relative to the total population. Patton (2013) examined the size of government from 1980 to 2012, a span of time that included five different US presidents. Patton's GE/P ratio indicates that the percentage of people working for the government held pretty steady until the end of Barack Obama's first term (when Patton's analysis ended). The GE/P ratio for Ronald Reagan was 7.2 percent; George H.W. Bush, 7.3 percent; Bill Clinton, 7.3 percent; George W. Bush, 7.4 percent; and Obama, 6.9 percent. Based on this analysis, the swamp had been drained quite a bit by the end of Obama's first term (something he never seems to get credit for doing, at least compared to his four predecessors) and yet 6.9 percent of the population working in the government sector is still quite a significant figure (Patton 2013).

Using more current data, when Obama left office the GE/P ratio was 6.84 (GE = 22.3 million/P = 325.7 million). In July 2019, the BLS reported that the number of employees hired by the government was 22,542,000. The total US population was at 329,345,464. If we apply GE/P ratio we learn that a little more that 6.8 percent of the total population was employed by the government (Federal Reserve Economic Data 2019). In other words, after his first two years as president, Trump has done no better at draining the swamp than his predecessor Barack Obama. Eric Bolling (2017) insists that the swamp must be drained and mistakenly believes that no one will miss the swamp if it is. The more than 22 million people employed in the swamp will surely disagree, and if these government-employed millions of people do lose their jobs, the unemployment rate would skyrocket, sending the economy into a tailspin.

The swamp has not been drained; it is deeper and murkier

No rational person actually believed that Trump would drain the swamp, but that did not stop many of his followers from reveling in "drain the swamp" chants at his political rallies. While it would have been impossible to drain the tens of millions of people that make up the swamp, Trump was in the position to appoint people of high ethical and moral quality to his presidential cabinet. And, if the opportunity should arise (which it has, twice so far) wherein he could nominate someone to the Supreme Court, he was free to choose someone with unquestionable qualifications and the ability to make fair, unbiased, and reasoned decisions on matters of great national importance. Furthermore, he could have made good on another campaign promise to enact and enforce ethics reforms designed to curtail the power of lobbyists.

In the following pages, we will examine whether or not Trump succeeded in any of these enlightened goals.

Circumventing ethics in lobbying

If a politician hopes to make good on promises to voters, it is best to limit statements to something specific, like proposing ethical reforms to lobbying, rather than to say something abstract like, "I will drain the swamp." Then again, if a politician has no real intention of following through on campaign pledges, conceptual rather than concrete promises are logical. To his credit, Trump did propose a detailed five-point list of ethical reforms to tighten the rules for lobbying in Washington, DC.

The reforms outlined by Trump in early 2017 included an executive order banning administrative officials from lobbying for five years after they leave office (Mackenzie 2017), which the president said he would ask Congress to turn into law "so that it cannot be lifted by executive order" (Meyer 2017). Trump also pledged to bar officials in his administration from lobbying on behalf of foreign governments for life; to ask Congress to ban former members and their staffs from lobbying for five years; to pass legislation broadening the definition of lobbying "so we close all the loopholes that former government officials use" by calling themselves consultants and advisers; and to ask Congress to ban lobbyists for foreign interests from making campaign contributions (Meyer 2017).

As of October 2017, Trump had delivered fully on just one of his five promises, signing an executive order a week after taking office that banned executive branch officials from lobbying for foreign governments and overseas political parties after they leave the administration. While this seems like a good start, it is unclear how the ban will be enforced (Meyer 2017). Trump has attempted to follow through on another pledge—to bar former executive officials from lobbying for five years. However, this was watered down in an executive order that prevents employees only from lobbying the agencies where they work. To date, there is no indication that Trump has pressured Congress to pass the ban into law. As for the other three reforms, Trump has given little attention to following through on those campaign promises (Meyer 2017).

As Mackenzie (2017) explains, relying on executive orders to curtail lobbying is not good enough, as President Obama found out when he began his first term in office in 2009. Obama signed executive orders barring officials from his administration from lobbying but the following year (2010) special-interest spending on lobbying reached what was then an all-time high— despite the fact that the number of registered lobbyists dropped from 14,000 in 2009 to just over 11,000 lobbyists on the books in 2010 (Mackenzie 2017).

Trump did not learn from Obama's error as his executive orders were also rendered useless, thus making the swamp murkier. Rather than draining the swamp of unethical lobbyists, many Washington, DC lobbyists say business is better than ever. "Spending on lobbying in Washington totaled almost $1.7 billion in the first half of the year [2017], the highest since 2012, according to the Center for Responsive Politics" (Meyer 2017). Brian Wild, a long-time Republican lobbyist and former aide to House Speaker John Boehner, said, "I don't think that anything's really changed. If anything, the lobbying business is booming right now" (Meyer 2017). As early as May 2018, "at least eight former Trump officials [had] found ways around the so-called ethics pledge" that Trump made his political appointees sign as a condition of taking office (Kravitz and Mierjeski 2018). Using unethical means to circumvent the pledge, some former officials obtained special waivers allowing them to go back to lobbying and others simply did not register as lobbyists (much like what happened when Obama was president). By February 2019, at least 33 former Trump officials had found ways to sidestep the administration's ethics pledge (Kravitz 2019).

The most prominent is former interior secretary Ryan Zinke, who resigned in December 2018 after a series of ethics investigations (Kravitz 2019). Zinke faced intense pressure from the White House to step down from his office because of "multiple probes tied to his real estate dealings in his home state of Montana and his conduct in office" (Eilperin, Dawsey, and Fears 2018). Zinke battled more than a dozen ethics investigations related to his leadership at the Interior Department, and especially his alleged misuse of charter aircraft (Stokols 2018b). Zinke, the first Montanan to have served in a presidential cabinet, became the fourth member of Trump's cabinet to resign under an ethics cloud in less than two years. "Health and Human Services Secretary Tom Price, Veterans Affairs Secretary David Shulkin and Environmental Protection Agency Administrator Scott Pruitt also relinquished their posts amid scrutiny on subjects including how they spent taxpayer money on their travel" (Eilperin, Dawsey, and Fears 2018).

Zinke drew the ire of environmentalists as well. Among other things, the inspector general's office investigated whether Zinke's decision in 2017 to allow oil and gas exploration on previously protected federal lands (accomplished by cutting the boundaries of the Grand Staircase-Escalante National Monument in Utah) improperly benefited a Republican state lawmaker whose land was removed from the monument (Stokols 2018b). In December 2017, he signed off on a plan to roll back federal protections on 2 million acres of land in Utah, overriding environmental protections established by the Obama administration. He also blamed "environmental terrorist groups" for "mismanaging" forests that resulted in a devastating wildfire that wrought havoc in California during the summer of 2018 (Stokols 2018b). Jennifer Rokala, executive director of the Center for Western Priorities, said of Zinke,

Ryan Zinke will go down as the most anti-conservation Interior Secretary in our nation's history. Surrounding himself with former lobbyists, it quickly became clear that Ryan Zinke was a pawn for the oil and gas industry. We can expect more of the same from Acting Secretary David Bernhardt, but without the laughable Teddy Roosevelt comparisons

(Eilperin, Dawsey, and Fears 2018)

Zinke had styled himself as a Teddy Roosevelt Republican; among other things, he rode a Park Police horse several blocks to his first day of work as secretary (Stokols 2018).

While it is arguably a great thing that Zinke is no longer the head of the Interior Department, Zinke announced that following his resignation he was joining the lobbying firm Turnbury Solutions, which was started in 2017 by several former Trump campaign aides (Kravitz 2019). Zinke was just one of at least 18 of the 33 former Trump officials to have registered as lobbyists, with the rest working at firms in jobs that closely resemble federal lobbying (Kravitz 2019).

At the conclusion of Trump's first three years as president it was safe to say that he had been unsuccessful in draining the swamp of unethical lobbying.

The muck of Trump's White House

Former Trump officials acting as lobbyists and quasi-lobbyists merely represent the beginning of the swamp that has flooded into the White House. By the time the Trump presidency had reached just two years of completion, his campaign, transition, inauguration, business, and presidency were all under investigation. In addition, nearly every organization he had led was also under investigation. Among the Trump organizations under scrutiny at this time (December 2018) and detailed by Fahrenthold, Zapotosky, and Kim (2018) were the following.

- Trump's private company is contending with civil suits digging into its business with foreign governments and with looming state inquires into its tax practices. Trump still owns his private company, although he says he's given up day-to-day control to his sons, Donald Trump, Jr. and Eric Trump. Trump's businesses have hosted parties for foreign embassies, which is a violation of Constitutional law.
- Trump's 2016 campaign was probed by special counsel Robert S. Mueller III, whose investigation into Russian interference has already led to guilty pleas by his campaign chairman and four advisers.
- Trump's inaugural committee probed by Mueller for illegal foreign donations. One specific instance involved an American political consultant, W. Samuel Patten, who admitted to steering $50,000 from a Ukrainian politician to the inaugural committee through a straw donor. Under federal law, foreigners are barred from donating money or making gifts to influence US elections.

- Trump's charity is under investigation by New York State, which accuses his foundation of "persistently illegal conduct" (p. B1). As an update, by July 2019, there were 29 investigations related to Trump's dealings in New York State, ten federal criminal investigations, eight state and local investigations, and eleven Congressional investigations (Buchanan and Yourish 2019).
- In November 2019, Roger Stone, a long-time friend and ally of President Trump and a person proud of his reputation as a practitioner of political dirty tricks who frequently boasted about the extent of his contacts and the depth of his insider information, was convicted of seven counts in a federal indictment (Associated Press 2019i). Stone is the sixth Trump aide or adviser to be convicted of charges brought forth during the Mueller Russia investigation.

These and many other unethical and possibly illegal activities conducted by Trump and his administration have contributed to his flooded White House. In the following pages we will take a quick look at some of the many examples of Trump's flooded White House.

We will first look at special counsel Robert S. Mueller III and the investigation of Trump and his administration, an investigation that Trump referred to as a "witch hunt." Mueller's investigation began in May 2017 after Trump fired FBI director James Comey. "The special counsel's mandate: to investigate Russian interference in the 2016 campaign and whether the Kremlin worked with Trump associates" (Fahrenthold, Zapotosky, and Kim 2018:B1). Mueller also examined whether the president sought to obstruct the Russia probe. By December 2018, this investigation into possible treasonous activity had led to 33 people being charged; this figure includes 26 Russian nationals—some of whom allegedly stole emails and other data from US political parties, others of whom allegedly sought to influence public opinion via phony social media postings (Fahrenthold, Zapotosky, and Kim 2018). As Virginia Heffernan wrote as early as July 2018,

> The "witch hunt" by special counsel Robert S. Mueller III keeps turning up actual witches. The coven of Russian military officers that Mueller indicted certainly seems to have put a whammy on U.S. democracy. The indictments charge a dozen military intelligence agents with conspiracy to attack the United States in 2016. They further connect at least one candidate for U.S. Congress to the Russian spies. And they suggest that any Americans who collaborated with Guccifer 2.0, a front for the Russian military operation, could be considered co-conspirators.
>
> *(Heffernan 2018a:A20)*

Adding to the murkiness of Trump's firing of former FBI director Comey was the claim by former deputy press secretary Sarah Huckabee Sanders (who has her own issues with the truth) claim that "countless members of the FBI" were grateful and thankful for the president's decision. This was a lie. She later told prosecutors working for Mueller that her comments were a mere "slip of the tongue" (Megerian

2019b:A1). Sanders felt the need to tell the truth to federal investigators, as it is a crime to lie to them or Congress, a lesson that many of Trump's associates learned the hard way (i.e., former national security advisor Michael Flynn or disbarred lawyer Michael Cohen). Unfortunately, it is not a crime to lie to reporters and the American people, something for which Sarah Huckabee Sanders, Trump, and those who work for Trump can be grateful (Megerian 2019b). It is impossible for a rational person to believe Sanders because she retold the "slip of the tongue" comment countless times.

Not all of Trump's associates are willing to lie for him. For example, "After a March 22, 2017, Oval Office meeting, the president asked Director of National Intelligence Dan Coats to say publicly that Trump didn't have any links to Russia," the Mueller report read, but "The claim would have been false since Trump sought to build a luxury skyscraper in Moscow while running for president" (Megerian 2019b:A8). Another Trump appointee to show some backbone was former deputy attorney general Rod Rosenstein. When Trump fired Comey (on May 9, 2017), he asked Rosenstein to hold a news conference stating that it was the decision of the Justice Department. The Mueller Report stated, "Rosenstein responded that this was not a good idea because if the press asked him, he would tell the truth that Comey's firing was not his idea" (Megerian 2019b:A8). The report also revealed that numerous others were willing to spread falsehoods on Trump's behalf.

Among the numerous others willing to lie on Trump's behalf were Paul Manafort, the president's former campaign manager, Trump's former lawyer-fixer Michael Cohen, conspiracy theorist and Trump "cheerleader" Jerome Corsi, and Trump Organization advisor Felix Sater (Heffernan 2018b). Each of these men "has at varying times had amply means and opportunity to connect President Trump with Russian authorities and agents" (Heffernan 2018b:A24). Manafort was found guilty in August 2018 of tax and bank fraud charges and pleaded guilty in September 2018 to conspiracy and obstruction charges unrelated to his work for the campaign. However, while he agreed to cooperate with Mueller's investigation, the special counsel's office asserted he would not be credible as he had been lying to investigators (prior to convictions) (Fahrenthold, Zapotosky, and Kim 2018:B1). Still, Manafort and Cohen signed plea deals with Mueller, though Manafort breached his. Corsi, who is best known as the leading force behind the false "birther" conspiracy theory (the lie repeated by Trump countless times that Obama was not born in the US) faced an indictment as a result of the Mueller Report (Ross 2019). As for Sater, he has already served time in prison for assault but avoided jail time as a criminal informant after pleading guilty to a $40-million stock scheme. "He has met more than once with the Mueller team and, according to reports, facilitated contacts between the Kremlin, Trump's business and his campaign" (Heffernan 2018b:A24). Sater was an executive who had worked on and off for the Trump Organization.

Michael Flynn was forced out of the Trump administration about three weeks after Trump's inauguration. He admitted to lying to the FBI about his conversations with the Russian ambassador during the presidential transition (Fahrenthold,

Zapotosky, and Kim 2018; Megerian 2019b). "Saying that he could not hide his 'disgust,' a federal judge publicly excoriated Michael Flynn ... before unexpectedly postponing his sentencing for lying to the FBI (Willman 2018:A1). US District Judge Emmet G. Sullivan "ripped into the retired three-star Army general for lying about his contacts with the Russian ambassador to Washington shortly after the 2016 election—and for secretly working as a lobbyist for a foreign government [Turkey] during the campaign and the presidential transition" (Willman 2018:A1). Adding to his verbal attack on Flynn, Sullivan said that he (Flynn) arguably undermined everything that the US flag stands for and that he had sold out his country. At one point, the judge even suggested that Flynn may have committed treason, although he later recanted and said that he did not mean to assert that (Willman 2018). Flynn's behavior was especially alarming because he had had access to some of the government's most closely held secrets. Flynn admitted under oath that he had intentionally lied to the FBI and knew that it was a crime when he did it (Willman 2018).

In addition to Flynn's lying to the FBI, Rick Gates, Trump's former deputy campaign chairman, admitted to conspiracy and lying to the FBI. Former foreign policy advisor George Papadopoulos pleaded guilty to lying to the FBI about his Russian contacts. Michael Cohen admitted to lying about efforts to build a Trump project in Moscow that lasted into Trump's presidential run (Fahrenthold, Zapotosky, and Kim 2018).

Michael Cohen's involvement with Trump involves a variety of unethical and illegal activities. Recall the quote from Cohen that began Chapter 3—"Blind loyalty [to Trump] led me to choose a path of darkness, over light." This quote also serves as an appropriate reminder here of Cohen's involvement in Trump's flooded White House swamp. While standing in federal court in November 2018, Cohen admitted that he had lied out of "loyalty" to help Trump's "political messaging" (Megerian 2018b:A1). Cohen had also previously implicated the president in a felony by admitting he had paid hush money to two women at Trump's direction during the campaign (Megerian 2018b). The Cohen misdeeds are numerous and the highlights include his (August 2018) pleading guilty to eight federal charges, including campaign finance offenses, bank fraud, and tax evasion (Day 2018; Megerian 2018b). Claiming that he did so on the behalf of Trump, Cohen paid hush money to buy the silence of porn actress Stormy Daniels and former Playboy model Karen McDougal, who both alleged they had had affairs with Trump (Day 2018). In December 2018, Cohen was sentenced to three years in prison for what a judge called a "veritable smorgasbord of criminal conduct" (Fahrenthold, Zapotosky, and Kim 2018:B3). However, "U.S. District Judge William H. Pauley III denied Cohen's plead for leniency because of his guilty pleas for bank fraud, tax evasion, campaign finance violations and lying to Congress" (Megerian and Sharp 2018a:A1). While Cohen insists that he acted on behalf of Trump, predictably, Trump disavowed such a claim. Trump stated, "I never directed him to do anything wrong. Whatever he did, he did on his own" (Fahrenthold, Zapotosky, and Kim 2018:B3).

In July 2019, the Trump and Cohen saga resurfaced as court documents revealed that the criminal investigation was wider than previously known. An affidavit revealed that the two former friends and associates had spoken on the phone shortly before Cohen began transferring money to buy the silence of Stormy Daniels. The affidavit was used to obtain warrants to search Cohen's home, hotel room, and office during the 2018 investigation (Megerian 2019c). The *National Enquirer*, a tabloid run by a Trump ally, was responsible for paying $150,000 to Karen McDougal. Federal prosecutors in New York said that Trump did indeed direct the scheme to pay off his mistresses and his alleged extramarital affairs but then they told Judge Pauley that they were closing the case. Pauley countered that if the case was closed, federal prosecutors should release the hundreds of pages of documents, including the affidavit, that had previously been heavily redacted, as the contents were a "matter of national importance" (Megerian 2019c:A7).

Many of Trump's appointees have left his administration either because they were fired, resigned, or because they felt they could no longer work with him. In November 2018, then-Attorney General Jeff Sessions was forced to resign, ending a "tortured relationship with President Trump" (Megerian and Wilber 2018:A1). Sessions was the forty-first high-ranking member of Trump's administration to leave his employ in less than two years. Defense Secretary Jim Mattis abruptly resigned the administration in December 2018 after Trump overruled his advice against pulling troops out of Syria. In his resignation letter, Mattis wrote to Trump explaining that he was leaving his administration because "you have a right to have a Secretary of Defense whose views are better aligned with yours" (Miller and Baldor 2018). Mattis also made it clear that the US should more strongly support its allies. Trump tried to claim that Mattis was retiring but that was not the case. In September 2019, Trump's national security adviser John Bolton resigned. (Trump later claimed that he had fired Bolton.) Bolton is a seasoned Washington player with a reputation as a hard-liner, especially when dealing with North Korea, Iran, Venezuela, and Afghanistan. However, Trump and Bolton had had too many disagreements (e.g., Trump's repeated meetings with North Korean leader Kim Jong Un) that would lead to Bolton being the third national security advisor to leave this position in less than three years (Michael Flynn and H.R. McMaster being the previous two). "Mr. Bolton's singular achievement was to dismantle a foreign-policymaking structure that had until then kept the president from running foreign policy by the seat of his pants" (Gans 2019). Shortly after Bolton's departure, Trump appointed Robert O'Brien as his next national security adviser. O'Brien, a like-minded Trump proponent who sought to destroy the Obama administration's approach to foreign policy (see his book *While America Slept: Restoring American Leadership to a World Crisis*), had most recently been a chief hostage negotiator and an established figure in the Republican policy circles. Among his "accomplishments" just prior to his promotion, O'Brien had negotiated a deal with Sweden to help secure the release of rapper A$AP Rocky (real name Rakim Mayers) from Swedish custody in July 2019 (Subramanian 2019).

The Democrats took control of the House of Representatives following the November 2018 mid-term elections. They vowed to put pressure on the Trump White House. Their ambition and power were countered by the continued Republican control over the Senate. Both the Republicans and the Democrats looked forward to the release of the Mueller Report ("Report On The Investigation Into Russian Interference In The 2016 Presidential Election"), which finally happened March 2019. When it was released, neither side got exactly what they wanted and yet both claimed a political victory. The full report is available to the public now but initially only a redacted version was available. Attorney General William Barr provided a summary report that made Trump look like he was fully exonerated from any wrongdoing. Trump proudly proclaimed, "No collusion" whenever he was asked by the press about the report. Mueller complained to Barr that his four-page summary letter did not "fully capture the context, nature and substance of this office's work and conclusions," a Justice Department official said (Megerian 2019d:A7). On May 1, 2019, Barr testified before the Senate Judiciary Committee on the Mueller Report. Democrats drilled Barr and attacked his credibility, or lack thereof. California Senator Kamala Harris said, "This attorney general lacks all credibility and has, I think, compromised the American public's ability to believe that he is a purveyor of justice" (Megerian and Wilber 2019:A6). The top-ranking Democrat on the committee, California Senator Dianne Feinstein, pressed Barr about his conclusion that Trump had not obstructed justice, saying, "Contrary to the declarations of the total and complete exoneration, the special counsel's report contained substantial evidence of misconduct" (Megerian and Wilber 2019:A6). Republicans rallied behind Barr and praised his handling of the Russia investigation. Barr refused to pass judgment on Trump's actions. A week later, Barr refused to comply with a Congressional subpoena and ignored a scheduled hearing at which he was supposed to deliver sworn testimony; he even dared lawmakers to do something about his deliberate stonewalling (Benen 2019). A month later, the Democratic-controlled House Oversight Committee did do something about it, voting 24–15 to advance contempt measures against Barr and Commerce Secretary Wilbur Ross. Representative Justin Amash of Michigan, who has said he supports an impeachment inquiry against Trump, was the only Republican to join the Democrats (Daly and Balsamo 2019). The swamp is deeper with Barr as a member of Trump's cabinet.

Yet another appointee of Trump with a highly questionable background is former labor secretary R. Alexander Acosta, who announced his resignation from the Trump administration in July 2019. Acosta was under mounting criticism because of a lenient plea deal he struck with a later-convicted sex offender, Jeffrey Epstein. Epstein was a wealthy financier when Acosta served as US attorney in Miami. After his soft sentence from Acosta, Epstein was allegedly involved in a number of other crimes including sex trafficking. While the billionaire financier was being held without bail pending trial on child sex trafficking charges, Epstein was found dead in his jail cell on August 10 having apparently committed suicide. Trump initially stood by Acosta, saying that he had done a good job as labor secretary. In his consistently odd and poor way of speaking, Trump said of Acosta, "He was a great student at Harvard. He's Hispanic, which I so admire, because maybe it was a little tougher for him and maybe not. That's what I know about him I know one thing—he did a great job" (Engelmayer and Bierman 2019:A1) While Acosta serves as yet another example of Trump's poor judgment in his choice of individuals serving in his administration, the real headline story here is the fact that Trump and Epstein were close friends. "Epstein was a regular visitor to Donald Trump's Mar-a-Lago [hotel], and the two were friends ... Trump was a frequent dinner guest at Epstein's home, which was often full of barely dressed models" (Callahan 2016). (Bill Clinton was another friend of Epstein's.) There are many videos of Trump saying how Epstein loved young beautiful women, some very young, as much as he did. Connecting yet another person of questionable ethics and morality to this peculiar story, Barr had refused to recuse himself from overseeing the Epstein case (prior to his alleged suicide). Barr's father Donald Barr had been the headmaster of the prestigious Dalton School, a prep school in Manhattan where Epstein taught calculus and physics from 1973 to 1975, despite lacking a college degree (Colvin and Fram 2019). The muck of this story would not be believable unless it was, in fact, true.

In August 2019, Chuck Park, an eight-year State Department veteran who was most recently posted to a US consulate in Mexico, became the latest American diplomat to publicly and pointedly call it quits when he said he could no longer be "complicit" in the Trump administration (Wilkinson 2019c). Park (2019) said, "Over three tours abroad, I worked to spread what I believed were American values: freedom, fairness and tolerance. But more and more I found myself in a defensive stance, struggling to explain to foreign peoples the blatant contradictions at home." Morale is sinking among State Department workers as American foreign policy is now being dictated unchecked by a shoot-from-the hip president (Wilkinson 2019c). This underscores the true harm of President Trump; he is not only the "Great Divider" home in the United States, but has also compromised the reputation of the US overseas. In this regard, the flooded swamp of the White House is spreading outside the national borders.

Judicial appointments and the potential for a long-term mess

Donald Trump has spread the White House muck with his political appointments, a number of whom have questionable character and threaten to impede the progress of enlightened thought. As detailed in the previous pages, Trump's often poor decision making has cost the US good will abroad and divided the country domestically. His constant support for Big Business, especially the fossil fuel industry, could cost the country dearly for generations to come. His decision to appoint Kelly Craft as the next US envoy to the United Nations (US Senate confirmation took place on July 31, 2019) despite Democratic concerns about her inexperience and potential conflict of interest because of her connections to the coal industry will surely hurt attempts to curtail the devastating effects of climate change. She and her husband, Joe Craft, have donated millions of dollars to Republican political candidates, and she will be the first major political donor to occupy the top United Nations post for any administration. Joe Craft is the chief executive of Alliance Resource Partners, one of the largest coal producers in the United States (Associated Press 2019d).

While the damage to enlightened and rational thought of Trump's cabinet positions and appointments may have a relatively long-term negative effect on the US and the world, we have also seen how many of these appointees do not have a long shelf life. Furthermore, once the darkness of the Trump regime is over, the next president has the ability to correct most of the damage caused by this inexperienced dark knight of American socio-political history. What concerns many people who promote enlightened rational thought, however, is the potential harm that Trump's judicial appointees may cause.

By mid-July 2018, Trump had appointed more federal appeals court judges so far during his presidency than Barack Obama and George W. Bush combined had appointed at the same point in theirs, according to a Pew Research Center analysis (Gramlich 2018). At this same time, Trump had had a lesser impact on lower-court judges. The 22 appeals court judges and 20 district judges Trump had appointed by July 12, 2018 represent a number of powerful judges who sit just below the Supreme Court level. Support or disapproval of Trump's appointees was divided along partisan lines. "About eight-in-ten Republicans and Republican-leaning independents (82%) said they had at least some confidence in Trump regarding judicial appointments, a view shared by just 19% of Democrats and Democratic leaners" (Gramlich 2018). There is some balance to Trump's appointees (a number that is sure to rise as time progresses) as among all the active federal judges, 58 percent were appointed by Democratic presidents, the largest number by Obama. As of mid-July 2018, the current federal judiciary overall consisted of 725 active judges across 94 district courts, 13 appeals courts, the Supreme Court, and one additional court, the Court of International Trade (Gramlich 2018).

It is the Supreme Court that generates the greatest interest as this nine-member judiciary is the most significant aspect of one of the three branches of US government, the Judicial branch (which consists of the nation's lower federal courts with the Supreme Court making final decisions when issues reach that level). The Judicial branch of the government is constitutionally designed to be equal with the Legislative (Congress) and the Executive (headed by the president). The Supreme Court can shift the balance of power as it has the ability to override decisions made by the president and Congress. The nine judges that make up the Supreme Court, then, are very powerful. They can make decisions that affect people's lives for multiple generations. For example, in the United States it is currently legal for a woman to control her own body and decide whether or not to have an abortion. For the Supreme Court to override this decision (a goal of conservatives), it would take a shift in power in the Supreme Court and this is likely, assuming that future proposals to eliminate legal abortions make it past the federal appeals courts. Supreme Court justices are supposed to be non-biased, impartial decision makers who act on behalf of the American public. However, Supreme Court justices are appointed by a president and the political whims and leanings that they possess. The appointee must make it through the confirmation process, which is generally very political as seldom does a nominated judge appear to be truly non-biased. The ability to appoint and get a confirmation of a judge on the Supreme Court is one of the lasting signs of power of a president and will often become the legacy of that president.

During the end of Obama's second term as president there was an opening on the Supreme Court (following the February 13, 2016 death of Antonin Scalia) and he and the Democrats wanted to fill that seat before the 2016 presidential election was held, especially just in case a Republican (and in the worst-case scenario a far-right Republican) became president. For Democrats, the worst case did occur: a shocking victory by a far-right candidate lacking completely in political and military experience and qualifications. Before the 2016 election, Obama tried to get his nominee—Merrick Garland—appointed to the Supreme Court. Garland, considered by most to be a moderate liberal judge, was chief judge of the US Court of Appeals in Washington, DC. "Garland's nomination lasted a total of 293 days—the longest period in Supreme Court history, by far—without ever getting a confirmation hearing, or a hearing of any kind, from Senate Republicans" (Ware 2017). Garland's opportunity to become a part of the US Supreme Court was blocked by the Republicans in the Senate as they did not want the high court to have a majority of liberal-leaning judges. The indignity experienced by Garland and the shameful behavior of the Republicans opened the door for Trump to nominate his own judge.

Predictably, Trump chose a conservative-leaning judge as his nominee for the Supreme Court, Neil Gorsuch. Gorsuch was a judge on the US Court of Appeals of the Tenth Circuit in Denver when he was nominated. He would become the 113th justice of the US Supreme Court in 2017 (Biography.com 2019c). The Democrats initially attempted to filibuster Gorsuch's confirmation in the Senate but they lacked enough Congressional seats to do so. That conservative Gorsuch took the place of another conservative judge (Scalia, who had been appointed by President Reagan) was not really a tide-turning moment. That Obama was not allowed to make an appointment to the Supreme Court but Trump was is a matter that will never sit well for Democrats and those who promote progressive, enlightened ideals.

The tide-turning moment occurred when suddenly Trump would be given an opportunity to appoint a second judge to the Supreme Court. Two major high-profile appointments in his first half-term, however, brought with them a chance to change the Supreme Court for years to come. The opportunity came about when Anthony Kennedy retired in 2018. Kennedy was often the swing vote in Supreme Court decisions, sometimes voting in the conservative mode but other times showing a liberal form of thinking (e.g., he voted in favor of legalized same-sex marriage in a 5–4 decision; he helped to preserve *Roe* v. *Wade*). However, with Kennedy's decision to step down, the Supreme Court was subject to transformation for generations as Trump would surely nominate a young, conservative jurist. Such an action would create a bloc of five staunch conservative justices and cement a conservative majority for the foreseeable future (Vogue 2018).

The fate of the Supreme Court as either an enlightened, rationally based group of thinkers who embraced democratic ideals of equality for all and who would promote science and reason, or a Court that would be dominated by conservative, sometimes reactionary forms of thinking, now rested with Donald Trump. How had the United States reached this point? As we know, Trump not only chose a conservative judge to sit on the Supreme Court; he picked a highly controversial one in Brett Kavanaugh.

Kavanaugh, at age 53 at the time of his selection as Trump's nominee for the Supreme Court, was young by the standards of the high court. He had been a long-time foe of former President Bill Clinton and a former aide to President George W. Bush. Kavanaugh was the lead author of the controversial Starr Report and a member of Independent Counsel Kenneth Starr's investigation that had ultimately resulted in Clinton being impeached (Nussbaum 2018). Kavanaugh is no stranger to the flooded swamp, having spent the vast majority of his career in the capital, having been born in Washington, DC and raised in Bethesda, Maryland. His wife Ashley had been a former personal secretary to George W. Bush (Nussbaum 2018). Kavanaugh was confirmed to the Court on October 6, 2018 in a hotly contested battle largely divided along party lines, 50–48. In addition to bitterly partisan debates, the nomination process was marred by allegations of sexual misconduct against Kavanaugh that began to surface the month prior to his confirmation (Segers, Watson, Nolen, and Erickson 2018). Kavanaugh's temperament and love of beer also became areas of concern, as highlighted in Box 4.

As potentially devastating as these two Supreme Court nominations are to the future of the United States as a leader in democratic principles centered on rational, reasoned, and scientific thought, imagine the fallout if Trump is allowed to make a third nomination. It's enough to make an enlightened person's mind blow. The possibility is all too real when we realize that the average age for retirement of the last 11 Supreme Court justices was 80, and in 2019 two justices were already past that age (Baker 2018). Ruth Bader Ginsburg turned 86 on March 15, 2019 and Stephen Breyer turned 81 on August 15, 2019. Both of these justices are considered to lean left in their ideological beliefs.

The acting government

Many examples of Trump's revolving cabinet doors were described earlier but more disconcerting than the fact that many of his appointees come and go is the realization that many more members of Trump's team are acting members of his administration. It is a sure sign of the murky White House swamp created by Trump when one realizes that temporary administrative members do not have to go through the approval process.

In April 2019, Secretary of Homeland Security Kirstjen Nielsen resigned and it became but a part of a pattern for the Trump administration. At that time, three of the president's cabinet members were serving in an acting capacity. Six months after Nielsen's resignation, her replacement, Acting Homeland Security Secretary Kevin McAleenan, resigned (October 11, 2019). He was criticized over family separations at the US–Mexico border. McAleenan is the eighteenth cabinet-level official to resign since Trump took office less than three years earlier in 2017; that compares to seven such departures in the first three years of the Obama administration and four for President George W. Bush (Naylor 2019). Trying to underscore the importance of an "acting" cabinet, Max Stier, CEO of the Partnership for Public Service, states, "We don't have established leaders in really important places in our government" (Naylor 2019). Stier compares the acting directors to substitute teachers; "They might be amazing educators or amazing leaders in their own right, but they're not set out for success. They're not going to be perceived as having complete and full authority by those that are around them" (Naylor 2019). Trump has said, "I am in no hurry" to fill the positions; "I like acting. It gives me more flexibility. Do you understand that? I like acting" (*Guardian* 2019).

The idea of so many acting positions within the Trump administration is troublesome and contributes to the deepening of the swamp as it means Trump would rather avoid Senate confirmation. Naylor (2019) explains, "It also means an end-around of the Senate, which the U.S. Constitution says has a role to advise and consent to the president's appointments." Stier adds, "It's not only the Senate that's voting on them. In some very real way, it's also a public vetting that's occurring when the Senate is performing this function" (Naylor 2019). The lack of public review and vetting are elements of a political swamp.

The clogged swamp

One of the many campaign promises made by Trump but left drastically unfulfilled is his promise to drain the swamp. He not only failed to drain the political swamp but, as documented here, the swamp has gotten deeper and murkier.

Trump promised that he would make ethical reforms to lobbying. He did detail a five-point list of ethical reforms but he only partially delivered only on one of them. In fact, spending on lobbying in Washington, DC has reached a record high under his watch. Trump not only failed at cleaning up lobbying by the time his presidency had reached just two years of completion; his campaign, transition, inauguration, businesses, and presidency were all under investigation. In addition, nearly every organization he had led was also under investigation. The "witch hunt" that was supposedly the Mueller investigation led to dozens of people being charged with wrongdoing, including possible treasonous activity. The Mueller Report essentially concluded that while the Trump team had tried to collude with Russians they were too inept to accomplish it; there were ten counts of obstruction identified. Trump has repeatedly hammered home a simple, powerful defense to any and all claims of collusion by saying, "No collusion!" Such a claim came under bipartisan fire on June 13, 2019, when Trump said he would gladly "listen" if a foreign government offered him dirt on a political opponent and asserted that there would be nothing wrong with doing so (Stokols and Bierman 2019). Trump's defiant comments during a "television interview suggest special counsel Robert S. Mueller III's final report—which found 'sweeping and systematic' Russian interference in the 2016 election aimed at helping Trump win—did not so much chasten Trump as embolden him" (Stokols and Bierman 2019:A1). "National security veterans warned that Trump's cavalier attitude all but invited foreign meddling in the 2020 race, raising the stakes as election officials and campaigns worry about sophisticated 'deep fake' videos and other disinformation aimed at influencing voters" (Stokols and Bierman 2019:A1). Robert Anderson, a former assistant director of the FBI's counter-intelligence, division said, "Every hostile intelligence service in the world is listening to that. Forget Russia, it's everybody. It's China, its Iran" (Stokols and Bierman 2019:A1). House Speaker Nancy Pelosi (D-San Francisco) said that Trump's comments shows that "he does not know the difference between right and wrong, and that's probably the nicest thing I could say about him" (Stokols and Bierman 2019:A9). Accepting foreign help to win an election is illegal, unethical, immoral, and Trump's statement is another sign that the level of muck in the swamp has risen under Trump's watch.

A number of former Trump associates found themselves incarcerated for wrongdoings on behalf of the president, although Trump insists they acted on their own. The president's cabinet has become somewhat of a revolving door with people coming and going, some having been fired, others who resigned because they felt they could no longer work for Trump. President Trump has made numerous federal appeals judge appointments, which is common for any president, and he also secured adding two new conservative judges to the Supreme Court, one with a very questionable background. His preference for an acting government has allowed him to circumvent the Senate confirmation procedures that are so vital to American democracy.

Trump himself seems enamored with autocrats. He often praises North Korean leader Kim Jong Un even though he is one of the world's most brutally repressive dictators. Trump said of the dictator, "Hey, he's the head of a country. And I mean he is the strong head. Don't let anyone think anything different. He speaks and his people sit up at attention. I want my people to do the same" (Bierman and Stokols 2018:A7). Does Trump really want Americans to treat him as a dictator? Do his supporters really want the United States to fall under the rule of dictator? Around the world everyone wonders and worries about the United States. Nicholas Burns, a former undersecretary of state and NATO ambassador, said, "It's been a troubling week for America's credibility in the world. Our leadership of the West has long been a moral leadership, that we will be the country that defends democracy" (Bierman and Stokols 2018:A7). Trump's supporters seem to be willing to ignore how Trump buddies up with Kim Jong Un and point to his hard-line message against certain other autocrats. While the Trump administration may target leftist autocrats in Cuba, Venezuela, and Nicaragua, it embraces right-wing autocrats in Columbia, Chile, and Brazil (Wilkinson 2018b). Some have suggested that Trump suffers from "dictator envy" (Bierman and Stokols 2018).

In sum, Trump's swamp is such a cesspool that it resembles a clogged drain filled with all sorts of nasty bits of sewage.

The Deep State

The concept of the "Deep State" has reached the consciousness of many people, from those who are seriously attempting to uncover the presumed reality of such an entity, to those who need to blame a scapegoat when their socio-political ideas are challenged by facts, to those who seem to be crackpots and need to self-publish on the topic because their ideas do not stand up to peer-reviewed scrutiny. The Deep State is the operating arm of neither the left nor the right, but it most certainly casts a shadow over "legitimate" government. Chaffetz (2018) describes the Deep State as an intentional, unconstitutional, and organized phenomenon that possesses "pure, unfettered power, and it gets very angry when it is even questioned" (p. xi). Jeremy Stone (2018) refers to

> the deep state as an internal and foreign Government that functions independently and in direct opposition to our sovereign "Nation State." This kind of shadow government is both internal and foreign because although its members currently function inside nearly every U.S. Government agency, they are foreign, as they operate as embedded moles from previous administrations and have been inserted from hostile foreign governments in an attempt to undermine our Republic.

Stone adds to his interpretation of the Deep State as a group of people attempting to establish a globalist-communist state. Not all interpretations of the "Deep State" are as extreme as Stone's, but thinking of such an entity as secretive and working in the shadows is very consistent.

As we shall learn in the following pages, there are those who think the Deep State is in fact real, in one shape or another, and exists to undermine the legitimate government of the US, and those who believe that the notion of the Deep State only exists in foreign nations and not the United States.

Explaining the Deep State

Mike Lofgren (2016) views the Deep State as a shadow government that exists alongside the legitimate government. On the one hand, there is a visible US government situated in buildings around the Mall in Washington, DC, and there is another more secretive and indefinable government that is not so readily visible. This shadowy government supposedly controls elections regardless of who is formally in power. In other words, the Deep State consists of those not necessarily working in the interests of any particular political party, but operates to meet its own goals. Lofgren (2016) cites Franklin D. Roosevelt's April 29, 1938 message to

Congress to help illustrate his point that there has been an awareness of the "Deep State" for a long time. Roosevelt states,

> The first truth is that the liberty of a democracy is not safe if the people tolerate the growth of private power to a point where it becomes stronger than their democratic State itself. That, in its essence, is fascism—ownership of government by an individual, by a group or by any other controlling private power
>
> *(Lofgren 2016:30)*

Lofgren (2016) believes that the Deep State has developed slowly over a period of nearly a century as he states: "Mountains of empirical evidence teach us that those features arose by tiny degrees over eons as random adaptations to chance and necessity" (p. 33). Emphasizing his point that the Deep State's origin does not come from a specific political party, Lofgren (2016) describes how in recent years the left viewed George W. Bush as a demonic figure put into power by those behind the scenes just as those on the right came to view Obama as a tyrant.

The components of the Deep State, according to Lofgren (2016), are a hybrid of national security and law enforcement agencies along with key members of other branches of government (i.e., the Department of Defense, the Department of State, the Department of Homeland Security, the Central Intelligence Agency, and the Department of the Treasury) and members of certain other key areas of the judiciary (i.e., the Foreign Intelligence Surveillance Court—appointed by the Chief Justice of the Supreme Court—whose actions are mysterious even to most members of Congress), whose roles give them membership in the Deep State. Powerful individuals and groups from Wall Street, Silicon Valley, and key corporate entities connected by a web of money, mutual goals, and careerism to specific and very powerful elements of corporate America, combined with all the other representatives previously described above, help to make up the governmental military–industrial complex.

Lofgren is not the first person, of course, to warn of the governmental military–industrial complex. Among the more notable persons to discuss this are former US president Dwight Eisenhower and American sociologist C. Wright Mills. Eisenhower warned the nation about what he described as a threat to democratic government—the military–industrial complex, a formidable union of defense contractors and the armed forces. Eisenhower, a retired five-star Army general, the man who led the allies on D-Day, made the remarks in his farewell speech from the White House in January 1961. He used this speech to warn about the "the immense military establishment" that had joined with "a large arms industry." Here's an excerpt from his farewell speech: "In the councils of government, we must guard against the acquisition of unwarranted influence, whether sought or unsought, by the military–industrial complex. The potential for the disastrous rise of misplaced power exists, and will persist" (*NPR* 2011). The concern that Eisenhower, or Ike, as he was known, had over those who control the decision making for the military–industrial complex also came at the expense of resources that could otherwise be allocated to building hospitals and schools—a concern that has been legitimized numerous times and especially with the wars waged since his time. Consider, for example, the recent wars waged by the United States and its allies in the Persian Gulf that have included the hiring of private contractors (i.e., Blackwater). These contractors are hired to fight wars, which in turn lead to greater profits for private industrial giants. This reality reeks of the Deep State.

> Private military contractors perform tasks once thought to be inherently governmental, such as raising foreign armies, conducting intelligence analysis and trigger-pulling. During the Iraq and Afghanistan wars, they constituted about 15 percent of all contractors. But don't let the numbers fool you. Their families have outsized impact on U.S. strategy.
>
> *(McFate 2016)*

The reliance on contracting private soldiers to fight wars is a result of the Deep State, which has convinced (or influenced) decision makers in the US government to continue to wage war so that they may profit from it. Many of the private contractors fighting for the US are not even American (McFate 2016). The United States is not the only government that has been duped into military action by the Deep State; a US Senate investigation in 2010 found that the United Kingdom also subcontracted private military companies such as the ArmorGroup who further sub-contracted two Afghan military companies called "Mr. White" and "Mr. Pink" to provide a guard force. "The investigation found evidence that they were linked to murder, kidnapping, bribery, and anti-coalition activities" (McFate 2016).

When looking for members of the Deep State from the perspective of a corrupt military–industrial complex it is useful to investigate who profits from war. With the Gulf Wars, private contractors are among those who profited; in any modern war, the private and corporate leaders of industries that make products for war, such as the war machine industries (e.g., tanks, helicopters, war ships, and war planes) and, of course, the gun industry are among those who profit from the death of innocent civilians and soldiers. Dow Chemical profited tremendously from producing chemical weapons of warfare including Agent Orange for the Vietnam War. Dow's development of napalm for wars previous to and including the Vietnam War was a huge moneymaker for the chemical company. Senior management at Dow Chemical initially denied any knowledge of napalm production for war (PBS 2019). If this is true, Dow executives did not know about their own company producing napalm, which would speak of infiltration at the decision making level. If the top executives knew about the production of napalm all along, that would speak to direct involvement in a consortium of power.

Before Eisenhower's warning, C. Wright Mills wrote about the "triangle of power" or "tripartite elite" in *The Power Elite* (1956) as an increasing threat to American democracy.

> The power elite is composed of men whose positions enable them to transcend the ordinary environments of ordinary men and women; they are in positions to make decisions having major consequences.... They rule big corporations. They run the machinery of the state and claim its prerogatives. They direct the military establishment. They occupy the strategic command posts of the social structure, in which are now centered the effective means of the power and the wealth and the celebrity which they enjoy.
>
> *(Mills 1956:3–4)*

Mills (1958) explained the unity of the power elite in psychological and economic terms. The members of the power elite generally share a similar origin, education, and style of life, and because of their similar social type, they easily intermingle. Additionally, since they are the "elites" of society, they share economic goals. The social context of the mid-1950s was clearly an influence on Mills' writings regarding the power elite. American military technology was superior, the economy was strong but becoming increasingly dependent on foreign markets, and a repressive political climate existed because of the Cold War; all contributed to Mills' "conspiracy" theory of the power elites (Delaney 2005). Since the time of Mills' writing on the topic of the power elite, the United States has been in a near-constant state of war, with military expenditures and budgets exploding to new highs and private corporations and power elites profiting from it all.

Prior to Mills' analysis of the power elites was Italian sociologist Vilfredo Pareto (1848–1923) and his concept of the "circulation of elites." Pareto wrote about this concept in three key publications with the primary articulation in *The Rise and Fall of the Elites: An Application of Theoretical Sociology* (1901). He uses the term "elite" mostly within the context of economics (the wealthy) and politics (those with power). The elites, then, are principally the bourgeoisie. The *circulation of elites* refers to Pareto's theory that while power elites come and go, there will in fact always be elites that rule over the masses. The elites are few in number but they remain in power because new elites take the place of older elites that die off. This "circulation of elites" assures that a limited number of people, often working in the shadows, will maintain power and influence. Thus, there is a domination of a very small minority over the majority (Pareto 2008).

Returning to Lofgren, he provides a socio-psychological perspective on how those in the Deep State can assure conformity among their subordinates. Lofgren (2016) cites the work of social psychologist Irving Janis and his concept of "groupthink." As described by Janis (1972, 1982), "groupthink" refers to the phenomenon of group members keeping their own opinions and ideas to themselves rather than expressing them to the group. They will do this even when they know that their private ideas are likely much better than those expressed by the most powerful person in the group. *Groupthink* occurs when members feel pressure to overconform (Delaney 2012). Group members feel so pressured to conform to the whims and desires of the group that they come to value conformity itself. This phenomenon occurs in friendship groups, the business world and in politics. In friendship groups some members feel the pressure to conform because of their sociopsychological need to be a part of a group even if that means giving up their voice. In the business world, subordinates are generally purposively kept out of the loop of full information and therefore risk looking ignorant if they express a view counter to the dominant one. Workers also feel the stress to conform because they do not want to risk losing their jobs if they are viewed as insubordinate. A famous quote from American socialist Upton Sinclair (1878–1968) helps to reinforce the idea that workers fear for their livelihoods if they challenge those with power—"It is difficult to get a man to understand something when his salary depends upon his not understanding it" (Lombardi 2019). Lofgren argues that the politics of Washington, DC is a universe wherein groupthink can thrive. This is true for a number of reasons including the fact that powerful people tend to surround themselves with like-minded thinking people and those who want to keep their jobs.

As demonstrated earlier in this chapter, President Trump has shown his willingness to fire those who do not support him 100 percent. Trump's demand for complete loyalty among the members of his inner circle results in a groupthink mentality. This pressure to conform was exposed again when it was revealed that his White House aides stood by silently for months even while Trump allegedly tried to strong-arm a foreign government (Megerian 2019e). The incident referenced here alludes to a whistleblower's complaint that the president attempted to get Ukraine to investigate his political enemies. In July 2019, Trump delayed nearly $400 million in foreign aid to Ukraine, a country that has been fending off Russia-backed separatists, and then told its president, Volodymyr Zelensky, a week later that he wanted a "favor" (Megerian 2019e). His subsequent orders to his underlings not to cooperate with any investigation led to a Democrat-led impeachment inquiry of Trump in September 2019. Early into the investigation, the Trump administration's Ukraine envoy, Kurt Volker, resigned after three congressional committees subpoenaed him to testify about the whistleblower complaint. Public impeachment hearings of Trump's alleged *quid pro quo* (granting a favor while expecting another favor in return) relationship with Ukraine began in November 2019. On December 10, 2019 the House Judiciary Committee moved to charge President Trump with at least two articles of impeachment: abuse of power and obstruction of Congress. Representative Jerrold Nadler (D-New York), the head of the committee, said, "We do not take this action lightly, but we have taken an oath to defend the Constitution" (Wire 2019:A1). On December 18, 2019, Trump was impeached on both counts. This was just the third time in US history that a president was impeached—forever staining Trump's already disgraced reputation. The articles of impeachment then went to the Republican-controlled Senate for trial. No impeached president has ever been removed from office. (Richard Nixon resigned before he was officially impeached by the House.) As expected, and based almost entirely on party affiliation (Republican Senator Mitt Romney of Utah was the lone GOP to break from the party), the Senate narrowly voted (52-48 favoring acquittal of abuse of power; 53-47 favoring acquittal of obstruction of Congress) not to remove Trump from office.

An unlikely source of light in the darkness of Trump's presidency came immediately following the impeachment as *Christianity Today*, an extremely conservative magazine serving evangelical interests, condemned Trump's use of "his political power to coerce a foreign leader to harass and discredit one of the president's political opponents … [this is] not only a violation of the Constitution; more importantly, it is profoundly immoral" (Galli 2009). The periodical, founded in 1956 by the late Rev. Billy Graham, stated that Trump should be removed from office and (if he is not removed) urged evangelical voters (a stronghold for Trump) not to vote for Trump in 2020.

Lofgren (2016) adds another interesting reason as to why people conform so easily and this is because of the very nature of most people's jobs—they are boring, mundane, uninspiring, and/or routine. This boredom leads to assimilation, which leads to complacency and an unwillingness to rock the boat. Look at nearly any place of employment, including politics, and you will find that many of the older employees simply want to put in their time until retirement and younger employees need their jobs to support their families. Employers generally prefer married employees who need to support a family because they know such workers are less likely to draw attention to improprieties. Challenging the power elite equates to a risk that many are afraid to accept. (And thus the value of tenure in occupations so that those with great knowledge of that particular workplace can feel the freedom to challenge the status quo without fear of being fired.) For Lofgren, all of these elements of the Deep State contribute toward an explanation as to why so few people are willing to be whistle-blowers; they are afraid of the consequences and the repercussions of the power elite and the Deep State. Repercussions extend beyond losing one's job as the power elites will use their advantageous position to harass and ridicule their accusers. Trump publicly ridiculed the whistle-blower that led to his impeachment inquiry as a coward and enemy of the state and suggested that it was the whistle-blower who had engaged in treasonous behavior. Beyond the fear of being fired and ridiculed is the realization that those who have knowledge of wrongdoing in their workplace are all too often afraid to speak out against injustices because they do not have the guts to shine the light on the darkness.

For the past few years, a number of writers for *The New York Times*, citing a variety of "experts" on the topic, have written articles about the "Deep State" and have essentially concluded that it does not exist in the United States. "American institutions do not resemble the powerful deep states of countries like Egypt or Pakistan, experts say. Nor do individual leaks, a number of which have come from President Trump's own team, amount to a conspiracy" (Fisher 2017). According to Fisher (2017), Trump's claims that the "Deep State" is responsible for leaks, internal conflict, and the politicization of institutions like intelligence agencies under his watch represent an attempt at damage control of his own shortcomings and poor leadership.

> Mr. Trump has put institutions under enormous stress. He has attacked them publicly, implied he would reject intelligence findings that cast his election in

a poor light, hobbled agencies by failing to fill critical positions and cut off bodies like the National Security Council from shaping policy. That has forced civil servants into an impossible dilemma: acquiesce, allowing their institution to be sidelined, or mount a defense, for example through leads that counter Mr. Trump's accusations or pressure him into restoring normal policy-maker practices.

(Fisher 2017)

Blaming a liberal-led Deep State weakens the US government's ability to perform its duties and jeopardizes the millions of Americans who depend upon it (Fisher 2017).

While blaming dysfunctional governance on partisan disputes and a Deep State seems to have solidified the loyalty of Trump's supporters to the president in the short term, it carries great risks in the long run.

Elizabeth N. Saunders, a George Washington University political scientist, compared this dynamic to the way that science had been "polarized" by fights over climate change. When opponents of environmental regulations disputed basic climate science, researchers felt compelled to push back. Science became an increasingly partisan issue, which hurt scientists' ability to shape public understand and government policy.

(Fisher 2017)

Saunders adds that government agencies and institutions could face a similar fate. "The more they're publicly drawn into these battles, the more there will be polarization and politicization of them, too" Saunders states (Fisher 2017). As a specific example, consider the Trump accusation that former President Barack Obama wire-tapped the White House phones, which forced the FBI into

an unappealing choice: Let the accusations slide, though it implies the bureau broke the law, or rebuke the president and risk the appearance of playing politics. Either way, the bureau loses some of its internal influence, public stature or, quite possibly, both. Losing stature can be especially dangerous, as the bureau needs public trust to effectively operate.

(Fisher 2017)

Intelligence agencies faced a similar situation under President Nixon as he had publicly attacked such agencies; those that sided with him would eventually have their reputations tarnished. Interestingly, it was an FBI official, W. Mark Felt, who leaked details of the Watergate break-in that led to Nixon's impeachment (Fisher 2017). Nixon's bravado and belief that he was above the law would lead to his impeachment and ultimately his humiliating evacuation of the White House.

There have been a number of leaks from government officials during Trump's presidency. In 2019, one such leak led to an impeachment inquiry (as described earlier in this chapter), and many others have contributed to the desperate and often effective tactic of Trump to blame the Deep State, which is now being labeled as a liberal, Democratic entity. However, it is not just liberals and Democrats questioning the legitimacy of a Deep State operating in the US and conspiring against President Trump. Experts say that countries such as Egypt, Turkey, and Pakistan have shadowy networks within government bureaucracies, often referred to as "Deep States," that undermine and coerce elected governments, but they question a Deep State in the United States (Taub and Fisher 2017). Taub and Fisher (2017) describe how leaks can be a normal and healthy check on a president's power but also risk developing an entrenched culture of conflict between the president and his own bureaucracy. Issandr El Amrani, an analyst who has written on Egypt's Deep State, does not believe that the US has reached the Deep State status of Egypt but warns that deep divisions within society create constant tensions (Taub and Fisher 2017). Tension gives rise to conflict. The conflict theory in sociology views society as composed of competing elements (interest groups) that fight over scarce resources (e.g., wealth, power, and prestige) with power differentials that ultimately determine the allocation and distribution of these scarce resources (Delaney 2014). The power elites will always act in a manner as to maintain their power positions in society and will attempt to impose their will on subordinate groups. It is the existence of multiple groups (which results in a stratified society) with different values, goals, and aspirations that results in tension, strain, and conflict between them. As Lewis Coser (1956) states, "Conflict sets boundaries between groups within a social system by strengthening group consciousness and awareness of separateness, thus establishing the identity of groups within the system" (p. 34). Democratic leaders are expected to try and find a way to secure compromises among the varying groups in an attempt to establish social cohesion or, at the very least, minimize open conflict. This expectation is especially important in the United States, a nation that attempts to export its brand of democracy across the globe. And yet, the US has a president that consistently does the opposite. When it comes to leaks, the president can either look at them as cries for attention on matters that need to be addressed in a different manner, or they can be viewed as attacks. We know how Trump looks at any criticism of his decision making. Taub and Fisher (2017) state, "Mr. Trump's tendency to treat each leak as an attack rather than an attempt to influence policy has created an atmosphere in Washington of open institutional conflict."

As a result of their research, Taub and Fisher (2017) have come to view the "Deep State" not as a shadowy conspiracy but instead as a political conflict between a nation's leader and its governing institutions. This perspective is very narrow in focus and ignores the power elite theory brought forth by Mills and other conflict theorists. Perhaps, at the very least, the notion of the Deep State as a conflict between a nation's leader and its governing institutions would be viewed as an aspect of the Deep State put forth by many conflict theorists.

Julie Hirschfeld Davis is another writer for the *New York Times* who has conducted research on the Deep State. Davis (2017) describes the concept of a "Deep State"—"a shadowy network of agency or military officials who secretly conspire to influence government policy"—as more often used to describe countries like Egypt, Turkey, and Pakistan. Davis (2017), like Taub and Fisher, describes how President Trump and his most trusted inner circle (some of whom are no longer a part of the inner circle) view attacks on his administration and leaks about his alleged corruption as attacks from within their own government. While neither Trump nor Steve Bannon (Trump's then chief strategist) uses the term "Deep State" publicly (as of the time of this article), Breitbart News, the conservative site Bannon used to run, uses the term frequently in its coverage. Reacting in kind, other right-leaning websites and conservative talk radio shows are increasingly using the "Deep State" concept as a means of inflaming the flock. (Bannon left his position with Trump on August 18, 2017 and rejoined Breitbart.) As for the legitimacy in the claim that a Deep State is trying to bring down President Trump, Michael V. Hayden, the former Central Intelligence Agency director under both Obama and former President George Bush, said, "'Deep state,' I would never use [that term]. That's a phrase we've used for Turkey and other countries like that, but not the American republic" (Davis 2017). Loren DeJonge Schulman, a former top official in Obama's National Security Council, also questions the idea that a Deep State operates in the United States.

> A deep state, when you're talking about Turkey or Egypt or other countries, that's part of government or people outside of government that are literally controlling the direction of the country no matter who's actually in charge, and probably engaging in murder and other corrupt practices. It's shocking to hear that kind of thinking from a president or the people closest to him.
>
> *(Davis 2017)*

Davis (2017) adds, "The deep state is a phrase often heard in countries where there is a history of military coups and where generals often hold power independent of elected leaders." James Jay Carafano, a fellow at the Heritage Foundation who advised Trump's transition, states,

> Just because you see things like leaks and interference and obstruction doesn't necessarily mean there's a deep state—that's something we've seen before, historically, and its nothing new. What would be different is if there were folks from the previous administration that were consciously orchestrating, in a serious way, inside opposition to the president. [In the absence of evidence, one way or the other] It's hard to know: Is this Trump using some strong political rhetoric, or an actual theory?
>
> *(Davis 2017)*

Constitutional attorney John W. Whitehead describes a different type of shadow government, one that has long been in the making and yet is "shrouded in secrecy, even to those elected to represent the American people in Congress that essentially exists and functions contrary to any concept of democratic government. The little [information] that has leaked out merely serves to reinforce concerns that an authoritarian government waits in the wings" (Whitehead 2011). This authoritarian government waiting to emerge from the shadows will reveal itself after a major life-threatening event such as a terrorist attack, Whitehead argues. While Whitehead's description of a shadow government may seem far-fetched and hard to believe, he does cite the specific Continuity of Government (COG) plan that has been in existence since the days of the Cold War, designed to keep the government of the United States operating following a catastrophic attack on the nation's capital. Found within the COG plan is the 102-page National Continuity Plan, which contains the strategy for the mass evacuation and relocation of every federal government agency including the White House and the military in response to an exceptional catastrophic event within the National Capital Region (White House Information 2019).

The designated individuals from every federal agency would be a part of an "Emergency Relocation Group" and taken to a secure bunker so that they could perform their duties in assuring that the government continue to operate. Selected individuals would also mean that non-elected persons would be in charge under a declared presidential emergency. The country would be subjected to martial law and the Constitution and Bill of Rights would be suspended. Among the hand-picked designees under President Ronald Reagan were Congressman Dick Cheney and Donald Rumsfeld, then a business executive with G.D. Searle & Co. "At least once a year during the 1980s, Cheney and Rumsfeld vanished on top-secret training missions, where each of the teams practiced evacuating and directing a counter nuclear strike against Russia" (Whitehead 2011). Plans changed following the September 11, 2001 attacks as it was deemed that the assumptions that drove COG planning during the Cold War were no longer applicable. "Instead of relying on part-time bureaucrats and evacuation schematics, the Bush administration permanently appointed executive officials, stationed outside the capital, to run a shadow government" (Whitehead 2011). The plans for the shadow government are very elaborate and include massive underground bunkers the size of small cities that are sprinkled throughout the country for the government elite to escape to in the event of a national emergency. Mount Weather near Bluemont, Virginia is one of these facilities and among other things it includes a hospital, crematorium, dining and recreation areas, reservoirs of drinking and cooling water, an emergency power plant, sleeping quarters, and a radio/television studio (Whitehead 2011). Such a revelation makes it a little easier to understand why the elites are not worried about an environmental nightmare as they will live safely in bunkers (or, if given enough time, on colonies away from Earth).

As the preceding discussion reveals, there is little wonder that the "Deep State" is shrouded in mystery. Its very existence is, on the one hand, denied and on the other hand treated as a given, albeit in varying form (e.g., it is the result of one political party out to get another; it belongs to no political party; it is really the power elites; it is the result of a military–industrial complex out to secure funds for its continued corporate growth; it is a concerted effort by some to undermine a standing president; or it refers to a shadow government waiting to emerge following a major catastrophic attack on the nation's capital).

Dangerous secret societies

The existence of a Deep State is difficult to confirm with full certainty but there appears to be enough evidence to conclude that such an entity does exist. That the Deep State is generally described as a shadowy body of powerful individuals with a like-minded goal of maximizing profits for a select few speaks of a secret society. The secretive nature of the Deep State makes it difficult to clearly identify specific individuals, although it is easy to speculate that it consists of the most powerful elites who value profits over the good of society as a whole. Furthermore, because many of the power elites that make up the Deep State come from other secret societies that are identifiable, we turn our attention to some of the most dangerous secret societies in the world.

A "secret society" is a relative term as clearly some people know about their existence, while most do not. By definition, a *secret* is something kept hidden or unexplained, it is mysterious, and involves keeping important bits of information concealed from others. *Secret societies* involve a membership wherein individuals have taken an oath or a vow to maintain allegiance to the group or organization; they may, or may not, attempt to conceal its existence but they do keep its primary activities suppressed. German sociologist Georg Simmel (1906) states that the first internal relation typical of the secret society is the reciprocal confidence among members. It is required because the purpose of secrecy is protection of the group members. The oath of secrecy is coupled with a very impressive schooling in the moral solidarity among members. With increased growth come more rituals, degrees of initiation, group egoism, centralization of group needs, and de-individualism. There are many secret societies; some, not so ironically, are unknown because they are secretive while others, such as college fraternities and sororities, are well-known fraternal orders recognized by the general public. While we know of the existence of such secretive organizations as fraternities and sororities, we do not know of all their private activities. Secret societies engage in rites and activities that are concealed from nonmembers. The term "secret society" is generally not applicable to covert groups, such as intelligence agencies, or guerrilla insurgencies. A number of lists of secret societies exist. Below are a few examples of some of the most dangerous secret societies that have been identified.

Writing for the *India Times*, an English-language daily newspaper owned by The Times Group and the third-largest newspaper in India by circulation and largest-selling English-language daily in the world (according to Audit Bureau of Circulations, India), Rishabh Banerji (2018) provides a list of nine of the most dangerous secret societies in the world:

1 **The Order of Skull and Bones.** Founded in 1832 by a community of students from Yale University, this secret society is famous for being a part of a

number of conspiracy theories, including the popular belief that the founders of the CIA were members of this group (Banerji 2018). Each year, only 15 juniors are chosen for lifetime membership; they reportedly have to divulge intimate personal details, including full sexual histories, before being inducted and they agree to give part of their estates to the club. In return, they receive a promise of lifelong financial stability (Sterbenz and Jackson 2015). Among the members of the Order of Skull and Bones are three former US presidents, William Howard Taft (his father Alphonso was the co-founder of this secretive society and would later become a Supreme Court of Ohio Justice), George Herbert Walker Bush and George W. Bush. Women were not allowed into this secretive society until 1991 (Sterbenz and Jackson 2015).

2 **The German Thule Society.** Founded in August 1919 in Munich, it is presumed to have been the real inspiration of Nazism as a number of Nazi leaders were a part of Thule. Adolf Hitler was associated with the society as a "visiting brother" (Banerji 2018). The Thule Society believed in killing people to reduce the world's population, practiced sexual magic and black magic, and partook in racist chants. "Some say that it was a demonic ritual on the sexually impotent Hitler that made him into the sadistic killer the world got to later know him as" (Banerji 2018). Today, the Thule Society considers Hitler as one of the greatest leaders of all time and describes him as a spiritual being and leader (Thule Society 2019).

3 **The Bilderberg Group.** This group would seem to epitomize the meaning of the "Deep State" as, according to Banerji (2018), it is compromised of the world's elite and hosts an annual private conference of 120–150 of the most influential people from the world of business, finance, academics, media, and even some presidents and prime ministers. Top military intelligence manages the security for its annual meeting of financial planning and plotting (Bilderberg Group 2019). Its purpose is to create an "aristocracy of purpose," mainly in the United States and Europe. Simply being rich is not enough to gain membership into this secretive society; members must be among the truly powerful elites. The Bilderberg Group has "been accused of conspiracy theories around the world, including the Great Depression and most of the world's biggest terrorist activities" (Banerji 2018).

4 **Freemasonry.** One might wonder how the Freemasons are included in a list of the most dangerous secretive societies as they are mostly known for their charitable work. Banerji (2018) states, "The 'G' used in their signs apparently stands for the Masonic gnosis or generation with Lucifer, and God as the main enemy of Christendom … [They] vow not to reveal the secret of the Masons to anybody outside their group, not even to their wives." Freemasons worship a generic Grand Architect of the Universe and not the Christian God, and this helps to explain why the Catholic Church condemns it. Curiously, while Freemasonry is not really a religion, agnostics and atheists cannot join. Compared to other secretive organizations with clear financial goals and the intent of solidifying power for the elites, it seems a little odd that Banerji lists them as

the fourth-most dangerous secret society in the world. Then again, the nature of secret societies may lead us to wonder what exactly the activities of this organization are.

5   **The Order of the Nine Angles (ONA).** This satanic group is based in the United Kingdom and its members are followers of Satanism and hold Neo-Nazi ideologies and activism. The ONA believes in human sacrifice as a way to eliminate weaknesses and claims that the evil tribes are an important part of the strategy of the devil to carry out the mission to disrupt and ultimately conquer the common people (Banerji 2018). The ONA also promotes rebellion against authority and challenges its members to upset the status quo of social and political society (Baciu 2015).

6   **The Assassins.** Banerji (2018) describes the Assassins, or Hashashin, as "one of the most fearful of all the secret societies in the world" as "they are known for striking down their targets regardless of the number of security personnel that guard them." The Assassins are an organization of the past, as the Mongols virtually destroyed them in the thirteenth century. The mystique of this group, however, has carried on throughout time. Regardless of their skill in assassination, they are no match for modern militaries. There is a 2015 movie called "The Assassin" that depicts this ancient dangerous secret society.

7   **The Ku Klux Klan.** This American cult, also known as the KKK or the Klan, strikes terror in countless innocent people, especially African Americans and Catholics. The KKK advocates extremist views such as white supremacy, white nationalism, and anti-immigration. Those who oppose them face possible terrorist reprisal. Founded in 1865 in Pulaski, Tennessee, the KKK "became a vehicle for white southern resistance to the Republican's Party's Reconstruction-era policies aimed at establishing political and economic equality for blacks. Its members waged an underground campaign of intimidation and violence directed at white and black Republican leaders" (History.com 2019). The Republican Party of Lincoln is far different today. Members of the KKK openly march at a number of Trump political rallies and feel empowered by his often-racist rhetoric.

8   **The Illuminati.** Made popular by Dan Brown's famous novel *The Da Vinci Code*, the Illuminati represent perhaps the most popular cult of modern society. As Banerji (2018) explains: "The Illuminati, which in Latin means the enlightened, refers to various organizations that claim to have links to the Bavarian Illuminati. The Bavarian Illuminati is an Enlightenment-era secret society, founded on May 1, 1776 that opposed superstition, obscurantism, religious influence over public life and abuses of state power." In the decades following its formation, Bavarian ruler Charles Theodore, with the encouragement of the Catholic Church, attempted to put to an end to the Illuminati, Freemasonry, and other secret societies. According to information provided on the homepage of the Illuminati's (2019) official website, "The Illuminati is an elite organization of world leaders, business authorities, innovators, artists, and other influential members of this planet." Such an admission lends this organization

as a possible aspect of the Deep State. Banerji (2018) adds that the Illuminati is "often alleged to conspire and control world affairs by masterminding events and planting agents in government and corporations to establish a New World Order and gain further political power and influence. The group has been depicted as working in the shadows with references being spotted in novels, movies, television shows, comics, video games, and music videos. Modern conspiracy theorists believe that the Illuminati are the ones who have been pulling the strings in most of the world's major events, including the Battle of Waterloo, the French revolution and President John F. Kennedy's assassination."

9 **Ashoka's Nine Unknown Men.** This is the final secret society that Banerji (2019) has included in his top nine most dangerous secret societies, even though it no longer exists. Ashoka is "India's only recorded secret society, perhaps the oldest, and the one that could change the world. Some believe that this was the most powerful society in the world, especially because there were only 9 members in it. King Ashoka of the Maurya dynasty in 270 B.C., who had a change of heart after his conquest of Kalinga, formed a secret society of 9 men who would hold the key to everything in this world." The Nine Unknown Men are widely suspected of manipulating political and societal trends in order to further the personal goals of the organization (Sullivan 2016).

Other lists of dangerous secret societies include many of the same examples provided by Banerji, although they may be ranked differently; they may also contain other organizations such as: The Knights of the Golden Circle; The Black Hand; The Order of the Golden Dawn; Ordo Templi Orientis; and The Knights Templar.

Of the secretive organizations described here, it is relatively easy to speculate that the Deep State consists of members of the Order of Skull and Bones, the Thule Society, the Illuminati, and especially the Bilderberg Group.

Too big to fail ... from flooding the swamp

The collective influence of "Big Business," "Big Tech," "Big Data," "Big Pharma," "Big Banks," and "Big Religion" in the global community is immense and contributes heavily to both the "swamp" and the "Deep State." The captains of these industries are among some of the most pivotal power elites that can have an undue influence political policy.

Big Business

"Big Business" is a term used to describe financial organizations considered as a group that are powerful, generate large profits, and exert a significant influence on social and political policy. "The term originated in the middle and late 19th century, when a large number of mergers and acquisitions consolidated many large companies that previously existed" (The Free Dictionary 2019b). Porter (2005) explains how Big Business grew from 1860 to 1920 due to a number of reasons, including primary shifts in technologies and markets, changing cultural values and sensibilities of Americans during that era, growing ties between emerging corporations and other American institutions, the nature of competition among giant firms, and the dawn of modern advertising and consumerism. Mass production in manufacturing, the development of efficient transportation systems, and industrialists such as Andrew Carnegie willing to put huge profits above all else would continue to assist the growth of Big Business and corporations throughout the twentieth century. In early twenty-first century, Big Business continues to grow. Tyler Cowen (2019), in his "love letter" to Big Business, states that Big Business has two straightforward and essential virtues: "First, business makes most of the stuff we enjoy and consume. Second, business is what gives most of us jobs" (p. 1). As a means of explanation, Cowen (2019) states that he uses the word "business" as "a commercial or sometimes an industrial enterprise" and uses the more legally precise word "corporation" interchangeably, even though the two concepts are not strictly the same. Cowen (2019) adds, "A kid with a lemonade stand is a business but not a corporation" (p. 2). As another aspect of his defense of Big Business, Cowen describes its overall performance, by global standards, as remarkably impressive. Part of the success of American Big Business, according to Cowen, is the fact that the American economy is accommodating to corporate enterprise and, compared to other countries, is relatively effective in weeding out the worst firms through competitive pressures. Cowen (2019) adds, "Compared with other major regions, the United States also does the best job of funneling labor and resources into the best-managed firms. That is, successful American businesses can grow and extend their reach" (p. 4). Furthermore, Cowen (2019) points out that business is less polarized and more virtuous than government. While few will argue that politics in many parts of the world and especially in contemporary United States is indeed polarizing, not everyone will agree that Big Business acts in an honorable manner.

It is certainly true that business, whether big or small, produces most of the products we enjoy and consume and it is the primary employer in the United States. According to the US Department of Labor's Bureau of Labor Statistics (BLS), there were more than 161 million jobs in the United States in 2018. In general categories, nearly 150 million (93 percent) of these jobs were in nonagricultural wage and salary work; 2.3 million (1.4 percent) in agriculture, forestry, fishing, and hunting; and nearly 9 million (5.5 percent) in self-employed nonagricultural work (BLS 2019). Some of the leading specific areas of business employment include: professional and business services, 20.9 million; health care and social assistance, 19.9 million; leisure and hospitality, 16.3 million; retail trade, 15.8 million; manufacturing, 12.6 million; and financial activities, 8.5 million (BLS 2019). The BLS (2019) reports that nearly 2.8 million Americans work for the federal government and nearly 20 million work for state and local governments.

While business in general has a number of positive benefits to the American and global economies, Cowen (2019) correctly points out that not all people are pro-Big Business.

> We live in an age when the reputation of business is under siege. Among Democrats, for instance, the word "socialism" now polls better than does "capitalism." But Republicans, while they pay greater lip service to some business ideals, are not in practice much better. Many of them have quite readily followed President Donald Trump into his attacks on free trade, immigration, outsourcing, and the American media (which is labeled "the enemy of the people")—all fundamentally anti-business stances.

Citing a 2016 Gallup poll, Cowen reveals how most Americans have little trust in Big Business. Just 6 percent said that they have "a great deal" of trust in Big Business, and 12 percent said they trust Big Business "quite a lot." In this same poll, it was revealed that zero percent of Americans have "a great deal" of trust in Congress, and just 6 percent have "quite a lot" of trust in Congress. The military is the highest-ranking institution among Americans, 41 percent of whom have "a great deal" of trust and 32 percent of whom have "quite a lot" of trust in it. Small business came in second among American institutions with 30 percent having "a great deal" of trust 38 percent reporting "quite a lot" of trust.

Small business remains as a vital aspect of the overall American economic sector. The US Small Business Administration (SBA) Office of Advocacy reports that small businesses generate 44 percent of US economic activity (SBA 2019). In US dollars, this 44 percent figure equated to $5.9 trillion in 2014. While the overall small business share of US GDP (gross national product is the market value of the goods and services produced by labor and property located in the United States) dropped from 48 percent to 43.5 percent from 1998 to 2014, the SBA (2019) states, "Over the same period, the amount of small business GDP has grown by about 25 percent in real terms, or 1.4 percent annually. However, real GDP for large businesses has grown faster, at 2.5 percent annually."

Despite the relative strength of small businesses in the overall US economy, they are just that—small in size, consisting of many varying industries. As a result, their ability to exert significant influence on the government is limited, especially when compared to Big Business. On the other hand, Big Business is dominated by a select few powerful industries, which is why it can have the greatest impact on politics and policy making decisions. Who are the largest corporations? According to *Fortune* (2019), the US "Fortune 500 companies represent two-thirds of the U.S. GDP with $13.7 trillion in revenues, $1.1. trillion in profits, $22.6 trillion in market value, and employ 28.7 million people worldwide." The top-ten largest corporations in the United States are: Wal-Mart (retail stores), Exxon Mobil (energy, chemical manufacturing, fossil fuels), Apple (electronics, technology), Berkshire Hathaway (Warren Buffet's conglomerate of well-known companies including Coca-Cola, Wells Fargo, and IBM), Amazon.com (e-commerce, data), United

Health Group, McKesson (largest drug distributor in the US), CVS Health (drug retailer), AT&T (communications), and AmerisourceBergen (drug distributors) (*Fortune* 2019). This top-ten list includes examples of Big Business, Big Tech, Big Data, and Big Pharma who all work with Big Banks.

The top 15 companies in the world by market value in 2019 were: Apple, Microsoft (systems and applications, electronics), Amazon.com, Alphabet (parent company of Google, data), Berkshire Hathaway, Facebook (social networking, data, tech), Alibaba (e-commerce, venture capital), Tencent Holdings (Chinese multinational conglomerate, internet services, artificial intelligence, technology), JPMorgan Chase (banking), Johnson & Johnson (pharmaceuticals), Visa (banking, technology), Exxon Mobil, ICBC (the world's largest bank), Wal-Mart, and Bank of America (banking) (Duffin 2019). Once again, we can see how all the "Big" industries of business, technology, data, pharma, and banks are represented in this list of powerful global businesses.

Recall the earlier discussions about the symbiotic relationship between the power elites and secret society members and the government, along with the discussion of the power elite theory, and we can see how top officials of Big Business can have a heavy influence on political matters. The ability of Big Business to impact politics and policy making is evident with all the largest corporations identified here. A number of specific examples from the various "Big" Businesses will be provided in the following pages, but our examination of the power of certain businesses that add to the flooding of the swamp begins here with a brief look at three specific industries as a whole—fossil fuels, tobacco, and guns.

That most of the world still has an antiquated dependency on fossil fuels as the primary source of energy is a sure testament to the power of "Big Oil" (a pejorative term used to describe the world's six-largest publicly traded oil and gas companies that especially have an impact on the US and the West; they are also known as supermajors) specifically, and the fossil fuel industry in general (OPEC and smaller gas and oil companies). The six corporations generally recognized as "Big Oil" are ExxonMobil, Royal Dutch, Shell, BP, Chevron Corporation, and ConocoPhillips. Globally, the largest oil and gas companies are: China Petroleum & Chemical Corporation (Sinopec), Royal Dutch Shell, China National Petroleum Corp (CNPC), BP Plc, ExxonMobil, Total, Chevron, Rosneft, Lukoil, and Phillips 66 (Offshore Technology 2019).

With the technological advancements made in scientific communities it is inconceivable that reliable and affordable alternative forms of energies that do not rely on fossil fuels are yet to have been developed. Further, instead of putting massive efforts into developing cleaner forms of energy, the fossil fuel industry has exerted great influence over politicians to support their agendas of petroleum, coal, and natural gas. The fossil fuel industry convinces politicians (that they have corrupted) into not only accepting the legitimacy of relying on outdated energy sources but also in supporting the notion that climate change, especially that which is caused by humans, is a hoax. The combined efforts of politicians on the payroll of the fossil fuel industry and its power elites have contributed to the promotion of labeling anything that goes against their doctrines as "alternative facts" or "fake news." This unfortunate reality has led to the irrational climate change denial movement across parts of the United States and the world. That the fossil fuel industry has this much power (in addition to dominating the world's supply of energy) is truly an example of darkened, irrational thinking.

Paul Buchheit (2018) charges fossil fuel companies with decades of ecological terror and states that "the World Health Organization, the American Lung Association, the United Nations, the Pentagon, cooperating governments, and independent research groups" all agree that human-induced climate change is killing people. He adds that

> the oil industry's intentionality and political motives have been demonstrated by their refusal to admit the known truth, starting with Exxon, which has covered up its own climate change research for 40 years, and continuing through multi-million dollar lobbying efforts by Amoco, the US Chamber of Commerce, General Motors, Koch Industries, and other corporations in their effort to dismantle the Kyoto Protocol against global warming.
>
> *(Buchheit 2018)*

(See Chapter 3 for a more in-depth look at the fossil fuel industry and its negative effects on the environment.)

Speaking of killing people, what industry is responsible for more deaths than Big Tobacco? The question has been asked repeatedly for decades, "Why is tobacco legal when it is responsible for so many premature deaths?" The government and health officials are quick to react in response to certain products that have led to death, and the public generally reacts in kind—if it is dangerous to people and leads to death, it should be banned. Consider, for example, that in the United States in 2019, dozens of people were suddenly dying from using electronic cigarette (vaping) products. *Vaping* is the act of inhaling and exhaling an aerosol, often referred to as vapor, produced by an e-cigarette or similar device. People are vaping for a number of reasons, some because they view the practice as a means of weaning off of tobacco products, others because they report enjoying the sensation; this is especially true with flavored vaping. E-cigarettes do not produce tobacco smoke but the aerosol/vapor actually consists of fine particles and any number of unknown chemicals. In October 2019 the Centers for Disease Control and Prevention reported more than 500 confirmed and probable cases of lung illnesses and nine deaths nationwide had been attributed to vaping (Associated Press 2019e). Health officials are especially alarmed by the growing numbers of high school students vaping, which increased from 10.5 percent in 2014 to 27.4 percent in 2018 (Associated Press 2019e). Young people seem to be attracted to flavored vaping and as a result of this (and of the few reported deaths from vaping) a number of health organizations, including the American Cancer Society and various state governments (i.e., Michigan, New York, and Rhode Island), moved quickly to pass legislation to ban vaping, especially flavored vaping. President Trump had also proposed a federal ban on flavored electronic-cigarettes (Associated Press 2019e) but, "under pressure from the industry and conservative activists, has reconsidered his Health and Human Services secretary's proposed ban on nearly all flavored e-cigarette products" (Wingrove and Porter, Jr. 2019).

While it may be viewed as an example of enlightened rational thought to ban vaping products because of the loss of life of a few people, we can ask the question again: how does tobacco stay legal when it kills nearly a half-million Americans and millions of other people around the world annually? According to the Centers for Disease Control and Prevention (CDC), tobacco use is the leading cause of preventable disease, disability, and death in the United States (CDC 2019a). While the number of Americans who smoke continues to dwindle, there are still nearly 40 million adults who defy logic and common sense by smoking cigarettes, and about 4.7 million middle and high school students who use at least one tobacco product, including e-cigarettes. "Each year, nearly half a million Americans die prematurely of smoking or exposure to secondhand smoke. Another 16 million live with a serious illness caused by smoking. Each year, the United States spends nearly $170 billion on medical care to treat smoking-related disease in adults" (CDC 2019a). Cardiovascular diseases (heart disease, hypertension, and stroke) cause the largest number of smoking-related deaths, followed by various cancers (e.g., lung and throat), respiratory diseases (e.g., chronic airway obstruction, pneumonia, bronchitis, and emphysema), and other causes, such as burn deaths.

Tobacco smoke contains more than 7,000 chemicals, including hundreds that are toxic and about 70 that can cause cancer (CDC 2019b). Tobacco smoke does not harm just the smoker but also anyone in close proximity via secondhand smoke. *Secondhand smoke* is smoke from burning tobacco products, such as cigarettes, cigars, or pipes; it is smoke that has been exhaled, or breathed out, by the person smoking. Exposure to any amount of secondhand smoke can be harmful to one's health. Since 1964, approximately 2.5 million nonsmokers have died from health problems caused by exposure to secondhand smoke (CDC 2019b). For children, secondhand smoke can lead to ear infections, more frequent and severe asthma attacks, respiratory symptoms, respiratory infections, and a greater risk for sudden infant death syndrome (SIDS). In adults, secondhand smoke can cause heart disease, lung cancer, and stroke (CDC 2019b).

The World Health Organization (WHO) reports that in 2015, over 1.1 billion people smoked tobacco, with males far more likely than females to do so. While the prevalence of smoking is decreasing globally, smoking appears to be increasing in the WHO Eastern Mediterranean Region and the Africa Region (WHO 2019b). Globally, tobacco is a major preventable cause of premature death and disease. "Currently, approximately 5.4 million people die each year due to tobacco-related illnesses—a figure expected to increase to more than 8 million a year by 2030" (CDC 2019c).

A discussion on the harmful effects of tobacco products could go on and on, but suffice it to say that the tobacco industry is responsible for millions of preventable deaths per year and yet its products are legal to persons of age. That an industry that creates products that cause so much harm to so many people is legal is a true testament of the political power that it wields and of the hypocrisy of politicians and policy makers who dare to claim that they care about the welfare of their representatives. The swamp is polluted by the tobacco industry and those politicians who accept payments from it and the deaths of millions of people per year are the result of their actions. Darkness surrounds the tobacco industry.

Another industry responsible for killing people is the gun industry. In the US, gun ownership is guaranteed by the US Constitution. Many scholars, historians, social policy makers, and individuals have debated the true meaning of the Second Amendment, which reads: "A well regulated Militia, being necessary to the security of a free State, the right of the people to keep and bear Arms, shall not be infringed." The second and third words of this amendment—"well regulated"—are emphasized by those who promote gun control and certain restrictions on ownership and types of guns that citizens should be allowed, while the last four words—"shall not be infringed"—are emphasized by those who do not want any restrictions on gun ownership. Most people tend to ignore that this amendment was directed toward the need of the new country to have a standing army—"Militia." Passions run deep on the topic of guns in the US, a nation with an incredibly high number of deaths due to guns. On one extreme are those who want no restrictions on gun ownership; on the other extreme are those who want a number of restrictions; in the middle are those who agree that citizens have the right to bear arms but primarily for the purpose of home protection, hunting, and target shooting. These same people tend to think that more advanced guns (e.g., automatic rifles) are not necessary for home protection or recreational use.

Every day, 100 Americans are killed with guns and hundreds more are shot and injured, and beyond that, gun violence shapes the lives of millions of Americans who witness it, know someone who was shot, or live in fear of the next shooting. Interestingly, nearly two-thirds of gun deaths are suicides (Everytown Research 2019). Far less common than suicides caused by guns are the total number of deaths caused by mass shootings. However, public mass shootings "are uniquely terrifying because they occur without warning in the most mundane places. Most of the victims are chosen not for what they have done but simply for where they happen to be" (Berkowitz, Alcantara, and Lu 2019). The number of people killed in war worldwide by guns is nearly immeasurable but is certainly high. In short, people with guns can more easily kill others. Counter to this fact is the idea that a person with a gun can more easily fend off attackers.

It is not the purpose of this discussion to debate the merits of gun ownership versus gun control, but rather to illustrate the power of the gun industry. The annual revenue of gun and ammunition manufacturing is $13.5 billion, with a $1.5 billion profit; the number of pistols, revolvers, rifles, shotguns, and miscellaneous firearms manufactured in the US in 2013 was nearly 11 million; the estimated number of guns in the US is over 300 million; there are nearly 300,000 full-time jobs related to the firearm industry; and the estimated overall economic impact of the firearms and ammo industry in the United States is nearly $43 billion (Popken

2015). The firearms industry has managed to become very powerful politically. Its de facto marketing arm, the National Rifle Association (NRA), has a huge impact on who gets elected in many areas of the nation. Anyone who is in favor of guns merely has to say so publicly and they can automatically expect support from the very vocal "pro-Second Amendment" contingent. Conversely, if a politician states that they want gun control or want to take away certain gun rights they can expect to endure the very vocal ire of the NRA and "pro-Second Amendment" supporters.

Big Tech

"Big Tech" is a term used to describe a number of large technology companies relating to computers that when combined form a single industry with great political influence. The five companies that make up Big Tech are Facebook, Google, Apple, Amazon, and Microsoft. Some classifications of Big Tech do not include Microsoft, instead using the term Gang of Four (Google, Amazon, Facebook and Apple). Facebook and Google dominate internet advertising, together collecting 63 percent of the US digital advertising dollars in 2017 (Lotz 2018). Both Google and Facebook "earn most of their revenue from advertising: 97 percent for Facebook and 88 percent for Google's parent company Alphabet in 2016. But what they offer to advertisers and what users want from them are very different" (Lotz 2018). While Google and Facebook earn their money from advertising, Apple earns most (84 percent) of its revenue from hardware sales of such products as the iPhone, iPad, and iMac computers. Amazon operates in many different business sectors but primarily it is a goods retailer (70 percent of its revenue). Microsoft blends many revenue streams, including cloud services, software, gaming consoles, and search engine advertising (Lotz 2018).

Microsoft has received criticism from some of its own employees who believe that it is unethical for its CEO Satya Nadella to sell its cloud computing services to fossil fuel companies. Microsoft and other tech giants have been competing with one another hoping to secure lucrative partnerships with ExxonMobil, Chevron, Shell, BP, and other energy firms, in many cases supplying them not just with remote data storage but also artificial intelligence tools for pinpointing better drilling sports or speeding up refinery production (O'Brien 2019). The oil and gas industry spends nearly $20 billion each year on cloud services, which accounts for about 10 percent of the total cloud market (O'Brien 2019). The clean energy proponents at Microsoft do not believe that their company should do business with the fossil fuel industry. Defending his actions, Nadella counters that the Big Oil companies are researching and developing more sustainable energy production methods (O'Brien 2019).

The Big Tech firms have all drawn great scrutiny from those outside their own ranks, including from the users of their services and products, the public, and some government agencies and politicians because of their influence on social and political issues and because of the huge amount of personal data they own. "The industry is being accused of excessive lobbying, monopolization and tax dodging. And the long-standing Silicon Valley business model of vacuuming up the data of unsuspecting users and leveraging it for profit is coming under sustained attack" (Halper 2019). President Trump has accused Google, Facebook, and other social media companies of censorship and bias against conservatives, and Democrats have accused Big Tech firms of exploiting workers and eroding digital privacy, and the failure of social media platforms to combat election disinformation on their sites (Halper 2019). Some politicians (i.e., Elizabeth Warren and Kamala Harris) have called for the break-up of Facebook and Google because of their heavy influence on societal matters (Bishop 2019). Amanda Lotz (2018) states, "public concern about Facebook's power in society—and in politics—has skyrocketed in the wake of revelations that users' data was analyzed by a U.K.-based marketing firm and used to construct highly targeted political propaganda in advance of the 2016 U.S. presidential election."

The concern over Facebook and Google and their possible role in political influence during the 2020 elections led to a September 2019 meeting between US intelligence officials (from the Department of Homeland Security, the FBI, and the Office of the Director of National Intelligence) and representatives from the two Big Tech firms. Representatives from Twitter and Microsoft were also in attendance. "The full-day meetings were arranged to discuss how tech companies like Facebook are preparing for election-related security issues, including government-backed online disinformation campaigns similar to the one Russia orchestrated ahead of the 2016 U.S. election" (Wagner 2019). CEO Mark Zuckerberg has been very vocal about Facebook's commitment to election-related security. "Facebook has been heavily criticized for unwittingly propagating past disinformation campaigns" (Wagner 2019). Mark Zuckerberg received even greater condemnation from many when he announced that Facebook would continue to allow deceptive (including flat-out false) ads on Facebook. He has shown that making money is of a greater importance than acting in a moral and ethical manner.

Big Tech firms have the capability to influence political elections and that is what makes them a contributor to the flooding swamp.

Big Data

"Big Data" refers to an accumulation of data from traditional and digital industrial sources that is too large and complex for processing by traditional database management tools, which can be analyzed computationally to reveal patterns, trends, and associations, especially relating to human behavior and interactions. The data collected come from traditional and digital sources inside and outside a specific company that represents a source for ongoing discovery and analysis (Arthur 2013). SAS Insights (2019) states, "It's not the amount of data that's important. It's what organizations do with the data that matters. Big data can be analyzed for insights that lead to better decisions and strategic business moves." Organizations collect data (e.g., structured, numeric data in traditional databases or unstructured text documents, email, video, audio, stock ticker data, and financial transactions) from a variety of sources, including business transactions, social media, and information from sensors or machine-to-machine (SAS Insights 2019).

Big Data is used by a variety of industries that can benefit from many streams of information including: banking (e.g., to assist them with their attempts to stay one step ahead of the game with advanced analytics); education (e.g., in their attempt to identify at-risk students, make sure students are making adequate progress, implement better systems of evaluation, and support of teachers and principals); government (e.g., to manage utilities, run agencies, deal with traffic congestion, or prevent crime); health care (e.g., for treatment plans and managed care); manufacturing (e.g., to boost quality and output while minimizing waste); and retail (e.g., to market to customers, handle transactions efficiently) (SAS Insights 2019). It is important for all industries and big businesses to fully understand how Big Data can help them.

Among the concerns over Big Data is how this information is being collected (people do not necessarily consent to data collection and having their private information shared) and what information is gathered for Big Data. Sources of collected data include information and communications being shared on social media sites, private emails, and purchasing histories. The databases are so large and hackers are so sophisticated that consumers, businesses, and governments must worry about the data, and thus their personal information, being hacked. While information on purchasing practices, for example, may be important to businesses looking for consumers to buy their products, personal information gained on individuals and shared with the government and varied businesses comes with ethical and moral concerns. Unethical and immoral behaviors go hand-in-hand with the rising level of the swamp.

Big Pharma

"Big Pharma" is a term that encompasses the largest global corporations in the pharmaceutical industry. Like the other industries labeled "big," such a nickname is meant to demonize an industry under increasing scrutiny from the general public, consumer watchdog groups, and governments. The ten largest pharmaceutical companies (based on 2018 revenue) are: Pfizer, $53.7 billion (headquartered in Connecticut; a research-based company); Roche, $45.6 billion (founded in Basel, Switzerland; develops innovative drugs and devices); Johnson & Johnson, $40.7 billion (New Brunswick, New Jersey; popular consumer products); Sanofi, $39.3 billion (Paris; pharmaceutical sales); Merck & Co, $37.7 billion (Kenilworth, New Jersey; pharmaceutical sales, drug, vaccine, and biologic drug development); Novartis, $34.9 billion (Swiss-based pharmaceutical company that focuses on a wide variety of disease areas); Abbvie, $32.8 billion (Lake Bluff, Illinois; drug manufacturer, multiple therapy areas); Amgen, $23.7 billion (Newbury Park, California; multinational biopharmaceuticals, novel human therapeutics); GlaxoSmith-Kline (GSK), $23 billion (a leading British pharmaceutical company; innovative drugs, a wide range of therapy areas); and Bristol-Myers Squibb (BMS), $22.6 billion (New York City-based pharmaceutical company specializing in therapy areas of oncology, cardiovascular, immunoscience, and fibrosis) (Ellis 2019).

The pharmaceutical industry is responsible for the development, production, and marketing of medications—activities that are very important. The business aspect of the global health market is immense as the total pharmaceutical revenues worldwide exceeded $1 trillion for the first time in 2014 (Mikulic 2019). North America is responsible for the largest portion (48.9 percent) of these revenues due to the leading role of the US pharmaceutical industry. However, like many other industries, the Chinese pharmaceutical sector has shown the highest growth rates over the past years (Mikulic 2019).

Big Pharma is not only responsible for the development, production, and marketing of medications; it is also under attack for the many instances of fraud that occur within this industry. Consider the following instances of Big Pharma fraud over the past decade.

- The GSK office in Beijing was the center of a 2013 scandal in which local managers were accused of paying millions of dollars in bribes to Chinese doctors to prescribe the company's drugs (Kessel 2014; Bio Spectrum Bureau 2013).
- Before the China bribery scandal, GSK became a part of the largest health care fraud settlement in US history; the drug maker paid $3 billion for promoting two drugs for unapproved uses and failing to report safety data about a diabetes drug to the US FDA (Bio Spectrum Bureau 2013). The settlement covered criminal fines as well as civil settlements with the federal and state governments (England 2012).
- Merck was involved in a case of fraudulently representing the mumps component of its MMR vaccine Pluseriz as an effective vaccine after studies proved its ineffectiveness (Bio Spectrum Bureau 2013). Merck's behavior is said to have left millions unprotected against mumps (England 2012).
- The UK medicines regulatory body MHRA claims that European medicines giant Roche did not evaluate about 80,000 reports, including over 15,000 death reports, suspecting that adverse patient reactions were caused by Roche drugs (Bio Spectrum Bureau 2013).
- In 2012, Pfizer paid $60.2 million to the United States to settle charges that the company bribed government officials, including hospital administrators, government doctors, and members of regulatory and purchasing committees in China, Russia, Italy, and a number of other European countries to approve and prescribe Pfizer products (Bio Spectrum Bureau 2013).
- Abbott Laboratories pleaded guilty and paid $1.5 billion for unlawfully promoting the prescription drug Depakote for uses not approved safe and effective by the US FDA (Bio Spectrum Bureau 2013). Depakote was promoted by Abbott as a drug to control agitation and aggression in elderly dementia patients and to treat schizophrenia when neither of these uses were approved by the FDA (England 2012).

- Top executives of Purdue Pharma, which makes OxyContin, pleaded guilty in 2007 to criminal charges for their role in deceptive marketing that downplayed the risk of abuse (Kristof 2015).
- Purdue Pharma, under attack for its role in the opioid addiction crisis in the US, reached a tentative agreement deal in September 2019. Facing more than 2,000 lawsuits by state and local governments, the pharma giant agreed to a structured bankruptcy and will pay as much as $12 billion over time, with about $3 billion coming from the controlling Sackler family. This figure involves future profits and the value of drugs currently in development. In addition, the family will have to give up its ownership of the company and contribute another $1.5 billion by selling another of its pharmaceutical companies, Mundipharma (Mulvihill and Collins 2019). Several attorneys general from about half of the states suing Purdue Pharma said "the agreement was a better way to ensure compensation from Purdue and the Sacklers than taking their chances if Purdue files for bankruptcy on its own" (Mulvihill and Collins 2019:A6).
- Just two days after the announced opioid settlement in the Purdue Pharma and Sackler family case, it was revealed that the Sacklers had transferred $1 billion to themselves in Swiss and other hidden accounts in an effort to maintain some of their wealth. "The transfers bolster allegations by New York and other states that the Sacklers worked to shield their wealth in recent years because of mounting worries about legal threats" (Associated Press 2019f:A5).
- Johnson & Johnson, already hit with numerous multimillion-dollar jury verdicts in recent years for serious health issues related to its talcum powder, hip implants, pelvic mesh, the antipsychotic drug Risperdal, and other products was hit with a $572 million fine in Oklahoma (September 2019) for misrepresenting the dangers of its opioid medications Nucynta and Duragesic, thereby causing a "public nuisance" (Sharp 2019). On October 1, 2019, Johnson & Johnson reached an agreement worth more than $20 million with two Ohio counties, "becoming the latest company to settle a lawsuit to get out of the first federal trial over the nation's opioids crisis" (Mulvihill 2019:A18).
- On October 21, 2019, the three biggest drug distributors in the US (AmerisourceBergen, Cardinal Health, and McKesson) and a major drugmaker (Israeli-based Teva) agreed to a $260-million settlement in an Ohio court (Associated Press 2019g). The settlement was made just prior to when the case brought about by two Ohio counties (Cuyahoga and Summit) was scheduled to go to federal court, averting the first federal trial over opioid crisis. The three distributors will combine to pay $215 million and Teva will contribute $20 million in cash and $25 million worth of generic Suboxone, a drug used to treat opioid addiction. The deal contains no admission of wrongdoing by the drug companies (Associated Press 2019g).

The opioid crisis represents a public health disaster in the United States. Opioids are a class of drug that includes prescription painkillers as well as heroin and illicitly made fentanyl, which have been lined to more than 400,000 deaths in the US since 2000 (Mulvihill 2019). Big Pharma has been mostly blamed for this predicament. While it's true that Big Pharma manufactures prescription painkillers such as OxyContin and Vicodin, not all the blame should be directed in their direction, at least according to some researchers. Big Pharma corporations such as Purdue continued to develop and market addictive drugs like Oxy as safe and doctors prescribed them to patients eager to relieve their suffering from pain. Sue Ogrocki (2019) writes, "Prescriptions flowed freely at 'pill mill' clinics, especially in Florida, where drug dealers would get drugs and spread them around the country" (p. A2). Thieves often broke into a number of pharmacies and stole the drugs to sell on the streets, according to Ogrocki (2019). Maia Szalavitz (2019) argues that individuals who take opioids, and not doctors, are the ones primarily responsible for the opioid crisis. Szalavitz (2019) states,

> 80 percent of those who begin misusing prescription opioids are taking drugs illegally—from theft, dealers, friends, relatives, the internet or other people's medicine cabinets, not from doctors. And nearly three out of four young people who misuse opioids have previously taken cocaine or crack repeatedly. Indeed, researchers say that prior recreational drug use is a much larger risk factor for opioid addiction than medical exposure. That is not to say that there aren't some whose addictions begin with a prescription—but this group is a decided minority.

Szalavitz (2019) does acknowledge that the pharma industry is the source for these opioids and its marketing convinced many doctors to write large prescriptions that helped to create the addiction epidemic, but reiterates the previous point that it isn't primarily pain patients who get hooked.

Despite the interesting perspectives of Ogrocki and Szalavitz described above, the consensus among attorneys general and the CDC is to blame Big Pharma's lobbying, manufacturing, and marketing efforts of opioid prescription drugs as being safe to the public. Vermont Senator Bernie Sanders states, "We know that pharmaceutical companies lied about the addictive impacts of opioids they manufactured," and consequently he blames their malicious intentions as the primary cause of the opioid crisis in the United States (Buchheit 2018).

Big Banks

The play on words used in this review of the "Big" industries (and their representation in the Deep State) and their effect on contributing to the rising levels of "the swamp" is a nod to the "too big to fail" concept that became in vogue a decade ago. "Too big to fail" is used to describe a situation in which the government will intervene in situations where a business has become so deeply ingrained in the functionality of an economy that its failure is perceived to be disastrous to the economy at large (Investopedia 2019b). The "too big to fail" mantra centers around the idea that certain businesses, such as the biggest banks, are so vital to the economy that if they failed it would cause a catastrophic crisis, and therefore they must be saved. The bailout funds would come from taxpayers via the government. The "'Lehman Brothers' collapse marked the peak of the financial crisis in September 2008. With its bankruptcy filing, government regulators discovered the biggest banking firms were so interconnected that only large bailouts would prevent a substantial portion of the financial sector from failing" (Investopedia 2019b; see also Onaran 2017). The Emergency Economic Stabilization Act (EESA) of 2008 was signed in October 2008 and established a $700 billion "Troubled Asset Relief Program" (TARP) to be managed by the US Treasury for the purpose of helping troubled banks (Investopedia 2019b).

The Big Banks are indeed intertwined with numerous other financial entities, businesses, and individual homeowners. The dominance of the Big Banks is illustrated by the realization that in the US, the biggest six banks have $10 trillion in assets, almost twice as much as the next 30 combined (Onaran 2017). The six biggest banks in the US and Europe have increased their assets more than five-fold since 1997 (to 2014). While the bailouts were arguably necessary, many people were enraged as a lot of homeowners and businesses went under (Onaran 2017). It is little wonder, then, that in the same Gallup poll cited by Cowen (2019), just 11 percent of Americans report having "a great deal" of trust in banks and another 16 percent report that they have "quite a lot" of trust in banks.

Following the 2008 financial crisis, President Barack Obama tried to curtail the activities of Big Banks via federal regulators. These regulators worked publicly and privately in an effort to keep giant banks such as JPMorgan, already deemed too big to fail, from getting even bigger. They snuffed out merger ambitions and discouraged plans to expand businesses, offer new products, and open branches. The goal of the Obama administration was to contain the Big Banks and their worst impulses without the glare of public scrutiny (Davis 2019). Containment efforts came to an end, however, under President Trump.

> The Trump administration has rolled back the stealth campaign. And the implications—for banks, their customers, investors and the economy—could be enormous. Interviews with more than two dozen current and former industry executives and regulators underscore how banks have managed to wriggle free from much of the strict oversight enacted to prevent another meltdown—all without any wholesale changes to the laws enacted on Wall Street after the crisis.
>
> *(Davis 2019:A7)*

Indeed, in May 2018, Trump signed into a law a measure that loosens key restraints for banks imposed by the landmark 2010 Dodd–Frank Act after the financial crisis of 2018. As a result, the Federal Reserve and the Office of the Comptroller of the Currency (OCC)—the industry's primary regulators—have adopted a friendlier approach, giving banks, including JPMorgan, more freedom to expand into new markets, introduce products, and make acquisitions (Davis 2019). Trump even picked a former chief executive of One West Bank, Joseph Otting, to head the OCC. Otting has run interference for his CEO buddies in the banking industry, concealing evidence of a potential replay of the Wells Fargo fake account scandal (Dayen 2018). Wells Fargo had just previously admitted to opening millions of accounts without customer consent. Of the 3.5 million unauthorized accounts, approximately 190,000 incurred fees and charges (McGrath 2017). It is truly shameful to charge customers fees and charges on accounts that they did not open.

Trump's obsession with undoing anything accomplished by Obama has harmed the country, and the world, in numerous ways (as demonstrated throughout this book) but allowing the Big Banks to operate freely represents yet another way in which he has flooded the swamp.

Big Religion

Karl Marx argued that religion was the "opiate of the masses" because it existed chiefly to pacify the poor by turning their attention away from the misery of their lives in this world toward a happier afterlife (Glock and Stark 1965; McLellan 1987). Marx argued that religion existed to help the ruling elite keep the masses docile, controllable, and exploitable. He referred to it as an explicitly evil form of slavery that hampered individuals' attempts to reach their full human potential (Carlebach 1978). The Republican Party in the United States especially relies on a conservative religious base in order to achieve political gain. Even Donald Trump, who has never been confused as a religious person, manages to dupe the conservative religious base. When Trump was campaigning for the presidency in 2016 he was asked to identify his favorite Bible verse and fumbled his response. Trying to help Trump, the friendly reporter then asked him to identify *any* Bible verse and he failed to come up with a single example. But, Trump does certainly know how to speak to the conservative religious base in a language they understand, a language that does not value science and higher education and does not seek facts and truth.

Trump is certainly not the first politician to rely on a religious base of followers to support him in his political campaigns and political agendas; however, nearly always it is these Christians politicians, or those who claim to be Christian, that benefit the most. This is understandable in that in the United States, 70.6 percent of Americans report belonging to a Christian religion; 5.9 percent claim a non-Christian faith (i.e., Jewish, 1.9 percent); and a growing number of Americans (22.8 percent) claim "unaffiliated" (religious "nones") status (Pew Research Center 2019). Interestingly, many of the "Christians" that support Trump do not practice fundamental principles of Christianity—helping to feed and clothe the poor (e.g., immigrants) and showing love and acceptance of all people (e.g., they discriminate against members of the LGBTQ+ community), for example.

The influence that religion enjoys in the US extends beyond exerting direct political pressure on politicians. The symbiotic relationship between Church and

State is akin to that of the Middle Ages and is, perhaps, best exemplified by the fact that no church in the US pays taxes. And what a shame that is, as "Big Religion" in America was said to be worth $1.2 trillion in 2016 (Markoe 2016). This figure makes American religion larger than the global revenues of the top ten tech companies and 50 percent larger than the six largest American oil companies' annual revenue (Markoe 2016). Estimates vary slightly, but the annual tax revenue on Big Religion would be worth $71 billion a year. And as any Christian, as well as any person of other or no affiliation, would tell you, that money could really help the poor. Megachurches, the exemplar of Big Religion, are the ones that capitalize the most on this tax-exempt financial enterprise. A megachurch is characterized by stadium seating and large projection screens. The sermons are devoid of rationality and reason and are designed to dupe the audience (through the use of psychology, patriotism, electronics, and visual effects) desperate for meaning, much in the manner described by Marx so many years ago.

Connecting enlightened rational thought with popular culture

BOX 4.1 "I LIKED BEER. I STILL LIKE BEER"—BRETT KAVANAUGH, US SUPREME COURT JUSTICE

When a US president has an opportunity to make a Supreme Court appointment, he (and some day, she) can cement his legacy for decades to come. After the February 13, 2016 death of Justice Antonin Scalia, then-president Barack Obama had 11 months to nominate and secure confirmation of an appointee of his choosing to replace him. However, the Republicans successfully impeded all of Obama's attempts. After Donald Trump won the 2016 presidential election the Republican-controlled Senate changed "rules to eliminate filibusters on Supreme Court nominees and narrowly pushed through Neil Gorsuch to take Scalia's place" (Roberts and Roberts 2019b:A4). In 2018, with the retirement of Justice Anthony Kennedy, an opportunity arose for Trump to secure a second appointee to the Supreme Court. Trump nominated Brett Kavanaugh, a long-time foe of President Bill Clinton and a former aide to President George W. Bush. A product of the Washington, DC swamp, Kavanaugh is a highly polarizing figure, with numerous allegations of sexual misbehavior and ethical complaints having been directed at him; and yet, his fellow Republicans pushed for his confirmation. The bitterly partisan divide between Democrats and Republicans qualifies for what Lord (2019) describes as a "swamp war."

While a debate on Kavanaugh's qualifications on matters of political philosophy (liberalism versus conservatism) was certainly expected during the confirmation hearings, there were other explosive and memorable occurrences as well. First, we have the multiple allegations of sexual misbehavior including the claim by Christine Blasey Ford (now a professor of psychology at Palo Alto

University) that Kavanaugh had attempted to rape her at a party in 1982 that they attended as teenagers (both were raised in the Washington, DC area). Deborah Ramirez was among more than a dozen people who said they could provide information about numerous drunken escapades (e.g., exposing himself to female classmates) that Kavanaugh participated in as a freshman at Yale. Interestingly, Kavanaugh was not a member of the Order of Skull and Bones at Yale but instead of the secret society called "Truth and Courage," a lofty name for what was, in reality, an all-male drinking club (Hensley-Clancy 2018). While Ford was given a chance to testify before the Judiciary Committee, the Republican majority committee refused to provide Ramirez with a public hearing (Calmes 2019). This information was known at the time of the Kavanaugh judiciary hearing but what was not publicly known until a year later was a revelation that the White House and Senate Republicans allegedly constrained the FBI investigation into the many allegations of sexual misconduct when Kavanaugh was a college freshman. The FBI did not investigate many former classmates of Kavanaugh that wanted to confirm that they witnessed sexual misconduct on the part of the future Justice (Calmes 2019). The second memorable occurrence of the Kavanaugh US Senate Confirmation Judiciary Committee hearing was the fact that he had 83 ethics complaints filed against him. However, a panel of federal judges later permanently dismissed (on the moment he was confirmed on October 6, 2018) all of the complaints claiming that Supreme Court justices are not subject to the federal judiciary's system of ethics review (Boboltz 2019).

Allegations of sexual misconduct and unethical behaviors on the part of a Supreme Court Justice are very serious concerns, but whether he is guilty or innocent these events can no longer be held against Kavanaugh. However, we are still left with the disturbing images of Kavanaugh's out-of-control behavior while he was questioned. Turning red and looking like he might explode during his questioning, Kavanaugh spoke of his high school buddies, lifting weights, football, and drinking beer. And oh how he loved his beer, and he still loves beer. In fact, the second most popular quote of 2018 (the most popular quote —"Truth isn't truth", uttered by Rudy Giuliani, was referenced in Chapter 2) came from Kavanaugh, who stated during the US Senate Confirmation Judiciary Committee hearing—"I liked beer. I still like beer" (Phillips 2019). Kavanaugh repeatedly shouted and ranted that he liked beer and said that sometimes he and his friends drank too much beer. Despite his love of beer, he insisted that he never blacked out from drinking too much beer and proclaimed that he never sexually assaulted anyone. During one of his rants Kavanaugh said, "Yes we drank beer, my friends and I, boys and girls. Yes, we drank beer, I like beer, I still like beer, we drank beer. The drinking age, as I noted, was 18, so the seniors were legal, senior year in high school people were legal to drink. Yeah, we drank beer, and I said sometimes, sometimes probably had too many beers, and sometimes other people had too many beers. We drank beer, I like beer" (Grasso 2018). Frank Bruni (2018b) summarizes Kavanaugh's behavior and demeanor this way: "He was painting himself as a martyr for maleness, and he was using beer—along with weight lifting, football, flatulence jokes and what he mendaciously insisted were inoffensive yearbook high jinks—to do it. Beer was his brand, and he was proud of it."

His lack of composure and professed love of beer and hijinks—during a job interview no less—was completely inappropriate for a Supreme Court Justice, but it certainly did provide a great deal of comic fodder for comedians and especially for "Saturday Night Live" (SNL), an American institution for 45 years of comedy, satirical skits, and musical guests. Sure enough, during the SNL 2018 season premiere actor Matt Damon impersonated Brett Kavanaugh as a "screaming man-child" (Reynolds 2018). Damon parodied the emotional behavior of Kavanaugh's testimony from just two days earlier (September 27, 2018) as he responded to an accusation of sexual assault from Dr. Blasey Ford. His impersonation of Kavanaugh was dead-on and references to liking beer flowed as if it were poured from a keg. Damon, as Kavanaugh, described himself as an optimist, saying, "I'm a keg-is-half-full kind of guy." He referenced his buddies from his youth by their nicknames. Damon then went on a tirade, saying, "Look, I like beer, OK? I like beer. Boys like beer. Girls like beer. I like beer. I like beer" (Reynolds 2018). In reference to both Kavanaugh's determination to be confirmed to the Supreme Court, as well as Blasey Ford's disturbing accusation, Damon's Kavanaugh character stated, "I don't know the meaning of the word 'stop.' Am I angry? You're damn right. But if you think I'm angry now, you just wait till I get on that Supreme Court, 'cause then you're all going to pay" (Reynolds 2018). Videos of this SNL skit are available on the internet and especially on YouTube.

Summary

A flooded swamp is a reference to the murkiness of politics and to those who have undue influence over policy making. It is common to refer to the "political swamp" as simply the "swamp." The swamp can be viewed as an environment wherein a variety of non-elected persons, including cabinet and judicial appointees, lobbyists, bureaucrats, and administrative staffs who help run the countless daily operations of a government and who have power to issue and enforce regulations as if they are law, hold positions of quasi-authority. The vast majority of those working in the swamp are people who work for the government in an attempt to keep it running smoothly. Appointees to political offices reflect the values and ideology of the person (e.g., the US president) who has the power to put them in charge of some government agency; such appointees become susceptible to lobbyists who attempt to influence them on the behalf of some other entity that has the support of those in charge of running the government. Some version of a swamp has been in existence since the earliest governments and it is an almost universal phenomenon.

There have been unfulfilled promises made by many top politicians that they will "drain the swamp." Any serious attempt to rid the political arena of corruptness should center on curtailing the influence of lobbyists and donors and weeding out crooked and unqualified persons that hold positions of high authority, assuring that cabinet and judicial appointees are highly qualified and ethical. When these goals are not met, we have a deeper and murkier swamp. Other indicators of a swollen swamp are an increase in the number of acting government appointees, as they do not have to go through the vetting process, and attempts by the Executive branch to impede Congressional investigations into Executive wrongdoing.

In addition to internal sources contributing to the swamp are external sources such as the "Deep State" and "Big Business." The concept of the "Deep State" is neither an operating arm of the Left or the Right, but it most certainly casts a shadow over "legitimate" government. The "Deep State" is an intentional, unconstitutional, and organized phenomenon that uses its power to corrupt government officials; it is a type of shadowy government that acts on behalf of the power elites that make up the entity. The governmental military–industrial complex has been identified by some as the "Deep State." Others believe that the true power elites are the Deep State and that they attempt to manipulate governments and policy making to assure their own fortunes and power. The shadowy nature of the Deep State leads us to an examination of dangerous secret societies as some of the most powerful people in the world belong to such organizations as "the Order of Skull and Bones," the German "Thule Society," and "the Bilderberg Group."

Another contributing external influence on the maintenance and deepening of the swamp is the collective influence of "Big Business," "Big Tech," "Big Data," "Big Pharma," and "Big Banks." The captains of these industries are among some of the most pivotal power elites that can have an undue influence on political policy. Each of these "big" variations of industry has been accused, in one form of another, of having too much influence over the public and private sectors.

The bottom-line concern over a "flooded swamp" is the realization that it represents a tremendous threat to enlightened, rational thought, and that it is a sign of the darkness that surrounds us.

5
WILL THE LIGHT OF RATIONAL THOUGHT CHASE AWAY THE DARKNESS?

Introduction

What does the future hold for the remainder of the twenty-first century—will enlightened rational thought prevail, or will the darkness that surrounds us eventually extinguish democracy and human rights? Enlightened rational thought, a reliance on science, the promotion of education and critical thinking skills coupled with democratic forms of government are all designed to secure human rights for all. However, as demonstrated throughout this book, there are numerous and significant challenges to reasoned thought prevailing as a guiding light of enlightened thinking. The political climate of the early twenty-first century appears to be a barrier to rational forms of thinking. While it is true that people and politicians have always held ideological differences in their perspectives on how society should best be designed, most democratic societies agreed on the idea of preserving human dignity and basic human rights. However, in the United States, which often promotes itself as the world-leader in spreading democratic idealism, the partisan divide is as cavernous as ever. In the United Kingdom, Brexit underscores the deep political divide that exists there. In fact, all nations that promote democratic ideals and yet have played witness to the spread of a type of populism that preaches intolerance and treats people unequally (e.g., Poland, Italy, Sweden, Hungary, and Greece; see Chapter 2 for a further review) are risks to enlightened, rational thought.

Signs of light

There are signs of light for the future of humanity. The Renaissance and Enlightenment eras discussed in Chapter 1 did stimulate scientific curiosity, a belief in progress, humanistic ideals, and such liberal notions as liberty, equality for all, and democracy, and such ideals and aspirations can still inspire us today.

Progress, guided by enlightened rational thought

Those of us who promote rational enlightened thought share a general belief that society is continuously progressing and that technology can assist in the cultural and moral growth of humanity. Since the time of the Industrial Revolution the human species has witnessed and enjoyed tremendous social improvements due to technological growth in many spheres of life, including advancements in the medical professions. Among these advancements are vaccines against once-deadly diseases; improvements in fighting existing diseases, such as heart disease; human genome discoveries; information technology; stem cell research; targeted therapies and drugs for fighting cancer; robotic techniques revolutionizing surgery; hormone replacement therapy; bionic limbs; brain–computer interfaces (BCI) for the paralyzed; and the "cyborg-craze" wherein people implant devices and technologies in their bodies.

Advancements in materials science have led to shifts in understanding in the development of goods. Among these advancements are: an international technology roadmap for semiconductors (ITRS); scanning probe microscopes; giant magnetoresistive (GMR) effects; semiconductor lasers and LEDs; nanotechnology; Li-ion (and lithium) batteries; carbon nanotubes; soft lithography; and metamaterials (Wood 2008). Technological advancements in materials science combined with ingenuity stimulate further progress in the form of advancements in everyday material goods (e.g., houseware products, smoke and CO_2 detectors, cordless tools, and lightweight warm clothing); travel (e.g., automobiles, trains, subways, airplanes); space travel (both manned and unmanned); space exploration (multiple countries have successfully landed probes on the Moon, with China in 2019 being the first to land one on the far/dark side of the Moon); improvements in food production (e.g., advanced farming equipment and the ability to grow massive amounts of food); industrial improvements (e.g., industrial robots); advancements in communications (e.g., fiber optics, satellites, cellular phones, the internet, and global positioning systems); the development of non-fossil fuel energy sources (e.g., solar energy, wind turbines, nuclear energy); a decrease in the reliance of coal in the United States (as predicted by Hillary Clinton but argued against by Donald Trump during the 2016 presidential election); and developments in family planning (e.g., in-vitro fertilization and birth control). It is true, however, that some of the benefits of the technology described here come with their own set of problems as, for example, the development of automobiles, trains and planes, and electricity has led to a dependence on fossil fuels that is contributing to the current sixth mass extinction period.

Social movements

A *social movement* is a persistent and organized effort on the part of a relatively large number of people who share a common ideology and try to bring about or resist change. In Chapter 3, the growing social movement to help eliminate our dependence on plastics was mentioned. An example of a persistent social movement is the women's rights movement, a movement that has found success in reaching some of its goals (e.g., securing the rights of women to vote), but is still fighting for equality in other areas (e.g., equal pay for men and women doing the same job with the same experience). In recent years, the women's rights movement has been directed toward securing equality and ending discrimination of those in the LGBTQ+ community (Mann and Patterson 2016).

Around the world, the younger generation is continuing the social movement of those raised in the 1970s in their attempt to save the environment. A great deal of legislation (e.g., the Clean Air Act of 1970 and Clean Water Act of 1972) designed to protect the environment was passed as a result of the baby boomers; however, as they would learn, the power elites managed to curtail all of their lofty goals. The current younger generation is energized by such climate activists as Greta Thunberg, a Swedish teenager who first became known for her activism in August 2018 (then aged 15) when she stood outside the Swedish parliament to protest climate change, calling for stronger action on global warming by holding up a sign that read: "School strike for the climate." Throughout 2019 she led a youth-spirited social movement in an attempt to halt the negative forces contributing to climate change. Thunberg's message has been so inspiring that *Time* magazine named the teenaged climate activist the 2019 "Person of the Year" (she is the youngest person to receive this prestigious honor). However, Thunberg and her peers are also learning first-hand of the resistance among conservatives and the power elite who wish to maintain the *status quo*. President Trump, for example, tweeted (upon learning that Thunberg had received the *Time* honor), "So ridiculous. Greta must work on her Anger Management problem, then go to a good old fashion movie with a friend! Chill Greta, Chill!" This is the type of ignorance this generation must overcome if they hope to be more successful than the previous generations.

Many American youths of the "School Shooting Generation" have become social activists and have started the #NeverAgain movement to curb gun violence and mass shootings via sensible gun control legislation and practices. Stoneman Douglas High School (Parkland, Florida) mass shooting survivors are among the activists. The documentary "After Parkland," describing the horrific events of the mass shooting, was released on November 27, 2019.

Other examples of social movements seeking equality and/or democracy include:

- he student-led pro-democracy movement in Hong Kong that seeks autonomy from China
- the 2019 decriminalization of homosexuality in Botswana following years of activism
- the election of Zuzana Caputova, the first female president of Slovakia, viewed as a sign of light in a region of Europe "that has seen a lurch toward right-wing populism in recent years" (King 2019f)

- student-led protests in Iran, Lebanon, and Chile triggered by a price increase for an economic staple, which led to significant social changes including calls for constitutional changes (Chile) and the right to use social media platforms (Lebanon) (Etehad 2019)
- growing unrest in Columbia, Bolivia, and Ecuador, as well as in Chile, which has led to protests against economic inequality (Etehad 2019)
- the resignation of far-right, anti-migrant Austrian populist leader Heinz-Christian Strache in May 2019, which became a light of hope for those promoting equality and democracy

These points of light give hope to the future of humanity, so long as they are not countered by signs of further darkness. Unfortunately, progress in the early twenty-first century is confronted by many dangerous social forces.

Signs of further darkness

Chapters 2–4 describes in detail the many examples of socio-political darkness that surround us, including: political leaders who constantly lie; attacks on journalists, even in democratic societies; populist, nationalist, and nativist social movements in many countries; the growing economic disparity between the haves and the have-nots; attacks on higher education; a growing disbelief in the legitimacy of science (e.g., those who deny the damage being caused to our environment) among the ignorant; people turning to pseudoscience; the flooded political swamp; and the deepening threat from Big Business, Big Tech, Big Data, Big Pharma, Big Banks, and Big Religion.

As we enter the 2020s, there are signs of further darkness ahead of us. The United States' withdrawal from the Paris Accord (upon the orders of President Trump) coincides with warnings from the United Nations of the immediate need for countries around the world to make steep cuts to their greenhouse gas emissions or risk even further global warming and environmental catastrophes. Some pro-environmentalists have called for Trump's impeachment for his climate crisis denial in light of the fact that the US is the only nation on the planet that has pulled out of the Paris Accord (Goodman and Moynihan 2019e).

There has been a rise of hate crimes in the United States since Trump became president and this is not surprising considering some of his supporters—including white nationalists, the "Alt-Right," Nazis, pro-Confederacy reactionaries, and white supremacists—feel empowered to participate in overt forms of racism (covert forms of racism were a part of the American landscape long before we became a nation). Hate crimes and hate incidents are also on the rise around the world as intolerance of immigrants has spearheaded a campaign of bigotry and narrow-mindedness. Internet sites such as 8chan, which posts such things as mass shooters' manifestos of hate (i.e., the March 2019 Christ Church, New Zealand mosque attack and the August 2019 El Paso, Texas mass shooting at a Wal-Mart), have also contributed to the spread of hate.

Another sure sign of continued darkness is the lunacy displayed by the Ohio House of Representatives who, in November 2019, passed the "Student Religious Liberties Act" which prevents teachers from penalizing students for giving incorrect answers on tests or other school work if their work is scientifically wrong so long as the reasoning is because of their religious beliefs (WKRC Staff 2019; Jensen 2019). "The bill's sponsor, Republican representative and ordained minister Timothy Ginter, has a history of attempting to write his religious beliefs into legislation" (Jensen 2019). Such ridiculous legislation speaks to the general disbelief in science held by some; the acceptance of nonsensical religious beliefs; and the failure of the education system, especially when political motivations interfere with the primary function of education (to teach critical thinking and provide factual information). The insane notion of this legislation represents a clear example of unenlightened thought and of the darkness that surrounds us.

Civil rights for women and members of the LGBTQ+ community still lag and in many countries are flat-out denied. While the US House passed legislation (April 2019) to reauthorize the Violence Against Women Act (first passed in 1994), 157 Republicans voted against it (along with one Democrat) because the National Rifle Association (NRA) was pushing them to oppose it over its gun safety provisions (Bendery 2019).

The power of the NRA is astonishing and has contributed greatly to a gun culture that, among other things, ignores the countless mass shootings that occur in the United States. Proponents of the gun culture make the completely useless gesture of offering "thoughts and prayers" to victims of gun violence rather than taking action to curtail the killings. So serious is the gun violence in the United States that more school-aged children in the US die as a result of guns than on-duty police officers or military personnel (Sanchez 2019).

The future

This book has provided a socio-political critique of society in early twenty-first century from the perspective that there is a decline in rational, enlightened thought as a result of a growing number of forces of darkness. So alarming are these forces of darkness that the very fabric of democracy, human rights, and rational thought are in jeopardy.

There have been others who have attempted to warn us of the potential demise of democracy, including long-time Republican politician and strategist Dick Rosenbaum (with whom I had the pleasure to meet personally and enjoy quality conversations). In 2008, Rosenbaum wrote, "Over the past twenty years, I've witnessed a metamorphosis in the GOP. I've seen my party move away from its middle-of-the-road position to the right, often the far right, a position that places the GOP in deep ideological opposition to many Democrats" (p. 247). Rosenbaum adds that this was not always the case as Democrats and Republicans have historically managed to find some common ground. Rosenbaum (2008) believes that the reason the GOP has changed so much can be explained in two words: "zealous ideology" (p. 247). This zealous ideology has led to many of the extreme views that I have detailed throughout this book (and significantly beyond what Rosenbaum describes).

Zealous ideology has also contributed to what Levitsky and Ziblatt (2018) describe as never-before-seen changes in the political climate of the United States; "Over the past two years, we have watched politicians say and do things that are unprecedented in the United States—but that we have recognized as having been the precursors of democratic crisis in other places" (p. 1). Unfortunately, this dire warning is not likely to be heeded by those responsible for the darkness that surrounds us. Levitsky and Ziblatt indicate that Americans' belief in the power of the Constitution will keep the nation strong and democratic; however, as I have pointed out here, there are currently many threats to the Constitution.

In the preface of his book *How Democracy Ends* (2018), David Runciman begins with this ominous statement, "Nothing lasts forever. At some point democracy was always going to pass into the pages of history" (p. 1). Runciman (2018) believes that the election of Trump is a major sign of the end of democracy but echoes the sentiments expressed by others that it is not simply Trump as president that is causing so many problems in the United States—problems that reverberate across the globe; it's the changing political climate "that appears increasingly unstable, riven with mistrust and mutual intolerance, fuelled by wild accusations and online bullying, a dialogue of the deaf drowning each other out with noise. In many places, not just the United States, democracy is starting to look unhinged" (pp. 1–2).

With major global elections looming in the very near future, the election of certain political leaders will be significant if we hope to see rational enlightened thought reign over the darkness. But even if certain extremist politicians do not remain in power, the undercurrent of intolerance, mistrust, and shameful and hateful actions will still exist. These signs of further darkness are so plentiful that it will require a future book to detail them all—and that is a task I have already begun.

BIBLIOGRAPHY

AAUP. 2019. "Dangerous Times For Public Higher Education in Alaska." Email sent to AAUP Members, July 10.
Abbott, Carl, 2017. "No, Washington Is Not Built on a Swamp." *City Lab*, March 8. Retrieved August 20, 2019 (www.citylab.com/equity/2017/03/waswashington-dc-really-a-swamp/519003/).
ABC7. 2018. "Beaches in Nassau County Reopen After Needles, Syringes Washed Ashore." Retrieved August 14, 2019 (https://abc7ny.com/health/hempstead- beaches-reopen-after-needles-syringes-wash-ashore/3990860/).
ABC News. 2019. "1969: Moon Shot." Original air date April 23.
Abrams, Stacey. 2019. "Live Interview on CBS This Morning." *CBS*, August 19.
Adams, Bert and R.A. Sydie. 2001. *Sociological Theory*. Thousand Oaks, CA: Pine Forge Press.
Al Jazeera. 2019. "Is it the End of Populism in Greece?" Inside Story, July 7. Retrieved July 26, 2019 (www.aljazeera.com/programmes/insidestory/2019/07/populism-greece-190 707200321896.html).
Ali, Lorraine. 2018. "Forget 'Fake News,' it's Propaganda." *Los Angeles Times*, November 18: E11.
Alterman, Eric. 2019. "Trump's Prodigious Lying Threatens Our Democracy." *The Nation*, May 16. Retrieved July 14, 2019 (www.thenation.com/article/trump-lies-eric-alterman/).
Alvarado, Denise. 2011. *The Voodoo Hoodoo Spellbook*. San Francisco, CA: Red Wheel/Weiser.
Amadeo, Kimberly. 2019. "Current US Federal Budget Deficit." *The Balance*, May 8. Retrieved July 15, 2019 (www.thebalance.com/current-u-s-federal-budget-deficit-33 05783).
American Chemistry Council. 2019. "How Plastics Are Made." Retrieved August 14, 2019 (https://plastics.americanchemistry.com/How-Plastics-Are-Made/).
American Cleaning Institute. 2009. "2009 National Clean Hands Report Card Survey Findings." Retrieved July 14, 2019 (www.cleaninginstitute.org/newsroom/surveys/92109-summary).
Andryszewski, Tricia. 2008. *Mass Extinctions: Examining the Current Crisis*. Minneapolis, MN: Twenty-First Century Books.

Armstrong, Elizabeth A. and Mary Bernstein. 2008. "Culture, Power, and Institutions: A Multi-Institutional Politics Approach to Social Movements." *Sociological Theory*, 26(1): 74–99.

Arthur, Lisa. 2013. "What is Big Data?" *Forbes*, August 15. Retrieved October 5, 2019 (www.forbes.com/sites/lisaarthur/2013/08/15/what-is-big- data/#6443b995c85b).

Ashcraft, Richard. 1987. *Locke's Two Treatises of Government*. London: Allen and Unwin.

Associated Press. 2014. "Joan Quigley, Astrologer for Ronald Reagan, Dies." As it appeared in *The Citizen*, October 25: A5.

Associated Press. 2018a. "What the President Says, and What the Facts Show." As it appeared in the *Los Angeles Times*, July 5: A2.

Associated Press. 2018b. "President Trump Says He Is 'the Least Racist Person.'" *Fortune*, January 14. Retrieved July 23, 2019 (https://fortune.com/2018/01/14/donald-trump-says-not-racist/).

Associated Press. 2018c. "'Truth Isn't Truth': Rudy Giuliani Wins Yale Quote-of-the-Year Nod." December 21. Retrieved April 20, 2019 (www.marketwatch.com/story/truth-isnt-truth-rudy-giuliani-wins-yale-quote-of-the-year-nod-2018-12-20).

Associated Press. 2018d. "Mayor Blocks Polish Nationalist March." As it appeared in the *Los Angeles Times*, November 8: A4.

Associated Press. 2018e. "U.N. Rebukes Venezuela." As it appeared in the *Los Angeles Times*, June 23: A4.

Associated Press. 2019a. "Far-Right Europe Leaders condemn Migration, Islam." As it appeared in the *Los Angeles Times*, April 26: A4.

Associated Press. 2019b. "Parents Sue Over Vaccine Mandate." As it appeared in the *The Citizen*, July 11: A3.

Associated Press. 2019c. "Global Groups See A 'Climate Emergency.'" As it appeared in the *Los Angeles Times*, July 11: A4.

Associated Press. 2019d. "Senate Confirms Craft to UN Post." As it appeared in the *The Citizen*, August 1: A6.

Associated Press. 2019e. "Court Blocks Flavored Vaping Ban." As it appeared in the *The Citizen*, October 4: A3.

Associated Press. 2019f. "NY: Sackler Family Hid $1B in Transfers." As it appeared in the *The Citizen*, September 14: A5.

Associated Press. 2019g. "Firms Settle Opiods Case for $260 million." As it appeared in the *Los Angeles Times*, October 22: A4.

Associated Press. 2019h. "Latino Man Says Acid Attacker Accused Him of Invading U.S." As it appeared in the *Los Angeles Times*, November 5: A9.

Associated Press. 2019i. "Long Time Trump Ally Stone Convicted." As it appeared in the *Los Angeles Times*, November 11: A5.

Astin, Alexander. 2019. "The Fallacy of 'Free College for All.'" *Los Angeles Times*, August 8: A11.

Ayers, Michael. 1999. *Locke*. New York: Routledge.

Ayers, Sabra. 2019. "2 Reported Killed in LGBTQ Purge in Chechnya." *Los Angeles Times*, January 15: A3.

Ayers, Sabra and Laura King. 2018. "Christian Rights Global 'Cultural War.'" *Los Angeles Times*, October 6: A1.

Baciu, Florin. 2015. "Order of the Nine Angles (O.N.A.)." *Occult Study*, September 17. Retrieved October 1, 2019 (https://occult-study.org/order-of-nine-angles- ona/).

Baker, Sinead. 2018. "Ruth Bader Ginsburg Celebrates 25 Years in the Supreme Court Today—Here's When She and Her Colleagues Could Retire." *Business Insider*, August 10. Retrieved September 2, 2019 (www.businessinsider.com/supreme-court-when-ginsberg-other- justices-could-quit-based-on-age-tenure-2018-6).

Baldor, Lolita C. and Robert Burns. 2019. "US to Protect Syrian Oil Fields." *The Citizen*, October 26: A5.

Baldor, Lolita C., Matthew Lee, and Robert Burns. 2019. "Trump Abandons Kurdish Fighters." *The Citizen*, October 8: A6.

Banerji, Rishabh. 2018. "9 of the Most Dangerous Secret Societies in the World." *India Times*, March 28. Retrieved October 1, 2019 (www.indiatimes.com/culture/who-we-are/9-of-the-most-dangerous- secret- societies-in-the-world-247678.html).

Banerji, Arun Kumar. 2019. "Age of Populism." *The Statesman*, June 23. Retrieved July 22, 2019 (www.thestatesman.com/opinion/age-of-populismi- 1502768796.html).

Barnosky, Anthony D., Nicholas Matzke, Susumu Tomiya, Guinevere O.U. Wogan, Brian Swartz, Tiago B. Quental, Charles Marshall, Jenny L. McGuire, Emily J. Lindsey, Kaitlin C. Maguire, Ben Mersey, and Elizabeth A. Ferrer. 2011. "Has the Earth's Sixth Mass Extinction Already Arrived?" *Nature*, 471 (7336): 51–57.

The Basics of Philosophy. 2019. "Voltaire (Francois-Marie Arouet)." Retrieved May 24, 2019 (www.philosophybasics.com/philosophers_voltaire.html).

Baumgaertner, Emily. 2019. "How Civic Discord can Lead to Lower Vaccinations Rates." *Los Angeles Times*, May 13: A2.

BBC News. 2019a. "Spike in Wildfires in Brazil's Amazon Rainforest," August 21. Retrieved August 23, 2019 (www.bbc.com/news/av/world-latin-america-49417171/spike-in-wildfires-in-brazil-s-amazon-rainforest).

BBC News. 2019b. "Wa Lone and Kyaw Soe Oo: Reuters Journalists Freed in Myanmar". Retrieved February 21, 2020 (www.bbc.com/news/world-asia-48182712).

Bendery, Jennifer. 2019. "157 Republicans Just Opposed Renewing the Violence Against Women Act." *Huff Post*, April 5, 2019. Retrieved November 29, 2019 (www.huffpost.com/entry/republicans-oppose-violence-against-women-act_n_5ca68295e4b047edf957b5e1).

Benen, Steve. 2019. "House Panel Holds AG Bill Barr in Contempt." MSNBC, May 8. Retrieved September 1, 2019 (www.msnbc.com/rachel-maddow-show/house-panel-holds-ag-bill-barr-contempt).

Bengali, Shashank and Zulfiqar Ali. 2019. "Polio Surges Back In Pakistan." *Los Angeles Times*, September 13: A1, A4.

Berkowitz, Bonnie, Chris Alcantara, and Denise Lu. 2019. "The Terrible Numbers that Grow with Each Mass Shooting." *The Washington Post*, August 31. Retrieved October 5, 2019 (www.washingtonpost.com/graphics/2018/national/mass-shootings-in-america/).

Bidwell, Allie. 2018. "Most Americans Say Higher Ed is Moving in the Wrong Direction." National Association of Student Financial Aid Administrators (NASFAA). Retrieved August 8, 2019 (www.nasfaa.org/news-item/15809/Most_Americans_Say_Higher_Ed_Is_Moving_in_the_Wrong_Di rection).

Bierman, Noah. 2018. "Macron Rebukes a Stance Taken by Trump." *Los Angeles Times*, November 12: A1, A4.

Bierman, Noah. 2019. "Trump Seeks to Disavow Chant." *Los Angeles Times*, July 19: A1, A6.

Bierman, Noah and Eli Stokols. 2018. "Dictator Envy? Trump Seems to Have It." *Los Angeles Times*, June 16: A7.

Bilderberg Group. 2019. "What are Bilderberg Conferences All About?" Retrieved October 1, 2019 (http://bilderberggroup.net/).

Bio Spectrum Bureau. 2013. "Recent 6 'Big Pharma' Frauds." Retrieved October 6, 2019 (www.biospectrumasia.com/analysis/25/6598/recent-6-big-pharma-frauds.html).

Biography.com. 2019a. "Petrarch." Retrieved April 27, 2019 (www.biography.com/scholar/petrarch).

Biography.com. 2019b. "Voltaire." Retrieved April 29, 2019 (www.biography.com/scholar/voltaire).

Biography.com. 2019c. "Neil Gorsuch." Retrieved September 2, 2019 (www.biography.com/law-figure/neil-gorsuch).

Birnbaum, Sarah. 2017. "President Donald Trump Isn't the Only World Leader Denying Climate Change." PRI.org, January 26. Retrieved August 12, 2019 (www.pri.org/stories/2017-01-26/president-donald-trump-isnt-only-world-leader-denying-climate-change).

Bishop, Tyler. 2019. "Singing the Praises of 'Big Business.'" *New York Times*, May 17. Retrieved October 5 2019 (www.nytimes.com/2019/05/17/books/review/big-business-tyler-cowen.html?searchResultPosition=1).

Black Demographics. 2019. "African American Income." Retrieved July 30, 2019 (https://blackdemographics.com/households/african-american-income/).

Blake, Aaron. 2017. "Kellyanne Conway Says Donald Trump's Team Has 'Alternative Facts.' Which Pretty Much Says It All." *Washington Post*, January 22. Retrieved April 20, 2019 (www.washingtonpost.com/news/the-fix/wp/2017/01/22/kellyanne-conway-says-donald-trumps-team-has-alternate-facts-which-pretty-much-says-it-all/?utm_term=.957cff22f4f5).

Boboltz, Sara. 2019. "Ethics Complaints Against Justice Brett Kavanaugh Dismissed Permanently." *Huffington Post*, August 2. Retrieved October 10, 2019 (www.huffingtonpost.ca/entry/brett-kavanaugh-ethics-complaints-dismissed_n_5d4442a1e4b0acb57fcb6356).

Bohrer, Becky. 2019. "University of Alaska Faces Major Cuts." *Los Angeles Times*, July 7: A8.

Bolling, Eric. 2017. *The Swamp: Washington's Murky Pool of Corruption and Cronyism and How Trump Can Drain It*. New York: St. Martin's Press.

Bondarenko, Veronika 2017. "Trump Keeps Saying 'Enemy of the People'—But the Phrase Has a Very Ugly History." *Business Insider*, February 27. Retrieved July 19, 2019 (www.businessinsider.com/history-of-president-trumps-phrase-an-enemy-of-the-people-2017-2).

Boot, Max. 2018. "Trump Keeps Lying Because it Works." *Post-Standard*, June 10: E3.

Borenstein, Seth. 2011. "Scientists: Thawing Permafrost Vents Worsens Warning." *Post-Standard*, December 1: A15.

Boundless World History. 2019. "The Scientific Revolution." Retrieved April 27, 2019 (https://courses.lumenlearning.com/boundless-worldhistory/chapter/the-scientific-revolution/).

Boyer, Jeremy. 2019a. "Newspaper Front Pages Stay Factual." *The Citizen*, May 16: A4.

Boyer, Jeremy. 2019b. "Some Progress Fighting Made-Up News." *The Citizen*, June 6: A4.

Boyle, Christina and Laura King. 2019. "Brexit Advocate Johnson is Britain's New Prime Minister." *Los Angeles Times*, July 24: A1, A5.

Brasovean, I., I. Oroian, C. Iederan, C. Oroian-Mihai, A. Fleseriu and P. Burduhos. 2010. "Legislative Framework and Objectives of Medical Waste Management." *Pro Environment*, 3: 301–304.

Breuninger, Kevin. 2018. "Trump Slams the Media as 'The True Enemy of the People' Days After CNN was Targeted with Mail Bombs." CNBC, October 29. Retrieved July 19, 2019 (www.cnbc.com/2018/10/29/trump-slams-media-as-true-enemy-of-the-people-days-after-cnn-targeted.html).

Brockell, Gillian. 2019. "Geronimo and the Japanese Were Imprisoned There. Now Fort Sill Will Hold Migrant Children—Again." *Washington Post*, June 12. Retrieved July 29, 2019.

Brokaw, Tom. 2019. *The Fall of Richard Nixon: A Reporter Remembers Watergate*. New York: Random House.

Bruni, Frank. 2018a. "Aristotle's Wrongful Death." *New York Times*, May 26. Retrieved August 8, 2019 (www.nytimes.com/2018/05/26/opinion/sunday/college-majors-liberal-arts.html).

Bruni, Frank. 2018b. "Brett Kavanaugh Loves His Beer: The Supreme Court Nominee Paired a Frothy Beverage with Identify Politics." *New York Times*, September 29 (www.nytimes.com/2018/09/29/opinion/brett-kavanaugh-beer-politics.html).

Buchanan, Larry and Karen Yourish. 2019. "Tracking 29 Investigations Related to Trump." *New York Times*, July 30. Retrieved September 1, 2019 (www.nytimes.com/interactive/2019/05/13/us/politics/trump-investigations.html).

Buchheit, Paul. 2018. "Meeting the Definition of Terrorism: Big Pharma, Big Oil, and Big Banks." *Nation of Change*, April 30. Retrieved October 4, 2019 (www.nationofchange.org/2018/04/30/meeting-the-definition-of-terrorism-big-pharma-big-oil-and-big-banks/).

Buckland, Raymond. 2002 (revised edition). *Buckland's Complete Book of Witchcraft*. St. Paul, MN: Llewellyn.

Bulos, Nabih. 2018. "A Rocky Road for Female Saudi Drivers." *Los Angeles Times*, August 2: A1.

Bulos, Nabih. 2019. "Is Another Arab Spring Starting to Unfold?" *Los Angeles Times*, April 14: A7.

Bureau of Labor Statistics (BLS). 2017a. "Newspaper Publishers Lose Half Their Employment from January 2001 to September 2016." Retrieved July 20, 2019 (www.bls.gov/opub/ted/2017/mobile/newspaper-publishers-lose-over-half-their-employment-from-january-2001-to-september-2016.htm?mc_cid=e73bf40429&mc_eid=e49f1168cb).

Bureau of Labor Statistics (BLS). 2017b. "Measuring the Value of Education." Retrieved August 5, 2019 (www.bls.gov/careeroutlook/2018/data-on-display/education- pays.htm).

Bureau of Labor Statistics (BLS). 2019. "Employment by Major Industry Sector." Retrieved October 4, 2019 (www.bls.gov/emp/tables/employment-by-major-industry-sector.htm).

Burke, Michael. 2019. "Trump Claims Wind Turbine 'Noise Causes Cancer.'" *The Hill*, April 3. Retrieved August 11, 2019 (https://thehill.com/homenews/administration/437096-trump-claims-noise-from- windmills-causes-cancer).

Burke, Peter. 1964. *The Renaissance*. New York: Barnes and Nobel.

Burleigh, Nina. 2018. "Trump Speaks at Fourth-Grade Level, Lowest of Last 15 U.S. Presidents, New Analysis Finds." *Newsweek*, January 8. Retrieved March 2, 2018 (www.newsweek.com/trump-fire-and-fury-smart-genius-obama-774169).

Byman, Daniel. 2019. "ISIS Reborn?" *Slate*, October 18. Retrieved October 19, 2019 (https://slate.com/news-and-politics/2019/10/isis-syria-trump-kurds-resurgence-comeback.html).

Caferro, William. 2011. *Contesting the Renaissance*. Malden, MA: Wiley-Blackwell.

Caldwell, Don. 2017. "Drain the Swamp." Retrieved August 24, 2019 (https://knowyourmeme.com/memes/drain-the-swamp).

Callahan, Maureen. 2016. "The "Sex Slave' Scandal That Exposed Pedophile Billionaire Jeffery Epstein." *New York Post*, October 9. Retrieved September 1, 2019 (https://nypost.com/2016/10/09/the-sex-slave-scandal-that-exposed-pedophile-billionaire-jeffrey-epstein/).

Calmes, Jackie. 2019. "Review of U.S. Justice Limited by FBI." *Los Angeles Times*, September 16: A1.

Canberra Times. 2008. "Creationist Sarah and the Politics of Extinction," October 31. Retrieved August 16, 2019 (www.canberratimes.com.au/story/820038/creationist-sarah-and-the-politics-of-extinction/).

Carcamo, Cindy, Hannah Fry, and Corina Knoll. 2018. "Killings by Migrants Fuel Political Attacks." *Los Angeles Times*, November 2: B1, B5.

Carlebach, Julius. 1978. *Karl Marx and the Radical Critique of Judaism*. Boston, MA: Routledge and Kegan Paul.

Case, William. 2017. *Populist Threats and Democracy's Fate in Southeast Asia*. New York: Routledge.

Cassirer, Ernst. 1951. *The Philosophy of the Enlightenment*. Princeton, NJ: Princeton University Press.

Catton, William R. 1980. *Overshoot: The Ecological Basis of Revolutionary Change*. Urbana, IL: University of Illinois Press.

CBS News. 2018. "Major Chickenpox Outbreak Seen in Anti-Vaccine Hot Spot," November 2018. Retrieved August 12, 2019 (www.cbsnews.com/news/north-carolina-chickenpox-outbreak-in-anti-vaccine-hot-spot-asheville-waldorf-school/).

CBS News. 2019. "King Vajiralongkorn of Thailand Marries His Security Chief Suthida, Makes Her Queen," May 2. Retrieved July 28, 2019 (www.cbsnews.com/news/vajiralongkorn-king-thailand-marries-queen-suthida-former-security-chief-today-2019-05-02/).

Celtic Connection. 2019. "What is Wicca?" Retrieved August 16, 2019 (https://wicca.com/celtic/wicca/wicca.htm).

Centers for Disease Control and Prevention (CDC). 1999. "Ten Great Public Health Achievements—United States, 1900–1999." Retrieved May 12, 2019 (www.cdc.gov/mmwr/preview/mmwrhtml/00056796.htm).

Centers for Disease Control and Prevention (CDC). 2019a. "Cigarette Smoking Remains High Among Certain Populations." Retrieved October 5, 2019 (www.cdc.gov/tobacco/data_statistics/index.htm?s_cid=osh-stu-home-nav-005).

Centers for Disease Control and Prevention (CDC). 2019b. "Smoking & Tobacco Use: Secondhand Smoke (SHS) Facts." Retrieved October 5, 2019 (www.cdc.gov/tobacco/data_statistics/fact_sheets/secondhand_smoke/general_facts/index.htm).

Centers for Disease Control and Prevention (CDC). 2019c. "Smoking & Tobacco Use: Global Tobacco Control." Retrieved October 5, 2019 (www.cdc.gov/tobacco/global/index.htm).

Chaffetz, Jason. 2018. *The Deep State: How an Army of Bureaucrats Protected Barack Obama and Is Working to Destroy the Trump Agenda*. New York: HarperCollins.

Chagaeva, Tamara. 2019. "Extreme Tourism: How The TV-Show Chernobyl Encouraged Influencers to Go Crazy." Society19.com, July 23. Retrieved August 17, 2019 (www.society19.com/extreme-tourism-how-the-tv-show-chernobyl-encouraged-influencers-to-go-crazy/).

Chapman, Matthew. 2019. "Trump's Racist Tweets Against 'The Squad' Helped Him with Republicans." *Salon*, July 18. Retrieved July 23, 2019 (www.salon.com/2019/07/18/trumps-racist-tweets-against-the-squad-helped-him-with-republicans_partner/).

Chapman, Simon. 2017. "Wind Farms are Hardly the Bird Slayers They're Made Out to Be—Here's Why." *Phys Org*, June 16. Retrieved August 11, 2019 (https://phys.org/news/2017-06-farms-bird-slayers-theyre-behere.html).

Chauran, Alexandra. 2014. *Clairvoyance for Beginners: Easy Techniques to Enhance Your Psychic Visions*. Woodbury, MN: Llewellyn Publications.

Chavern, David. 2018. "We are Pressing On." *The Citizen*, July 12: A4.

Cillizza, Chris. 2017. "Donald Trump Just Claimed He Invented 'Fake News.'" CNN

Politics, October 26. Retrieved April 20, 2019 (www.cnn.com/2017/10/08/politics/trump-huckabee-fake/index.html).

Cillizza, Chris. 2019. "Donald Trump Lies More Often than You Wash Your Hands Every Day." CNN Politics, June 10. Retrieved July 14, 2019 (www.cnn.com/2019/06/10/politics/donald-trump-lies-fact-check/index.html).

Clark, Laura. 2015. "The First State of the Union Address: Way Shorter, Way Less Clapping." *Smithsonian.com*, January 20. Retrieved August 11, 2019 (www.smithsonianmag.com/smart-news/first-state-union-address-way-shorter-less-clapping-180953954/).

Clawson, Laura. 2018. "Union Popularity Hits 15-Year High Amid Republican Attacks." *Daily Kos Labor*, August 30. Retrieved July 30, 2019 (www.dailykos.com/stories/2018/8/30/1792156/-Union-popularity-hits-15-year-high-amid-Republican-attacks).

Clive, Geoffrey. 1973 [1960]. *The Romantic Enlightenment*. Westport, CT: Greenwood Press.

Cloud, David S., Jennifer Haberkorn, and Nabih Bulos. 2019. "Trump's Syria Pull Back Plan Imperils Allies." *Los Angeles Times*, October 8: A1, A4.

Coan, Andrew. 2019. "Trump Is No Nixon. He's Worse." *Los Angeles Times*, April 23: A9.

Cohen, Jennie. 2018. "History's Worst Nuclear Disasters." History.com. Retrieved August 17, 2019 (www.history.com/news/historys-worst-nuclear-disasters).

Cohen, Patricia. 2016. "A Rising Call to Promote STEM Education and Cut Liberal Arts Funding." *New York Times*, February 21. Retrieved August 8, 2019 (www.nytimes.com/2016/02/22/business/a-rising-call-to-promote-stem-education-and-cut-liberal-arts-funding.html).

Colvin, Jill and Alan Fram. 2019. "Trump Defends Acosta." *The Citizen*, July 10: A6.

Colvin, Jill, Jonathan Lemire, and Calvin Woodward. 2019. "Trump Digs in on Tweets." *The Citizen*, July 16: A6.

Committee to Protect Journalists (CPJ). 2016. "CPJ's 2016 Global Impunity Index Spotlights Countries Where Journalists are Slain and the Killers Go Free." Retrieved July 21, 2019 (https://cpj.org/reports/2016/10/impunity-index-getting-away-with-murder-killed-justice.php).

Committee to Protect Journalists (CPJ). 2019. "CPJ to Honor Journalists with International Press Freedom Awards." Retrieved July 16, 2019 (https://cpj.org/).

Conserve Energy for Future. 2019a. "Causes, Effects and Solutions of Food Waste." Retrieved August 14, 2019 (www.conserve-energy-future.com/causes-effects-solutions-food-waste.php).

Conserve Energy for Future. 2019b. "What is Agricultural Pollution?" Retrieved August 14, 2019 (www.conserve-energy-future.com/causes-and-effects-of-agricultural-pollution.php).

Cooper, Preston. 2018. "Republicans, Democrats, Disagree About the Point of Higher Education." *Forbes*, May 22. Retrieved August 8, 2019 (www.forbes.com/sites/prestoncooper2/2018/05/22/republicans-democrats-disagree-about-the-point-of-higher-education/#3293d5a17ae6).

Coser, Lewis. 1956. *The Functions of Social Conflict*. New York: Free Press.

Coser, Lewis. 1977. *Masters of Sociological Thought, Second Edition*. New York: Harcourt, Brace and Jovanovich.

Cowen, Tyler. 2019. *Big Business: A Love Letter to an American Anti-Hero*. New York: St. Martin's Press.

Cranston, Maurice. 1986. *Philosophes and Pamphleteers: Political Theorists of the Enlightenment*. Oxford: Chaucer Press.

Creamer, Robert. 2013. "How the GOP Hopes to Take Away Americans' Right to Collective Bargaining." *Huffington Post*, July 15. Retrieved July 30, 2019 (www.huffpost.com/entry/how-the-gop-hopes-to-take_b_3597960).
Crocker, Lester G. 1968. *Jean-Jacques Rousseau: The Quest, 1712–1758, Vol. 1*. New York: Macmillan.
Croyle, Johnathan. 2018. "SU's 1898 Class Day Marred by 'Battle.'" *Post-Standard*, June 7: A2.
Crumley, Jack S. II. 2016. *Introducing Philosophy: Knowledge and Reality*. Tonawanda, NY: Broadview.
Cullen, Daniel E. 1993. *Freedom in Rousseau's Political Philosophy*. DeKalb, IL: Northern Illinois University Press.
Daalder, Ivo. 2019. "Impeachment Inquiry: Why So Many People in U.S. Diplomacy?" *Post-Standard*, November 24: E3.
D'Antonio, Michael. 2016. *The Truth About Trump*. New York: St. Martin's Griffin.
D'Antonio, Michael. 2018. "A Check on Trump? Expect Him to Go Low." *Los Angeles Times*, November 8: A 17.
Daly, Matthew and Michael Balsamo. 2019. "Officials Held in Contempt." *The Citizen*, June 13: A6.
Date, S.V. 2019. "In Turkey Vs. Kurds Dispute, Trump Chooses The Side Where He Has a Condo Complex." *Huffington Post*, October 7. Retrieved October 8, 2019 (www.huffpost.com/entry/trump-kurds-turkey-istanbul_n_5d9b82ffe4b03b475f9de498).
Davis, Julie Hirschfeld. 2017. "Rumblings of a 'Deep State' Undermining Trump? It Was Once a Foreign Concept." *New York Times*, March 6. Retrieved September 30 (www.nytimes.com/2017/03/06/us/politics/deep-state-trump.html?searchResult Position=2).
Davis, Michelle F. 2019. "Unshackled, Banks Prowl for Deals." *Los Angeles Times*, July 22: A7.
Day, Chad. 2018. "Road to Cohen's Guilty Plea." *The Citizen*, December 1: B5.
Dayen, David. 2018. "Bank Error? Or Scandal?" *Los Angeles Times*, June 18: A13.
De la Torre, Carlos. 2018. *Populism: A Quick Immersion*. Kindle edition. Tididabo Publishing.
Delaney, Tim. 2004. *Classical Social Theory: Investigation and Application*. Upper Saddle River, NJ: Prentice Hall.
Delaney, Tim. 2005. *Contemporary Social Theory: Investigation and Application*. Upper Saddle River, NJ: Pearson.
Delaney, Tim. 2008. *Shameful Behaviors*. Lanham, MD: University Press of America.
Delaney, Tim. 2012. *Connecting Sociology to Our Lives*. Boulder, CO: Paradigm.
Delaney, Tim. 2014. *Classical and Contemporary Social Theory: Investigation and Application*. Boston, MA: Pearson.
Delaney, Tim. 2016. "Ethics and Sportsmanship." Keynote Address, Saint Thomas More Lecture Series, St. John Fisher College, March 14.
Delaney, Tim. 2017. *Social Deviance*. Lanham, MD: Rowman & Littlefield.
Delaney, Tim. 2019. *Common Sense as a Paradigm of Thought: An Analysis of Social Interaction*. London: Routledge.
Delaney, Tim and Tim Madigan. 2014. *Beyond Sustainability: A Thriving Environment*. Jefferson, NC: McFarland.
Delaney, Tim and Tim Madigan. 2016. *Lessons Learned From Popular Culture*. Albany, NY: State University of New York Press.
Dennis, Brady. 2019. "EPA Will Allow Use of Pesticide Very Toxic to Bees." *Post-Standard*, July 16: A10.

Deutsch, Gotthard. 2011. "Bonald, Louis-Gabriel-Ambroise." *Jewish Encyclopedia*. Retrieved May 4, 2019 (www.jewishencyclopedia.com/articles/3498-bonald-louis-gabriel-ambroise).

Diaz, Alexa. 2019. "EPA to Roll Back Regulations on Methane Leaks." *Los Angeles Times*, August 30: A2, A7.

DivinationandFortuneTelling.com. 2017. "Methods of Divination and Fortune- Telling." Retrieved August 15, 2019 (https://divinationandfortunetelling.com/articles/methods-of-divination-and-fortune-telling).

Doob, Christopher Bates. 1999. *Racism: An American Cauldron*. New York: Longman.

Dornan, Geoff. 2019. "Nevada State Employees Now Have Collective Bargaining." *Nevada Appeal*, June 12. Retrieved July 30, 2019 (www.nevadaappeal.com/news/government/nevada-state-employees-now-have-collective-bargaining/).

Doyle, Alison. 2019. "What is the Difference between Internships and Apprenticeships?" *The Balance Careers*, July 4. Retrieved August 4, 2019 (www.thebalancecareers.com/what-are-apprenticeship-programs-2061927).

Drake, Frances. 2000. *Global Warming: The Science of Climate Change*. New York: Oxford University Press.

Duffin, Erin. 2019. "Top Companies in the World by Market Value 2019." *Statista*, August 12. Retrieved October 4, 2019 (www.statista.com/statistics/263264/top-companies-in-the-world-by-market-value/).

Dwyer, Colin and Andrew Limbong. 2019. "'Go Back to Where You Came From': The Long Rhetorical Roots of Trump's Racist Tweets." *NPR*, July 15. Retrieved July 23, 2019 (www.npr.org/2019/07/15/741827580/go-back-where-you-came-from-the-long-rhetorical-roots-of-trump-s-racist-tweets).

EarthDay.org. 2018. "Fact Sheet: Single Use Plastics." Retrieved August 14, 2019 (www.earthday.org/2018/03/29/fact-sheet-single-use-plastics/).

Edelman, Adam. 2016. "A Look at Trump's Most Outrageous Comments About Mexicans as He Attempts Damage Control By Visiting with Country's President." *Daily News*, August 31. Retrieved August 12, 2019 (www.nydailynews.com/news/politics/trump-outrageous-comments-mexicans-article-1.2773214).

Eilperin, Juliet, Josh Dawsey, and Darryl Fears. 2018. "Interior Secretary Zinke Resigns Amid Investigations." *Washington Post*, 2018. Retrieved August 29, 2019 (www.washingtonpost.com/national/health-science/interior-secretary-zinke-resigns-amid-investigations/2018/12/15/481f9104-0077-11e9-ad40-cdfd0e0dd65a_story.html).

Ellis, Monique. 2019. "Who are the Top 10 Pharmaceutical Companies in the World? (2019)." *Proclinical*, March 20. Retrieved October 5, 2019 (www.proclinical.com/blogs/2019-3/the-top-10-pharmaceutical-companies-in-the-world-2019).

Eltis, David and David Richardson. 2010. *Atlas of the Transatlantic Slave Trade*, foreword by David Brion Davis. New Haven, CT: Yale University Press.

Elving, Ron. 2019. "With Latest Nativist Rhetoric, Trump Takes America Back to Where it Came From." *NPR*, July 16. Retrieved July 23, 2019 (www.npr.org/2019/07/16/742000247/with-latest-nativist-rhetoric-trump-takes-america-back-to-where-it-came-from).

Encyclopedia Britannica. 2019a. "Cesare Beccaria." Retrieved May 2, 2019 (www.britannica.com/biography/Cesare-Beccaria).

Encyclopedia Britannica. 2019b. "Benjamin Henry Day." Retrieved May 4, 2019 (www.britannica.com/biography/Benjamin-Henry-Day).

Engelmayer, Caroline S. and Noah Bierman. 2019. "Labor Chief Quits Over Criticism of Epstein's Plea Deal." *Los Angeles Times*, July 13:A1, A8.

England, Christina. 2012. "7 Shameful Examples of Big Pharma Fraud." VacTruth.com, July 9. Retrieved October 6, 2019 (https://vactruth.com/2012/07/09/7-examples-pharma-fraud/).

Environmental Protection Authority (EPA) South Australia. 2019. "E-waste." Retrieved August 14, 2019 (www.epa.sa.gov.au/environmental_info/waste_management/e_waste).

Epps, Garrett. 2018. "Why Jim Acosta Got His Pass Back." *The Atlantic*, November 16. Retrieved July 19, 2019 (www.theatlantic.com/ideas/archive/2018/11/cnns-jim-acosta-has-right-his-press-pass/576109/).

Estelle, Emily. 2019. "Chaos in North Africa Opens Door for Extremists." *Los Angeles Times*, May 10: A9.

Etehad, Melissa. 2019. "Around the Globe, Political Grief Boils Into Mass Protest." *Los Angeles Times*, November 25: A2.

Everytown Research. 2019. "Gun Violence in America." Retrieved October 5, 2019 (https://everytownresearch.org/gun-violence-america/).

Fahrenthold, David A., Matt Zapotosky, and Seung Min Kim. 2018. "Nearly Every Organization Trump Has Led Is Now Under Investigation." *Post-Standard*, December 16: B1, B3.

Fain, Paul. 2019. "Philosophy Degrees and Sales Jobs." *Inside Higher Ed*, August 2. Retrieved August 3, 2019 (www.insidehighered.com/news/2019/08/02/new-data-track-graduates-six-popular-majors-through-their-first-three-jobs).

Farrell, John A. 2017. *Richard Nixon: The Life*. New York: First Vintage Books.

Federal Pay. 2019. "Military Pay Raises – 2014 to 2019." Retrieved July 15, 2019 (www.federalpay.org/military/raises).

Federal Reserve Economic Data (FRED). 2019. "All Employees: Government (USGOVT)." Economic Research Federal Reserve Bank of St. Louis. Retrieved August 24, 2019 (https://fred.stlouisfed.org/series/USGOVT).

Finnegan, Michael and Mark Z. Barabak. 2018. "Trump's History with Racial Comments." *The Citizen*, January 17: B5.

Finnegan, Michael and Maya Sweedler. 2018. "Knight Ad Features Man who Posts Racist Facebook Rants." *Los Angeles Times*, November 1: A1, A9.

Fisher, Max. 2017. "What Happens When You Fight a 'Deep State' That Doesn't Exist?" *New York Times*, March 10. Retrieved September 30, 2019 (www.nytimes.com/2017/03/10/world/americas/what-happens-when-you-fight-a-deep-state-that-doesnt-exist.html?searchResultPosition=6).

Fisher, Mischa. 2013. "The Republican Party Isn't Really the Anti-Science Party." *The Atlantic*, November 11. Retrieved August 11, 2019 (www.theatlantic.com/politics/archive/2013/11/the-republican-party-isnt-really-the-anti-science-party/281219/).

Flemr, Jan. 2019. "Czechs Alarmed as Populist Leaders Take Aim at Public Media." *Yahoo News*, June 15. Retrieved July 26, 2019 (https://news.yahoo.com/czechs-alarmed-populist-leaders-aim-public-media-190216557.html;_ylt=A0geKYz2ijtdDcQA2PBXNyoA;_ylu=X3oDMTEyOXFyYzAyBGNvbG8DYmYxBHBvcwM2BHZ0aWQDQjc2NzVfMQRzZWMD c3I-).

Flesher, John. 2019. "Clean Water Rule Lifted." Associated Press as it appears in *The Citizen*, September 13: A6.

Fortune. 2019. "Fortune 500." Retrieved October 21, 2019 (https://fortune.com/fortune500/?sortBy=revchange&sortDir=desc).

The Foundation for Critical Thinking. 2019. "Defining Critical Thinking." Retrieved May 5, 2019 (www.criticalthinking.org/pages/defining-critical-thinking/766).

Fox News. 2019. "Who's in Trump's Cabinet" A Full List of the President's Top Advisers," July 12. Retrieved August 11, 2019 (www.foxnews.com/politics/whos-in-trumps-cabinet-a-full-list-of-the-presidents-top-advisers).

Frank, Philipp. 1947. *Einstein: His Life and Times*. New York: Alfred A. Knopf.

Frank, Robert. 2017. "Richest 1% Now Owns Half the World's Wealth." CNBC, November 14. Retrieved July 30, 2019 (www.cnbc.com/2017/11/14/richest-1-percent-now-own-half-the-worlds-wealth.html).

The Free Dictionary. 2019a. "Lobbying." Retrieved August 24, 2019 (https://legal-dictionary.thefreedictionary.com/Lobbying).

The Free Dictionary. 2019b. "Big Business." Retrieved October 1, 2019 (https://financial-dictionary.thefreedictionary.com/Big+Business).

Freedom House. 2018a. "About Freedom in the World: An Annual Study of Political Rights and Civil Liberties." Retrieved July 28, 2019 (https://freedomhouse.org/report-types/freedom-world).

Freedom House. 2018b. "Freedom in the World 2018: Thailand." Retrieved July 28, 2019 (https://freedomhouse.org/report/freedom-world/2018/thailand).

Freedom House. 2018c. "Mexico." Retrieved July 28, 2019 (https://freedomhouse.org/country/mexico).

Freedom House. 2019a. "About Us." Retrieved July 21, 2019 (https://freedomhouse.org/about-us).

Freedom House. 2019b. "Mexico: Aggregate Freedom Score." Retrieved July 28, 2019 (https://freedomhouse.org/report/freedom-world/2019/mexico).

Freedom House. 2019c. "Democracy in Retreat: Freedom in the World 2019." Retrieved July 28, 2019 (https://freedomhouse.org/report/freedom-world/freedom-world-2019).

Freedom House. 2019d. "Freedom in the World 2019: United States." Retrieved July 29, 2019 (https://freedomhouse.org/report/freedom-world/2019/united-states).

Friedman, Lisa and Coral Davenport. 2019. "Curbs on Methane, Potent Greenhouse Gas, to Be Relaxed in U.S." *New York Times*, August 29. Retrieved August 29, 2019 (www.nytimes.com/2019/08/29/climate/epa-methane-greenhouse-gas.html?searchResultPosition=1).

Friedman, Zack. 2018. "Student Loan Debt Statistics In 2018: A $1.5 Trillion Crisis." *Forbes*, June 13. Retrieved August 9, 2019 (www.forbes.com/sites/zackfriedman/2018/06/13/student-loan-debt-statistics-2018/#c0e5b247310f).

Fritze, John. 2019a. "Trump Used Words Like 'Invasion' and 'Killer' to Discuss Immigrants at Rallies 500 Times: USA Today Analysis." *USA Today*, August 9. Retrieved August 10, 2019 (https://news.yahoo.com/invasion-killers-donald-trump-describes-204632866.html;_ylt=A0geKaPsx05dJpsADApXNyoA;_ylu=X3oDMTByMjB0aG5zBGNvbG8DYmYxBHBvcwMxBHZ0aWQDBHNlYwNzYw--).

Fritze, John. 2019b. "How Well Does Trump Know $1 Million Donors like Gordon Sonnland? Some Now Work for Him." *USA Today*, November 20. Retrieved February 23, 2020 (www.usatoday.com/story/news/politics/2019/11/20/donald-trump-dismisses-relationship-1-million-donor-gordon-sondland/4252260002/).

Gajanan, Mahita. 2017. "The True Story Behind *The Post*." *Time*, December 26. Retrieved July 31, 2019 (https://time.com/5079506/the-post-true-story/).

Galli, Mark. 2019. "Trump Should Be Removed from Office." *Christianity Today*, December 19. Retrieved December 20, 2019 (www.christianitytoday.com/ct/2019/december-web-only/trump-should-be-removed-from-office.html).

Gans, John. 2019. "How John Bolton Broke the National Security Council." *New York Times*, September 10. Retrieved September 10, 2019 (www.nytimes.com/2019/09/10/opinion/john-bolton-trump.html?action=click&module=Opinion&pgtype=Homepage).

Garner, Roberta, editor. 2000. *Social Theory*. Orchard Park, NY: Broadview.

Garrand, Danielle. 2019. "Parts of the Amazon Rainforest are on Fire—and Smoke can be Spotted from Space." CBS News, August 22. Retrieved August 22, 2019 (www.cbsnews.

com/news/amazon-wildfire-parts-of-amazon-rainforest-on-fire-smoke-seen-from-space-2019-08-20/).

Glock, Charles and Rodney Stark. 1965. *Religion and Society in Tension*. Chicago, IL: Rand McNally.

Gomez, Filiberto Nolasco. 2018. "Organized Labor Resoundingly Rejects Kavanaugh's Nomination for the Supreme Court." *Workday Minnesota*, July 10. Retrieved July 30, 2019 (https://workdayminnesota.org/articles/organized-labor-resoundingly-rejects-kavanaughs-nomination-supreme-court).

Goodman, Amy and Denis Moynihan. 2019a. "Trump Blends McCarthy Tactics with Overt Racism." *The Citizen*, July 20: A4.

Goodman, Amy and Denis Moynihan. 2019b. "Resist the Racist in Chief." *The Citizen*, March 2: A4.

Goodman, Amy and Denis Moynihan. 2019c. "The Assange, Manning Crusade." *The Citizen*, June 15: A4.

Goodman, Amy and Denis Moynihan. 2019d. "Attacks on Press Must Stop." *The Citizen*, October 19: A4.

Goodman, Amy and Denis Moynihan. 2019e. "Impeach Trump for Climate Denial." *The Citizen*, November 9: A4.

Gordon, James. 2018. "Trump Speaks at a Fourth-Grade Level According to New Analysis but Linguists Say it may Make Him More 'Authentic, Relatable and Trustworthy.'" *Daily Mail*, January 8. Retrieved March 2, 2018 (www.dailymail.co.uk/news/article-5248567/Trump-speaks-fourth-grade-level-according-new-analysis.html.).

Gramlich, John. 2018. "With Another Supreme Court Pick, Trump Is Leaving His Mark on Higher Federal Courts." *Pew Research Center*, July 16. Retrieved September 2, 2019 (www.pewresearch.org/fact-tank/2018/07/16/with-another-supreme-court-pick-trump-is-leaving-his-mark-on-higher-federal-courts/).

Grasso, Samantha. 2018. "Brett Kavanaugh Can't Stop Shouting 'I like Beer' at His Hearing Today." *The Daily Dot*, September 27. Retrieved October 12, 2019 (www.dailydot.com/irl/brett-kavanaugh-beer-memes/).

Greenslade, Roy. 2016. "13 Countries Where Journalists Have Been Killed with Impunity." *Guardian*, October 27. Retrieved July 21, 2019 (www.theguardian.com/media/greenslade/2016/oct/27/13-countries-where-journalists-have-been-killed-with-impunity).

Gresko, Jessica. 2019. "Court Frees Up Wall Funds." *The Citizen*, July 27: A5.

Greywolf, Anastasia. 2016. *A Handbook of Magic, Spells, and Potions*. New York: Quarto Publishing Group.

Grynbaum, Michael M. 2017. "Trump Calls the News Media the 'Enemy of the American People.'" *New York Times*, February 17. Retrieved July 19, 2019 (www.nytimes.com/2017/02/17/business/trump-calls-the-news-media-the-enemy-of-the-people.html).

Guardian. 2019. "Trump Says Acting Cabinet Members Give Him 'More Flexibility,'" January 6. Retrieved September 1, 2019 (www.theguardian.com/us-news/2019/jan/06/trump-acting-cabinet-members-give-him-more-flexibility).

Guinness Book of World Records. 2019. "Oldest Higher-Learning Institution, Oldest University." Retrieved August 5, 2019 (www.guinnessworldrecords.com/world-records/oldest-university).

Hadden, Richard W. 1997. *Sociological Theory*. Orchard Park, NY: Broadview.

Hafner, Josh. 2016. "Donald Trump Loves the 'Poorly Educated'—and They Love Him." *USA Today*, February 24. Retrieved August 10, 2018 (www.usatoday.com/story/news/politics/onpolitics/2016/02/24/donald-trump-nevada-poorly-educated/80860078/).

Hagenmeier, 2017. "Namibia: The End of Rapid Growth Helps Populism To Rise." Day Trading Academy, August 29. Retrieved July 27, 2019 (https://daytradingacademy.com/namibia-end-rapid-growth-helps-populism- rise/).

Halper, Evan. 2019. "Silicon Valley No Longer Eludes Candidate Scrutiny." *Los Angeles Times*, October 8: A1, A10.

Hance, Jeremy Leon. 2019. "As Bolsonaro Takes the Helm in Brazil, Environmental Organizations Ramp Up Efforts to Protect the Amazon." Retrieved August 14, 2019 (https://ensia.com/features/bolsonaro-brazil/).

Harrington, Rebecca. 2016. "Here's What Trump Means When He Says 'Drain the Swamp'—Even Though It's Not an Accurate Metaphor." *Business Insider*, November 11. Retrieved August 20, 2019 (www.businessinsider.com/what-does-drain-the-swamp-mean-was-dc-built-on-a-swamp-2016-11).

Harvard University. 2019. "Francis Petrarch (Francesco Petrarcha, 1304–1374)." Retrieved April 26, 2019 (https://chaucer.fas.harvard.edu/pages/francesco- petrarcha-1304–1374).

Hawking, M.G. 2018. *Foundations of Psychokinesis: The Essential Knowledge* (Kindle). Wisdom Masters Press.

Haynes, Suyin. 2019. "President Trump Said Revolutionary War Troops 'Took Over the Airports' In His Fourth of July Speech." *Time*, July 5. Retrieved July 5, 2019 (https://time.com/5620936/donald-trump-revolutionary-war-airports/).

Hazard, Paul. 1954. *European Thought in the Eighteenth Century*. New Have, CT: Yale University Press.

Head, Tom. 2019. "How South Africa has Become 'The World's Second-Most Populist Country.' " *The South African*, May 2. Retrieved July 27, 2019 (www.thesouthafrican.com/news/what-is-populism-south-africa-populists/).

Healy, Melissa. 2018. "No Lie: Voters Tolerate Politicians' Fibs." *Los Angeles Times*, December 24: A5.

Heffernan, Virginia. 2018a. "It's Not a 'Bias,' Just Reality." *Los Angeles Times*, July 15: A20.

Heffernan, Virginia. 2018b. "All the President's Moronic Men." *Los Angeles Times*, December 2: A24.

Henager, Robin, Melissa J. Wilmarth, and Teresa Mauldin. 2016. "The Relationship Between Student Loan Debt and Financial Wellness." *Consumer Interests Annual*, vol. 62: 1–2. Retrieved August 9, 2019 (www.consumerinterests.org/assets/docs/CIA/CIA2016/cia%20abstract_ro bin%20melissa%20teresa.pdf).

Hensley-Clancy, Molly. 2018. "The Yale Secret Society Brett Kavanaugh Joined Was Mostly About Drinking, Yale Alumni Say." Buzzfeed News, July 11. Retrieved November 13, 2019 (www.buzzfeednews.com/article/mollyhensleyclancy/the-yale-secret-society-brett-kavanaugh-joined-was-mostly).

Hiltzik, Michael. 2019. "Trump's Unending Assault on Labor." *Los Angeles Times*, July 24: C1.

History.com. 2010. "Freed U.S. Slaves Depart on Journey to Africa." Retrieved July 23, 2019 (www.history.com/this-day-in-history/freed-u-s-slaves-depart-on-journey-to-africa).

History.com. 2019a. "Thomas Paine." Retrieved May 4, 2019 (www.history.com/topics/american-revolution/thomas-paine).

History.com. 2019b. "Ku Klux Klan." Retrieved October 1, 2019 (www.history.com/topics/reconstruction/ku-klux-klan).

Ho, Dale. 2016. "Will the 2016 Presidential Election Be Decided by Voter Suppression Laws?" ACLU, January 14. Retrieved August 19, 2019 (www.aclu.org/blog/voting-rights/fighting-voter-suppression/will-2016-presidential-election-be-decided-voter).

Hookway, Christopher. 2002. *Truth, Rationality, and Pragmatism*. Oxford: Clarendon Press.

Horkheimer, Max. 1947. *Eclipse of Reason.* New York: Seabury Press.
Howell, Evan A., Steven J. Bograd, Carey Morishige, Michael P. Seki, and Jeffrey J. Polovina. 2012. "On North Pacific Circulation and Associate Marine Debris Concentration." *Marine Pollution Bulletin,* 65: 16–22.
Hruby, Denise. 2019. "Far-Right Poles' Assault on Restitution." *Los Angeles Times,* December 2: A3.
Human Rights Watch. 2019a. "Hungary." Retrieved July 27, 2019 (www.hrw.org/europe/central-asia/hungary).
Human Rights Watch. 2019b. "Turkey: Events of 2018." Retrieved October 9, 2019 (www.hrw.org/world-report/2019/country-chapters/turkey).
IFEX. 2018. "ARTICLE 19 Calls for Governments to Act on Crimes Against Journalists." November. Retrieved July 21, 2019 (https://ifex.org/article-19-calls- for-governments-to-act-on-crimes-against-journalists/).
Illuminati. 2019. "Official Website of the Illuminati: Welcome." Retrieved October 1, 2019 (www.illuminatiofficial.org/#).
IMDb. 2019a. "The Post." Retrieved July 31, 2019 (www.imdb.com/title/tt6294822/).
IMDb. 2019b. "Chernobyl." Retrieved August 17, 2019 (www.imdb.com/title/tt7366338/).
Inequality.org. 2019. "Global Inequality." Retrieved July 31, 2019 (https://inequality.org/facts/global-inequality/).
Institute for Policy Studies. 2019. "Facts: Income Inequality in the United States." Retrieved July 30, 2019 (https://inequality.org/facts/income-inequality/).
International Air Transport Association (IATA). 2019. "IATA Forecasts Passenger Demand to Double Over 20 Years." Retrieved May 13, 2019 (www.iata.org/pressroom/pr/Pages/2016-10-18-02.aspx).
International Monetary Fund (IMF). 2017. "IMF Fiscal Monitor: Tackling Inequality, October 2017." Retrieved July 31, 2019 (www.imf.org/en/Publications/FM/Issues/2017/10/05/fiscal-monitor-october-2017).
Internet Encyclopedia of Philosophy. 2019. "David Hume." Retrieved May 3, 2019 (www.iep.utm.edu/hume/).
Investopedia. 2019a. "Student Loan Forgiveness." Retrieved August 9, 2019 (www.investopedia.com/terms/s/student-loan-forgiveness.asp).
Investopedia. 2019b. "Too Big to Fail." Retrieved October 5, 2019 (www.investopedia.com/terms/t/too-big-to-fail.asp).
Islam, Salma. 2018. "Egypt Leads in Arrests over 'Fake News.'" *Los Angeles Times,* December 18: A3.
Jackson, Brandon A. and John R. Reynolds. 2013. "The Price of Opportunity: Race, Student Loan Debt, and College Achievement." *Sociological Inquiry,* 83 (3): 335–368.
Jacob, Margaret C. 1991. *Living the Enlightenment: Freemasonry and Politics in Eighteenth-Century Europe.* Oxford: Oxford University Press.
Janis, Irving L. 1972. *Victims of Groupthink.* Boston, MA: Houghton Mifflin.
Janis, Irving L. 1982. *Groupthink: Psychological Studies of Policy Decisions and Fiascoes.* Boston, MA: Houghton Mifflin.
Jarvie, Jenny. 2018. "U.N. Has More Hard Words for U.S." *Los Angeles Times,* June 23: A5.
Jeffrey, Terence P. 2015. "21,995,000 to 12,329,000: Government Employees Outnumber Manufacturing Employees 1.8 to 1." CNS News.com, September 8. Retrieved August 23, 2019 (www.cnsnews.com/news/article/terence-p-jeffrey/21955000-12329000-government-employees-outnumber-manufacturing).
Johnson, Paul. 2000. *The Renaissance: A Short History.* New York: Random House.
Johnson, L.A. 2007. "How Tacky Can We Get?" *Post-Standard,* May 20: I1, I2.

Kaleem, Jaweed. 2018. "A Surge in Anti-Semitism." *Los Angeles Times*, October 30: A2.

Kavanagh, Jennifer, William Marcellino, Jonathan S. Blake, Shawn Smith, Steven Davenport, and Mahlet G. Tebeka. 2019. "News in a Digital Age: Comparing the Presentation of News Information over Time and Across Media Platforms," published by the RAND Corp. Retrieved July 20 (www.rand.org/pubs/research_reports/RR2960.html).

Kessel, Mark. 2014. "Restoring the Pharmaceutical Industry's Reputation." *Nature Biotechnology*, 32: 983–990.

Khan, Amina. 2019. "Microplastic in the Atmosphere is Making its Way to the Pristine Arctic." *Los Angeles Times*, August 15. Retrieved December 11, 2019 (www.latimes.com/environment/story/2019-08-14/microplastic-is-significant-source-of-air-pollution).

Kim, Seung Min and Mike DeBonis. 2019. "Trump Tries to Distance U.S. from Syrian Crisis." *Post-Standard*, October 17: A18.

King, Laura. 2017. "In Poland, A Right-Wing, Populist, Anti-Immigrant Government Sees an Ally in Trump." *Los Angeles Times*, July 5. Retrieved July 27, 2019 (www.latimes.com/world/la-fg-poland-trump-2017-story.html).

King, Laura. 2018a. "Trump's No. 1 Fan in Brazil." *Los Angeles Times*, November 30: A2.

King, Laura. 2019b. "'Incredibly Grim' Prognosis on Global Warming by a U/N. Group Includes Clarion Call for World's Action." *Los Angeles Times*, October 9: A1.

King, Laura. 2019a. "Trump's Tweets Criticized as Racist." *Los Angeles Times*, July 15: A1, A10.

King, Laura. 2019b. "Hungarian Strongman to Visit Trump." *Los Angeles Times*, May 13: A3.

King, Laura. 2019c. "Polish President Unlikely to Get Earful from U.S." *Los Angeles Times*, June 12: A3.

King, Laura. 2019d. "Another Snag in Turkish–U.S. Relationship." *Los Angeles Times*, October 9: A3.

King, Laura. 2019e. "Ire Over Brexit Report Delay." *Los Angeles Times*, November 15: A2.

King, Laura. 2019f. "A Sign of Change Ascends in Slovakia." *Los Angeles Times*, April 6: A3.

Kirchgaessner, Stephanie. 2018. "Italy: Populist Government Sworn in as Political Deadlock Ends." *Guardian*, June 1. Retrieved July 26, 2019 (www.theguardian.com/world/2018/may/31/italys-populist-leaders-strike-deal-resurrect-coalition).

Knowles, David. 2019. "Number of Trump's 'False or Misleading Claims' Rose Dramatically in 2019." *Yahoo News*, December 16. Retrieved December 16, 2019 (www.aol.com/article/news/2019/12/16/number-of-trumps-false-or-misleading-claims-rose-dramatically-in-2019/23882025/).

Koerner, Claudia and Julia Reinstein. 2019. "How a Group For Jewish Moms Spread Anti-Vax Propaganda Before New York's Measles Outbreak." BuzzFeed News, April 15. Retrieved August 13, 2019 (www.buzzfeednews.com/article/claudiakoerner/anti-vaccine-peach-measles-new-york-propaganda-outbreak).

Krakow, Morgan and Tim Elfrink. 2019. "Reagan Called Nixon to Complain About Africans." *The Post-Standard*, August 1: A15.

Krannawitter, Thomas L. 2017. *Save The Swamp: Career Guidebook for Budding Bureaucrats*. Speakeasy Ideas.

Krastev, Ivan. 2011. "The Age of Populism: Reflections on the Self-enmity of Democracy." *European View*, 10: 11–16.

Kravitz, Derek. 2019. "Former Trump Officials Are Supposed to Avoid Lobbying. Except 33 Haven't." *ProPublica*, February 14. Retrieved August 29, 2019 (www.propublica.org/article/the-lobbying-swamp-is-flourishing-in-trumps-washington).

Kravitz, Derek and Alex Mierjeski. 2018. "Trump's Appointees Pledged Not to Lobby After They Leave. Now They're Lobbying." *ProPublica*, May 3. Retrieved August 29, 2019 (www.propublica.org/article/trump-appointees-pledged-not-to-lobby-after-they-leave-now-lobbying).

Kristeller, Paul Oskar. 1951. *Renaissance Thought: The Classic, Scholastic, and Humanist Strains*. New York: Harper and Row.

Kristof, Nicholas. 2015. "Heroin Doesn't Have to Be a Killer." *Post-Standard*, June 11: A–14.

Laloggia, John. 2019. "Republicans Have Doubts that Colleges, K-12 Schools are Open to Range of Viewpoints." Pew Research Center, July 19. Retrieved August 8, 2019 (www.pewresearch.org/fact-tank/2019/07/19/republicans-have-doubts-that-colleges-k-12-schools-are-open-to-range-of-viewpoints/).

La Torre, Carlos de. 2018. *Populisms: A Quick Immersion*. New York: Tibidabo.

Labropoulou, Elinda. 2019. "Greek Elections: Victory for New Democracy Party Signals End of Left-Wing Populism." CNN, July 7. Retrieved July 26, 2019 (www.cnn.com/2019/07/07/europe/greece-elections-new-democracy-intl/index.html).

Lemon, Jason. 2017. "5 Bromance Moments Between Trump and Sisi." Step Feed, May 5. Retrieved July 16, 2019 (https://stepfeed.com/5-bromance-moments-between-trump-and-sisi-8744).

Levitsky, Steven and Daniel Ziblatt. 2018. *How Democracies Die*. New York: Crown.

Lewis, Tanya. 2013. "World's E-Waste to Grow 33% by 2017, Says Global Report." *Live Science*. Retrieved August 14, 2019 (www.livescience.com/41967-world-e-waste-to-grow-33-percent-2017.html).

Lilienfeld, Scott O. 2019. "Foreword: Navigating a Post-Truth World: Ten Enduring Lessons from a Study of Pseudoscience," pp. xi–xvii in *Pseudoscience: The Conspiracy Against Science*, edited by Allison B. Kaufman and James C. Kaufman. Cambridge, MA: Massachusetts Institute of Technology (MIT) Press.

Lofgren, Mike. 2016. *The Deep State: The Fall of the Constitution and the Rise of a Shadow Government*. New York: Penguin Books.

Lombardi, Esther. 2019. "Upton Sinclair Quotes." *ThoughtCo.com*, March 2. Retrieved September 25, 2019 (www.thoughtco.com/upton-sinclair-quotes-741426).

Long, Cindy. 2011. "Behind the Right-Wing Attacks on Collective Bargaining." National Education Association, March 4. Retrieved July 30, 2019 (http://neatoday.org/2011/03/04/behind-the-right-wing-attacks-on-collective- bargaining/).

Lord, Jeffrey. 2019. *Swamp Wars: Donald Trump and the New America* (Kindle Edition). New York: Bombardier Books.

Los Angeles Times. 2018. "Editorial: Taking Kids from Their Parents." June 19: A8,

Los Angeles Times. 2019a. "Editorial: Boris Johnson's Brexit Dilemma." July 24: A8.

Los Angeles Times. 2019b. "The Sexist 'Billy Graham Rule.'" *Los Angeles Times*, July 16: A10.

Los Angeles Times. 2019c. "Administration Variable on Winds." August 27: C2.

Lotz, Amanda. 2018. "'Big Tech' Isn't One Big Monopoly—It's 5 Companies All In Different Businesses." *The Conversation*, March 23. Retrieved October 5, 2019 (http://theconversation.com/big-tech-isnt-one-big-monopoly-its-5-companies-all-in-different-businesses-92791).

Lyons, Gene. 2019. "Trump's Ugly Brand of Racism." *The Citizen*, July 19: A4.

Mackenzie, Chris. 2017. "Trump's Lobbying Ban Was Step Towards 'Draining the Swamp.'" *The Hill*, January 30. Retrieved August 29, 2019 (https://thehill.com/blogs/pundits-blog/the-administration/316843-trumps-lobbying-ban-was-big-step-towards-draining-the).

Maguder, Natasha and Tom Page. 2017. "World's Oldest University, Library, Meets 21st Century with Massive Restoration." CNN Style, April 3. Retrieved August 5, 2019 (www.cnn.com/style/article/fez-al-qarawiyyin-medina-restoration-unesco/index.html).

Mahr, Krista. 2019. "Measles Makes a Comeback." *Los Angeles Times*, October 26: A2.

Mann, Susan Archer and Ashly Suzanne Patterson. 2016. *Reading Feminist Theory: From Modernity to Postmodernity*. New York: Oxford University Press.

Mansfield, Harvey. 2019. "Niccolo Machiavelli: Italian Statesman and Writer." *Encyclopedia Britannica*. Retrieved April 27, 2019 (www.britannica.com/biography/Niccolo-Machiavelli).

Marger, Martin N. 2006. *Race and Ethnic Relations: American and Global Perspectives*, 7th edn. Belmont, CA: Thomson/Wadsworth.

Markoe, Lauren. 2016. "What's U.S. Religion Worth? $1.2 Trillion, Says New Study." *Salt Lake Tribune*, 2016. Retrieved November 29, 2019 (https://archive.sltrib.com/article.php?id=4354308&itype=CMSID).

Marks, Andrea. 2017. "Trump's 5 Most 'Anti-Science' Moves." Scientific American, January 18. Retrieved August 11, 2019 (www.scientificamerican.com/article/trumps-5-most-ldquo-anti-science-rdquo-moves/).

Mazza, Ed. 2019. "Jon Meacham: Trump Now Tied for 'Most Racist President in American History.'" *Huff Post*, July 16. Retrieved July 23, 2019 (www.huffpost.com/entry/donald-trump-andrew-johnson- racist_n_5d2d6e41e4b085eda5a0d7fa).

McCarthy, Juliana. 2018. *The Stars Within You: A Modern Guide to Astrology*. Boulder, CO: Roost Books.

McFate, Sean. 2016. "America's Addiction to Mercenaries." *The Atlantic*, August 12. Retrieved on October 21, 2019 (www.theatlantic.com/international/archive/2016/08/iraq-afghanistan-contractor-pentagon-obama/495731/).

McGrath, Maggie. 2017. "Wells Fargo Admits to More Unauthorized Accounts, Increasing Tally to 3.5 Million." *Forbes*, August 31. Retrieved October 6, 2019 (www.forbes.com/sites/maggiemcgrath/2017/08/31/wells-fargo-admits-to-more-unauthorized-accounts-increasing-tally-to-3-5-million/#46e38ab1f1b6).

McLellan, David. 1987. *Marxism and Religion*. New York: Harper & Row.

McManus, Doyle. 2019a. "A War on Transparency." *Los Angeles Times*, May 1: A2.

McManus, Doyle. 2019b. "Trump's Doctrine is Simple." *Los Angeles Times*, October 9: A2.

Mead, Alyson. 2015. *Astrology Made Simple: A Beginner's Guide to Interpreting Your Birth Chart and Revealing Your Horoscope*. Zephyros Press.

Media Matters. 2018. "On Fox Business, Sean Spicer Says the White House Needs to Treat Journalists 'Like Children.'" November 20. Retrieved July 19, 2019 (www.mediamatters.org/stories-and-interests/trumps-war-press).

Megerian, Chris. 2018a. "Russia's Invasion Into U.S. Politics." *Los Angeles Times*, July 15: A1, A12.

Megerian, Chris. 2018b. "Cohen Says He Lied About Russia Project." *Los Angeles Times*, November 30: A1, A10.

Megerian, Chris. 2019a. "Trump Indifferent to Hong Kong Protests." *Los Angeles Times*, August 16: A6.

Megerian, Chris. 2019b. "Mueller Report Exposes All the President's Liars." *Los Angeles Times*, April 21: A1, A8.

Megerian, Chris. 2019c. "Papers Reveal Broader Probe." *Los Angeles Times*, July 19: A7.

Megerian, Chris. 2019d. "Mueller Criticized Barr's Framing of Report." *Los Angeles Times*, May 1: A7.

Megerian, Chris. 2019e. "Scandal Reveals How Loyalists Shield Trump." *Los Angeles Times*, September 27: A6.

Megerian, Chris and Jennifer Haberkorn. 2019. "Trump Not Experienced, Mueller Says." *Los Angeles Times*, July 25: A1, A8.

Megerian, Chris and Sonja Sharp. 2018. "Former Trump Lawyer Cohen Sentenced to 3 Years in Prison." *Los Angeles Times*, December 13: A1.

Megerian, Chris and Del Quentin Wilber. 2018. "Trump Forces Sessions Out." *Los Angeles Times*, November 8: A1.

Megerian, Chris and Del Quentin Wilber. 2019. "Barr Hearing Stokes Acrimony With Congress." *Los Angeles Times*, May 2: A1, A6.

Mehta, Nirav J. and Ijaz A. Khan. 2002. "Cardiology's 10 Greatest Discoveries of the 20th Century." *Texas Heart Institute Journal*, 29 (3): 164–171.

Melendez, Pilar. 2019. "Trump Hates Windmills—and It Has Nothing to Do with His Bogus Cancer Claims." *Daily Beast*, April 3. Retrieved August 11, 2019 (www.dailybeast.com/trump-hates-windmills-and-it-has-nothing-to-do-with-his-bogus-cancer-claims).

Meyer, Robinson. 2019. "The Unprecedented Surge in Fear About Climate Change." *The Atlantic*, January 23. Retrieved February 22, 2020 (www.theatlantic.com/science/archive/2019/01/do-most-americans-believe-climate-change-polls-say-yes/580957/).

Meyer, Theodoric. 2017. "Has Trump Drained the Swamp in Washington?" Politico, October 19. Retrieved August 24, 2019 (www.politico.com/story/2017/10/19/trump-drain-swamp-promises-243924).

Meza, Summer. 2017. "'Fake News' Named Word of the Year." Newsweek, November 2. Retrieved April 20, 2019 (www.newsweek.com/fake-news-word-year-collins-dictionary-699740).

Mezzofiore, Gianluca. 2018. "Why Italy's U-turn on Mandatory Vaccination Shocks the Scientific Community." CNN Health, August 7. Retrieved August 12, 2019 (www.cnn.com/2018/08/07/health/italy-anti-vaccine-law-measles-intl/index.html).

Mikulic, Matej. 2019. "Global Pharmaceutical Industry – Statistics & Facts." *Statista*, August 13. Retrieved October 5, 2019 (www.statista.com/topics/1764/global-pharmaceutical-industry/).

Miller, Chaz. 2012. "Profiles in Garbage: Food Waste." *Waste Age*, 43 (2). Retrieved August 14, 2019 (www.waste360.com/food-waste/profiles-garbage-food-waste).

Miller, Zeke and Lolita Baldor. 2018. "Mattis to Resign After Clashes with Trump." *Los Angeles Times*, December 21: A6.

Miller, Zeke, Jill Colvin, and Catherine Lucey. 2018. "President: Summit All About 'Attitude.'" *The Citizen*, June 8: A6.

Mills, C. Wright. 1956. *The Power Elite*. New York: Oxford University Press.

Mills, C. Wright. 1958. "The Structure of Power in American Society." *British Journal of Sociology*, 9 (1): 29–41.

Mitchell, Dan. 2016. "In One Phrase, Everything that You Need to Know about the Failure of Big Government." *International Liberty*, March 23. Retrieved August 24, 2019 (https://danieljmitchell.wordpress.com/2016/03/23/in-one-phrase- everything-that-you-need-to-know-about-the-failure-of-big-government/).

Mohan, Geoffrey. 2019. "California Defies Trump, Moving to Ban Pesticides." *Los Angeles Times*, August 15: C1, C5.

Moore, Mark. 2018. "Giuliani: 'Truth Isn't Truth.'" *New York Post*, August 19. Retrieved April 20, 2019 (https://nypost.com/2018/08/19/giuliani-truth-isnt- truth/).

Moran, Lee. 2019. "Donald Trump Calls New York Times 'A True Enemy of the People.'" *Huffington Post*, February 20. Retrieved July 18, 2018 (www.huffpost.com/entry/donald-trump-declares-new-york-times-a-true-enemy-of-the-people_n_5c6d61f2e4b0e2f4d8a16333).

Morello, Carol. 2018. "UN Chief: White House's Policy on Migrant Kids 'Unconscionable.'" *The Post-Standard*, June 19: A12.

MoveForHunger.org. 2019. "The Environmental Impact of Food Waste." Retrieved August 14, 2019 (www.moveforhunger.org/the-environmental-impact-of-food-waste/).

Muller, Jan-Werner. 2016. *What is Populism?* Philadelphia, PA: University of Pennsylvania Press.

Mulvihill, Geoff. 2019. "Johnson & Johnson Settles with 2 Counties Over Opioids." *The Citizen*, October 3: A18.

Mulvihill, Geoff and Dave Collins. 2019. "Purdue Pharma: Gets Tentative Deal." *The Citizen*, September 12: A6.

Munck, Thomas. 2000. *The Enlightenment: A Comparative Social History 1721–1794*. London: Arnold.

Munro, Andre. 2019. "Populism: Political Program or Movement." *Encyclopedia Britannica*. Retrieved July 22, 2019 (www.britannica.com/topic/populism).

MSN. 2019. "Trump to Migrants: 'We Can't Take You Anymore… Our Country is Full.'" April 6. Retrieved July 29, 2019 (www.msn.com/en- us/news/politics/trump-to-migrants-we-cant-take-you-anymore-our-country-is-full/ar-BBVGh2k#page=2).

Myers, Gregory. 2017. "10 Most Reliable News Sources." *Top Tenz*, February 20. Retrieved July 9, 2019 (www.toptenz.net/10-reliable-news-sources.php).

Nadworny, Elissa. 2019. "College Completion Rates Are Up, But the Numbers will Still Surprise You." NPR, March 13. Retrieved August 9, 2019 (www.npr.org/2019/03/13/681621047/college-completion-rates-are-up-but-the-numbers-will-still-surprise-you).

NASA. 2013a. "The Decision to Go to the Moon: President John F. Kennedy's May 25, 1961 Speech Before a Joint Session of Congress." Retrieved May 14, 2019 (https://history.nasa.gov/moondec.html).

NASA. 2013b. "Space Debris and Human Spacecraft." Retrieved August 14, 2019 (www.nasa.gov/mission_pages/station/news/orbital_debris.html).

Nauert, Charles G., Jr. 1995. *Humanism and the Culture of Renaissance Europe*. Cambridge: Cambridge University Press.

National Academy of Sciences. 2019a. "Greatest Engineering Achievements of the 20th Century." Retrieved May 5, 2019 (www.greatachievements.org/).

National Academy of Sciences. 2019b. "Automobile." Retrieved May 12, 2019 (www.greatachievements.org/?id=2950).

National Center for Education Statistics (NCES). 2019. "Fast Facts: Graduation Rates." Retrieved August 9, 2019 (https://nces.ed.gov/fastfacts/display.asp?id=40).

National Geographic. 2018. "Here's How Much Plastic Trash is Littering the Earth." Retrieved August 14, 2019 (www.nationalgeographic.com/news/2017/07/plastic-produced- recycling-waste-ocean-trash-debris-environment/).

National Oceanic and Atmospheric Administration (NOAA). 2019a. "About the Arctic Report Card." Retrieved August 13, 2019 (www.arctic.noaa.gov/Report-Card).

National Oceanic and Atmospheric Administration (NOAA). 2019b. "Global Snow and Ice – May 2018." Retrieved August 13, 2019 (www.ncdc.noaa.gov/sotc/global-snow/201805).

National Oceanic and Atmospheric Administration (NOAA). 2019c. "Trends in Atmospheric Carbon Dioxide." Retrieved August 13, 2019 (www.esrl.noaa.gov/gmd/ccgg/trends/).

National Oceanic and Atmospheric Administration (NOAA). 2019d. "Ocean Acidification: The Other Carbon Dioxide Problem." Retrieved August 13, 2019 (www.pmel.noaa.gov/co2/story/Ocean+Acidification).

National Oceanic and Atmospheric Administration (NOAA). 2019e. "What is Marine Debris?" Retrieved August 14, 2019 (https://oceanservice.noaa.gov/facts/marinedebris.html).

Naylor, Brian. 2019. "An Acting Government for the Trump Administration." NPR, April 9. Retrieved September 1, 2019 (www.npr.org/2019/04/09/711094554/an-acting-government-for-the-trump-administration).

New World Encyclopedia. 2017. "David Hume." Retrieved May 3, 2019 (www.newworldencyclopedia.org/entry/David_Hume).

Newsday. 2019. "Trump's Divisiveness." As it appeared in *The Citizen*, July 20: A4.

New York State Department of Environmental Conservation. 2019. "What is Solid Waste?" Retrieved August 14, 2019 (www.dec.ny.gov/chemical/8732.html).

New York Times. 1921. "Einstein Sees Boston; Fails on Edison Test; Asked to Tell Speed of Sound He Refers Questioner to Text Books," May 18. Retrieved August 7, 2019 (www.nytimes.com/1921/05/18/archives/einstein-sees-boston-fails-on-edison-test-asked-to-tell-speed-of.html).

Norris, Pippa and Ronald Inglehart. 2018. *Cultural Backlash: Trump, Brexit, and the Rise of Authoritarian Populism*. New York: Cambridge University Press.

Novak, Tony. 2017. "Republican Attacks Against Labor Unions." Retrieved July 30, 2019 (http://tonynovak.com/republican-attacks-against-labor-unions/).

NPR. 2011. "Ike's Warning of Military Expansion, 50 Years Later," January 17. Retrieved September 22, 2019 (www.npr.org/2011/01/17/132942244/ikes-warning-of-military-expansion-50-years-later).

Nussbaum, Matthew. 2018. "Brett Kavanaugh: Who Is He? Bio, Facts, Background and Political Views." Politico, July 19. Retrieved September 2, 2019 (www.politico.com/story/2018/07/09/brett-kavanaugh-who-is-he-bio-facts-background-and-political-views-703346).

NW Creation Network. 2019. "Biblical Young Earth Creationism." Retrieved August 16, 2019 (www.nwcreation.net/ageyoung.html).

Nunez, Christina. 2019. "Deforestation Explained." *National Geographic*. Retrieved August 14, 2019 (www.nationalgeographic.com/environment/global-warming/deforestation/).

O'Brien, Matt. 2019. "Big Tech Still Pursues Deals with Big Oil." *The Post-Standard*, October 3: A18.

Ocean Acidification. 2012. "The Other CO2 Challenge." Retrieved August 14, 2019 (http://oceanacidification.net/).

Offshore Technology. 2019. "The World's Biggest Oil and Gas Companies." Retrieved October 4, 2019 (www.offshore-technology.com/features/largest-oil-and-gas-companies-in-2018/).

Ogrocki, Sue. 2019. "Deadly, Costly Opioid Crisis." *Los Angeles Times*, August 30: A2.

Onaran, Yalman. 2017. "Too Big to Fail." Bloomberg, December 8. Retrieved October 5, 2019 (www.bloomberg.com/quicktake/big-fail).

Opoien, Jessie. 2017. "Wisconsin Lawmaker: Response to Belief Earth is 6,000 Years Old Shows Need for UW Speech Bill." *The Capital Times*, June 8. Retrieved February 23, 2019 (https://madison.com/ct/news/local/govt-and-politics/election-matters/wisconsin-lawmaker-response-to-belief-earth-is-years-old-shows/article_4a06eb1b-26f9-5dbb-9185-f3c4ef2a6fce.html).

Organization for Economic Cooperation and Development (OECD). 2001. "Glossary of Statistical Terms: Nuclear Waste Pollution." Retrieved August 14, 2019 (https://stats.oecd.org/glossary/detail.asp?ID=1859).

Organization for Economic Cooperation and Development (OECD). 2018. "General Government Spending." Retrieved August 24, 2019 (https://data.oecd.org/gga/general-government-spending.htm).

Orlik, Tom and Justin Jimenez. 2018. "Strong-Arm Governments Are Taking Over the Global Economy: Populists and Authoritarians Now Oversee the Biggest Chunk of G20 Output. How Could that Affect Economic Performance?" Bloomberg, August 10. Retrieved July 26, 2019 (www.bloomberg.com/news/features/2018-08-10/populists-oversee-the-biggest-slice-of-g20-gdp-whither-growth).

Pareto, Vilfredo. 2008 [1901]. *The Rise and Fall of Elites: An Application of Theoretical Sociology*, with an introduction by Hans L. Zetterberg. New Brunswick, NJ: Transaction Publishers.

Park, Chuck. 2019. "I Can No Longer Justify Being a Part of Trump's 'Complacent State.'" *The Washington Post*, August 8. Retrieved September 1, 2019 (www.washingtonpost.com/opinions/i-can-no-longer-justify-being-a-part-of-trumps-complacent-state-so-im-resigning/2019/08/08/fed849e4-af14-11e9-8e77-03b30bc29f64_story.html).

Patton, Mike. 2013. "The Growth of Government: 1980 to 2012." *Forbes*, January 24. Retrieved August 24, 2019 (www.forbes.com/sites/mikepatton/2013/01/24/the-growth-of-the-federal-government-1980-to-2012/#642f956e17b6).

Paul, Richard and Linda Elder. 2007. *The Miniature Guide to Critical Thinking: Concepts and Tools*. Dillon Beach, CA: The Foundation for Critical Thinking.

PBS. 2001. "Humans: Origins of Human Kind." Retrieved August 15, 2019 (www.pbs.org/wgbh/evolution/humans/hunankind/index.html).

PBS. 2019. "Napalm and the Dow Chemical Company." American Experience. Retrieved September 29, 2019 (www.pbs.org/wgbh/americanexperience/features/two-days-in-october-dow-chemical-and-use-napalm/).

The Pew Research Center. 2017. "Sharp Partisan Divisions in Views of National Institutions." July. Retrieved August 8, 2019 (www.people- press.org/2017/07/10/sharp-partisan-divisions-in-views-of-national-institutions/).

The Pew Research Center. 2019. "Religious Landscape Study." Retrieved October 21, 2019 (www.pewforum.org/religious-landscape-study/).

Phillips, Dom, Jason Burke, and Paul Lewis. 2019. "How Brazil and South Africa Became the World's Most Populist Countries." *Guardian*, May 1. Retrieved July 27, 2019 (www.theguardian.com/world/2019/may/01/how-brazil-and-south-africa-became-the-worlds-most-populist-countries).

Phillips, Kristine. 2019. "They Said What?" *Post-Standard*, January 1: A14.

Pickrell, John. 2006. "Introduction: Human Evolution." *New Scientist*, September 4.

Pierson, David. 2019a. "Singapore Passes Law Targeting Fake News Online. Critics Warn of a Chilling Effect." *Los Angeles Times*, May 9: A3.

Pierson, David. 2019b. "Journalists Lose Myanmar Case." *Los Angeles Times*, April 24: A4.

Pomeau, Rene Henry. 2019. "Voltaire: French Philosopher and Author." *Encyclopaedia Britannica*. Retrieved May 22, 2019 (www.britannica.com/biography/Voltaire).

Popken, Ben. 2015. "America's Gun Business, By the Numbers." NBC News, June 30. Retrieved October 5 (www.nbcnews.com/storyline/san-bernardino- shooting/americas-gun-business-numbers-n437566).

Porter, Glenn. 2005. *The Rise of Big Business 1860–1920, Third Edition*. Malden, MA: Wiley-Blackwell.

Porter, Roy. 1991. *The Enlightenment*. Atlantic Highlands, NJ: Humanities Press International.

Porter, Sandra J. 2013. "Why Earth's Rising Carbon Dioxide Levels Matter." *Post- Standard*, June 6: A21.

Porter, Tom. 2019. "Karen Pence has Just Taken a Job at a School that Bans LGBT Pupils." *Newsweek*, January 16. Retrieved July 29, 2019 (www.newsweek.com/karen-pence-has-just-taken-job-school-bans-lgbt-pupils-1293513).

Posner, Michael. 2019. "Why the Gannett-Gatehouse Merger Will Speed the Demise of Local News." *Forbes*, August 8. Retrieved August 10, 2019 (www.forbes.com/sites/michaelposner/2019/08/08/why-the-gannett-gatehouse-merger-will-speed-the-demise-of-local-news/#1b5dfe4c67f0).

Post-Standard. 2019. "The Kurds Feel Betrayed. Not for the First Time," October 13: E5.

Quora. 2017. What are the Most Empirically Neutral, Objective, Nonpartisan and Unbiased News Sources in the US?" Retrieved July 9, 2019 (www.quora.com/What-are-the-most-empirically-neutral-objective-nonpartisan-and-unbiased-news-sources-in-the-US).

Radu, Sintia. 2019. "Media Facing Suppression Worldwide, Report Says." U.S. News, June 5. Retrieved July 21, 2019 (www.usnews.com/news/best-countries/articles/2019-06-05/suppression-of-media-around-the-world- increasing-report-says).

Ralph, Pat and Eliza Relman. 2018. "These are the Most and Least Biased News Outlets in the US, according to Americans." *Business Insider*, September 2. Retrieved July 9, 2019 (www.businessinsider.com/most-biased-news-outlets-in-america-cnn-fox-nytimes-2018-8).

Ralston, Shane. 2019. "American Enlightenment Thought." Internet Encyclopedia of Philosophy. Retrieved May 3, 2019 (www.iep.utm.edu/amer-enl/).

Rappler.com. 2017. "Philippines Worst in Impunity in Global Index." Retrieved July 21, 2019 (www.rappler.com/nation/182915-global-impunity-index-2017-philippines-ranking).

Redd, Nola Taylor. 2018. "Nicolaus Copernicus Biography: Facts & Discoveries." Space.com, March 20. Retrieved April 27, 2019 (www.space.com/15684-nicolaus-copernicus.html).

Reid, Thomas. 2000 [1764]. *An Inquiry Into the Human Mind: On the Principles of Common Sense, Fourth Edition*. Edinburgh: Edinburgh University Press.

Reporters Without Borders (RWB). 2017. "2017: Least Deadly Year for Journalists in 14 Years." Retrieved July 20, 2019 (https://rsf.org/en/journalists-killed).

Repucci, Sarah. 2019. "Freedom and the Media: A Downward Spiral." Freedom House. Retrieved July 21, 2019 (https://freedomhouse.org/report/freedom- media/freedom-media-2019).

Reynolds, Daniel. 2018. "Matt Damon Impersonates Brett Kavanaugh on *SNL* as Screaming Man-Child." *Advocate*, September 30. Retrieved October 12, 2019 (www.advocate.com/comedy/2018/9/30/matt-damon-impersonates-brett-kavanaugh-snl-screaming-man-child).

Riedel, Bruce. 2017. "Who are the Houthis, and Why are We At War with Them?" Brookings, December 18. Retrieved July 29 (www.brookings.edu/blog/markaz/2017/12/18/who-are-the-houthis-and-why-are-we-at-war-with-them/).

Ritzer, George and Jeffrey Stepnisky. 2018. *Sociological Theory, Tenth Edition*. Thousand Oaks, CA: Sage.

Roberts, Cokie and Steven Roberts. 2019a. "America Is Not 'Full.'" *The Citizen*, April 12: A4.

Roberts, Cokie and Steven Roberts. 2019b. "A Bad Idea In D.C." *The Citizen*, April 18: A4.

Rodriguez, Sabrina. 2018. "Mexico's Trumpian Populist Could Mean Trouble for Donald Trump." Politico, January 7. Retrieved July 28, 2019 (www.politico.com/story/2018/01/07/mexico-trump-populism-209089).

Rosen, Edward. 1971. "Copernicus and Renaissance Astronomy," pp. 96–105 in *Renaissance Men and Ideas*, edited by Robert Schwoebel. New York: St. Martin's Press.

Rosenbaum, Richard M. 2008. *No Room for Democracy: The Triumph of Ego over Common Sense*, with a foreword by Henry A. Kissinger. Rochester, NY: RIT Press.

Ross, Chuck. 2019. "Jerome Corsi, Who is Suing Mueller, Praises Special Counsel Following Roger Stone Indictment." Business and Politics, January 26. Retrieved September 1, 2019 (www.bizpacreview.com/2019/01/26/jerome-corsi-who-is-suing-mueller-praises-special-counsel-following-roger-stone-indictment-717696).

Rosoff, Matt. 2015. "The Growing Anti-Science Movement is Making People in Silicon Valley Nervous." *Business Insider*, March 1. Retrieved August 12, 2019 (www.businessinsider.com/anti-science-movement-hurts-america-2015-3).

Roth, Kenneth. 2019. "The Dangerous Rise of Populism: Global Attacks on Human Rights Values." *Human Rights Watch: World Report 2017*. Retrieved July 26, 2019 (www.hrw.org/world-report/2017/country-chapters/dangerous-rise-of-populism).

Roth, Madeline. 2016. "Ever Wondered Why the VMA Statue is a Moonman?" MTV News, August 27. Retrieved May 14, 2019 (www.mtv.com/news/2924701/vma-statue-moonman/).

Rouse, Margaret. 2019. "E-waste." Search Data Center. Retrieved August 14, 2019 (https://searchdatacenter.techtarget.com/definition/e-waste).

Rousseau, Jean-Jacques. 1992 [1755]. *Discourse on the Origin of Inequality*. Indianapolis, IN: Hackett Publishing.

Rugaber, Christopher. 2019. "As Economy Grows, Wealth Gap Widens." *Los Angeles Times*, July 7: C3.

Runciman, David. 2018. *How Democracy Ends*. New York: Basic Books.

Said, Sammy. 2013. "The Top 10 Deadly Diseases Cured in the 20th Century." The Richest, June 13. Retrieved May 12, 2019 (www.therichest.com/rich-list/most-influential/the-top-10-deadly-diseases-cured-in-the-20th-century/).

Salhani, Justin. 2017. "Italy's Populist Movement Isn't Like the Others in Europe. And that's Worrisome." Think Progress, May 18. Retrieved July 26, 2019 (https://thinkprogress.org/meet-the-italian-populist-right-c9fca24557f2/).

Samuels, Brett. 2019. "Trump Declares *New York Times* 'Enemy of the People.'" The Hill, February 20. Retrieved July 18, 2019 (https://thehill.com/homenews/administration/430716-trump-declares-new-york-times-enemy-of-the-people).

Sanchez, Ray. 2019. "More US School-Age Children Die From Guns than On-Duty US Police or Global Military Fatalities, Study Finds." CNN, March 22. Retrieved November 29, 2019 (www.cnn.com/2019/03/22/health/gun-deaths-school-age-children-trnd/index.html?fbclid=IwAR08C5C_EFiTjNMMm3X4iazc_GdZT8BGETWOKeguXft8bATdG1kRW6VV29o).

SAS Insights. 2019. "Big Data: What It Is and Why It Matters." Retrieved October 5, 2019 (www.sas.com/en_us/insights/big-data/what-is-big-data.html).

Sasse, Ben. 2018. *Them: Why We Hate Each Other—and How to Heal*. New York: St. Martin's Press.

Saunders, Peter. 2005. *The Poverty Wars: Reconnecting Research with Reality*. Sydney: University of New South Wales Press.

Savage, David G. 2018. "'Georgia is Ground Zero' For Voting Rights." *Los Angeles Times*, November 4: A14.

Sawhill, Isabel V. and Christopher Pulliam. 2019. "Six Facts about Wealth in the United States." Brookings, June 25. Retrieved July 30, 2019 (www.brookings.edu/blog/up-front/2019/06/25/six-facts-about-wealth-in-the-united-states/).

Schultheis, Emily. 2018. "Sweden's Far Right is on the Rise in Elections." *Los Angeles Times*, September 10: A3.

Schwoebel, Robert, editor. 1971. *Renaissance Men and Ideas*. New York: St. Martin's Press.

Scotland.org. 2019. "Climate Change & Renewables." Retrieved August 11, 2019 (www.scotland.org/about-scotland/scotlands-stories/renewable-energy).

Scott, Eugene. 2019. "Reagan Tapes Not Surprising to a Lot of Black Americans." *The Post-Standard*, August 1: A18.

Segers, Grace, Kathryn Watson, John Nolen, and Bo Erickson. 2018. "Kavanaugh Sworn in as Supreme Court Justice." CBS News, October 6. Retrieved September 2, 2019 (www.cbsnews.com/live-news/brett-kavanaugh-vote-live-stream-senate-confirmation-today-2018-10-06/).

Seidman, Steven. 1983. *Liberalism and the Origins of European Social Theory*. Los Angeles, CA: University of California Press.

Sharp, Kathleen. 2019. "Legal Fights Against Pharma Aren't Enough." *Los Angeles Times*, September 8: E2.

Shaw, Steve. 2012. "JFK and the So-Called Religious Issue." *Huffington Post*, March 7. Retrieved July 19, 2019 (www.huffpost.com/entry/jfk-the-socalled-religiou_b_1305721).

Simmel, Georg. 1906. "The Sociology of Secrecy and of Secret Societies." *The American Journal of Sociology*, 11 (4): 441–498.

Small Business Administration (SBA). 2019. "Small Businesses Generate 44 Percent of U.S. Economic Activity: Release No. 19–1 ADV." Retrieved October 4, 2019 (https://advocacy.sba.gov/2019/01/30/small-businesses-generate-44-percent-of-u-s-economic-activity/).

Smith, Elizabeth. 2012. "Deforestation and the Effects It Has on a Global Scale." *National Geographic*. Retrieved August 14, 2019 (http://greenliving.nationalgeogrpahic.com/deforestation-effects-global-scale- 2214.html).

Smith, Noah. 2019. "Education is for Everyone, but College Isn't." Bloomberg, as it appeared in *Post-Standard*, July 30: A12.

Snopes.com. 2016. "Was Donald Trump Never Accused of Racism Before Running Against Democrats?" Published, May 18, 2016. Retrieved July 23, 2019 (www.snopes.com/fact-check/donald-trump-racist-meme/).

Somers, Darian and Josh Moody. 2019. "10 College Majors with the Best Starting Salaries." *U.S. News & World Report*, February 7. Retrieved August 6, 2019 (www.usnews.com/education/best-colleges/slideshows/10-college-majors-with-the-highest-starting-salaries?onepage).

Spivak, Joshua. 2019. "The Electoral College is a Failure." *Post-Standard*, April 14: E1.

Statista. 2019a. "Statistics & Facts on the Global Automotive Industry." Retrieved May 12, 2019 (www.statista.com/topics/1487/automotive-industry/).

Statista. 2019b. "Richest People in America: Estimated Net Worth of the 20 Richest People in 2019 (in billion U.S. Dollars)." Retrieved July 30, 2019 (www.statista.com/statistics/201426/the-richest-people-in-america/).

Statista. 2019c. "Global Plastic Production." Retrieved August 14, 2019 (www.statista.com/statistics/282732/global-production-of-plastics-since-1950/).

Sterbenz, Christina and Abby Jackson. 2015. "The 13 Most Powerful Members of 'Skull and Bones.'" *Business Insider*, December 6. Retrieved October 1, 2019 (www.businessinsider.com/the-10-most-powerful-members-of-skull-and-bones-2015-12).

Stokols, Eli. 2018a. "Trump Makes False Claim." *Los Angeles Times*, December 28: A7.

Stokols, Eli. 2018a. 2018b. "Zinke Set to Leave Cabinet Post." *Los Angeles Times*, December 16: A1, A9.

Stokols, Eli. 2018a. 2019. "Technology's Not His Thing." *Los Angeles Times*, March 14: A2.

Stokols, Eli and Noah Bierman. 2018. "Trump is Defiant on Immigrants." *Los Angeles Times*, June 19: A1, A6.

Stokols, Eli and Noah Bierman. 2019. "Trump Comment Sets Off Alarms." *Los Angeles Times*, June 14: A1, A9.

Stone, Jeremy. 2018. *History of the Deep State*. Independently published.

Subramanian, Courtney. 2019. "Robert O'Brien Helped Free A$AP Rocky. Here's What to Know About Trump's Newest Senior Adviser." *USA Today*, September 18. Retrieved September 20, 2019 (www.usatoday.com/story/news/politics/2019/09/18/robert-obrien-trump- security-adviser-helped-free-asap-rocky/2363454001/).

Stobbe, Mike. 2019. "'Tough Year' for Measles." *The Citizen*, December 28: A1, A5.

Sullivan, Kerry. 2016. "The Mysterious Secret Society of Ancient India and The Nine Unknown Men of Ashoka." Ancient Origins, September 25. Retrieved October 1, 2019 (www.ancient-origins.net/myths-legends-asia/mysterious-secret-society-ancient-india-and-nine-unknown-men-ashoka-006714).

Swallow, Phillip S. 2018. "Explaining the Rise of Populism in Poland: The Post- Communist Transition as a Critical Juncture and Origin of Political Decay in Poland." *Inquiries*, 10 (7). Retrieved July 26, 2019 (www.inquiriesjournal.com/articles/1740/explaining-the-rise-of-populism-in-poland-the-post-communist-transition-as-a-critical-juncture-and-origin-of-political-decay-in-poland).

Swift, Art. 2017. "Democrats' Confidence in Mass Media Rises Sharply From 2016." Gallup, September 21. Retrieved July 20, 2019 (https://news.gallup.com/poll/219824/democrats-confidence-mass-media-rises- sharply-2016.aspx).

Szalavitz, Maia. 2019. "Johnson & Johnson Twisted the Truth. Here Are the Facts." *The New York Times*, August 29 (www.nytimes.com/2019/08/29/opinion/johnson-and-johnson-lawsuit.html)

Tansley, Arthur. 1935. "The Use and Abuse of Vegetational Concepts and Terms." *Ecologist* 16.

Tate, Karl. 2012. "How the Apollo 11 Moon Landing Worked." Space.com. Retrieved May 12, 2019 (www.space.com/17411-apollo-11-moon-landing-explained-infographic.html).

Taub, Amanda and Max Fisher. 2017. "As Leaks Multiply, Fears of a "Deep State' in America." *New York Times*, February 16. Retrieved September 30, 2019 (www.nytimes.com/2017/02/16/world/americas/deep-state-leaks-trump.html?searchResultPosition=3).

Thomas Jefferson Foundation. 2019. "Jefferson and the Enlightenment" Retrieved May 3, 2019 (www.monticello.org/slavery-at-monticello/liberty-slavery/jefferson-and-enlightenment).

Thomson, Garret. 1993. *Descartes to Kant*. Prospect Heights, IL: Waveland Press.

Thornton, William E., Jr. and Lydia Voigt. 1992. *Delinquency and Justice, Third Edition*. New York: McGraw-Hill.

Thule Society. 2019. "Thule Society: Philosophy." Retrieved October 1, 2019 (https://thulesociety.nfshost.com/).

Tondo, Lorenzo. 2019. "Matteo Salvini Replaced by Migration Specialist in New Italy Coalition." *The Guardian*, September 4. Retrieved September 7, 2019 (www.theguardian.com/world/2019/sep/04/matteo-salvini-replaced-by-migration-specialist-in-new-italy-coalition).

Torpey, Elka. 2018. "Measuring the Value of Education." Bureau of Labor Statistics (April). Retrieved August 5, 2019 (www.bls.gov/careeroutlook/2018/data-on-display/education-pays.htm).

Touchkoff, Svetlana A. 1992. *Russian Gypsy Fortune Telling Cards*. New York: HarperCollins.

Tripathi, Salil. 2019. "Singapore: Laboratory of Digital Censorship." *The New York Review of Books*, July 19. Retrieved July 19, 2019 (www.nybooks.com/daily/2019/07/19/singapore-laboratory-of-digital-censorship/).

Tubman, Kadia. 2019. "Fox News Host Presses WH Adviser Stephen Miller on 'Send Her Back! Chant at Trump Rally." Yahoo News, July 21. Retrieved July 21, 2019 (https://news.yahoo.com/fox-news-host-stephen-miller-racist-send-her-back-chant-trump-rally-165723025.html;_ylt=A0geK.WKRDddl7AATgFXNyoA;_ylu=X3oDMTEyM jc4ZmpjBGNvbG8DYmYxBHBvcwMyBHZ0aWQDQjc2NzVfMQRzZWMD c3I-).

Turrentine, Jeff. 2018. "Who is Andrew Wheeler? (And Why You Should Be Afraid of Him)." National Resources Defense Council (NRDC), April 13. Retrieved August 11, 2019 (www.nrdc.org/onearth/who-andrew-wheeler-and-why-you-should-be-afraid-him).

Tyson, Alec and Shiva Maniam. 2016. "Behind Trump's Victory: Divisions by Race, Gender, Education." Pew Research Center, November 9. Retrieved August 10, 2019 (www.pewresearch.org/fact-tank/2016/11/09/behind-trumps-victory-divisions-by-race-gender-education/).

Union of Concerned Scientists (UCS). 2011. "A Brief History of Nuclear Accidents Worldwide." Retrieved August 17, 2019 (www.ucsusa.org/nuclear-power/nuclear-power-accidents/history-nuclear-accidents).

Union of Concerned Scientists (UCS). 2019. "The State of Science in the Trump Era (2019)." Retrieved August 11, 2019 (www.ucsusa.org/center-science-and-democracy/state-of-science-trump-era).

United States Census Bureau. 2018. "Income, Poverty and Health Insurance Coverage in the United States: 2017." Press release, September 12. Retrieved July 30, 2019 (www.census.gov/newsroom/press-releases/2018/income-poverty.html).

US Department of Education. 2019. "Science, Technology, Engineering, and Math." Retrieved August 8, 2019 (www.ed.gov/Stem).

US Department of Health & Human Services. 2019. "2019 Poverty Guidelines." Retrieved July 30, 2019 (https://aspe.hhs.gov/2019-poverty-guidelines).

US Environmental Protection Agency. 2018. "Summary of the Toxic Substances Control Act." Retrieved August 14, 2019 (www.epa.gov/laws- regulations/summary-toxic-substances-control-act).

US Government Spending. 2019. "Federal Debt Clock." Retrieved July 15, 2019 (www.usgovernmentspending.com/debt_clock).

Van Helden, Albert. 2019. "Galileo: Italian Philosopher, Astronomer, and Mathematician." *Encyclopedia Britannica*. Retrieved April 27, 2019 (www.britannica.com/biography/Galileo-Galilei).

Vogue, Ariane de. 2018. "Justice Anthony Kennedy to Retire from Supreme Court." CNN Politics, June 27. Retrieved September 2, 2019 (www.cnn.com/2018/06/27/politics/anthony-kennedy-retires/index.html).

Voltaire Foundation. 2017. "About Voltaire." Retrieved February 21, 2020 (www.voltaire.ox.ac.uk/about-voltaire/about-voltaire).

Wagner, Kurt (and Bloomberg). 2019. "Facebook and Google Met with U.S. Intelligence About Online Security for the 2020 Presidential Election." *Fortune*, September 4. Retrieved October 5, 2019 (https://fortune.com/2019/09/04/facebook-google-fbi-meeting-2020-election- security/).

Ware, Doug G. 2017. "Nomination Expires for Obama Supreme Court Appointee Merrick Garland." UPI.com, January 3. Retrieved September 2, 2019 (www.upi.com/Top_News/US/2017/01/03/Nomination-expires-for-Obama-Supreme-Court-appointee-Merrick-Garland/4841483472115/).

Washington Post. 2019. "In 869 Days, President Trump Has Made 10,796 False or Misleading Claims," June 7. Retrieved July 14, 2019 (www.washingtonpost.com/graphics/politics/trump-claims-database/?utm_term=.04d8612aee8e).

Watson, Richard A. 2019. "Rene Descartes: French Mathematician and Philosopher." *Encyclopedia Britannica*. Retrieved April 27, 2019 (www.britannica.com/biography/Rene-Descartes).

Watts, Jonathan. 2018. "Brazil's New Foreign Minister Believes Climate Change is a Marxist Plot." *Guardian*, November 15. Retrieved July 14, 2019 (www.theguardian.com/world/2018/nov/15/brazil-foreign-minister-ernesto-araujo-climate-change-marxist-plot).

Welsh, Melinda. 2019. "Trump Hates Science, Sad!" *Los Angeles Times*, March 4: A11.

Wemple, Erik. 2018. "True—But Negative—Stories Called 'Fake News.'" *Post-Standard*, January 18: A17.

Wernick, Adam. 2019. "Brazil's New President Targets Amazon Rainforest, Indigenous Peoples." Pri.org, January 28. Retrieved August 14, 2019 (www.pri.org/stories/2019-01-28/brazils-new-president-targets-amazon-rainforest-indigenous-peoples).

Weschcke, Carl Llewellyn and Joe H. Slate. 2013. *Clairvoyance for Psychic Empowerment*. Woodbury, MN: Llewellyn Publications.

White, Peter. 2019. "'Chernobyl' Scores 19 Emmy Noms Including Limited Series Nod As Brits Clean Up In Short-Run Categories." Deadline.com, July 16. Retrieved August 17, 2019 (https://deadline.com/2019/07/chernobyl-emmys-19-nominations-1202646849/).

White House Information. 2019. "Continuity of Government – 2019." Retrieved September 30 (https://whitehouse.gov1.info/continuity-plan/).

Whitehead, John W. 2011. "America's Shadow Government: Part One." *Huff Post*, May 25. Retrieved November 14, 2019 (www.huffpost.com/entry/americas-shadow-governmen_b_131218).

Wilkinson, Tracy. 2018a. "U.S. Quits U.N. Human Rights Council." *Los Angeles Times*, June 20: A6.

Wilkinson, Tracy. 2018b. "White House Slams 'Troika of Tyranny' In Latin America." *Los Angeles Times*, November 2: A1, A4.

Wilkinson, Tracy. 2019a. "Brazil Inaugurates Far-Right President." *Los Angeles Times*, January 2: A3.

Wilkinson, Tracy. 2019b. "U.S. Redefining Human Rights." *Los Angeles Times*, July 24: A3.

Wilkinson, Tracy. 2019c. "More U.S. Diplomats Are Calling It Quits." *Los Angeles Times*, August 22: A6.

Wilkinson, Tracy and Noga Tarnopolsky. 2019. "Israel's Move to Bar 2 Democrats Riles Even Allies." *Los Angeles Times*, August 16: A1, A5.

Williams, Matt. 2012. "Republican Congressman Paul Broun Dismisses Evolution and Other Theories." *Guardian*, October 6. Retrieved August 11, 2019 (www.theguardian.com/world/2012/oct/06/republican-congressman-paul-broun-evolution-video).

Willman, David. 2018. "Judge Rebuffs Flynn, Delays His Sentencing." *Los Angeles Times*, December 19: A1, A4.

Wingrove, Josh and Gerald Porter, Jr. 2019. "Vaping Crackdown Delayed As Trump Considers Impact." *Los Angeles Times*, November 16: C2.

Wire, Sarah D. 2019. "House Democrats Unveil Articles of Impeachment." *Los Angeles Times*, December 11: A1, A7.

Wiseman, Richard. 2019. "The Mindset Behind the Moon Landing." *Science Focus*, January 31. Retrieved May 12, 2019 (www.sciencefocus.com/space/the-mindset-behind-the-moon-landing-richard-wiseman/).

Witchel, Elisabeth. 2018. "CPJ's 2018 Global Impunity Index Spotlights Countries Where Journalists Are Slain and their Killers Go Free." Committee to Protect Journalists. Retrieved July 21, 2019 (https://cpj.org/reports/2018/10/impunity-index-getting-away-with-murder-killed-justice.php).

WKRC Staff. 2019. "Ohio House Passes Bill Allowing Student Answers to Be Scientifically Wrong Due to Religion," November 15. Retrieved November 16, 2019 (www.richarddawkins.net/2019/11/ohio-house-passes-bill-allowing-student-answers-to-be-scientifically-wrong-due-to-religion/).

Wolchover, Natalie. 2012. "'One Small Step for Man': Was Neil Armstrong Misquoted?" Space.com, August 27. Retrieved May 14, 2019 (www.space.com/17307-neil-armstrong-one-small-step-quote.html).

Wolf, Zachary B. 2019. "Why Not Take Political Dirt from a Foreign Government? So Many Reasons." CNN, June 13. Retrieved June 15, 2019 (www.cnn.com/2019/06/13/politics/oppo-research-donald-trump-foreign-powers/index.html).

Wood, Jonathan. 2008. "The Top Ten Advances In Materials Science." *Materials Today*, 11 (1–2): 40–45.

Woolfson, Lisa. 2016. "10 Dumbest Things Trump Has Said." Odyssey, August 8. Retrieved July 22, 2019 (www.theodysseyonline.com/10-dumbest-things-trump-has-said).

World Atlas. 2019a. "Fossil Fuel Dependency By Country." Retrieved August 12, 2019 (www.worldatlas.com/articles/countries-the-most-dependent-on-fossil-fuels.html).

World Atlas. 2019a. 2019b. "Countries Least Dependent On Fossil Fuel Sources for Energy Needs." Retrieved August 12, 2019 (www.worldatlas.com/articles/countries-least-dependent-on-fossil-fuel-sources-for-energy-needs.html).

The World Bank. 2018. "Nearly Half of the World Lives on Less than $5.50 a Day." Press release, October 17. Retrieved July 31, 2019 (www.worldbank.org/en/news/press-release/2018/10/17/nearly-half-the-world-lives-on-less-than-550-a-day).

The World Health Organization (WHO). 2019a. "Ten Threats to Global Health in 2019." Retrieved August 12, 2019 (www.who.int/emergencies/ten-threats-to-global-health-in-2019).

The World Health Organization 2019b. "Prevalence of Tobacco Smoking." Retrieved October 5, 2019 (www.who.int/gho/tobacco/use/en/).

World Nuclear Association. 2019. "Nuclear Power in the World Today." Retrieved August 14, 2019 (https://world-nuclear.org/information-library/current-and- future-generation/nuclear-power-in-the-world-today.aspx).

The World Poverty Clock. 2019. "Real Time Poverty Estimates." Retrieved July 31, 2019 (https://worldpoverty.io/index.html).

Wright Brothers Aeroplane Company. 2010. "A History of the Airplane." Retrieved May 12, 2019 (www.wright- brothers.org/History_Wing/History_of_the_Airplane/History_of_the_Airpla ne_In tro/History_of_the_Airplane_Intro.htm).

Wu, Nicholas. 2019. "Department of Energy Refers to 'Freedom Gas' and 'Molecules of U.S. Freedom' in Press Release." *USA Today*, May 29. Retrieved August 13, 2019 (www.usatoday.com/story/news/politics/onpolitics/2019/05/29/department-energy-uses-freedom-gas-refer-natural-gas/1270444001/).

Yeung, Jessie and Kevin Liptak. 2019. "India Denies that Trump was Invited to Mediate Kashmir Conflict after Social Media Firestorm," CNN Politics, July 23. Retrieved July 24, 2019 (www.cnn.com/2019/07/23/politics/trump-kashmir-india-intl-hnk/index.html).

Zadrozny, Brandy. 2019. "Brooklyn Measles Outbreak: How a Glossy Booklet Spread Anti-Vaccine Messages in Orthodox Jewish Communities." NBC News, April 12. Retrieved August 13, 2019 (www.nbcnews.com/news/us-news/brooklyn-measles-outbreak-how-glossy-booklet-spread-anti-vaccine-messages-n993596).

Zantow, Emily. 2018. "Wisconsin Unions Fight Collective Bargaining Limits." *Wausau Pilot & Review*, February 28. Retrieved July 30, 2019 (https://wausaupilotandreview.com/2018/02/28/wisconsin-unions-fight-collective-bargaining-limits/).

INDEX

Acosta, Jim 51
acting government, the 161–3, 195
Adams, John 1, 22, 34
Age of Populism 55–7
Age of Reason 1, 25, 33–4
air pollution 108, 114, 122, 125
alternative facts 35–7, 46, 90, 116, 181
anti-vaccination 114–15
apprenticeship 93, 98
Ashoka's Nine Unknown Men 177
Assange, Julian 48
The Assassins 176
astrology 131–3, 140

Bacon, Francis 9, 15, 34
Beccaria, Cesare 20–1, 34
Big Banks 177, 180, 189–91, 195, 199
Big Business 31, 104, 148, 158, 177–80, 186, 195, 199
Big Data 177, 180, 185–6, 195, 199
Big Pharma 177–80, 186–9, 195, 199
Big Religion 177, 191–2, 199
Big Tech 45, 177, 180, 184–5, 195, 199
The Bilderberg Group 175, 177, 195
Bolsonaro, Jair 73, 129
Bolton, John 156
Brexit 56, 58, 64–5, 68, 196

Carbon dioxide (CO_2) 113, 120–1, 124, 127, 129
carrying capacity 118, 122
celestial pollution 125–6
Century of Criticism 25–7

chemical pollution 124
Chernobyl Nuclear Power Plant 125, 137–9
clairvoyance 131–3, 140
climate change 73, 108–10, 112–14, 116, 118–21, 126–7, 129, 139–40, 158, 170, 180–1, 198
Clinton, Hillary 40, 48, 58, 105, 197
Cohen, Michael 41–2, 63, 154–5
Collective bargaining 85–7
conservatism 21–2, 26, 105, 192
conservative reaction 22, 26, 34
Copernicus, Nicolaus 5, 33
critical thinking 26–8, 34, 92, 97–9, 139, 196–200

da Vinci, Leonardo 2, 176
"Dark Ages" 91, 106
Day, Benjamin Henry 24, 34
Deep State, the 43, 164–77, 189, 195
de Montesquieu, Charles 1, 10, 13–14, 34
Descartes, René 9, 34
deterioration of the environment 112, 116
deterioration of freedom and human rights 75–81, 85, 90–1
disbelief in science 91, 106, 114, 139–40, 200
"drain the swamp" 147–50, 162, 195

economic disparity 82, 90, 199
ecosystem 117–18, 120–2, 126, 128, 141
electricity 22, 28–9, 111, 124, 197
enemy of the people 46–8, 50, 55, 75, 90, 179

enlightened rational thought 1–3, 11, 29–31, 33–4, 49, 89, 106, 137, 159, 182, 192, 195–7
The Enlightenment 1–2, 5, 8, 10–16, 18–19, 21–3, 25–6, 28, 33–4
environment 66, 73, 91–2, 108–9, 112–13, 116–19, 121–31, 140, 146, 151, 167, 181, 194, 198–9
Environmental Protection Agency (EPA) 109, 123–4, 127

Facebook 44–6, 80, 84, 180, 184–5
fake news 24, 35, 37–8, 43, 45–50, 53, 63–4, 90, 112, 181
Flynn, Michael 41, 154–6
fortune telling 131, 133, 140
fossil fuels 102, 110, 113–14, 116, 118–22, 124, 126–7, 131, 137, 139–40, 179–80, 197
Franklin, Benjamin 1, 21–3, 34
freedom gas 119
Freedom House 53–4, 73–8, 90
Freemasonry 175–6
Freedom in the World 73–5, 76, 90
French Revolution 1, 13, 15, 26, 177

Galilei, Galileo 8–9, 34
The German Thule Society 175, 177, 195
Giuliani, Rudolph "Rudy" 36, 193
Global economic inequality 87–8
globularist 137
Google 37, 45, 180, 184–5
guns 183–4

higher education 7, 26–8, 30, 34, 91–105, 131, 136, 139, 144, 191, 199
Hobbes, Thomas 9–11, 34, 145
Horkheimer, Max 136
Human Rights Watch 56, 68–9
humanism 5–7, 33
Hume, David 17, 34
hydraulic fracturing (fracking) 108, 122, 126–7, 140

The Illuminati 176–7
immigration 61–2, 64–7, 72–3, 77–9, 88, 90, 104, 112, 128, 176, 179
Impunity Index 51–2
intellect 27, 93, 97, 99, 139
intellectuals 11–12, 25–6, 34
ISIS 70–1

Jefferson, Thomas 1, 21, 23, 34
Johnson, Boris 56, 64
journalism 48–50, 77

journalists 12, 36, 38, 45–53, 67–9, 74–6, 80, 90

Kant, Immanuel 1, 19–20, 34
Kavanaugh, Brett 87, 161, 192–4
The Ku Klux Klan 176
Kurds, the 69–71

laissez faire 10, 19
land pollution 123–4, 126
Law and Justice Party (PiS) 65
liberalism 10, 21–2, 25, 192
lies, falsehood and misleading claims 37, 40, 43–4, 46, 49, 59, 75, 111
lobbying 81, 83, 143–4, 150–2, 162, 181, 185, 189
Locke, John 10–11, 15, 22, 25, 34
Lopez, Andres Manuel 74
Luther, Martin 2, 5, 27–8, 33, 104

Machiavelli, Niccolo 4–5, 33
Macron, Emmanuel 57
Madison, James 22, 24, 34
Manafort, Paul 41, 154
Marx, Karl 59, 191–2
mass extinction 117–21, 126, 130, 140, 197
media 35–6, 38, 48–53, 55, 67, 69, 75–6, 97, 105, 107, 139, 175, 179, 185
methane 120, 126–8
Middle Ages 2–3, 7, 26, 30, 33–4, 94, 106, 192
Mills, C. Wright 165–7, 171
Moon landing 30–3
More, Thomas 6, 8, 33
Mueller Report 40–1, 154, 157, 162
Mueller, Robert 36, 40
Mueller Report, the 40–1, 154, 157, 162

NASA 30, 33, 84, 125–6
National Rally party 66
nationalism 12, 54–7, 64, 75, 90, 176
Newton, Isaac 8, 11, 34
noise pollution 125
Nuclear energy 116, 124–5, 137, 197

Obama, Barack 39, 43, 48, 62–3, 79, 105, 107, 109–10, 123, 127, 149–51, 154, 156, 159–60, 162, 165, 170, 172, 190–2
Orbán, Viktor 67–8, 76
The Order of Skull and Bones 174–5, 177, 193, 195
The Order of the Nine Angles (ONA) 176
overpopulation 118, 122

paradigms of thought 2, 105–6

Pareto, Vilfredo 167
Petrarch, Francis 2–4, 6–7, 33
philosophes 12, 15, 25
populism 54–8, 69, 72, 75, 90, 196–7
poverty 8, 82, 84–5, 88–9
power elite, the 28, 99, 127, 139, 166–74, 177, 180, 195, 198
pseudoscience 30, 91, 107, 131–7, 139–40, 199

quid pro quo 168

racism 55, 62–4, 199
R. Alexander Acosta 157–8
reason 1, 6, 8, 12, 15, 17, 19–23, 25–8, 31, 33–4, 36–7, 90–1, 97, 104–6, 113, 123, 136–7, 140, 161, 192
Reid, Thomas 17, 34
The Renaissance 2–8, 11, 28, 33–4, 196
Reporters Without Borders 45, 51–2
Rousseau, Jean-Jacques 1, 13, 15–17, 34
Russia 19, 36, 39–41, 46–7, 52, 56, 66, 68, 71, 77, 80, 133, 152–5, 157, 162–3, 168, 173, 185, 187

science 1, 7–9, 11, 16, 20, 22, 25, 28–34, 36–7, 56, 91, 94, 96–7, 99–100, 105–14, 120, 131–3, 137, 139–40, 161, 170, 191, 196–7, 199–200
Scientific Revolution 2, 5, 8, 11, 33
Secondhand smoke 182
secret societies 61, 174–7, 195
shameful behavior 31, 37, 43, 46–7, 160
Sisi, Abdel Fattah 45, 68
Smith, Adam 17–18, 34
solid waste 122, 125
Social media 36, 40, 44–5, 49, 69, 76, 97, 115, 139, 153, 185–6, 199
social stratification 82, 90
STEM 96, 98–103, 139

Stone, Roger 153
superstition 15, 134–6, 140, 176
the (political) swamp 31, 37, 141–52, 155, 157–8, 161–4, 177, 180, 183, 185–6, 189, 191–2, 194–5, 199
Sweden Democrats 67

thrivability 117–18
tobacco 30, 143, 180–3
Todd, Chuck 36
"triangle of power" 166
Trump, Donald 35–48, 50–1, 54–71, 73, 78–82, 87, 90, 104–12, 116, 120, 123–4, 127, 129, 146, 149–64, 168–72, 176, 179, 181, 185, 190–2, 197–9, 201
truth isn't truth 35–7, 46, 90, 193
Twitter 38, 44–6, 50, 110, 185

Un, Kim Jong 68, 111, 156, 163
unemployment 39–40, 69, 83–4, 95, 97, 149
unenlightened and irrational thinking 91, 100, 106, 111–13, 116, 140
Union of Concerned Scientists (UCS) 108
unions 85–7

vaping 181–2
Voltaire, Francois-Marie Arouet 1, 13–15, 34
voodoo 134, 140
voter suppression 77–8

water pollution 122–3
wealth disparity 84, 90
witchcraft 134–5, 140
World Health Organization (WHO) 114–15, 122, 181–2

Zinke, Ryan 151–2

For Product Safety Concerns and Information please contact our EU
representative GPSR@taylorandfrancis.com
Taylor & Francis Verlag GmbH, Kaufingerstraße 24, 80331 München, Germany

www.ingramcontent.com/pod-product-compliance
Lightning Source LLC
Chambersburg PA
CBHW071826300426
44116CB00009B/1453